Dams, Displacement, and the Delusion of Development

NEW AFRICAN HISTORIES

SERIES EDITORS: JEAN ALLMAN AND ALLEN ISAACMAN

Books in this series are published with support from the Ohio University National Resource Center for African Studies.

David William Cohen and E. S. Atieno Odhiambo, *The Risks of Knowledge: Investigations into the Death of the Hon. Minister John Robert Ouko in Kenya, 1990*

Belinda Bozzoli, *Theatres of Struggle and the End of Apartheid*

Gary Kynoch, *We Are Fighting the World: A History of Marashea Gangs in South Africa, 1947–1999*

Stephanie Newell, *The Forger's Tale: The Search for Odeziaku*

Jacob A. Tropp, *Natures of Colonial Change: Environmental Relations in the Making of the Transkei*

Jan Bender Shetler, *Imagining Serengeti: A History of Landscape Memory in Tanzania from Earliest Times to the Present*

Cheikh Anta Babou, *Fighting the Greater Jihad: Amadu Bamba and the Founding of the Muridiyya in Senegal, 1853–1913*

Marc Epprecht, *Heterosexual Africa? The History of an Idea from the Age of Exploration to the Age of AIDS*

Marissa J. Moorman, *Intonations: A Social History of Music and Nation in Luanda, Angola, from 1945 to Recent Times*

Karen E. Flint, *Healing Traditions: African Medicine, Cultural Exchange, and Competition in South Africa, 1820–1948*

Derek R. Peterson and Giacomo Macola, editors, *Recasting the Past: History Writing and Political Work in Modern Africa*

Moses Ochonu, *Colonial Meltdown: Northern Nigeria in the Great Depression*

Emily Burrill, Richard Roberts, and Elizabeth Thornberry, editors, *Domestic Violence and the Law in Colonial and Postcolonial Africa*

Daniel R. Magaziner, *The Law and the Prophets: Black Consciousness in South Africa, 1968–1977*

Emily Lynn Osborn, *Our New Husbands Are Here: Households, Gender, and Politics in a West African State from the Slave Trade to Colonial Rule*

Robert Trent Vinson, *The Americans Are Coming! Dreams of African American Liberation in Segregationist South Africa*

James R. Brennan, *Taifa: Making Nation and Race in Urban Tanzania*

Benjamin N. Lawrance and Richard L. Roberts, editors, *Trafficking in Slavery's Wake: Law and the Experience of Women and Children*

David M. Gordon, *Invisible Agents: Spirits in a Central African History*

Allen Isaacman and Barbara Isaacman, *Dams, Displacement, and the Delusion of Development: Cahora Bassa and Its Legacies in Mozambique, 1965–2007*

Dams, Displacement, and the Delusion of Development

*Cahora Bassa and Its Legacies
in Mozambique, 1965–2007*

⤳

Allen F. Isaacman and Barbara S. Isaacman

OHIO UNIVERSITY PRESS ⤳ ATHENS

Ohio University Press, Athens, Ohio 45701
ohioswallow.com
© 2013 by Ohio University Press
All rights reserved

Printed in the United States of America
Ohio University Press books are printed on acid-free paper ⊚ ™

23 22 21 20 19 18 17 16 15 14 13   5 4 3 2 1

Library of Congress Cataloging-in-Publication Data
Isaacman, Allen F.
Dams, displacement, and the delusion of development : Cahora Bassa and its
legacies in Mozambique, 1965–2007 / Allen F. Isaacman and Barbara S. Isaacman.
   p. cm. — (New African histories)
Includes bibliographical references and index.
ISBN 978-0-8214-2033-1 (pb : alk. paper) — ISBN 978-0-8214-4450-4 (electronic)
1. Cahora Bassa Dam (Mozambique)—History. 2. Economic development
projects—Mozambique. 3. Zambezi River Valley—Rural conditions. 4. Forced
migration—Zambezi River Valley. I. Isaacman, Barbara. II. Title. III. Series: New
African histories series.
 HC890.Z65I83 2013
 333.71509679—dc23
                              2012049113

We dedicate this book to the people of the lower Zambezi valley, whose lives have been forever altered by the Cahora Bassa Dam.

Contents

Illustrations

TABLES

Acknowledgments

We began this project on Cahora Bassa in 1997, while conducting fieldwork for our book, *Slavery and Beyond: The Making of Men and Chikunda Ethnic Identities in the Unstable World of South-Central Africa, 1750–1920.* In the fifteen years we were working on this project, many friends and colleagues, through their intellectual insights and thoughtful critiques, helped us sharpen our arguments and avoid embarrassing errors.

We owe a special debt of gratitude to four scholars. Richard Beilfuss, who shared with us his vast knowledge of the ecology of the Zambezi Valley, was a generous and patient teacher. His influence is apparent in our numerous citations of his work and that of his colleagues. Arlindo Chilundo helped plan the initial phase of oral research, and, together with a team of students from the Universidade Eduardo Mondlane—Xavier Cadete, Germano Mausse Dimande, Eulésio Viegas Felipe, Paulo Lopes José, and António Tovela—participated with Allen in the fieldwork conducted in 2000 and 2001. The oral interviews collected in the lower Zambezi valley by this research brigade provided much of the data on which this study rests. Chilundo's commitment to higher education in Mozambique prevented him from continuing on this project. Wapu Mulwafu, working with two students from the University of Malawi—John Mandala and Donald Khembo—and one from the Universidade Eduardo Mondlane—Xavier Cadete—interviewed peasants living near the confluence of the Zambezi and Shire Rivers in 2000. Their research provided valuable insights about the social, ecological, and cultural effects of Cahora Bassa in that region. Finally, David Morton interviewed farmers living near Mponda Nkuwa, the site of a proposed new dam downriver from Cahora Bassa.

When we began this project, we knew very little about the construction and far-reaching consequences of large dams. Besides Richard Beilfuss, we were extremely fortunate to consult with and learn from Carlos Bento, Bryan Davies, Leila Harris, Patrick McCully, Lori Pottinger, Daniel Ribeiro, Thayer Scudder, and Chris Sneddon. Together, they patiently answered our questions and identified critical bodies of literature for us to consult.

A number of scholars read various drafts of our manuscript. The final product is far better, thanks to the detailed comments of Heidi Gengenbach, Leila Harris, Jim Johnson, Premesh Lalu, Elias Mandala, Stephan Miescher, David Morton, and Derek Peterson. Portions of this project were presented as lectures and seminars at the Center for Advanced Studies in the Behavioral Sciences (Stanford University); Colgate University; Cornell University; the Rockefeller Study and Conference Center (Bellagio); the Universidade Eduardo Mondlane; the University of California, Santa Barbara; the University of Michigan; the University of Minnesota; and the University of the Western Cape. Participants and audience members at all of these institutions, including James Campbell, Laura Fair, Jim Ferguson, M. J. Maynes, Anne Pitcher, Helena Pohlandt-McCormick, Daniel Posner, Arvind Rajagopal, Anupama Rao, Ciraj Rasool, Richard Roberts, Abdi Samatar, Joel Samoff, Eric Sheppard, Ajay Skaria, France Winddance Twine, and Eric Worby, offered critiques and suggestions that helped us sharpen our thinking. Finally, we commend Jean Allman, coeditor of the Ohio University New African Histories series, for her thoughtful and supportive comments. It was a pleasure to work with her and Gillian Berchowitz, the editorial director at Ohio University Press.

The staff of the Arquivo Histórico de Moçambique, the Arquivo Nacional da Torre do Tombo, and the Hoover Institution always happily assisted us. We are also grateful to the International Rivers Network and Justiça Ambiental for sharing their considerable holdings on Cahora Bassa.

We wish to thank the American Council of Learned Societies, the Center for Advanced Studies in the Behavioral Sciences, the Rockefeller Foundation (Bellagio), and the University of Minnesota for their generous support. The idyllic conditions at the Center make it the perfect place to work on a manuscript, and there is no better ambiance in which to complete such a project than Bellagio. We also received the assistance of the Cartography Laboratory at the University of Minnesota, whose maps grace our book.

Finally, we owe an incalculable debt to the hundreds of men and women — peasants, fisherfolk and dam workers — who readily shared their memories, experiences, and perspectives. They were our best teachers, and we hope that we have done justice to their stories. It is to them that we dedicate this book.

Abbreviations

AIM	Agência de Informação de Moçambique (Mozambique Information Agency)
ANC	African National Congress
EDM	Electricidade de Moçambique (Mozambique's public electricity utility)
Eskom	Electricity Supply Commission (South Africa's public electricity utility)
FIVAS	Foreningen for Internasjonale Vannstudier (Association for International Water Studies)
Frelimo	Frente de Libertação de Moçambique (Mozambican Liberation Front)
GPZ	Gabinete do Plano do Zambeze (Zambezi Valley Planning Office)
HCB	Hidroeléctrica de Cabora Bassa (Cabora Bassa Hydroelectric)
IMF	International Monetary Fund
JA!	Justiça Ambiental
MFPZ	Missão de Fomento e Povoamento de Zambeze (Mission for the Promotion and Development of the Zambezi)
PIDE	Polícia Internacional e de Defesa do Estado (International and State Defense Police)
Renamo	Resistência Nacional Moçambicana (Mozambican National Resistance)
UTIP	Unidade Técnica de Implementação dos Projectos Hidroeléctricos (Technical Unit for Implementation of Hydropower Projects)

WCD	World Commission on Dams
WNLA	Witwatersrand Native Labour Association
Zamco	Zambeze Consórcio Hidroeléctrico Lda. (consortium that built Cahora Bassa)
ZANU	Zimbabwe African National Union
ZAPU	Zimbabwe African People's Union
ZESA	Zimbabwe Electricity Supply Authority

Cahora Bassa Timeline

May 1956	The Salazar regime dispatches Professor Alberto Manzanares to conduct a preliminary survey of the Cahora Bassa gorge.
September 1969	Lisbon signs a $515 million agreement with Zamco for it to build the Cahora Bassa Dam.
September 7, 1974	Frelimo and Portugal sign the Lusaka peace accord, which set the terms for the eventual transfer of the Cahora Bassa Dam to Mozambique.
December 6, 1974	The dam's gates close, blocking the Zambezi River from flowing freely downstream to the Indian Ocean.
April 1975	The reservoir at Cahora Bassa is filled, forming a 2,600-square-kilometer lake.
June 23, 1975	Portugal and Mozambique sign the agreement giving the HCB 82 percent ownership of the Cahora Bassa Dam.
June 25, 1975	Mozambique formally becomes independent.
January 1987	Mozambique implements the structural adjustment program known as the Program of Economic Rehabilitation (PRE).
October 4, 1992	The Mozambican government signs a peace accord with Renamo in Rome.
May 2002	The Mozambican government holds an investors' conference, seeking bids for

	the construction of the Mphanda Nkuwa hydroelectric project.
November 27, 2007	Mozambique purchases majority ownership of Cahora Bassa from the HCB.
2014	It is anticipated that Mozambique will own 100 percent of the dam by then.

1 ⤳ Introduction

Cahora Bassa in Broader Perspective

DAMS HAVE histories that are located in specific fields of power. Unlike the dams themselves, however, these histories are never fixed; whether celebrated or contested, they are always subject to reinvention by state and interstate actors, corporate interests, development experts, rural dwellers, and academics. Too often, though, the viewpoints of people displaced to make room for a dam are lost or silenced by the efforts of the powerful to construct its meaning in narrow terms of developmental or technical success. Yet, the voices of the displaced endure, carried by memories as powerful as the river itself. Such is the case of Cahora Bassa,[1] a grandiose dam project on the Zambezi River in Mozambique (see maps 1.1 and 1.2).

The Zambezi River is the fourth-largest waterway in Africa and the largest river system flowing into the Indian Ocean. Although the Cahora Bassa Dam and reservoir are entirely inside Mozambique, the vast bulk of its drainage basin lies outside the country. "Rising in Angola it has a catchment area of 1,570,000 [square kilometers], drains the southern borders of the Democratic Republic of Congo (DRC) and traverses Botswana, Zambia, Zimbabwe, Tanzania, Malawi and Moçambique."[2] Because Mozambique is furthest downstream, it depends on its neighbors for access to the Zambezi's waters.

Before the Zambezi or any of its tributaries were dammed by the Europeans in the twentieth century, the rate of the river's flow varied considerably in the catchment area. In much of the basin, located on the Central African plateau (termed the upper Zambezi by hydrologists), the water moved slowly through low plains and swamps. The undulating topography changed radically at Victoria Falls, where the river plunged more than one hundred meters and became the middle Zambezi. It was on this stretch, downstream from Victoria

MAP 1.1. Zambezi catchment. *University of Minnesota Cartography*

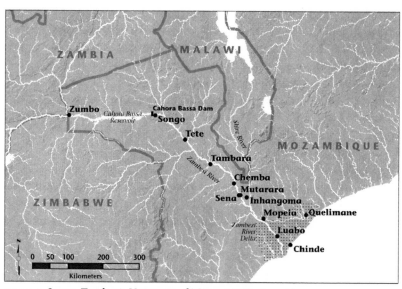

MAP 1.2. Lower Zambezi. *University of Minnesota Cartography*

Falls, that the British built Kariba Dam in 1958. Approximately one hundred kilometers further downstream, at the Cahora Bassa gorge, the river plunged once again, down a long succession of rapids and cascades, turning into a powerful and volatile force. The gorge marked the beginning of the lower Zambezi, which extended 650 kilometers to the Indian Ocean. Drawing from the British experience at Kariba, colonial planners decided that Cahora Bassa would be an ideal location for Portugal's hydroelectric project.[3]

When built, in the early 1970s, during the final years of Portuguese colonial rule, Cahora Bassa attracted considerable international attention. Engineers and hydrologists praised its technical complexity and the skill required to construct what was then the world's fifth-largest dam. For them, Cahora Bassa confirmed that nature could be conquered and biophysical systems transformed to serve the needs of humankind. Portuguese colonial officials recited a litany of benefits they expected from the $515 million megadam and the managed environment it would produce—expansion of irrigated farming, European settlement, and mineral output; improved communication and transportation throughout the Zambezi River valley; reduced flooding in this zone of unpredictable and sometimes excessive rainfall. In slick brochures and public pronouncements, they claimed that Cahora Bassa would "foster human progress through an improved standard of living for thousands of Africans who live and work there."[4] Above all, Cahora Bassa would generate a substantial influx of hard currency, since 82 percent of its electricity would go to South Africa—making it the largest dam in the world producing energy mainly for export. As a follow-up to this technological triumph, Portuguese planners envisioned building a second dam, sixty kilometers south of Cahora Bassa, at Mphanda Nkuwa (see map 1.3).

In June 1975, six months after the dam's completion, Mozambique gained its independence, ending a decade of warfare between the colonial regime and

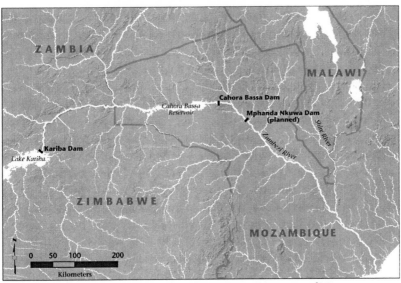

MAP 1.3. Mphanda Nkuwa and Cahora Bassa Dams. *University of Minnesota Cartography*

the guerrilla forces of Frelimo (Frente de Libertação de Moçambique). The newly installed Frelimo government—after years of claiming that Cahora Bassa, by providing cheap energy to apartheid South Africa, would perpetuate white rule throughout the region—radically changed its position. Hailing the dam's liberating potential, it expressed confidence that Cahora Bassa would play a critical role in Mozambique's socialist revolution and its quest for economic development and prosperity.

Even after Frelimo abandoned its socialist agenda, in 1987,[5] the dam remained central to Mozambique's postcolonial development strategy. Serious economic problems, stemming in part from the ongoing military conflict with South African–backed Renamo forces[6] and mounting pressure from the International Monetary Fund (IMF) and the World Bank, compelled the Mozambican government to introduce market-oriented reforms to lure foreign investment. What did not change was its continued celebration of the transformative potential of Cahora Bassa, whose provision of cheap electricity to new privately owned plants and factories would stimulate rapid industrial growth. Moreover, its announced intention, in the late 1990s, to implement the colonial plan to build a second dam at Mphanda Nkuwa underscored Frelimo's belief that large energy-producing dams were essential for national economic development.

Thus, despite their very different economic agendas and ideological orientations, the Portuguese colonial regime, the postindependence socialist state, and its free-market successor all heralded the developmental promise of Cahora Bassa. Whether Portuguese or Africans held the reins of state power, the dam symbolized the ability of science and technology to master nature and ensure human progress.[7] Moreover, to the extent that official versions of Cahora Bassa's history became the dominant reading of the past, they suppressed alternative voices that questioned the state's interpretive authority.[8]

The African communities living along the Zambezi River, however, tell a markedly different story. When the three hundred Zambezi valley residents interviewed for this book speak of the dam, their accounts rarely evoke images of prosperity or progress. Instead, Cahora Bassa evokes memories of forcible eviction from historic homelands, of concentration in crowded resettlement camps, and of unpredictable discharges of water that destroyed their crops and flooded their fields. Many also describe in detail the results of the river's altered flow regime—the devastating erosion of fertile riverbanks, the destruction of wildlife vital to their food security, and the dramatic decline of fish populations.

This book advances three central arguments. First, over the past three and one-half decades, Cahora Bassa has caused very real ecological, economic, and social trauma for Zambezi valley residents. All this is conspicuously absent from the widely publicized developmentalist narratives of Mozambique's colonial and postcolonial states, which have been a critical feature of state efforts to dam the Zambezi River in Mozambique. Elderly African peasants,[9] who had a long and intimate relationship with the Zambezi River, graphically describe how the dam devastatingly affected their physical and social world and recount their resiliency in coping and adjusting. These memories, which speak so powerfully about the daily lives and lived experiences of the rural poor, are either discounted or ignored in dominant discourses touting Cahora Bassa's centrality to national development. This silencing is indicative of the unequal field of power in which the histories of the rural poor are typically embedded.

The second argument is that extreme and continual violence has been a critical feature of state efforts to dam the Zambezi River in Mozambique. Bluntly stated, the history of Cahora Bassa reveals the willingness of an authoritarian but embattled colonial state, facing an armed nationalist movement and mounting criticism from the outside world, to put the full weight of its coercive power behind economic and strategic objectives it believed would strengthen its permanent hold over Mozambique. The forced labor used to build the roads to the dam site, the harsh labor regime at the dam itself, the displacement of thousands of peasants, and Renamo's prolonged destabilization campaign demonstrate the extent to which violence is deeply implicated in the history of Cahora Bassa.

The deleterious social and ecological consequences of this massive state-imposed project never figured in the political calculus of colonial planners. Nor do they seem to matter in current discussions about the building of a second dam, at Mphanda Nkuwa. This disregard for peasants' concerns about Mphanda Nkuwa is yet another example of the state's continuing efforts to silence the voices of the rural poor—a form of epistemic violence. In this respect, the present neoliberal government mimics the ways in which the late colonial state exercised and rationalized power.[10]

The history of Cahora Bassa also reveals the persistence of "colonialism's afterlife."[11] Under the 1974 Lusaka peace accord, which set the stage for Mozambique's independence, in return for assuming the $550 million debt incurred in building Cahora Bassa, Hidroeléctrica de Cahora Bassa (HCB), a Portuguese parastatal, received 82 percent of the shares, with the remainder going to the Mozambican government. The Constitution of the Cahora Bassa Dam, signed between Portugal and Frelimo on June 23, 1975, which memorialized this agreement, granted the HCB the right to manage the dam until Mozambique repaid the construction debt.[12] Because it was unable to do so until 2007, for thirty-two years after independence a Portuguese company retained effective control of the hydroelectric project (see chapter 6)—operating the dam, determining the outflows of water, and negotiating the sale of virtually all its electricity to South Africa.

That the newly independent socialist government could not use this energy for domestic purposes, such as electrifying the countryside, exposed the neocolonial reality—which persisted even after Frelimo adopted a neoliberal agenda in 1987 and needed cheap energy from Cahora Bassa to attract foreign investments and promote a free-market economy. Throughout, HCB management ignored these needs. For Mozambicans, Cahora Bassa was a living symbol of the violent and oppressive past and a constant reminder that independence did not guarantee resource sovereignty.[13]

In the mid-1990s, Frelimo began a campaign to wrest control of Cahora Bassa and its energy from Portugal. Lisbon, however, summarily rejected all Mozambique's attempts to reduce or erase the price it would have to pay to own the dam. To enhance its bargaining power, the Mozambican government then threatened to revive a colonial plan to build a second dam downriver at Mphanda Nkuwa, which would reduce Cahora Bassa's profitability. In 2007, under increasing pressure from Mozambique and its postapartheid South African ally, Portugal finally agreed to sell two-thirds of its shares in Cahora Bassa for $700 million (see chapter 6).

By this time, the Mozambican government had decided that two dams on the Zambezi were better than one, despite the human suffering and ecological destruction Cahora Bassa had inflicted. The rationale for constructing another dam at Mphanda Nkuwa was, as before, that foreign exchange would come from the sale of its energy—to South Africa and other energy-starved nations in the region. Rural electrification remained a secondary consideration, notwithstanding that only 7 percent of Mozambican households had access to electricity. In this regard, postindependence Mozambique continued the colonial ways of seeing, thinking, and acting. The persistent links between the postcolonial present and the colonial past is the third argument we advance.

We first became interested in the history of Cahora Bassa in 1997, when we visited Songo, the town adjacent to the dam site, to attend a Ministry of Culture–sponsored conference about the dam.[14] The list of participants was impressive. It included the manager of Cahora Bassa, who recounted the engineering feat of the dam's construction and the valiant attempts to keep it functioning, despite repeated Renamo attacks. Prominent scientists provided richly detailed accounts of the effects of the postdam river flow regime on the flora and fauna of the lower Zambezi valley. Historians presented papers on topics ranging from changing Zambezi flood patterns to the political economy of the dam. While more than fifty experts participated in the Songo colloquium,[15] absent were the voices of the African workers whose labor actually built Cahora Bassa and of the rural poor whose lives it changed forever—except through the presentations of a few sympathetic Europeans, who could offer, at best, only partial renditions of what local people remembered of the dam's history.[16] We quickly realized how little we knew about its impact on Songo-area workers and peasants, not to mention the rural communities downriver, whose gardens and grazing lands no longer benefited from the Zambezi's seasonal irrigation and whose fishing lagoons Cahora Bassa had greatly reduced.

This study presents an alternative history of Cahora Bassa—one that seeks to recover, or bring to the surface, what the master narratives of Mozambique's colonial and postcolonial state actors have suppressed.[17] This version clearly demonstrates that human and environmental well-being are inextricably intertwined, that development projects cannot be separated from the politics of control over scarce resources, and that the critical question of what is being "developed"—and for whom—is shaped as much by transnational as national or local actors.

Environmental policies and practices can never be divorced from relations of power. This is especially true when what is at stake is control over water, since no other natural resource is more important for the maintenance of life, society, and stable government. It is no surprise, then, that control of aquatic resources has provoked, and continues to provoke, conflict at local and national levels in Mozambique and elsewhere, especially in the global South.[18]

In the final analysis, most large state-driven development projects—whether dams or other initiatives that facilitate resource extraction and the export of cheap commodities—have not only failed to alleviate poverty and promote sustainable livelihoods but also often imperiled the lives of the poor. As long as such planned interventions lead to growing disparities in wealth and concomitant increases in hunger and poverty, which are the natural consequences of their market-driven calculus, for the overwhelming majority of people living in the global South there remains nothing but the delusion of development.

THE DAM REVOLUTION IN AFRICA

In the second half of the twentieth century, worldwide construction of large dams[19] increased exponentially—from approximately five thousand by 1950 to over fifty thousand by 2000.[20] According to Professor Kader Asmal, chair of the World Commission on Dams (WCD), "We dammed half our world's rivers at unprecedented rates of one per hour, and at unprecedented scales of over 45,000 [large] dams."[21] As a result, dam reservoirs submerged more than four hundred thousand square kilometers of the world's most fertile land.[22] Although the pace of construction has slowed, a number of new dams—most notably China's Three Gorges—were erected in the first decade of the twenty-first century.

In his monumental study of dams, Patrick McCully describes the appeal of such projects for political leaders as different as Jawaharlal Nehru, Mao

Tse-tung, Franklin Roosevelt, and Joseph Stalin: "The gargantuan scale of large dams, and their seeming ability to bring powerful and capricious natural forces under human control, gives them a unique hold on the human imagination. Perhaps more than any other technology, massive dams symbolize the progress of humanity from a life ruled by nature and superstition to one where nature is ruled by science, and superstition vanquished by rationality."[23] Nehru, for instance, invoked a sense of national pride, when observing the 226-meter-high Bhakra Dam, in northern India: "What a stupendous, magnificent work—a work which only that nation can take up which has faith and boldness!"[24]

The international community provided both material and moral support for these megaprojects. The World Bank, the largest financier of dams, funded more than six hundred dam projects in ninety-three countries during this period.[25] Other major lenders included the Inter-American and Asian Development Banks.[26] The Agricultural Organization of the United Nations (FAO) and the UN Development Programme (UNDP) also financed dam construction, as did the United States Agency for International Development (USAID) and the British Overseas Development Administration (ODA).[27]

These dam proponents, however, uniformly ignored the fact that the construction of large dams also brought intense suffering for an estimated 30 to 60 million people worldwide—many already poor and disenfranchised.[28] Most large dams forced poor rural populations to abandon their historic homelands, which the river's displaced water then submerged. In several cases, dams even had lethal consequences—the most tragic, perhaps, occurring in China's Hunan Province, where a number of dam bursts in 1975 left more than two hundred thousand people dead.[29]

Africa, too, became part of the dam revolution. In the name of modernization and prosperity, especially in the developmentalist years after World War II, European colonial governments constructed major hydroelectric complexes—as well as other large infrastructural projects.[30] Ghana's Akosombo Dam, for example, although originally conceived in the late colonial period, was erected under the leadership of Kwame Nkrumah shortly after independence.[31] Nkrumah used the language of national development to explain his unequivocal support for this colonial project: "Newer nations, such as ours, which are determined by every possible means to catch up in industrial strength, must have electricity in abundance before they can expect any large-scale industrial advance. . . . That, basically, is the justification for the Volta River Project."[32]

African leaders of all political persuasions embraced these projects with unbridled enthusiasm, as did their postcolonial successors. After all, dams reinforced the consolidation of state power in the countryside and were highly visible symbols of modernity and development. During the second half of the twentieth century, African governments constructed more than one thousand dams, including twenty megaprojects such as the Akasombo Dam in Ghana, the Lagdo Dam in Cameroon, the Kainji and Bakolori Dams in Nigeria, the Kossou Dam in Ivory Coast, and the Masinga Dam in Tanzania. Some of the most highly publicized dams in Africa—the Aswan High Dam, the Kariba Dam, and the Lesotho Highlands Water Project—cut across territorial frontiers.[33] By the end of the twentieth century, South Africa alone had more than 550 dams in operation.[34]

As elsewhere, the construction of large dams in Africa often had deleterious consequences. Megadams at Akasombo, Aswan, and Kariba flooded hundreds of thousands of hectares of fertile farmland.[35] The Akasombo, for example, which permanently inundated 4 percent of Ghana's land area, forced more than eighty thousand Ghanaians to abandon their communities adjacent to the Volta River.[36] Similarly, the Aswan dam uprooted one hundred twenty thousand people in Egypt and Sudan, and, in the area of the Kariba Dam, fifty-seven thousand Gwembe Tonga lost their homelands.[37] In these and many other cases around the continent, the physical, social, and cultural worlds of displaced peoples turned upside down.

People located downriver from the dams also found their livelihoods in jeopardy and critical natural resources degraded.[38] Damming permanently altered a river's flow regime—particularly the timing and extent of flooding along its banks. This disruption jeopardized long-established agricultural production systems that depended on seasonal flooding to enrich alluvial soils.[39] It also destroyed downriver fishing industries, increased waterborne diseases, eroded the shoreline and coast, degraded aquatic ecosystems, and caused declines in riparian animal and plant life.[40] Among the conclusions of a highly influential 2000 report by the WCD was the recognition that "in too many cases an unacceptable and often unnecessary price has been paid to secure these benefits [of dams], especially in social and environmental terms, by people displaced, by communities downstream, by taxpayers and by the natural environment."[41] Rural Mozambicans living adjacent to the Zambezi River certainly paid that price.

Although the construction of Cahora Bassa shares much in common with hydroelectric projects elsewhere in both Africa and other regions of the global South, the political context and social dynamics of Mozambique's megadam were unique. Cahora Bassa was the last "great" colonial infrastructure project in Africa. Whereas post–World War II British and French colonial planners tried to reshape the rural landscape of their African possessions through far-reaching river basin schemes and other large development projects,[42] Portuguese authorities invested little in Mozambique's rural infrastructure—or those of its other African colonies of Angola, Guinea-Bissau, and São Tomé. That all changed in the early 1960s when Portugal, as part of its antiguerrilla policy, began a number of infrastructural projects in the central and northern regions of the colony.

Military exigencies also explain why Cahora Bassa has the dubious status of being the world's largest national hydroelectric project created to export energy.[43] Mozambique's megadam, which cost so many rural families their livelihoods, land, and homes, existed solely to cement military ties between the Portuguese colonial administration and its apartheid neighbor, by exporting cheap energy to South Africa. In the process, the Mozambican countryside—even areas adjacent to the dam site—remained in the dark.

While the construction of large dams in Africa and elsewhere involved the forcible relocation by the state of large numbers of indigenous people, only in Mozambique were the victims of relocation herded into barbed-wire encampments (*aldeamentos*) to prevent them from aiding Frelimo guerrillas. The government also forcibly evicted several thousand more Africans living on the salubrious highlands near the dam site to make room for the construction of a segregated town for white workers and their families.

But it was not only peasants who suffered. Local African men who were conscripted to build the roads leading to the dam experienced another form of violence for the sake of Cahora Bassa, and the dam itself was literally built on the backs of thousands of African laborers enmeshed in a coercive and highly regimented labor regime.

These harsh realities highlight the central role of violence as a defining feature of Cahora Bassa's history. Unlike in India and Brazil, for instance, where domestic struggles shaped the politics of dam construction,[44] in Mozambique external political and security considerations generated this violence. Because the hydroelectric project symbolized the military alliance between the Portuguese colonial state and apartheid South Africa, the surrounding region became a highly contested zone of confrontation between Frelimo guerrillas seeking to sabotage it and the Portuguese military, which, with logistical support from Pretoria, unleashed a wave of violence against the peasant population allegedly to prevent them from aiding Frelimo.

Even after both the dam's completion and Mozambique's independence, the violence continued. When South African–backed Renamo forces launched a military campaign to destroy the new nation's economic infrastructure, Cahora Bassa's power lines were inviting targets—since the apartheid economy did not require the energy at that moment. These attacks lasted for over fifteen years.

THE LITERATURE ON LARGE DAMS

The dam revolution generated a voluminous body of scholarly literature, detailed discussion of which falls outside of the scope of this study. Broadly speaking, there are two diametrically opposed schools of thought: one celebrating and promoting these megaprojects as developmentalist triumphs and the other highlighting their damaging social and environmental consequences.

Engineers, economists, development experts, state officials, and representatives of the dam industry have been the most vocal proponents of the celebratory school. Their influential publications date back to the completion of the Hoover Dam, in the 1930s.[45] For half a century thereafter, they controlled the terms of public debate, while promoting dams in all corners of the globe. Using a narrow cost-benefit analysis, they emphasized the transformative potential of hydroelectric projects, even while acknowledging some of their unintended negative consequences. Dams, they stressed, provided a source of cheap energy that would stimulate industrial production and electrify areas with no previous access to power. Harnessing rivers, in their view, would promote irrigation and flood control, facilitate river transport, and ensure a secure supply of clean water. Many also predicted a sharp increase in the number of fish in dam reservoirs, thereby increasing the potential income of commercial anglers. More recently, the dam industry and its allies have appropriated the discourse of the green energy movement to claim that hydroelectric projects are a cleaner source of fuel than coal, thermal, oil, or natural gas.[46]

In the 1970s, geographers and anthropologists concerned about the social costs of dislocation and the worrisome environmental effects of recently erected dams began to challenge this dominant narrative. They pointed to the devastating ecological and health consequences of a river's inability to flow freely, since large dam reservoirs flooded fertile farmlands and rich forests, drowned wildlife, and destroyed medicinal plants. Downriver, altered flow regimes increased erosion, destroyed subsidiary channels, disrupted fish populations, increased salinization, and threatened vital mangrove forests. Human populations occupying river valleys also suffered sharp spikes in waterborne diseases, such as schistosomiasis, malaria, and gastroenteritis.[47]

Mounting evidence of large dams' damaging effects helped fuel indigenous protest movements, particularly in Brazil, India, Nigeria, Thailand, Turkey, and Zambia, and added urgency to academic debates.[48] These local insurgencies, supported by a growing transnational antidam movement,[49] highlighted for the world the traumatic social and cultural costs to riverine communities. Concerned scholars followed the lead of antidam activists, publishing accounts of forced displacement and the ways in which postdam flow regimes undermined traditional agricultural systems.[50] Other academics questioned whether providing cheap energy for cities and export industries at the expense of the rural poor was a sustainable development strategy or simply a reflection of who controlled the levers of state power.[51]

Although most of these debates focused on large dams in Asia and Latin America, Africanist scholars contributed by challenging the "heroic and often arrogant, modernizing dam-building agenda of the 1960s to the 1980s."[52] Foremost among them was the eminent anthropologist Elizabeth Colson, whose foundational 1971 study *The Social Consequences of Resettlement*, based on her extensive fieldwork in the 1960s, described in painful detail how the world of more than fifty-seven thousand Gwembe Tonga was turned upside down by their forcible removal from their homelands in southern Zambia during construction of the Kariba Dam. Thayer Scudder, who worked with Colson, extended her analysis by publicizing the dam-induced poverty in the area surrounding Lake Kariba, one of the largest artificial lakes and reservoirs in the world.[53] Geographer William Adams, in his continentwide study, *Wasting the Rain*, documented how river development schemes disrupted floodplain ecologies and subverted farming and fishing.[54] Most recently, feminist scholar Dzodzi Tsikata's *Living in the Shadow of the Large Dams* analyzed the experiences of lakeside and downstream communities affected by Ghana's Volta River Project.

Other Africanists, both north and south of the Sahara, opened up new areas of inquiry. Timothy Mitchell's provocative *Rule of Experts*, using the case of the Aswan High Dam to explore the inner world of technopolitics in the Egyptian state, showed how colonial and postcolonial experts celebrated the transformative power of dams while sidelining peasants' concerns.[55] JoAnn McGregor's innovative study, *Crossing the Zambezi*, situated the Kariba Dam's construction within the 150-year history of the politics of landscape in the middle Zambezi, while Julia Tischler's doctoral dissertation on Kariba analyzed the politics of development in the turbulent era of decolonialization.[56] Tsikata's work on the Volta Dam raised important questions about the gendered effects of Africa's hydroelectric projects, and Stephan Miescher's current research, extending the analysis beyond political economy and ecology, will explore its cultural symbolism and Ghanaian attitudes toward modernity, development, and nationhood.[57]

Our work is informed by both the scholarly debate on Africa's large dams and prior scholarship on Cahora Bassa, much of which focused on either the dam's strategic dimensions or its effects on downriver flora and fauna. João Paulo Borges Coelho's 1993 doctoral thesis, "Protected Villages and Communal Villages in the Mozambican Province of Tete (1968–1982)," detailed how the forced relocation of thousands of peasants—both those living in the area adjacent to Cahora Bassa and others residing in adjacent regions not affected by the dam—was a critical dimension of Lisbon's counterinsurgency program.[58] Keith Middlemas's 1975 study, *Cabora Bassa: Engineering and Politics in Southern Africa*, documented the challenges of financing and constructing the dam, drawing on official government reports, correspondence between Lisbon and prospective investors, and over one hundred interviews with dam officials, African workers, Portuguese military commanders, and Frelimo guerrillas.[59] In his carefully researched doctoral thesis, "The Regulation of the Zambezi in Mozambique," Peter Bolton examined the initial impact of the dam on the Zambezi River valley.[60]

Professor Brian Davies, a University of Cape Town zoologist, was part of a Portuguese research team in the 1970s investigating the anticipated ecological impacts of Cahora Bassa. After conducting pioneering studies downriver, he predicted that the dam would cause appreciable environmental destruction.[61] He spent the next thirty years mapping out the actual consequences, which were even worse than what he had predicted.[62] His work has been extended by Richard Beilfuss, a hydrologist who, with a team of Mozambican and foreign scientists, extensively researched environmental flows and sustainable management of the Zambezi River over the last two decades.[63] Their extremely important studies of wetland and wildlife conservation, particularly in the Zambezi delta, have provided invaluable information on the long-term ecological effects of Cahora Bassa. Our debt to all these scholars, but particularly to Beilfuss and his colleagues, is evident in the frequency with which we cite their work.

The present study makes three contributions to the literature on Cahora Bassa and the broader scholarship on the impact of large hydroelectric projects in Africa and the global South. Most writings on large dams have a strong presentist bias. Investigators typically begin their analyses either just before a dam's construction or shortly thereafter. By contrast, we treat Cahora Bassa as part of a much longer history, dating back to the sixteenth century, of Portuguese attempts to colonize the Zambezi valley and domesticate one of Africa's mightiest rivers. In summarizing that history, we also explore how European travelers and Portuguese functionaries forged a master narrative of the river as wild and dangerous—one that stands in stark contrast to indigenous representations of the Zambezi as a source of life and prosperity, which could be dangerous if not respected. Additionally, we look ahead—examining how the dam's history may affect Mozambique's decision to build a second dam at Mphanda Nkuwa, sixty kilometers downriver.

Just as we have extended the temporal parameters of our study beyond the relatively short history of the Cahora Bassa Dam, so too have we broadened its spatial dimensions by extending our gaze downriver from the dam site and reservoir to the Zambezi delta and estuary. Most studies of large dams tend to explore the social and ecological consequences either around the dam site or in the river delta, rather than examining the entire river system. As part of this expanded geographic perspective, we also include material on the Kariba Dam, located approximately eight hundred kilometers upriver on the Zimbabwe-Zambia border, since the amount of water it discharged has had a significant impact on Cahora Bassa and the area downriver. To understand the changing fields of power in which Cahora Bassa's history is embedded, it is necessary to consider the wider regional, transnational, and global forces operating during this period. Cold war geopolitics, the apartheid regime's aggressive efforts at bolstering its hegemonic position in the region, Lisbon's efforts to maintain a significant presence in postcolonial Mozambique, and pressure from the World Bank and the IMF have all figured prominently in the history of the dam.

Finally, we have shifted our principal angle of vision from a state-centric developmental approach to one that explores the linkages between power inequities and environmental change—particularly the difficulties of securing water for the Zambezi valley's rural poor and ecosystems. We focus on the interconnection between livelihood vulnerability and environmental changes provoked by the dam, and, because our emphasis is on the daily lives of affected rural communities, peasants' stories, rather than the official modernizing discourse of the colonial regime or the postcolonial state, are at the center of our analysis.

In adopting this strategy, we do not dismiss the role of the colonial state or its successor. Nor do we ignore the possibility of dissenting voices within the Portuguese and Frelimo administrations. To the contrary, we examine whatever critical debates and divergent views about the dam periodically surfaced. Although some documentation from the colonial period exists, because Mozambique's postcolonial archives remain closed, and producing cheap hydroelectric power continues to be a high priority of the Frelimo government, high-level disagreements about Cahora Bassa and the proposed dam at Mphanda Nkuwa generally remain shrouded in secrecy.[64]

Thanks to the work of such authors as Timothy Mitchell, James Scott, and James Ferguson, we know a great deal about "the rule of experts," what it means to see like a state, and the totalitarian aspects of modernist state planning.[65] Using these concepts, we have sought to write a social history of a development project in which the rural poor are not simply objects of state planning but play a significant role as actors in the story. This shift in the angle of vision helps us to understand how top-down developmentalism affected the organization of agriculture, the utilization of labor, the exploitation of microecological systems, the development of innovative fishing techniques, and the general resiliency of affected populations.

DISPLACEMENT FOR DEVELOPMENT

In the name of development, state-planned and -executed large dam projects have disrupted the lives and livelihoods of millions of people throughout the global South. "Development-induced displacement," to borrow the language of Peter Vandergeest, most often affects the poorest and most marginalized communities.[66] It also can have calamitous consequences for the physical and cultural worlds in which poor communities reside. Displacement for development certainly happened at Cahora Bassa, and the history of that destructive process is the narrative core of this study.

In the chapters that follow, we employ the term *displace* in two slightly different ways.[67] In its most conventional usage, as described in the next several paragraphs, *displace* means to remove or shift someone or something from its customary physical location. We use *displace* in this sense to capture the lived experiences of riverine communities that were violently dislodged and relocated to so-called protected villages when Lake Cahora Bassa inundated their historic homelands. *Displace* also refers to the forced removal of African villages located on the salubrious Songo highlands when those lands were taken over by Zamco, the multinational corporation that constructed the dam.[68] The term *displacement* also captures the experience of peasants living downriver who had to abandon fertile alluvial plains and island gardens when unpredictable discharges from the dam flooded these highly valued cultivated spaces.

In addition to people, Cahora Bassa literally displaced animals, plants, and soils. A few examples will illustrate this point. Herds of elephant, wildebeest, and kudu, among other wildlife that roamed the savannas and forests in the region adjacent to the river, either drowned or fled when the dam reservoir was filled. By sharply reducing the volume of river flow in the lower Zambezi, the dam increased salinization in the biologically diverse delta wetlands, leading over time to the replacement of freshwater grasses with more salt-tolerant species, able to thrive in the brackish water. And, because Cahora Bassa dramatically impeded the silt from traveling downriver, the mineral-starved water below the dam recaptured sediment loads by eating away at the riverbanks. This caused erosion that displaced large quantities of precious alluvial soil.

By converting the natural power of the Zambezi River into electricity for South Africa, the dam also displaced energy from Mozambique. Its primary function was to produce electricity, but not for local consumption. Instead, Cahora Bassa transported up to 1,450 megawatts over a 1,800-kilometer network of pylons stretching from Songo to the power grids of South Africa. This energy was, and continues to be, used to power South African mines, farms, and cities, while the vast majority of Mozambicans who live in the lower Zambezi valley remain without access to electricity and the economic activities it makes possible. In short, the dam converted one of Mozambique's most vital natural resources into an export commodity, principally for the economic benefit of its powerful neighbor.

The dam robbed energy from the region in another, less obvious way. By harnessing the once powerful Zambezi so that it no longer flowed freely, the dam prevented the river from accomplishing all its previous essential work. In addition to blocking the flow of water and silt, the dam walls trapped substantial amounts of organic and inorganic material that had previously fertilized the alluvial soils of the floodplains, creating optimal conditions for agriculture in an environment where erratic rainfall and poor soils made farming a precarious enterprise. As a result, riparian human communities as well as other forms of plant and animal life permanently lost essential energy-supplying nutrients.

We employ the term *displace* in a second, very different way to connote a less tangible process of dislodging and replacing. Here we have in mind the ways in which dominant colonial and postcolonial narratives of Cahora Bassa's history have rendered inaudible the stories and experiences of the Zambezi valley's riverine peoples. This silencing is due, of course, to the asymmetrical power relations surrounding the production and dissemination of knowledge about state-sponsored development projects. The Portuguese colonial state and its postcolonial successors all maintained a wall of silence around Cahora Bassa, authorizing only official representations of the dam in public discussions. Absent from public discourse were the experiences, conversations, and ideas of peasants who lived with the consequences of its existence. Official adulation for the hydroelectric project muted the voices of these men and women, in a form of displacement whose epistemological violence was no less painful than the physical violence peasants experienced because of the dam.

That Portuguese authorities silenced critical discussion of Cahora Bassa is hardly surprising, given the colonial regime's highly authoritarian character and its tendency to stifle any dissent. For all the fanfare about improving the quality of life for rural Mozambicans, Cahora Bassa's ultimate purpose was to cement a security alliance between the Portuguese colonial state and apartheid South Africa. The dam was integral to Portugal's antiguerrilla military strategy and a symbol of its commitment to retain its African empire. Even in government circles, there could be no debate about Cahora Bassa. European planners, scientists, or district administrators who raised questions about the potentially devastating effects of the megadam on local communities and environments were ignored, censored, or removed from their positions.[69]

The colonial version of history rested on the premise that the Portuguese were the guardians of progress, civilization, and modernity.[70] In its master narrative, the colonial state produced order, as opposed to the chaos and disorder of the precolonial past, which left no place for state-sanctioned violence. To the extent that colonial authorities acknowledged the violence that did occur, they cast it as an unintended or unfortunate, but necessary, consequence of "progress." Thus, Lisbon claimed that, compared to the dislocations caused by other large dam projects in Africa, only twenty-eight thousand people—a relatively small number—would be relocated due to Cahora Bassa and that problems associated with peasant relocation were amenable to technical solutions, such as selecting fertile sites and digging wells and boreholes. Colonial officials also contended that the inconvenience of forced resettlement was a trivial price to pay for the wide-ranging benefits Cahora Bassa would deliver.

Since the state prohibited scholars, journalists, and international observers from entering the areas of the Zambezi valley where aldeamentos (protected villages) were located, rural families herded into the protected villages had no channel through which to communicate their version of events to the outside world and no power to challenge the sanitized fiction of official discourse. Like displaced peasants, the African workers whose labor built Cahora Bassa could share stories of suffering only with one another. Portuguese accounts of the dam's construction similarly displaced evidence of the ongoing violence and exploitation and depicted the construction site as a harmonious multiracial workplace. No one reported the coercion and intimidation, the grueling work schedules and inadequate living conditions, or the industrial accidents that were an integral part of African dam workers' daily lives.

Even when, after independence, scholars and journalists documented the forced internment and labor abuses, the Frelimo government reproduced the colonial narrative that portrayed Cahora Bassa as an icon of economic development and progress and expressed confidence in the dam's ability to transform the Zambezi valley and spread the fruits of socialism to rural populations. Yet, like all developmentalist states, postindependence Mozambique paid scant attention to the voices of the rural poor—the riverside communities whose concerns about the effects of the dam were lost in the noise surrounding socialist transformation. In 1987, when Frelimo abandoned its socialist project and implemented an IMF–World Bank structural adjustment program, Cahora Bassa figured prominently in its neoliberal development agenda. The optimistic discourse of Mozambican leaders—engineers and economists, stressing the untapped potential of the dam as a source of hydroelectricity—perpetuated the state's developmentalist ideology and, once again, marginalized peasant concerns.[71]

In general, displacement is an inherent part of large-state development initiatives, and, whether intended or not, violence regularly accompanies massive infrastructural projects, such as dams. Nevertheless, development, as originally conceived in the aftermath of World War II,[72] was not supposed to involve the violent disruption of rural societies. Instead, it was built on the premise that "foreign aid and investment on favorable terms, the transfer of knowledge or production techniques, measures to promote health and education, and economic planning would lead impoverished countries to be able to become 'normal' market economies."[73] Since development was a strategy to alleviate poverty, the rise in per capita GNP, which accompanied development would, according to economist Arthur Lewis, give "man greater control over his environment and thereby increase his freedom."[74] At a global level, accelerated economic growth would narrow the gap between rich and poor, precipitating "modernization and economic take off."[75] By the 1970s, advocates of neoliberalism were proclaiming that unfettered markets were the key to development and to the optimal allocation of resources.[76]

Theorists on the left disagreed, pointing to the failures of large infrastructural projects, like dams—one prominent and typically destructive form of development—to alleviate poverty.[77] They contended that, rather than closing the gap, the unfettered functioning of the global market actually widened disparities between rich and poor.[78] This argument was sharpened by critical theorists who stressed that the "uneven development" inherent in capitalism had far-reaching and unequal social and spatial consequences that reinforced global hierarchies of power. By heightening the "contradictory relations of class, of gender, of town and countryside, of ethnicity and nationality," uneven development created conflicts over scarce resources and struggles for social justice.[79] Other Marxist critics took a slightly different approach, maintaining that a capitalist modernization agenda further oppressed the working classes, while facilitating capitalist accumulation.[80] In its place, they offered a socialist model of development that would promote prosperity and social equality.[81] Feminist scholars, drawing on a variety of different social theories, instead focused on the power of patriarchy and the subordination of women under both developmental paths, which ignored or undervalued production for sustenance and survival in which women and children figured most prominently.[82]

Proponents of sustainable development—primarily environmental economists for whom the construction of megadams provoked obvious concerns—also criticized the tendency of developmentalists to privilege large infrastructural projects. They insisted that any analysis had to consider the long-term resilience, vulnerability and regenerative capacity of ecological systems, which were essential for sustained economic growth, along with inter- and intragenerational equity.[83]

In the past two decades, postdevelopmental theorists have argued that development cannot be equated with enlightenment and progress. Ferguson, for example, has maintained that Western notions of modernity were little more than "a set of discourses and practices that has produced and sustained the notion of 'the Third World as an object' to be developed" and that developmentalism shaped and legitimated the practices of both the postcolonial state and international development agencies, whose interests were closely aligned.[84] Arturo Escobar similarly criticizes developmentalism as a strategy by capitalist countries in the global North to secure control over scarce resources and former colonial subjects, which simultaneously intensified hunger and poverty in the very communities being "developed."[85] The dam revolution is a case in point—the quintessential example of the delusion of development.

Although our study is informed by these criticisms of development, it would be an oversimplification to assume that development "is a self-evident process, everywhere the same and always tainted by its progressivist European provenance."[86] In fact, local, national and transnational factors produce substantial variations over time and space, and even development's coercive power, while still inseparable from larger processes of economic transformation and power relations, is rooted in local history and social relations.[87]

While not rejecting the notion of development per se, we recognize its inadequacy as an analytical concept.[88] For us, the critical issue is what exactly is being developed and for whom. Throughout the text, we employ the concept of sustainable livelihoods—itself a product of development theory—which stresses the inextricable interconnection between power, poverty, and environmental degradation,[89] since neither communities nor nations can ultimately sustain themselves if they pursue policies that adversely affect the nonhuman world.[90] In this study, we explore how the socioeconomic and ecological changes caused by Cahora Bassa adversely affected both people's access to scarce resources and their capacity to use these resources effectively to enhance their daily lives.[91] To the extent that the dam limited peasants' ability to achieve positive livelihood outcomes, it brought with it, instead, the delusion of development.

READING CAHORA BASSA—THE CHALLENGE OF SOURCES

Archival sources provide much of the evidentiary base for chapters 2, 3, and 4. The Arquivo Histórico de Moçambique (AHM) in Maputo, Mozambique, and the Arquivo Nacional da Torre do Tombo (ANTT) in Lisbon, Portugal, are the most important repositories of written documentation on the planning and construction of Cahora Bassa. The AHM contains numerous engineering and financial reports, as well as brief ecological and ethnographic surveys of the area to be affected by the dam, prepared under the auspices of the Missão do Fomento e Povoamento do Zambese (MFPZ), the state agency charged with overseeing the dam project. The archive is also a repository for reports from local administrators and military officials describing the forced resettlement scheme, rural opposition to the aldeamentos, the war effort against Frelimo, and official concerns about Frelimo's advance along both margins of the Zambezi River.[92]

The ANTT houses the largest body of material on the strategic dimensions of the dam. Reports by the Portuguese secret police (Polícia Internacional e de Defesa do Estado, or PIDE) and other security branches, along with those of colonial administrative officials, document the forced removal of peasants, the conditions of the proposed resettlement sites, and internal debates about the strategic desirability of relocating thousands of people from their home-lands to protected villages. These sources reveal fissures within the Portuguese colonial regime, particularly between civilian administrators, who favored per-suading rural communities to relocate voluntarily, and military commanders, who simply wanted to use force. Colonial intelligence reports, often based on accounts from African spies, describe the growing rural opposition to forced resettlement, the difficult position of loyalist chiefs who had to implement the villagization policy, and government fears that Frelimo would organize workers at the dam site. The ANTT also contains significant documentation of Portugal's negotiations with South Africa concerning financial and secu-rity matters and of efforts by competing multinational corporations to win construction contracts. Additionally, there is an entire dossier about Lisbon's attempts in the early 1970s to infiltrate and discredit the antidam movement, which had organized an international boycott of Cahora Bassa.

This voluminous documentation, however, has serious limitations. The most obvious is that colonial officials typically considered the opinions and experiences of the rural poor insignificant, rarely recording them for poster-ity. Even at the local level, European personnel tended to ignore the critical factors affecting the lives of African workers and peasants. For example, there were only passing references to labor conditions at the dam site, all concerning white workers. Moreover, because the dam site and the town of Songo were the domain of two Portuguese companies—Zamco, the consortium that built the dam, and Hidroeléctrica de Cahora Bassa (HCB), which subsequently owned and operated it—the limited extant labor documentation is in their archives, which remain closed to the public.[93] Nor did colonial authorities consider reporting on either life within the aldeamentos or the social and ecological consequences of Cahora Bassa's construction.

More fundamentally, these sources are problematic because they are colonial texts produced by chroniclers whose perceptions and agendas were shaped by their race, nationality, class, gender, and status within the colonial hierarchy. While it is sometimes possible to discern faint echoes of African voices in the written words of colonial personnel—as, for example, in adminis-trators' reports of conversations with African chiefs—teasing out subaltern per-spectives from such documents is very difficult. As Premesh Lalu argues, "to claim that subaltern consciousness, voice or agency can be retrieved through colonial texts is to ignore the organization and representation of colonized sub-jects as a subordinate proposition within primary discourses."[94] Thus, one must read even the richest archival documents from the colonial period carefully and critically, "against the grain."[95] While archival sources do not present a monolithic image of Cahora Bassa, the dominant narrative that emerges from these writings tends to obscure or disguise the realities of African rural life.

The wall of silence Lisbon imposed around Cahora Bassa during and after its construction compounds the inherent difficulty of utilizing colonial-era archival sources. The Portuguese government buried the findings of its own researchers when they raised concerns about the project and allowed only trusted journalists and international reporters to enter the region, which they classified as a strategic military zone. Even journalists and researchers with official clearance found their movements restricted to Songo and a few model aldeamentos. A Portuguese anthropologist studying the Tawara, a community living adjacent to the dam, acknowledged that he often had to rely on secondhand information, since "participant-observation was reduced to a minimum."[96]

This policy of secrecy and nondisclosure continued into the postcolonial period. Despite nominal oversight by Mozambique's energy ministry, the HCB still treated the dam as its own private domain and released almost no information about it. The Frelimo government, fearing Rhodesian sabotage, declared Cahora Bassa off-limits to most foreign researchers and journalists. Ideologically predisposed to pursuing rural development through large state projects, Frelimo's Marxist-Leninist leadership discouraged public debate about the dam, labeling it a symbol of socialist transformation and modernity. In the 1980s, Renamo military campaigns turned the Zambezi valley into a major battleground whose violence disrupted all local social and environmental research efforts. That Mozambique's national archives are not yet open for this period and that the Frelimo archives are in disarray[97] exacerbate the evidentiary limitations. In chapters 6 and 7, when discussing Mozambique's negotiations with Portugal over ownership of Cahora Bassa, its efforts to pressure the postapartheid South African state to increase the price paid for its electricity, and the status of the projected dam at Mphande Nkuwa, we had to rely on the publicly reported announcements of Mozambican officials. This was because the authorities, citing their confidential nature, were unwilling to speak candidly about these issues.

To address these challenges, we have relied on several reports concerning the feasibility of building a second dam at Mphanda Nkuwa produced by state-sponsored consultants, which include background material on the social and environmental effects of Cahora Bassa.[98] We have also examined documents and reports commissioned by nongovernmental organizations, environmental groups, and antidam activists, which, while often failing to capture the full complexity of realities on the ground, advance powerful critiques of the hydroelectric project.[99] The most valuable written sources for the postcolonial period are the meticulously researched hydrological and ecological research about the Zambezi River valley, on whose findings we draw throughout this book.[100]

The more than three hundred oral interviews of residents of riverside communities, missionaries, scientists, state officials, and antidam activists provide the principal evidence for most of this study. We began this project in 1998, while completing fieldwork for a book on runaway Chikunda slaves.[101] Two years later, Arlindo Chilundo, a Mozambican historian, and Allen Isaacman directed a research team from Universidade Eduardo Mondlane that studied the social and ecological consequences of Cahora Bassa.[102] Over two summers the team interviewed more than two hundred peasants and fisherfolk, living primarily on the southern margins of the Zambezi, whose recollections were recorded in public spaces, where members of the larger community could offer their thoughts. The interviews were public because, in rural communities, remembering and storytelling are preeminently social acts, in which both performance style and audience play crucial roles. In fact, the audience often intervened—either to elaborate on how their recollections were similar or different or to move the conversation to topics they thought were more interesting or significant.

We encountered several key informants by chance. Claúdio Gremi, an Italian Jesuit priest, was in the audience at the Songo conference. During the question-and-answer session, he wondered why none of the presenters had described the forced removal of peasants living near the lake and their internment in aldeamentos. He also mentioned the harsh working conditions at the dam site. When we approached him at the conference's conclusion, he informed us that he had been stationed at Songo in the early 1970s, where he ministered to the peasants and workers living in the area. Although a critic of Portuguese colonialism, he was committed to historical accuracy and, for that reason, he would only report what he had witnessed firsthand or had heard directly from one of his parishoners.[103] We have relied heavily on his observations.

Padre Gremi introduced us to parishioners who were, or had been, employed by the HCB. Absent his intervention, many of the aging employees would probably have been reluctant to speak about past or present working conditions. We interviewed them outside the earshot of company officials, at either our residence or their homes, often accompanied by Padre Gremi. These men detailed the harsh labor regime under which they worked, the major industrial accidents that went unreported in the colonial press, and their substandard living conditions. One of the most outspoken was Pedro da Costa Xavier, who had worked for the colonial state and the HCB for more than forty years. Although he had previously been a government tax collector and a company overseer, he described in detail the harsh working conditions at Songo and on the dam site.[104]

Our project also benefited from fieldwork conducted by Professor Wapu Mulwafu and three students from the University of Malawi's Chancellor College. The recollections of elders residing near the confluence of the Shire and Zambezi Rivers contained valuable information about the social and ecological effects of Cahora Bassa on communities along the northern margin of the Zambezi, the effects of South Africa's destabilization campaign on the region, and the plight of war refugees who sought sanctuary in Malawi.[105] Additionally, we draw on the voluminous fieldnotes of interviews British researcher Keith Middlemas conducted with colonial authorities, dam workers and managers, and Frelimo officials in 1970 and 1976.[106]

Upon analyzing this material, we realized that we could appreciate the full impact of Cahora Bassa on the peoples and environments of the lower Zambezi valley only if we understood how local communities perceived the proposed new dam at Mphanda Nkuwa. Toward that end, in 2008 and 2009, David Morton, an advanced graduate student at the University of Minnesota, interviewed peasants in Chirodzi-Sanangwe and Chococoma, villages near the dam site. Between 2009 and 2011, to learn more about this project, we also met with antidam activists and officials of the construction company planning Mphanda Nkuwa.

Because our study, above all else, concerns the lived experiences of riverside communities, their stories, memories, and representations figure most prominently. At the outset, we must stress that many of these memories gloss over the challenges and hardships that have characterized life along the Zambezi River for centuries. After all, irregular rainfall, periodic flooding, and other natural calamities, along with the uneven quality of the soils, imposed limits on agricultural production in the region. That many males had to leave the Zambezi valley in order to earn enough to pay their annual taxes and provide for their families clearly suggests the impoverished nature of the region, whose agricultural productivity was often insufficient. While life was less precarious for those who farmed along the alluvial plains adjacent to the river, these problems never entirely disappeared.[107] In fact, even in the rosier accounts of life before Cahora Bassa, there are muted references to seasonal hunger, food shortages, and natural disasters.

Such nostalgia about the predam period is understandable, since the elders with whom we spoke believe that Cahora Bassa is responsible for recent hardships. Given the stark reality of their present existence, it is hardly surprising that they failed to report recollections that ran counter to their characterization of life after Cahora Bassa. Even so, there are hints of such realities even in the more nostalgic accounts, which we do our best to present.

Despite the limitations of such interviews as historical evidence,[108] we are convinced that these oral texts, read critically, not only challenge the prevailing colonial and postcolonial formulations of Cahora Bassa's history but also offer an alternative narrative—a detailed interior view of life before and after the construction of the dam. Taken together, they tell a story about the changing social and environmental worlds of the lower Zambezi—one that would have been completely lost to us were we limited to conventional documentary evidence.

The recollections of the women and men who know the river best provide important evidence of the centrality of the Zambezi ecosystems to African lives and livelihoods. Their stories offer unique insights about the agricultural capacity, biodiversity, and livability of the Zambezi floodplains when the river still ran free. Because of our concern that their nostalgic memories romanticized the predam period, wherever possible we corroborate their stories with earlier or contemporary written accounts.

The elders' recollections also cast a revealing light on the devastating ecological, economic, social, and cultural consequences for peasant households of the colonial state's appropriation of the river's life-sustaining waters. Significantly, peasants' ecological memories of the perturbations in hydrology and ecology wrought by the dam confirm the preliminary observations of environmental scientists, both at the time of its construction and more recently.[109] These accounts also reveal how peasants perceived, explained, and coped with the ecological changes caused by Cahora Bassa and creatively adapted to changing life in the river basin.[110]

Additionally, oral accounts highlight the ways in which local notions of time were radically different from those of the colonial and postcolonial authorities. In the collective memories of most rural elders, the divide between "life before" and "life after" the dam was a critical temporal marker.[111] State planners, on the other hand, operated on a developmental time scale. They stressed that Cahora Bassa had a "natural life" of well over fifty years before problems of sedimentation would pose a threat to the mammoth project. During this period, in their view, the dam would remain a potent symbol of state-driven development and an integral part of the drive toward modernity.

Like all oral testimonies, our interviews are constrained by, but also benefit from, their interior positionality. Because there is no single "authentic" voice capable of capturing the tumultuous lived experiences of people living along the river and because the impacts of the harnessed river varied dramatically from one microecological zone to another, we tried to conduct as broad a range of interviews as possible throughout the Zambezi valley. That the dam ended seasonal flooding, for instance, had far greater consequences in the Zambezi delta, where the majority of residents farmed in the vast floodplain, than it did in the area around Tete, where the narrower band of alluvial soil supported only a small rural elite. Gender, age, and occupation further contributed to the variety in rural perceptions of Cahora Bassa, and the testimonies of women and men, old and young, peasant farmers and fisherfolk, hunters and herbalists focused on very different dimensions of daily life.[112] Thus, for example, women, who were responsible for the household's food security, stressed that, after construction of the dam, they coped with hunger by planting more cassava and searching the shoreline for roots and tubers—recalling that *nyika* (water lily) roots pounded into porridge were essential to their families' survival. Fisherfolk, on the other hand, described the steady decline in their catch and their desperate use of finer and finer nets to trap young fish, even though they knew that this strategy would further deplete future fish stocks. Herbalists spoke of their inability to treat the sick, because the floods created by the dam's unpredictable release of reservoir waters destroyed their medicinal plants. All these stories provided rare glimpses of fear, loss, and the indelible memory of impending chaos—moments of subjective reflection that historians have often found difficult to capture.[113]

We treat the diverse oral accounts produced through our interviews as significant social texts with hidden, multiple, and often contradictory meanings. Memories, whether individual or collective, do not exist outside the present; and problems of memory loss, repression, and reconstruction compound the challenges of interpretation, as does the impact of the interviewer's perceived social position. Understanding why people remember what they do at particular moments, and why they narrate those memories in particular ways, requires not only recognizing the nostalgia for what it is, but also probing what might have been at stake for the men and women we interviewed at the time of our meeting. As John Collins reminds us, we need to be aware of "the overdetermination of memory by immediate events."[114] In the case of Cahora Bassa, many elders may have also romanticized what life was like before the dam,[115] either because they were, at the time they were interviewed, involved in ongoing efforts to pressure the government to restore the predam flow regime or because they knew about plans to construct a second dam at Mphanda Nkuwa. Other villagers deployed this claim to support their demand that the ruling party take responsibility for environmental recovery in the Zambezi valley. Similarly, antidam activists and some living near Mphanda Nkuwa invoked a pre–Cahora Bassa golden age, as part of a broader political discourse opposing construction of the new dam.[116]

This nostalgia probably also explains the tendency of some elders to attribute to the dam's existence a variety of other ills, even when there is little evidence to support them. Several villagers, for example, asserted that, because the uncertain flows of the river discouraged animals from coming there in search of water, the small game they used to hunt had disappeared.[117] This explanation failed to consider the impacts of increasingly dense human settlements on the river's margins and the destruction of wildlife habitats by relocated villagers who cleared the riverine woodlands for firewood, building materials, and to make charcoal.[118]

The politics of forgetting also complicates the present-day meaning of oral narratives. Sometimes individuals and groups forget simply because of the limitations of memory—as when people make the past more manageable by blending the specifics of everyday life into a set of more "generic memories."[119] Indeed, accounts of patterned, normative behavior devoid of daily variations—as reflected in descriptions of "what we used to do"—characterized many of the stories about life before the dam. Forgetting, however, can also be a profoundly political act. As debates regarding memories of the Holocaust remind us, denial and suppression are common ways of reconfiguring both fragments of a collective past and the consciousness of individual historical actors.[120] Some of the elders we interviewed, for example, tended to downplay the more disturbing elements of their histories, such as the social tensions among aldeamento residents. Many were also reluctant to talk about adultery or witchcraft in these camps, although, when pressed, they acknowledged the presence of both. There was a similar tendency to gloss over the fact that male family members had worked as *sipais* (African police) or had fought in the colonial army. Such distortions require that we listen carefully and critically not only to the multiple voices in oral sources but also to the silences.[121]

Interpreting Zambezi valley oral sources becomes even more problematic due to the forced relocation of peasants into protected villages between 1970 and 1975 and the massive displacement of rural communities fleeing from Renamo attacks during the 1980s. These related processes destroyed communities, filled refugee villages with people from many different places, and severed their attachments to the specific physical sites associated with a remembered past. Since many stories about the past were grounded in particular "memory places" or "memoryscapes,"[122] displacement may have discouraged some from regularly reciting their historical memories—an activity necessary for their retention. Given the extraordinary instability in Mozambique during this period, we must be sensitive to Isabel Hofmeyr's position that oral traditions lose much of their substance when divorced from the geographical and social setting of their performance.[123] That her position may be somewhat overstated is suggested by Heidi Gengenbach's brilliant and comprehensive study of southern Mozambican women whose lives and communities were ravaged by Renamo attacks which forced them to flee their homelands.[124] Contrary to Hofmeyr, she found that physically displaced people did not necessarily cease to remember their past[125] and that, even where some loss of memory occurred, its rate was uneven.[126] Thus, scholars must be sensitive both to the circumstances under which displaced people manage to hold on to their memories and to the strength of their remaining recollections.

How people reconstruct, interpret, and use the past has powerful relevance for the present and future, and awareness of what might be at stake in speaking publicly about Cahora Bassa certainly influenced responses to our questions. After many of these sessions, outspoken individuals—some angry, others solicitous—asked us to stress to government officials in Maputo how much rural people had suffered because of Cahora Bassa. Beatriz Maquina, for example, expressed her frustrations as follows:

We are very tired of being interviewed. Many people have come here [from the government and NGOs] to ask us questions, and they promised to bring us seeds, corn, other cereals and blankets. But, until today, we have not received anything and we continue to suffer. These promises were made during the time of the war with Renamo and even today. They promised us many things and promised to help us, but nothing ever happened. We do not have schools, a hospital, or anything else. We are tired of all these interviews. We want to know when we will receive these things promised to us. You in the city eat well and live well, and we continue to suffer.[127]

A few raised the issue of compensation, although most simply wanted the authorities to make the river run freely again.[128] Although we insisted that we were not working for the government and had no direct links to state officials, these exchanges underscore the ways in which research and representation cannot be divorced from relations of power, which meant, at a minimum, that they saw us as having access to and influence with those who mattered.[129]

Whatever the contemporary overtones and difficulties of interpretation, these oral accounts constitute the richest and most accurate body of evidence about both the changing world of the lower Zambezi valley and the lived experience of its rural residents. Like all other forms of historical evidence, however, oral testimonies require careful and critical reading.

THE BOOK'S ARCHITECTURE

This study focuses on the period from the 1960s, when the Portuguese began planning for Cahora Bassa, to 2007, when Mozambique finally gained majority ownership of the dam. We situate it, however, within a broader historical framework, beginning with Portuguese efforts, dating back to the sixteenth century, to dominate the Zambezi River valley and ending with the ever-present effect of Cahora Bassa on the daily lives of people living adjacent to the river.

Chapter 2 documents Portuguese efforts, dating back to the sixteenth century, to conquer and domesticate the Zambezi River and its hinterland. Through the long history of their encounters with the waterway and riverine communities, colonial authorities, travelers, geographers, and development experts forged a narrative that stressed the dangers of the unharnessed river and constructed the region as an insalubrious backwater occupied by primitive people and half-breed Portuguese with neither the will nor the capacity to exploit nature's bounty. This chapter also explores local representations of the river before the dam, in which the idea of the Zambezi as a source of life coexisted with the notion of a capricious river that could flood their fields and destroy both their livelihoods and their lives.

Chapter 3 examines the construction of Cahora Bassa. Here we document the enormous technical problems the Portuguese had to overcome in a remote corner of Mozambique without any infrastructure. The chapter focuses on the labor process at the dam site, the highly racialized and regimented organization of work, and the contrasting experiences of European and African employees.

Chapter 4 explores the forced displacement of more than thirty thousand peasants from their ancestral homelands, which were later submerged under the man-made lake. Reconstruction of aspects of daily life within the aldeamentos relies primarily on the oral narratives of men and women who were herded into these barbed-wire encampments.

Chapter 5 shifts the angle of vision downriver. Cahora Bassa had far-reaching effects on the ecology of the Zambezi River valley and on the communities living adjacent to the waterway. The change in the river's flow regime—above all the unpredictable discharges from the dam—jeopardized the alluvial farming practices on which hundreds of thousands of people had relied in the predam era. The dramatic decline in its sediment load, trapped behind the walls of the dam, also robbed farmlands of valuable nutrients and precipitated massive erosion along the riverbanks. Plant and animal life that had depended on the river for sustenance suffered as well. Our discussion of Cahora Bassa's ecological effects relies heavily on both the oral testimonies and the scientific findings of a handful of researchers. While we have tried to assess and summarize the scientific data, as social historians we lack the technical expertise to explain fully the dam's impact on the ecology of the Zambezi valley.

Chapter 6 focuses on displaced energy. It documents Cahora Bassa's unique role as the largest dam in the world constructed to produce energy for export. Even after the end of Portuguese colonial rule and until today, virtually all its energy goes to South Africa. The chapter also details Frelimo's long struggle to gain control over the dam, which remained in Portugal's hands until 2007—thirty-two years after Mozambique achieved independence.

In "Legacies," the final chapter, we review the impact of the dam on both the riverine communities and the biosphere. Despite Cahora Bassa's traumatic history, the Frelimo government remains committed to a colonial-era plan to erect a second dam approximately seventy kilometers downriver. There are many striking parallels, and several significant differences, between the colonial and postcolonial projects. After examining the current rationale for the second dam, and the opposition that has emerged from a small but vocal antidam movement in the Mozambican capital, we discuss the concerns of and the expected outcomes for the two thousand residents who will have to make way for Mphanda Nkuwa, should this project proceed.

2 ⌒ The Zambezi River Valley in Mozambican History

An Overview

WELL BEFORE the Portuguese arrival in the Zambezi valley, in the sixteenth century, the Zambezi River had attracted Shona- and Chewa-speaking peoples who settled permanently along the banks of the river (see map 2.1),[1] as well as hunters, traders, and adventurers in search of gold, some of whom remained in the region. For over three centuries, the waterway also figured prominently in Portugal's plans to control the Mozambican interior. The Cahora Bassa Dam was merely its most recent effort to colonize the Zambezi valley and domesticate the river.

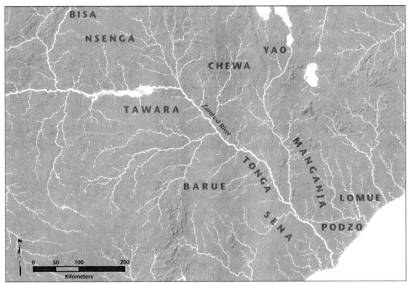

MAP 2.1. Zambezi ethnic groups. *University of Minnesota Cartography*

During these centuries, the Zambezi was a porous frontier that both separated and connected the peoples living near the river.[2] While communities on each side recognized it as a boundary, people also traded across it, fished in it, and sometimes even farmed on both banks. Gradually the river became less significant as a frontier than as a zone of settlement. As these groups of African and other immigrants domesticated the Zambezi valley, they transformed the waterway into a valuable resource.

We start this chapter with an overview of the Zambezi valley's strategic and changing significance as a highway into the interior, a home to the *prazo* estates, a zone of imperialist competition, and a site of unfulfilled economic development—themes that encapsulate much of the larger world's encounters with the region. From this history, Europeans forged a master narrative—portraying the river as "wild and dangerous," the indigenous population as "primitive," and the descendants of the Portuguese and Goan settlers as "half-breeds" who fostered the slave trade and stunted economic development by failing to exploit the area's natural resources. Portugal used these images of instability and violence to justify its conquest of the Zambezi valley, toward the end of the nineteenth century.

We then shift the angle of vision from a regional and transnational perspective and explore the impact of the Zambezi on the daily lives of the local populations. Their stories, based on a more sustained and intimate relationship with the river, are markedly different. For them, the river was, above all else, a source of life and prosperity, even though unusually large floods sometimes destroyed their fields and swept away their homes.

THE ZAMBEZI AS A HIGHWAY INTO THE INTERIOR

Long before the Portuguese arrival, the Zambezi River was a strategic highway for a vibrant commerce in gold, ivory, and slaves. Coastal Muslim traders, who had long served as the point men of Indian Ocean merchant capital, were already operating there by the fifteenth century. A century later, in 1511, António da Saldanha, a Portuguese chronicler, described dhows traveling up the Zambezi from the coastal port of Quelimane to the Lupata gorge. There, coastal traders paid the local Tonga land chiefs for the right to offload their wares, which local porters then carried to inland markets south of the Zambezi where Indian Ocean merchants exchanged cloth and a variety of other imported goods for gold, copper, ivory, and wax.[3]

For the Portuguese, the Zambezi valley was a wild and unfamiliar landscape—a malaria-infested, yellow fever–ridden frontier zone characterized by social disorder and decay. In the colonial imagination, it was both a landscape of fear and the gateway into the untapped mineral wealth of the interior. Their goals were to push the boundaries of civilization, dislodge the infidel Muslim traders, and exploit the region's gold and silver, which those merchants were already purchasing. By the 1570s, Lisbon had established fortified settlements along the Zambezi at Sena and Tete that became the region's administrative centers and garrison towns.[4] From Sena, located approximately two hundred kilometers from the coast, they were able to control river navigation between it and the Shire River. Tete, a further two hundred kilometers upriver, was a strategic point of entry into the south-central African interior. Lisbon later built a small commercial and military post further inland at Zumbo, on the northern bank of the Zambezi at its confluence with the Luangwa River (see map 1.2).

For almost three hundred years Sena, Tete, and Zumbo were at the center of the Portuguese commercial network. Portuguese and Goan merchants and *prazeiros* (Portuguese estate holders) dispatched caravans, ranging from ten to several hundred slaves, into the interior from these river-based trading stations. Each caravan, directed by a *misambadzi* (local trading specialist), traded both at fixed markets—like the fairs at Manica and Aruangua (see map 2.2)—and at villages along the route. By the end of the eighteenth century, these Zambezi-based caravans were traveling as far north as the Lunda homelands in the Congo and as far west as the rich gold producing areas in present-day Zimbabwe.[5] Incomplete statistics suggest that, for much the century, gold and ivory made up over 80 percent of the value of exports from the Zambezi valley.[6]

The nature of the trade changed dramatically in the nineteenth century, when the Zambezi valley became a major slave-trading zone. While only several hundred captives reached the coast in the 1750s, by 1821 the number was over five thousand—representing almost 90 percent of the value of exports.[7] Despite Lisbon's 1836 abolition decree, sending slaves to the sugar plantations in Brazil, Cuba, and Mauritius continued for most of the century.[8] Because many of the slaves exported during this period came from communities living along both margins of the river, the lives of these villagers had become much more precarious.[9]

While commerce in gold, ivory, and slaves was extremely lucrative, often providing the merchants with profits of 500 percent or more,[10] for the local African canoemen, who were hired to transport these goods up and down the Zambezi on large canoes, it was quite dangerous.[11] They faced a tangle of challenges, not the least of which was its powerful current, especially during the rainy season. Canoeing downstream in the swollen river could be quite hazardous. When a canoe confronted a fast-moving current, it was nearly impossible for the paddlers to retain control of their boat, and, if it struck a submerged object, both their cargoes and their lives could be lost. Attacks from crocodiles and hippopotami posed additional threats. Daniel Rankin graphically described seeing "a canoe crunched like matchwood and flung

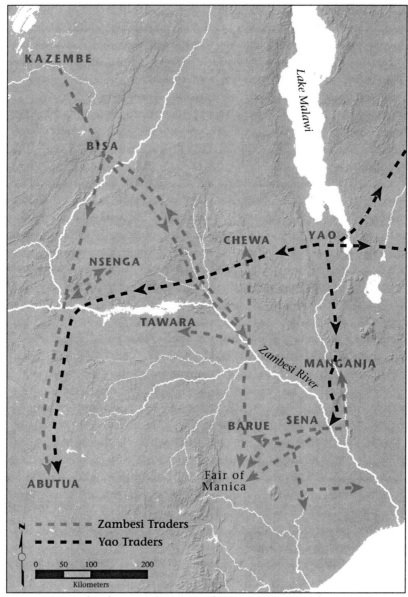

MAP 2.2. Principal trade routes. *University of Minnesota Cartography*

with its occupants high in the air by one of these [hippos]."[12] There were also numerous rapids in the river, each with its own form of jutting rocks and swirling current. Getting caught in a whirlpool could bring the journey to a crashing end. The treacherous thirty-five-kilometer Lupata gorge between Sena and Tete—the "horror of canoe men"—took the lives of many boatmen, when their canoes crashed against the rocks.[13] Surviving the Lupata gorge was no guarantee of a safe arrival in Tete, however. "The currents as we near Tete seem as strong as those of the Lupata," wrote John Kirk, and "are even more dangerous."[14] Further upriver, the notorious cataracts at Cahora Bassa were still worse.[15]

THE ZAMBEZI AS HOME OF THE PRAZOS

While a small military presence at Sena, Tete, and Zumbo may have been sufficient to protect commerce along the river, it did not ensure Portugal's political control over the strategic Zambezi waterway and its environs. To establish such sovereignty, Lisbon sought to co-opt the Portuguese nationals already residing there and to turn them into agents of the state. As early as the 1580s, Portuguese merchants and adventurers had begun to amass large tracts of land along both margins of the Zambezi. With the aid of armed slaves, whom they had acquired through trade and previous conquests, they imposed their rule over the local populations living adjacent to the river and upland.[16] Although these individuals were not initially acting in the name of the crown, Lisbon quickly came to appreciate their potential as colonial agents. In return for swearing fealty, paying annual rents, and providing soldiers to reinforce the small garrisons in Sena and Tete, the settlers received royal titles to their crown estates, called *prazos da corôa.*

By the middle of the eighteenth century, there were more than 125 prazos,[17] mostly between Tete and the mouth of the Zambezi. The prazeiros lived off both the taxes (*musonkho*) and agricultural produce paid by the peasants who resided on their estates and the profits they derived from trading in slaves and ivory. The owners of the largest estates, such as Cheringoma and Gorongoza, collected taxes from more than two thousand peasant villages[18] and commanded slave armies of several thousand.[19]

The crown estates had a long history, spanning almost three centuries, but did little to consolidate Lisbon's political control over the Zambezi valley. While the prazeiros were supposed to be loyal subjects, they were not,[20] and officials trying to enforce Lisbon's dictates often felt their wrath. According to one knowledgeable observer, among any "group of twenty *prazeros* each one has nineteen enemies; however, all are the enemy of the governor."[21] Nor could the governor muster the military force needed to challenge the autonomy of the prazeiro community and impose Lisbon's authority, since, until the late nineteenth century, the one hundred to three hundred soldiers stationed in the valley[22] were poorly armed, poorly trained, and poorly organized.[23]

The prazeiros' changing racial and cultural identities further subverted Lisbon's claim of sovereignty over the Zambezi valley. By 1777, 67 percent of the settler population was racially mixed; twenty-five years later it was 10 percent higher.[24] Miscegenation typically led to a profound shift in the cultural practices of prazeiro families. The longer they lived in the Zambezi, the more likely they were to adopt local languages, artifacts, practices, and worldviews.[25] This cultural hybridity further intensified the prazeiros' ambivalence toward the metropole.[26]

Between 1800 and 1850, the colonial presence in the Zambezi region declined even further. Due to growing absentee ownership, severe droughts, and locust attacks, Gaza Nguni raids, and the tendency of the prazeiros to enslave their subjects—which precipitated peasant flight and Chikunda slave revolts— the prazo system declined dramatically; by the middle of the century, only twenty prazos were still functioning.[27] Lisbon's hold over Zumbo was equally precarious, and in 1836 attacks by the Mburuma Nsenga forced the Portuguese to withdraw.[28] By the middle of the century, only the towns of Tete and Sena, both of which were in a state of decay and under siege from surrounding chieftaincies and renegade prazeiros,[29] remained in Portuguese hands.

THE ZAMBEZI AS A CONTESTED COLONIAL TERRAIN

Despite its declining economic significance, the Zambezi River valley remained politically strategic. Although Portugal's political influence and presence were effectively limited to the two enclaves at Sena and Tete, it used their existence to justify its claims to a vast swath of territory extending well into contemporary Malawi and Zimbabwe. Lisbon even imagined that it could forge a Central African empire from the Atlantic to the Indian Ocean, connecting its holdings in Angola and Mozambique. These imperial assertions, however, were challenged by Great Britain, by powerful mestizo warlords, and by inland African states like the Barue, whose chiefs vowed never to accept European rule.

England posed the most serious threat. Already dominating key sectors of the Portuguese metropolitan economy, British imperialists hoped to bring the fertile Manica highlands, the Shire valley, and the Zambezi valley into its empire. Beginning with David Livingstone in 1856, a wave of British explorers and missionaries "invaded" the Zambezi.[30] They wrote widely publicized books and newspaper articles detailing the horrors of the slave trade, the failure of the Portuguese to "civilize the natives," and the racial and cultural degeneration of the prazeiros.[31] The subtext of their publications was that Lisbon was unable to govern the Zambezi valley effectively—making its colonial claims illusory.

By the 1870s, British interests had made inroads in the region. The Scottish missionaries forged a religious community in the Shire highlands, and the African Lakes Company, an English commercial venture, challenged Portugal's trade monopoly by operating its own ships on the Zambezi River.[32] During the next decade, the British also incorporated portions of the Manica highlands, which Portugal considered an integral part of its territory, into their holdings in Southern Rhodesia. In 1890, to avert a looming war with Great Britain, Portugal had to renounce its claim to territory inland from the Zambezi in what later became Malawi and Zimbabwe[33] This effectively destroyed its dream of creating a Central African empire linking Mozambique and Angola.

At the same time, Portugal faced serious military challenges from rebellious warlords who controlled powerful military states. The southern margin of the Zambezi River between Tete and the Indian Ocean was divided between Massangano and Gouveia's Tonga confederation; Carazimamba, Kanyemba, and Matakenya dominated the zone from Tete to Zumbo; and Makanga and Massingire and the Makololo state[34] controlled the region between the Shire River and the Undi's territory, opposite Tete.[35] These conquest states built large stone fortresses, known as *aringas*, to defend their territory and control trade along the Zambezi, and all but the Makololo relied on large well-armed Chikunda forces to impose their hegemony over the indigenous populations.[36] They prospered by enslaving thousands of villagers living adjacent to the river.[37]

In an effort to co-opt these warlords and transform them into colonial conquerors, Portuguese officials provided them with sophisticated weapons and closed their eyes to the warlords' clandestine involvement in slaving.[38] When this strategy failed, Lisbon had no choice but to bolster its military presence and aggressively attack the renegades. To do otherwise might have led to a British takeover of this region—a fear reinforced by British negotiations with the Makololo, Kanyemba, and the Barue kingdom.[39] Despite stiff opposition, between 1886 and 1901 Portuguese forces defeated one state after another.[40]

The warlords' defeat and the retreat of the Gaza Nguni southward left the Barue as the only major regional state outside Portugal's control.[41] In August 1902 an elite Portuguese force, aided by several thousand African infantry soldiers, launched a major attack on the Barue. The five thousand Barue soldiers proved no match for the heavily armed colonial army, which subdued them by the end of the year.[42] Sixteen years later, descendants of the Barue rebels rose up to protest *chibalo* (conscripted African labor), which they equated with slavery. It took Lisbon a year to crush the insurrection.[43] Only then, more than three hundred years after the Portuguese crown had claimed sovereignty over the Zambezi, did Lisbon effectively control this region.

THE ZAMBEZI AS A ZONE OF UNREALIZED WEALTH

From the moment the first Portuguese traders and adventurers moved up the river, Lisbon expected the Zambezi valley someday to yield handsome profits. Colonial officials believed the rumors of rich gold and silver deposits and later were confident that plantation agriculture would flourish along the river's fertile floodplains. Their dreams of transforming the Zambezi valley into a vibrant economic zone, however, were never realized.

Portugal initially sought to control the river to gain access to the large gold mines it believed to exist in the interior. While explorers and traders never discovered the fabled mines of the queen of Sheba,[44] they did encounter a thriving local mining industry. In the southern hinterland's streams and rivulets, Africans panned for gold, which they sold to Muslim traders at the inland fairs. By the seventeenth century, Portuguese adventurers were also prospecting for gold, both there and on the northern bank. Through conquest or rental agreements with local land chiefs, they obtained control of gold-producing areas, where they established *bares* (permanent mining camps). Because *bare* owners failed to introduce modern mining technology, yields from shallow veins and rivulets were low, and only a trickle of gold reached the coast. In fact, in 1821 gold represented less than 2 percent of the total value of exports.[45] The reputed silver mines proved even more illusory, and exploitation of the rich coal deposits at Moatize, across the river from Tete, began only in the early twentieth century.[46]

Colonial efforts to promote agriculture were no more successful, despite the rich alluvial soils adjacent to the river. For centuries, Portuguese officials had presumed that plantation agriculture would anchor the prazo system. While periodically decreeing that prazeiros grow coffee, sugar, rice, tobacco, and other cash crops, they bemoaned the settlers' failure to select appropriate soils and seeds or to irrigate fields adjacent to the Zambezi.[47] With the exception of a handful of prazos in the delta producing rice, sugar, and wheat, commercial agriculture was nonexistent. In 1806 only twenty thousand kilograms of food were exported from the entire region,[48] and by 1821 such exports had declined by 90 percent.[49] Little changed during the remainder of the century, due to the prazeiros' ignorance of modern farming methods, their unwillingness to invest in technology, the lack of transport and accessible markets, and the much higher returns from trading in slaves and ivory.[50]

Portugal's decision in the 1870s to open the region to international commerce and Europe's soaring demand for vegetable oils for soap and candle making spurred an agricultural revolution based on peasant production.[51] Nevertheless, by the end of the century, Lisbon had reversed its policy and begun again promoting plantation agriculture[52] through long-term grants to concessionary companies. These firms employed conscripted African labor, which worked the fields to satisfy their tax obligations. In 1899 promulgation of a native labor code, which codified the existing system of unfree African labor in Mozambique, known as chibalo,[53] assured the concessionary companies an ample supply of workers.[54] This secure labor supply, especially in the Zambezi delta, allowed sugar production to skyrocket from 605 tons in 1893 to almost thirty thousand tons two decades later and ensured the profitability of the copra and sisal plantations that sprang up along the coast.[55]

Upriver cash crop production, by contrast, was negligible. Writing in the 1920s, the governor of Tete complained that the "practical effects of development [projects] was zero."[56] To stimulate additional agricultural and mineral production in this region, Portugal built the Trans-Zambézia Railway in 1922 and, in 1935, the railway bridge across the Zambezi at Sena, thereby effectively linking the region, with its large coal deposits at Moatize, to the port of Beira.[57] Even with these limited state initiatives, economic development outside the delta remained illusory.[58]

Despite the new railroad, upriver transport continued to be problematic. Most goods traveling between Tete and the Indian Ocean went on canoes of various sizes, barges, and flat-bottomed boats. These small craft were subject to the vagaries of the mighty river and could carry only limited quantities. A small number of steamboats also plied the river, but, even for them, Tete was the end of the journey. The gorge at Cahora Bassa blocked passage to the interior, which, Portuguese officials believed, prevented development of the region. After World War II, colonial planners concluded that other large projects were necessary to promote modernization in the Zambezi. Within a decade, constructing a dam at Cahora Bassa had become the panacea for economic takeoff.

CONSTRUCTING A COLONIAL NARRATIVE

From more than three centuries of contact with the Zambezi valley, Portuguese officials and European explorers constructed a comprehensive narrative of the river and its environs, which was framed by racial and cultural stereotyping and ideas about the degenerative nature of the tropics[59] and further shaped by their local guides and translators. While constraints of space preclude in-depth exploration of these themes, we will highlight three interrelated tropes that structured this narrative.

According to the first trope, before the region's vast resources could be extracted, it was necessary to tame the wild, malaria-infested river. Explorers and officials repeatedly documented the dangers posed by the powerful currents, jutting rocks, and menacing gorges, which jeopardized commerce and blunted passage inland. For commerce and Christianity to flourish, the river had to be domesticated and the natural barriers destroyed. Writing about the limitations imposed by the Cahora Bassa gorge, Livingstone noted, "if we can blast away the rocks which obstruct the passage, [i]t will be like opening wide the gates which barred the interior for ages."[60] Colonial authorities also lamented the unpredictable floods, which washed over the banks and destroyed peasants' fields and, more recently, company plantations. From the middle of the sixteenth century, they documented rainy-season floods, which seemed to recur every ten years or so.[61] Flood control, in fact, became one argument for constructing the Cahora Bassa Dam (see chapter 3).

That the degenerate settler community and the backward indigenous population had both failed to take advantage of the well-endowed Zambezi region was the second trope. According to Kirk, "there is not one white man or one who may call himself white, in the whole district . . . without venereal diseases. . . . The consequence is that all have skin diseases and when they have children, they are miserably syphilitic both in mind and body."[62] A century later, a senior colonial official echoed this assessment—lamenting that the indolent and ignorant estate holders "do not go in for any physical exercise, nourish themselves on a heavy and excessive diet, and delight in the abuse of sexual pleasures."[63] Portuguese authorities regularly complained that the debauchery of the estate holders subverted development.[64] According to Governor Sebastião Xavier Botelho, writing early in the nineteenth century, so did their ignorance: "The [prazeiros along the coast] plant the cane out of season and without any knowledge of the most appropriate and suitable lands for this endeavor; and the crop failure is then attributed to the quality of the land rather than the ignorance of the cultivator. If the production of sugarcane is poorly planned, it is no worse than the sugar cultivation on the Tete prazos in which they use inappropriate machinery, which conserves neither time nor manpower."[65]

Others attributed the lack of productivity in the fertile river valley to the ignorance and laziness of the Africans. Consider how Livingstone wove together themes of the region's divine-given fecundity with its unproductiveness: "The cultivated spots are mere dots compared to the broad fields of rich soil which is never either grazed or tilled. Pity that the plenty in store for all, from our Father's bountiful hands, is not enjoyed by more."[66] Colonial authorities shared his views, which became the ideological justification for forced labor. "It was imperative," wrote Joaquim Mousinho de Albuquerque, a Portuguese high commissioner in 1899, "to instill a work ethic among the indigenous population and eliminate the indolent habits of the savages."[67] Twenty-five years later, the governor of Tete echoed these sentiments, characterizing many of the "tribes" under his jurisdiction as "ill-disposed to work," "docile," and "thieves."[68] To compensate for the slothful Africans, development required that more Portuguese migrate to the Zambezi valley.[69]

The ability of technology and science to overcome the obstacles of the river and permit exploitation of the region's resources was the third trope. The time and dedication explorers and government officials devoted to cartographical, geological, and agronomic notations of the Zambezi were just one indication of their faith in scientific knowledge. Carl Peters, a German explorer, predicted that "European science would easily succeed in revolutionizing the country."[70] Portuguese officials saw the growth of modern plantations, construction of new railways, and development of the river as keys to unlocking the region's wealth and ensuring progress under the Portuguese flag.[71] In 1912, for example, the governor of the district of Quelimane argued passionately that "the salvation of the Zambezi and its transformation into a major agricultural zone" depended on the construction of several railway lines.[72] The completion of the Trans-Zambezi Railway a decade later, followed by the railroad bridge across the Zambezi at Sena, were steps in that direction. Nevertheless, eliminating the Cabora Bassa gorge as a barrier into the interior and constructing a dam on that site remained prerequisites to effective domestication of the river and exploitation of the Zambezi valley's rich natural resources.

LOCAL PERSPECTIVES:
"IN THE PAST, THE ZAMBEZI GAVE US WEALTH"[73]

For the Shona- and Chewa-speaking communities who had settled on the southern and northern margins of the Zambezi well before the arrival of the Portuguese (see map 2.1),[74] the river was neither a dangerous force of nature requiring domestication nor a form of wealth waiting to be tapped by scientists who, alone, knew the value of the riches it contained. While examples of livelihood insecurity—the river's erratic character and the hardships that flooding, crocodiles, and hippopotami caused, for example—are embedded in their oral narratives of environmental harmony in the pre-Cahora Bassa period, their stories about the Zambezi emphasized the river's positive meanings for the rural communities living near its shores.

From their perspective, for centuries the Zambezi had provided a safe and bountiful supply of fresh running water for drinking, cooking, washing, and bathing. It had nourished the reeds African men used to weave mats and baskets and the trees they needed to build homes and canoes. It was also an important waterway that facilitated local commerce in agricultural produce, honey, wax, fish, meat, iron, and indigenously produced cloth, and, even before the Portuguese arrived, a flourishing trade with Indian Ocean merchants. Additionally, the river yielded powerful medicines that combated illness and infection and was the location of many sacred sites. Above all else, it provided the nutrients needed to fertilize cultivators' alluvial gardens and to support the fish populations that were a crucial source of protein in African diets.

In short, the Zambezi, despite its unpredictability, had "given wealth" to African communities by sustaining and providing life. Thus, despite the nostalgia that is evident in their recollections, representations of the river in contemporary oral narratives highlight its intrinsic benefits and life-giving properties, rather than the hazards—or development potential—stressed by outsiders, making them an important counter to European discourses about the Zambezi.

In the following section, we highlight how Africans living in the lower Zambezi valley described the river's role in their everyday lives before the construction of Cahora Bassa. Based on oral and archival materials from the area stretching downriver from the dam to the Zambezi delta, this summary provides insights into the river's history and its varied impacts on local communities, environments, and production systems. Oral accounts stress the extraordinary agricultural capacity, biodiversity, and livability of the Zambezi floodplains while the river remained in African hands and provide glimpses of the devastating microecological and economic consequences that followed for peasant households when the colonial state appropriated control over its life-sustaining waters.

THE LOWER ZAMBEZI ECOSYSTEM

The lower Zambezi extends from Cahora Bassa to the expansive delta and enters the sea through a mosaic of alluvial grasslands and swamp forest, covering an area of 225,000 square kilometers. In the mountainous area, from Cahora Bassa to Tete city, the river runs through a narrow valley (five hundred meters wide) with bedrock outcrops adjacent to the waterway. Downstream from Tete, it broadens to a width of several kilometers. Only at the fast-swirling Lupata gorge, 320 kilometers from its mouth, does the river narrow appreciably. Otherwise, the banks are low and fringed with reeds, with alluvial gardens located along both shores. The Shire River flows from Lake Malawi into the Zambezi about 160 kilometers from the sea. Just south is the fertile delta, a triangular area covering 1.2 million hectares. The rich delta floodplain, whose width can reach several hundred kilometers, historically supported hundreds of thousands of rural villages. The delta's savanna and woodlands provided wood for fuel and housing along with wild fruits and medicinal plants and sustained a wide variety of wildlife, including the largest population of Cape buffalo in Africa.[75]

Before the construction of any upriver dams, the most important factor shaping the physical environment of the lower Zambezi valley—and the welfare of all species inhabiting the river and its neighboring lowlands—was the Zambezi's annual flood cycle. The complex ecological dynamics of the lower Zambezi's main channel, the associated floodplains, and the biologically rich delta and coastal estuary regions[76] had coevolved, in the predam period, with a very particular flood regime connected to the bimodal pattern of annual rainfall.[77]

Under normal climatic conditions, Zambezi flow patterns were fairly predictable. Flooding occurred in two stages after the onset of the rainy season, in late November or December. A week or two later, flow rates began to increase, creating small peaks in response to local rainfall runoffs in the lower Zambezi basin. While flows in December could reach as high as 6,740 cubic meters per second, the principal flood normally began in January and peaked between late February and late March (see fig. 2.1). During this period, the river swelled to several times its normal size, overflowing its banks virtually every year between 1930 and 1958—the period for which records of the flow rate exist.[78] The floodwaters began to recede in April, leaving behind a rich deposit of organic and inorganic nutrients on the lowlands adjacent to the river. During the dry season, from late April through October, water levels diminished rapidly, until the river's flow returned to its average low point of approximately 400 cubic meters per second. The flooding cycle began anew with the onset of the next rainy season.

The magnitude and duration of the seasonal floods varied over time and from one zone to another. For the forty years preceding Cahora Bassa's construction, the maximum annual peak flow ranged from five to twenty thousand cubic meters per second , although the extremes were infrequent—occurring only twice.[79] Even at the lower end, however, the runoff was sufficient to inundate the plains and deposit valuable silt. Table 2.1 documents the maximum flood levels measured at two locations on the lower Zambezi before the construction of Kariba and Cahora Bassa. Mutarara is located about 150 kilometers downriver from the Cahora Bassa gorge, and Marromeu sits in the

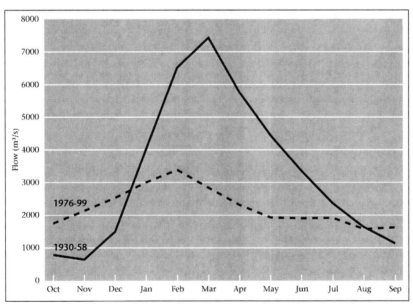

FIGURE 2.1. Pre-Kariba and Post–Cahora Bassa mean flows of Zambezi River at Mutarara. *Beilfuss and Santos "Hydrological Change," fig. 2.61*

delta. Despite the annual variability of flood levels, at both sites they were always sufficient to overflow the river's banks and inundate alluvial fields.

The Zambezi's annual flooding critically affected the topography and natural-resource base of both the valley and the vast wetlands of the delta. The seasonal runoff ensured high groundwater levels throughout the region and fed channels, tributaries, and lakes—most dramatically in the delta, where it formed a wide riverine landscape with "open mosaics of marsh, pond, oxbows and shallow wetlands."[80] During the rainy months of December through March, the width of the inundated floodplains varied from place to place. Carlos Churo of Chicoa Velha, for instance, remembered stretches of the river where floodwaters stretched for seven to nine kilometers on both banks.[81] In parts of the delta where the alluvial plains were much larger, the floodwaters could span twenty to thirty kilometers.[82] Some lowland areas, such as the northern floodplains near the confluence of the Zambezi and Shire Rivers, had a spillover that nourished more than eighty thousand hectares of land, while, in nearby Inhangoma, the Zambezi inundated fifty-five thousand choice hectares.[83] Many of the islands dotting the river also benefited from this extensive seasonal irrigation, as did lowlands adjacent to both the Zambezi's tributaries and streams flowing into it.

These alluvial lowlands, particularly in the delta, contained some of Mozambique's most biologically diverse ecosystems. For this reason, the delta itself has long been vital to Mozambique's national economy and is a wetland of international significance.[84] A massive eighteen-thousand-square-kilometer zone of flooding and silt deposition, it stretches almost three hundred kilometers along the Mozambique coastline and 160 kilometers inland to the Zambezi's confluence with the Shire River. For millennia its vast seasonally flooded grasslands supported a wide variety of birds, mammals, and reptiles, while the floodplains themselves were spawning grounds for riverine and anadromous fish and provided dry-season grazing for wildlife.[85] Coastal estuaries and mangrove forests, central elements of the delta and estuarine environment, were also a fertile breeding ground for shrimp.[86] The Zambezi flood flows played an extremely important role in maintaining the delicate biochemistry of this unique ecosystem—the pulsing floodwaters during the rainy season flushed accumulated salt from the coastal floodplains, helping to ensure the proper balance between tidal saltwater and riverine freshwater.

For the human residents of the lower Zambezi valley, however, the most valuable effect of the annual flooding cycle was the supply of life-sustaining nutrients deposited along the alluvial plains as the floodwaters receded every April, which, for centuries, supported farming communities and aquatic ecosystems. The annual replenishment of nutrients from the flooding Zambezi was responsible for the rich dark soils (known in local languages as *makande*, *ndrongo*, or *matope*) of the river-fed plains, whose high moisture retention and rich mineral content made them the most desirable agricultural sites in the region. Like fish, wildlife, and other elements of the Zambezi ecosystem, which depended for their survival on the regularity of the natural flow regime, peasant households historically relied on the annual inundation of the flood-plains for the very basics of life—fertile soil for growing food crops, dry-season pasture for livestock, and habitats that produced abundant supplies of fish and game. For all these reasons, before Cahora Bassa's construction, flood-ing was considered a normal, welcome phase of the agricultural year, around which riverine communities planned their food supply and other household routines, rather than a destructive or traumatic event. "The water used to flood once a year," recalled José Jone. "People moved to the *murumucheias* [higher lands] until the waters disappeared. Then we returned home."[87] This seasonal pattern of flooding underpinned the organization and viability of a "diversi-fied production system that incorporated flood recession agriculture, livestock management, fishing, gathering and hunting,"[88] all of which were essential for the food security of peasant households throughout the lower Zambezi valley.

At times, however, the river was also an extremely destructive force—a fact generally not stressed in the oral narratives. The earliest report of flooding in the Zambezi delta was in the mid-1500s, and extreme flooding occurred pe-riodically over the next three centuries.[89] In the twentieth century there were reports of twenty-one large floods,[90] and hydrological data collected between 1925 and 1955—a period about which most elders would have heard—at Mutarara, on the northern bank of the Zambezi River opposite Sena, and at Marromeu, further downriver in the delta, indicate nine seasons of extreme flooding provoked by heavy rains before the construction of Cahora Bassa (see table 2.1). Richard Beilfuss and David dos Santos describe the catastrophic flooding in the delta in the mid-twentieth century:

> In 1939, the delta reached its highest water levels in recorded history . . . , overtopp[ing] the dikes that were built in 1926 to protect the sugar estates at Marromeu and Luabo, and inundat[ing] most of the 1.2 million ha. delta. The dikes were overtopped again in 1940 and 1944, during what was probably the wettest period in the twentieth century. The most prolonged flooding on record occurred in 1952 . . . , caus[ing] extensive damage to houses and crops on the delta plains. . . . For the fourth time since 1926, the dikes protecting Marromeu and Luabo were overtopped. . . . In 1958, . . . the delta again experienced extreme flooding. . . . Water levels in the delta reached near-record levels, and exceeded catastrophic flood levels for 26 days. Large numbers of Cape buffalo and waterbuck were purport-edly drowned by these large floods.[91]

TABLE 2.1 Maximum flood levels, lower Zambezi, 1938–55

| | Mutarara, max. discharge | | Marromeu, max. water level | |
Year	(m3/s)	Rank[a]	(m amsl)[b]	Rank
1925–26	—	—	7.85[c]	6
1938–39	18,700	3	8.01	1
1939–40	13,200	5	7.91	5
1943–44	18,200	4	7.92	4
1947–48	12,600	8	7.85[c]	8
1951–52	22,300	2	8.00	2
1957–58	22,500	1	7.97	3
1962–63	13,200	5	7.85[c]	7
1954–55	12,300	9	7.77	9

Source: Beilfuss and Santos, "Hydrological Change," 69.

[a]The rankings reflect the absence of data from Mutarara in 1925–26, which received a ranking of 6 in Marromeu.

[b]amsl = above mean sea level.

[c]The authors of the table based their rankings on more precise information than is presented here.

Since the delta's flooding was due to heavy rainfall and runoff upriver, the destructive flooding of the river during these years necessarily would have adversely affected those living and farming in the Tete-Sena area.

RECESSION AGRICULTURE IN THE FLOODPLAIN

Everywhere, those interviewed agreed that the floodplain's rich, dark soil made it the most sought after and densely populated agricultural zone in the region.[92] One elder described the fertility of riparian land in almost magical terms: "We used to just have to drop a seed in to the soil here and it would grow into a tree."[93] Beatriz Maquina, an elderly woman who had farmed in the Chipalapala region her entire life, stressed the agricultural significance of the rich alluvial soils: "Makande land located near the banks of the river always gave us good production. We cultivated a great deal of sorghum as well as some maize."[94] Joaquim Sacatucua of Caia echoed her view: "We call the soil ndrongo. It is very fertile, which is why so many people settled here. Because of the rich land we had food, even when the rains did not come."[95] Writing in the mid-1960s, a Portuguese planner working for the Missão de Fomento e Povoamento de Zambeze (MFPZ) observed that adjacent to the Zambezi River the population density was much higher, because the environment there "permit[ted] the cultivation of a number of crops throughout the year on the alluvial plains" and provided much more food than "in the rain-fed interior where peasants practice[d] shifting agriculture"[96] (see fig. 2.2).

So desirable were floodplain plots that, in areas where the band of alluvial soil was narrow, competition for access to makande soil was intense. In the

FIGURE 2.2. Alluvial garden, 1967. *Ricardo Rangel*

Chirodzi-Sanangwe region, for instance, a handful of powerful families jealously guarded their claims to river-fed gardens that had passed down from one generation to another.[97] In the delta, families residing in upland areas historically forged marriage alliances with those living near the river so that they would have access to food in times of famine.[98] Peasants living on the southern side of the Zambezi often traveled long distances to work floodplain gardens, sometimes even traversing the river to cultivate small alluvial plots on the northern bank.[99] Ernest Kalumbi, who lived near Sena, recounted that, long ago, "we would cross the river to the other side [Inhangoma]—that's where we had our pumpkins and maize. These fields were good because they could stay wet for a long time and we would have a very good food crop each year."[100] In 1961 colonial scientists surveying the delta confirmed the area's fertility: "On the Inhangoma, the Zambezi floods ensure that the soils, which already are very rich in the principal nutrients, have a water content that permits the cultivation cycle to continue year after year without large decreases of the yields."[101]

Drawing on shared experiential and historical knowledge of local environments, acquired through years of trial and error, rural communities along the Zambezi had adapted their farming practices to the fluctuating rainfall, uneven soil quality, and seasonal flood cycle that defined the region's growing season. The result was a food production system calibrated to the Zambezi's flood regime, which rested on the cultivation of multiple fields in different microecological zones to minimize risk and maximize the benefits of varying soil, moisture, and light conditions. Peasants worked river-fed plots in a rotating sequence with upland fields in the somewhat less fertile mixed clay-loam soils of the floodplain's upper terrace—known as *mpumbo* and *tchetca*—or in the rocky *ntchenga* soils of the surrounding savanna and uplands, which were the most difficult to farm and produced significantly lower yields than riverside gardens.[102] As Paulo Mayo recalled, pointing to his floodplain garden from his hillside field, in the past "we could gather crops like maize, sorghum, and millet in our fields here, we could grow maize, [sweet] potatoes, and beans in another field in the floodplains, and the third field could be rice. We did this because it afforded us food guarantees and protection."[103] David Livingstone's observations of the region confirm these assertions. He found "the country . . . fertile in the extreme" with "old gardens continu[ing] to yield after they are uncared for."[104] Writing thirty years later, Frederick Selous observed that "the natives seemed very well off for food; and the soil . . . must be very fertile."[105] Local officials and travelers agreed with his assessment, reporting that sorghum, millet, corn, beans, sugar, and rice would easily grow there.[106]

Others confirmed the agronomic wisdom of this time-tested system. Maurício Alemão, an elderly peasant who had lived in Chicoa Velha, before he was displaced by the dam, remembered the reliable bounty of the cluster of alluvial and upland fields he had left behind: "In Chicoa Velha we could farm the entire year. In the dry season, we farmed on the banks of the river, and in the rainy season we farmed far from the river, because our riverine gardens were flooded. We grew corn, sweet potatoes, tomatoes, beans, and even tobacco. These were small fields, like gardens. But they produced a great deal."[107] Carlos Churo, his neighbor, told a similar story:

> Before Cahora Bassa, each family had several fields. The number and size varied depending on the strength of a person and the size of his family. . . . On the ntchenga soils we planted sorghum, which does not require as much water. The mixed ntchenga-makande soils were better for maize, which needs more moisture than sorghum. Some people planted peanuts in their maize fields. We harvested these crops in June and July and then returned to our gardens. . . . The land near the river, called makande, was very fertile. When the river rose and then receded in June, the area that had been covered with water was where we farmed. There, we first planted maize. We cultivated beans in the same field as the maize. Beans needed something to rest on and the maize stalks served well. Nearby we cultivated a second small plot with sweet potatoes, tomatoes, cabbage, and more beans. We harvested our gardens in September and October, before the rains and flooding.[108]

As this account suggests, intercropping—growing multiple crops simultaneously in a single field—was another key element of indigenous farming systems throughout the lower Zambezi valley.[109] It rested on the recognition that agricultural success in a difficult environment depended on peasant families' ability to make good use of limited resources while maximizing the returns on their labor. Intercropping offered several advantages to small-scale cultivators. Nitrogen-fixing legumes, such as beans and peanuts, were excellent companion crops for heavy nitrogen-consuming cereals, such as maize and sorghum. In exchange for functioning as a natural trellis for bean plants, maize and sorghum benefited from the restoration of nitrogen to the soil and achieved higher productivity when mixed with legumes than if planted on their own. Sowing maize or sorghum in the same mound as beans or peanuts also enabled cultivators to control pests and weeds for multiple crops at the same time—thereby reducing their labor requirements.

Just as important to local food production systems was the social organization of agricultural labor. A clearly defined gender division of labor was already in place by the early nineteenth century.[110] Historically, the agricultural season began in late July or August, when men felled trees in the upland areas, cleared the terrain of any major obstructions, and burned their fields, collecting the ashes for later use as fertilizer. Households with sufficient available labor might prepare a second and even a third upland plot. In October women burned whatever shrubbery remained on these plots and tilled the soil in preparation for planting. After the rains began, in November, they planted sorghum and bush millet, which were more drought resistant than maize, intermingled with smaller amounts of cowpeas, peanuts, and beans.[111] During the following months, women cut the surrounding grass and weeded the fields to remove parasites that threatened their crops.[112] With the help of their husbands and children, they harvested the grains and legumes in February and March.[113] Back in the village, women pounded the grains into a fine substance from which they prepared porridge, the mainstay of the local diet. This first harvest, known as *tchaca*, helped alleviate seasonal hunger, which occurred regularly.[114]

By April the water of the Zambezi was receding, and villagers with access to riverine land turned their attention to these plots. Although typically smaller then the upland fields,[115] riverine gardens were more productive. A wide variety of crops were cultivated on the floodplains, including several types of beans, sweet potatoes, tomatoes, okra, pumpkins, greens, and maize, along with tree crops, such as papayas.[116] Women gathered these foodstuffs in August and September. This harvest, known as *murope*, was typically a time of plenty. In most years, growers got more than one harvest from their alluvial gardens. Fatima Mbivinisa recounted how she and the other women in her village "often managed to grow crops twice a year."[117] When conditions were favorable, a second harvest might occur just before the November rains arrived.

Another important dimension of this gendered labor process was reliance on mutual assistance networks. Throughout the Zambezi region, cultivators historically organized work groups and exchanges for pressing tasks or those that were tedious or daunting when performed alone, such as tree cutting, burning, weeding, and harvesting.[118] Women, especially, depended on such collective labor arrangements, relying on kinship networks and neighbors to alleviate production bottlenecks during times of labor stress. Maquina remembered that in Chicoa Velha "neighbors would help me in the harvest," and then she would "brew *phombi* [local beer] and we would all have a party and celebrate."[119] During the colonial period, labor exchanges provided critical assistance to wives of migrant workers, who would have been hard pressed to cultivate their fields alone. As Peter Phiri, a peasant from Inboque, explained, "This practice in the local language is called *dhomba*. Women brewed phombi and invited their neighbors to help them weed their fields. Afterward they prepared chicken or goat, which they served in the field. This was how women managed two fields [one near the river and one upland] with their husbands working in Zimbabwe."[120]

Such time-honored practices as planting dispersed fields in different ecological zones, intercropping, and dhomba were important strategies for blunting the vagaries of nature, minimizing the risk of crop failure, and enabling rural households to avoid the devastating effects of subsistence crises.[121] Although not all interviewees shared identical memories of food security before the construction of Cahora Bassa, they agreed that the Zambezi River had been critical to the human ecology of survival and that indigenous farming systems were well adapted to local environmental conditions. Reliance on river-fed gardens and cultivation of multiple fields in different ecological zones provided a critical margin of food security to most households and dramatically reduced the risk of long-term hunger.[122] Francisco Manuel summed it up best: "My family survived because we had two *machamba* (fields). During periods of drought we relied on our gardens, and, when large floods destroyed my gardens, we got by on the reserves collected from my field in the hills."[123] Other long-time residents painted a much rosier picture: "In the past there was not any real hunger. We relied on food from the first harvest, which fed us until we collected grains from the second."[124] According to Maurício Alemão, "When we lived in Chicoa Velha, there was no hunger. We always had something to eat."[125] Even Senteira Botão, whose more nuanced account recognized that "in those times, occasionally there was hunger," credited long-standing local farming practices with ameliorating it: "There could be a shortage of corn, but then we had some sorghum. There could be a shortage of both, but then we would eat sweet potatoes and other products from our gardens near the river. If someone lacked food, then neighbors would provide it in exchange for labor or something else. . . . No one ever died from hunger."[126]

Inácio Guta and his friends in Chetcha gave a similar account: "In the past, when there were droughts, we experienced some hunger, but because we lived near the river we did not suffer too much."[127] Their neighbor Pezulani Mafalanjala mused about the decades just before the dam was built: "Even when we were forced to grow cotton, there was no hunger because, if our fields far from the river had low yields, we could always rely on our river gardens."[128] This recollection does not completely reflect reality, given that the colonial state forced peasants in the Zambezi valley, as elsewhere in Mozambique, to cultivate cotton between 1938 and 1964, provoking widespread food crises and famines throughout the colony.[129]

Despite the nostalgia evident in some of these memories, there is no doubt that the success of the Zambezi valley's agroecological system rested on peasants' access to the alluvial fields enriched by the annual flood cycle of the Zambezi. In most years, households with river gardens could both feed their families and produce some grain to trade for basic amenities. "In the past," recalled Joaquim Sacatucua, "I might have two sacks of maize or I might have five sacks of maize that I could sell to buy school books for my five children, as well as soap, medicine, and cigarettes."[130] When households with alluvial plots did experience food shortages, their intensity and duration were more limited. For them, seasonal shortfalls "typically lasted about a month, whereas in the region inland from the river, famines were more severe and persisted up to five months."[131]

As this recollection suggests, while recession agriculture with its double-field system offered a measure of food security, it did not provide ironclad protection against hunger. The fields could still be ravaged by droughts, insect infestations, and other natural disasters, which occurred with some regularity,[132] and the region's uncertain and relatively brief rainy season could still cause food shortages during the hungry months of February and March, when families had already typically consumed last year's grain harvest and were anxiously awaiting this year's first cereals. A number of elders stressed that, even before the construction of the dam, villagers were at the mercy of a sometimes capricious climate.[133] Moreover, when we raised the question of predam flooding, several elderly villagers acknowledged that the river could be unpredictable and dangerous and a threat to the stable productive agronomic system that had been practiced for centuries in the region.[134]

Local chroniclers gave catastrophic floods in the Zambezi valley powerfully descriptive names to ensure that people remembered their world gone awry.[135] The longest and most devastating flood was the 1952 Cheia M'bomane ("the flood that destroyed everything"). Marosse Inácio and his neighbors recounted how the waters "descended on their village suddenly at night. Although, in desperation, people climbed to the roofs of their huts to get away from the water, the storm swept the huts into the river. Many people drowned in the raging water. Few had canoes to escape."[136] Six years later, Cheia N'sasira ("the flood that forced people to live on top of termite mounds") devastated numerous communities living adjacent to the river. Limpo Nkuche explained how "many people died, while those who were fortunate enough to survive lost all their worldly possessions, including their livestock."[137] Hydrological data confirm that severe flooding occurred in those years (see table 2.1).

Even when the river did not reach such levels, it still inundated many fields and could undermine the food security of hardworking families, as occurred in 1948 and 1963.[138] Bento Estima and Joseph Ndebvuchena, for instance, remembered how periodic flooding caused life to be uncertain along the river's edge: "Before the dam, sometimes there was hunger. It depended on the rains. In times of drought, people cultivated maize, sugarcane, and vegetables on their plots near the river. When they farmed near the river, however, they faced the possibility of having their crops destroyed by the floods."[139]

Thus, living adjacent to the river was more precarious than most villagers at first acknowledged. While capricious floods increased the possibility of losing an entire year's agricultural production,[140] wildlife posed a more frequent threat to their food security. Without firearms, which the state prohibited them from owning, cultivators could do little to protect their alluvial gardens from hippopotami that ravaged their crops. As Luís Manuel recalled, "the only thing we could do was to go to the administration and ask them to send European hunters to kill these beasts."[141] Such assistance was not always forthcoming, causing frustrated peasants sometimes to abandon their riverine gardens.[142]

Yet elders also stressed how the Zambezi valley ecosystem and the river itself helped hard-pressed families survive in times of scarcity. Oral recollections of foraging for wild fruit during droughts suggest the great diversity of tree species that could provide minimal sustenance.[143] During the hungry season, women and children regularly augmented their food supply by gathering edible roots, tubers, plants, and berries that grew along the river's edge.[144] The most common wild foods harvested in the Tete region during these months were *nyika* (water lily roots), *mpambadza* (wild lily bulbs), *mboa* (wild mushrooms), *nyezi* (a cocoyam tuber), wild sorghum, and the berries of the *maçanica* bush.[145] Nyika was a significant famine food that grew in abundance near the river in the Mutarara-Inhangoma region, particularly in Lake Nbazema and in the riverine zone around Sena.[146] When gatherers returned home with nyika, they dried the root, peeled off the hard exterior, and pounded the flesh into a fine grain for porridge. In the nearby Shire valley colonial authorities reported in 1948 that "whole communities have lived on [*nyika*] without any other food at all for weeks at a time."[147] In addition, according to João Raposo of Caia, aquatic plants could be harvested from the river waters and consumed when food was scarce.[148] Nevertheless, to get through the year, many had to rely on wage remittances from kin working in Zimbabwe, South Africa, and Malawi.[149] A Portuguese official estimated that over ten thousand people from the Songo region alone were working in Zimbabwe in the 1960s.[150]

FISHING

The Zambezi's rich and varied fish population also played a vital role in the local food economy by supplying an extremely important source of protein.[151] The more than forty species of fish[152] living in the river system in the predam period also depended on the Zambezi's annual flood cycle for their survival. "The qualities of a river change drastically from the low-water to the high-water season. . . . During floods . . . the water spreads over a large area, where there is an abundance of inundated and rapidly growing vegetation serving both as food and shelter for the fish, and there is a large amount of insects, worms and mollusks available to the fish which migrate onto the flood plains. . . . Floods appear to be essential for reproductive success, and growth and survival of the young fish is improved during years with large floods."[153] From December through April, rising floodwaters triggered crucial changes in the feeding and reproductive behavior of fish and other aquatic organisms. "Reproduction, feeding and growth show seasonal variations depending on the water level. Reproduction of most species occurs just before or during the floods. . . . Feeding is most intense during the floods and most fish are then in peak conditions."[154]

Although the principal fisheries were located both in the floodplains between the Lupata gorge and the Zambezi's confluence with the Shire River and in the lower floodplains and delta extending to the sea, fishermen also exploited the rich lakes, rivulets, and estuaries connected to the Zambezi. According to one study, the estimated total catch in the delta alone—before the construction of Cahora Bassa—ranged from thirty to fifty thousand tons per year.[155] Even on the lower-yielding southern bank of the river near Tete, fishing provided a significant source of food for riparian households.[156]

Historically, fishing was a gendered economic activity to which many men devoted much time, energy, and skill (see fig. 2.3). Drawing on knowledge handed down by their fathers and grandfathers, fishermen deployed numerous intricate techniques to maximize their catch. Not surprisingly, men's fishing stories highlighted, and possibly exaggerated, the tremendous bounty of the river, rather than the labor and expertise required for successful fishing. Khumbidzi Pastor, for example, recalled proudly that most adult men simply baited *machonga* (fishing weirs), moored them in the river each evening, and

FIGURE 2.3. Fisherman, 1967. *Ricardo Rangel*

"the next day we would remove the machonga and they would be filled with fish."[157] Skilled canoemen were said to spear fish while standing on the sides of their boats, while young boys caught fish with hooks and lines—and even with their hands—in dammed-up pools and rivulets adjacent to the Zambezi.[158] These combined efforts yielded substantial catches of prized bream, tigerfish, catfish, and eel, which fishermen hauled back to their temporary villages for drying or smoking.[159] Women typically sold excess fish at inland markets.

An understudied subject in the environmental history of southern and Central Africa, fishing required considerably more ingenuity and skill than these simple narratives suggest.[160] For one thing, the labor process and choice of technique were highly dependent on location and time of year. During the dry season, groups of fishermen established temporary camps on the edges of the floodplains or on the small islands adjacent to their villages. When the river was low, they waded in with simple gill nets and baskets to catch their prey, sometimes with the assistance of their wives and older children. Floodplain fishing was attractive because it neither required substantial investments in nets or canoes nor was labor intensive. Although the fish were smaller during the dry season, yields were still relatively high, and fishermen were less likely to be attacked by crocodiles or hippos hidden in the water.[161] Women also participated in dry-season fishing, through a practice known as *mlembwe*, in which groups of women converged in the shallow pools and grasslands near the water's edge and scooped up the fish in sheets and baskets.[162] Although this allowed women to contribute substantial quantities of protein to their family's diet, it was not considered a serious form of fishing: "Women during that time could not seriously go into the water to catch fish. We could only go into the water to do mlembwe. We would stretch sheets, sink them under water, and move around; we would then fold them when the fish were inside. This is what we called mlembwe. Men would do the real fishing out there while we did mlembwe."[163]

Rainy-season fishing offered the possibility of larger catches. Khaki Mwandipandusa remembered that "when the [annual Zambezi] floods came, we were very happy. . . . We were catching a lot of fish because, when the river flowed at a faster rate, fish at the bottom would now come to the shallow waters."[164] From December through April, both the fish population and the number of large fish increased substantially. The faster-flowing currents, however, made catching fish harder and more dangerous.[165] "We worked very hard," stressed Aniva João, a fisherman from Inhangoma, "the river moved very quickly and there were so many fish that came out of the *bhande* [reeds]. We had to change our methods in order to capture them. During the floods we relied on a variety of different nets depending on where we were fishing, and [on] the types of fish."[166] Most fishermen used dugout canoes to harvest their catch, while some individually trawled with nets along the shoreline.[167] They generally fished at night, when the water was calmer and the fish stayed closer to the surface, returning home with their catch before dawn.[168] Boatmen who were more skilled searched the Zambezi for rich fishing beds further afield.[169]

To ensure their safety against the dangers of the mighty river, fishermen— and mlembwe women—relied on the sheltering power of spirits to protect them from harm. Fishermen embarking on long river journeys made special offerings (*ntsembe*) to their deceased relatives. To avoid drowning in the river, some "sprinkle[d] libations into the water as an offering to ancestor spirits."[170] According to Alberto Rapazolo, "in the past, before women went in work parties to catch fish, the chief and the elders would ask permission of the *mudzimu* [family ancestor spirits] to allow the women to enter the water and to protect them."[171]

Because rainy-season fishing in the rivulets and streams connected to the Zambezi was much less time consuming and dangerous than in the swiftly moving river, it attracted both professional and part-time fishermen. During the seasonal floods, when water from the Zambezi filled these smaller channels, it carried in large schools of fish. Men in canoes set *weiro*, large traps made from bamboo reeds, at strategic points in the smaller channels. The floodwaters sweeping into the rivulets thrust fish into the traps, from which escape was impossible. Most fishermen using this technique returned daily to secure their catch until the river receded.[172] Others, working in groups of five to six, used nets to trap fish in the adjacent wetlands and marshes.[173]

Many peasants who lived near these inlets also took advantage of the high fish population during flood season to supplement their household food supply. These men used *nkhonga*, smaller triangular weirs they wove out of thick grass, bound with palm strings, and baited with porridge. After paying homage to their ancestors, they placed them with their openings facing the fast-moving water at the edges of waterways and in shallow ponds.[174] The men typically remained at these locations for a week or two, collecting and drying the fish and ensuring that crocodiles and other animals neither destroyed their weirs nor consumed the catch. Some, like Bernardo Gona, returned to his fishing site once every three or four days. On a good night, when the fish were running well, he could "bring home five or six sacks stuffed after only four hours." He gave some of his catch to the people who worked with him in his garden, sold some to local traders, and consumed the rest.[175] After these part-time fishermen were satisfied that they had caught enough, they resumed working in the fields with their wives and children.[176]

As Gona's account suggests, for many households the especially rich supply of fish the Zambezi provided during the rainy season both augmented protein intake and fueled local labor and commodity markets. Bene Ngoca, who lived on the opposite bank from Gona, painted a similar picture: "In a single day I could fill my entire canoe with large fish—bass, catfish, bream, and many others."[177] In fact, the Zambezi valley's fishing economy expanded considerably in the first part of the twentieth century due to the development of new fishing techniques, most notably the *kokota* seine nets and the *psyairo* (encircling fishing fence).[178] By the middle of the twentieth century, many families were selling fish at nearby markets, even though in some areas fishing for profit ran up against long-standing cultural prohibitions against overexploiting natural resources for individual gain.[179] As Marita Zhuwao explained, "In the past if one continued to fish even after one caught sufficient fish for one's family, the spirit [of the river] would get angry. Then, if one threw in the nets to catch more fish, maybe one would catch a dead baby or [receive] some other bad omen."[180]

Even if some exaggerated the size of the catch, there is no question that fishing was one of the twin pillars of the Zambezi valley's economy, both for those who fished regularly and for many who primarily cultivated the land. Together with farming, it sustained riverside communities and fueled local trade. All this would change with the building of the dam.

WILDLIFE AND FOREST RESOURCES

The riparian ecosystems of the lower Zambezi valley also supported an impressive variety of animal and tree species. Guinea fowl, bushpig, kudu, and waterbuck were everywhere, and eland, buffalo, gazelles, elephants, and rhinoceroses also roamed the region,[181] seeking nourishment, especially in the dry season, in the grasslands, floodplains, marshes, and caves near the river and regularly visiting its edge for water and food. The Zambezi delta, with its predictable episodes of massive flooding and silt deposits, and its abundant supplies of fresh water and food, also attracted a spectacular array of large mammals, including zebras, elephants, waterbuck, hippopotami, and buffalo,[182] and the river's islands offered a particularly friendly habitat for many bird species, including the now-endangered wattled crane.

During the rainy season, when wild game that roamed the forests and scrublands of the floodplain stopped at the river to drink in the early mornings and late evenings, they became easy prey for local hunters.[183] Oral testimonies confirm the importance of hunting as both a source of food and an affirmation of male status in riverine communities. Zhuzi Luizhi reported that it was common to snare small animals as they "[sought] green grass along the river."[184] Chidasiyikwa Mavungire remembered that "during the time we were young, people could . . . hunt in the floodplains. In the area between the two rivers, the Shire and the Zambezi, there used to be shrubs where [small] animals could be found."[185] Other accounts highlighted both the prodigious supply of large game in the past (frequently expressed in the form of lists of animal species) and the community's collective pride in the skill of talented hunters. Maurício Alemão, for instance, explained that "there were many animals for us to hunt, including elephants, buffalo, giraffes, and eland."[186]

There were also two groups of renowned hunting specialists living on the margins of the river, who regularly provided meat to villages nearby. Those known as *mukumbalumi* killed elephants and larger game with homemade guns, called *gogodas*.[187] Their return to the village after a successful hunt was an occasion for great festivities and the consumption of large quantities of beer and meat—some distributed by the hunters among their relatives and the remainder exchanged for grain.[188] Phodzo canoemen armed with iron harpoons, by contrast, focused their hunting activities on hippopotami. After a kill, they removed the valuable hippo tusks for sale to the Europeans and sold some of the meat in nearby villages.[189] In a region inhospitable to livestock, the meat provided by all these hunters was a highly desired protein.

Rural communities also valued, and carefully managed, the timber and plant resources found in the savanna woodlands near the river. These river-nourished soils supported many species of trees, whose decomposing leaves were a natural fertilizer. Trees also supplied necessary materials for home construction, canoe building, fuel, and, the numerous wild fruits, roots, and tubers that supplemented rural diets.[190] Through the controlled use of fire, peasants balanced their dependence on these forest products with their knowledge that well-timed burns of wooded areas made other food sources available. Thus, fires at the conclusion of the harvest cleared land for next year's agricultural cycle, while early-season fires were effective both at flushing game out of the forest for hunting and at creating paths through the bush for easy travel.

Additionally, floodplain habitats yielded many medicinal plants used by respected herbalists[191] to treat rural families' common illnesses and serious diseases—from ailing bodies to complications during childbirth, childhood illnesses, diarrhea, venereal disease, sexual impotence, convulsions, and nervous disorders. Herbalists, most of whom were women, gathered therapeutic plant materials in and near the Zambezi during the seasonal floods, drawing upon detailed knowledge learned from family members and other practitioners. In the delta, some consulted with Nzunzu, the spirit of the water, before exploring remote corners of the Zambezi in search of medicinal plants.[192] *Curandeiras* also provided medications to protect their patients against witchcraft, to prevent attacks by crocodiles and hippopotami, and to treat common rural mishaps, such as snakebites.[193] João Raposo, for instance, recalled using a plant in Caia called *mghangha* to treat the bite of the *tchipiri* snake.[194] In short, these villagers used their expert knowledge to promote health and sustain life in the rural communities they served.

Moreover, the natural flow regime of the Zambezi River itself helped to regulate the health of rural communities in the centuries before construction of Cahora Bassa. The annual flood cycle, for instance, flushed out stagnant water bodies, thereby reducing the fecundity of disease vectors, such as malarial mosquitoes. The river's rapid flow also temporarily cleansed the water of schistosomiasis and other waterborne diseases.

～

Long before the construction of Cahora Bassa, the Zambezi played a critical economic and social role in the lives of the people living and working adjacent to its shores. While European administrators and travelers generally saw the river very differently than the indigenous population, occasionally they agreed. Thus, when the British explorer Frederick Selous wrote, "there's life in a draught of Zambesi water,"[195] and Carl Peters, his German counterpart, observed that the river's "arteries infused life into whole countries,"[196] their narratives overlapped with indigenous representations. For most foreign observers and government officials, however, the river had to be tamed before the region could prosper—which was the dominant development narrative that inspired the building of Cahora Bassa.

3 ⌐ Harnessing the River

High Modernism and Building the Dam, 1965–75

ON DECEMBER 6, 1974, two pressure-driven steel gates, each weighing 220 tonnes, stopped the mighty Zambezi River in its course. After five years of toil by more than five thousand workers, the construction of Cahora Bassa was complete.[1] Portuguese colonial officials, representatives of the new Frelimo-led government, church leaders, engineers, hydrologists, and journalists who were present on that day marveled at the dam's majestic 170-meter-high walls, its five massive General Electric turbines, and the vast man-made lake that would cover more than twenty-six hundred square kilometers.[2] The technical complexity and skill needed to erect the world's fifth-largest hydroelectric installation in a remote corner of Mozambique also attracted considerable international attention. For its proponents, Cahora Bassa represented high modernism at its best—the ultimate confirmation that science and technological expertise, in the hands of a strong state, could conquer nature and reorder biophysical systems to serve humankind.[3]

Yet casting Cahora Bassa as a high-modernist triumph obscures a great deal more than it reveals. As Mitchell demonstrated in his study of colonial Egypt, capitalist modernization projects undertaken by authoritarian states tend to be permeated with violence or its ever-present threat.[4] In fact, coercion was a central feature of Cahora Bassa's construction. Local African communities were forced to abandon their homes in the Songo highlands to make way for the construction of a segregated town for white workers recruited from abroad. Additionally, state officials often relied on conscripted labor to build both the infrastructure around the dam site and the dam itself. Moreover, even within the increasingly fortified confines of the dam site, colonial authorities used coercion to silence, repress, and discipline angry workers and suspected militants whom they feared might disrupt construction in some way.

The centrality of violence to the process of colonizing the Zambezi River and building Cahora Bassa demonstrated that the Portuguese regime had neither the political power nor the material resources to accomplish its ambitious economic goals. Frelimo's determined diplomatic and military campaign to stop the dam's construction, combined with the fiscal uncertainty of the chronically cash strapped colonial state, drove Portugal once again into the arms of South Africa, Mozambique's wealthy neighbor. The resulting transnational alliance enabled Portugal to hold nationalist forces at bay long enough to complete the dam, although at the cost of developmental goals that were supposed to improve the lives of African communities in the area.

This chapter examines the origins of the dam project Portugal hoped would economically transform the Zambezi River valley. It chronicles the local, national, and transnational factors compelling Portugal to scale back its plans, making Cahora Bassa simply a provider of cheap energy for South Africa. Most of the chapter, however, explores the very different lived experiences of European and African workers, embedded in unequal ways in a highly racialized and inherently coercive labor process. The final section highlights Frelimo's diplomatic and military efforts, with significant international support, to thwart Cahora Bassa's construction. While the brutality of Portugal's counterinsurgency measures ensured the triumphant unveiling of Cahora Bassa, in late 1974, as both a marvelous technical accomplishment and a symbolic defeat of the nationalist challenge, the dam's completion was, in many ways, a pyrrhic victory, won at the expense of the region's economy, environment, rural population, and, ultimately, control over Mozambique itself.

THE PLAN: A STUDY IN HIGH MODERNISM

For centuries, the mammoth Cahora Bassa gorge, located about 650 kilometers from the mouth of the Zambezi River, had both awed and frustrated Portuguese colonial planners[5] and merchants, who complained that its falls were an impenetrable obstacle to their use of the Zambezi as a highway into the rich interior. Only in 1955—after the British had decided to construct a large hydroelectric project at Kariba, another 650 kilometers upriver from Cahora Bassa, between colonial Zambia and Zimbabwe—did Lisbon realize that taming the great river might be achievable.[6]

The symbolic power and economic promise of Kariba immediately captured the imagination of the Portuguese Overseas Ministry, which in May 1956 ordered its engineers in Mozambique to investigate the possibility of impounding the Zambezi at Cahora Bassa. Two months later, the ministry dispatched Professor A. A. Manzanares, a close adviser to the Portuguese leader António de Oliveira Salazar, to Mozambique, where he flew by helicopter—the only form of access—to the Cahora Bassa gorge. After he enthusiastically endorsed the project upon his return to Lisbon,[7] the Overseas Ministry, embracing his findings, issued a highly influential and optimistic report:

> The basin of the Zambezi in Portuguese territory contains more eco-
> nomic possibilities for the future than any other river in Africa or even
> in the rest of the world. We must appreciate that in the Mozambique
> basin the potential energy of the river is roughly 50 billion KWH
> [50,000 megawatts] of which more than half can be achieved in a rela-
> tively short space. . . . The floods, when [Kariba and Cahora Bassa]
> are built, will become a memory, a spectre from past nightmares; and
> the lowlands formed over billions of years by the alluvial silt from
> Central Africa, product of primeval erosion, will be turned to produc-
> tive use by the patience and tenacity of men.[8]

Acting with dispatch, it immediately established a river-basin authority under its direct control, which meant that, in effect, "the upper Zambesi basin, a quarter of all Mozambique, was to be taken out of the sphere of the adminis-tration in Lourenço Marques and run directly from Lisbon."[9]

The Missão de Fomento e Povoamento de Zambeze (MFPZ)—which sub-sequently became the Gabinete do Plano do Zambeze (GPZ)—was charged with coordinating research, initiating feasibility studies, and establishing the blueprints for the development of the Zambezi.[10] Although both understaffed[11] and underfunded for this mammoth task, between 1957 and 1961 it published twenty-seven preliminary studies of the climatic, geological, topographical, hydrological, and economic conditions in the Zambezi River basin. This vast region, which was twice the area of Portugal, covered approximately 185,000 square kilometers.[12] Five years later, in 1966, the MFPZ produced a fifty-six-volume final report that confirmed the prior assessment that a dam would be highly beneficial to Mozambique.[13]

The core ideological rationale for Portugal's decision to invest in large in-frastructural projects, such as Cahora Bassa in Mozambique and the Cunene Dam in Angola, was its belief that the colonies in Africa (Mozambique, An-gola, Guinea Bissau, Cabo Verde, and São Tomé) and Asia (Goa and Mação) were an integral part of the Portuguese nation. In the 1950s, to justify its continued colonialism in the face of decolonization elsewhere in Africa, the Salazar regime promoted Gilberto Freyre's theory of lusotropicalism, which stressed the exceptional character of Portuguese colonialism and its absence of racism.[14] After relabeling the colonies as "overseas provinces," Portugal could claim the unique status of being a transcontinental, multiracial state, which, it imagined, would make it a force in world politics and undermine the push for independence by nationalist movements in its colonies. Thus, for the Salazar regime, damming the Zambezi was both a powerful symbol of patriotic pride and a reaffirmation of Portugal's long-term commitment to maintaining its African colonies at all costs. In 1970, Dr. Joaquim da Silva Cunha, the overseas minister, underscored the dam's centrality to the future of the metropole: "Through [the construction of Cabora Bassa] we seek to create a further dynamic factor for the progress of Mozambique, for the good of all who live here, integrated in the Portuguese Homeland . . . without any discrimination of race or religion."[15] The governor of Tete District,[16] site of the proposed dam, concurred. "Cabora Bassa is a very strong statement from our country," he told a reporter from the *Washington Post*, which "means we are not going to give [Mozambique] up. It is determination shown on the ground."[17]

In scale, rationale, and the political economy of its origins, the proposed dam at Cahora Bassa was radically different from its British counterpart. Kariba had ten turbines—double the number of the Portuguese project—and the reservoir was triple the size of the one at Cahora Bassa.[18] Kariba's purpose was to fuel postwar industrialization and commercial agriculture in the recently established Federation of Rhodesia and Nyasaland, by providing cheap electricity for the copper mines in colonial Zambia and for the European industries and farms in colonial Zimbabwe—the priority sectors of the federation's economy.[19] The site of the region's first large hydroelectric project was the subject of intense debate. Although building a dam at Kafue gorge made more technological and economic sense and would have required the relocation of only one thousand Tonga villagers,[20] Southern Rhodesian interests, which had greater political strength, prevailed, and Kariba became the site of the dam.[21]

By contrast, there was no debate within the Portuguese colonial state over the site or goals of Cahora Bassa, which, as originally conceived, were far more ambitious than Kariba. Portuguese planners saw Cahora Bassa as a multipurpose megadam designed to achieve a number of far-reaching economic, social, and political objectives—expanding regional productivity, enhancing the living conditions of the indigenous population, substantially increasing the number of Europeans in the Zambezi valley, and ending flooding.[22] With the rise of Frelimo, which began its military campaign in 1964,[23] added to the list was preventing Frelimo guerrillas from advancing beyond the Zambezi River into the economic heart of the colony. Along with a future dam to be built further downriver at Mphanda Nkuwa, colonial planners hoped that Cahora Bassa would generate a boundless source of cheap energy—energy that would both transform the colonial economy and bind Mozambique permanently to the Portuguese state.[24]

The dam at Cahora Bassa was originally supposed to provide hydroelectric power to stimulate agriculture, forestry, and industrial production in the Zambezi valley and to foster development of a commercial fishing industry on Lake Cahora Bassa.[25] Colonial planners additionally expected this new energy supply to facilitate the exploitation of abundant coal, iron, copper, and titanium deposits located in Tete District, and of bauxite and chrome in neighboring regions. Transporting these minerals down the Zambezi River to Chinde would transform this sleepy coastal port into a major gateway to international markets and the Zambezi itself into a bustling highway linking the rich interior to both the Indian Ocean and the wider world.[26]

Portuguese planners also expected local African communities to benefit greatly from the dam. They projected that the spin-off effects of its construction would improve the region's roads and other physical infrastructures, stimulate commerce, and generate income that would be used to construct a network of rural schools and health posts.[27] By the early 1960s, Portugal's colonial development narrative included a moral responsibility to improve the lives of its "backward subjects" and bring colonized peoples into the twentieth century under the "civilizing" tutelage of the Portuguese state.[28] Dr. Silva Cunha, during his visit to Cabora Bassa in November 1970, stressed the transforming social and cultural potential of the dam, declaring that Lisbon's objective was "to tame the great river and transform it into a source of enhancement of the vast region contained within its river base, a resource that would be capable of giving the progress of the whole area a rapid, dynamic impulse."[29] In short, the hydroelectric project reflected both Portugal's "civilizing mission" and its commitment to remain in Africa indefinitely. Plans to build the dam also fit within the global discourse on development, which stressed that increasing per capita GNP would alleviate poverty.[30]

Colonial authorities further predicted that the economic development stimulated by Cahora Bassa would dramatically increase the size of the white settler population in the Zambezi valley. To house the up to eighty thousand Portuguese immigrants projected to join the planned agricultural communities (colonatos) on both banks of the Zambezi River downstream from Tete, they identified 1.5 million hectares suitable for irrigation and conducted agronomic and climatic investigations to determine which cash crops would best thrive there.[31] Like the mineral wealth to be exported through Chinde, the planners expected that agricultural and forest commodities produced on the colonatos would be channeled down the Zambezi for sale abroad.

Seasonal flooding was another ongoing problem the dam was supposed to solve. On four occasions between 1926 and 1958, the river overflowed the levees constructed by Sena Sugar Estates in 1926, causing serious losses. Located at Luabo and Mopeia, these plantations were an important source of foreign exchange for the colonial regime, and protecting their sugar crop was an important rationale for building Cahora Bassa.[32] Colonial officials also claimed that flooding regularly destroyed several million dollars worth of peasant produce.[33]

The last critical objective of the Cahora Bassa project—again, absent from Kariba—was to keep Frelimo out of the economic heart of the colony. Mounting pressure from the nationalist movement, which began operating in central Mozambique in 1966, drove much of the later planning and elevated the project's urgency. Portuguese officials believed that the dam would help blunt guerrilla advances south of the strategic Zambezi River in two significant ways. First, they theorized that the lake behind the dam, stretching from Songo to Zumbo, which would be five hundred kilometers long and several kilometers wide, would pose a formidable geographic barrier to Frelimo's otherwise easy access to the heart of Mozambique from its bases in Zambia and Malawi. Second, they envisioned the colonatos, which would include many former soldiers,[34] as armed settler communities that would provide a first line of defense against African guerrillas seeking to reach the capital, Lourenço Marques, and overthrow the colonial regime.

From the beginning, however, skeptics in Lisbon and Mozambique questioned whether a megadam was economically viable, arguing that its expense would place a heavy burden on the national budget and that substantial Portuguese investment either in the dam or in commercial agriculture and mining was unlikely. Critics also stressed that the scheme rested on unsubstantiated assumptions—that the dam would draw European settlers to the malaria-infested Zambezi valley, that the agricultural commodities those settlers produced would be competitive on the world market, and that the region's minerals were both substantial and accessible. Mozambique's inability to consume even 10 percent of the projected 2,075-megawatt output from Cahora Bassa's turbines merely increased concerns about its viability.[35]

The escalating conflict with Frelimo posed a more immediate and concrete threat to the project's feasibility. Until the mid-1960s, nationalist forces had focused their military activities on the northern districts of Cabo Delgado and Niassa (see map 3.1). In 1968, however, Frelimo launched a coordinated diplomatic and military campaign to thwart the construction of Cahora Bassa—including a guerrilla offensive in Tete District, the dam's home. It made no effort to conceal its intentions, vowing in *Mozambique Revolution*, Frelimo's English-language periodical, to destroy Cahora Bassa because it represented "a hostile act against the Mozambican people."[36] The colonial government found the Tete offensive especially worrisome; not only did it actually endanger Cahora Bassa, but, if Frelimo were able to cross the Zambezi River, it would gain access to the more populous southern half of Mozambique—a region that included the white highlands of Manica and Sofala and the cities of Beira and Lourenço Marques.

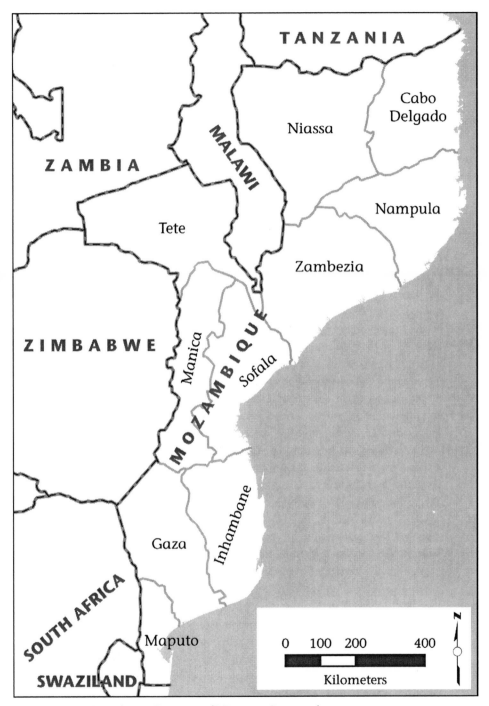

MAP 3.1. Mozambique. *University of Minnesota Cartography*

The combination of economic uncertainty and mounting security threats compelled planners to rethink both the purpose and timeline of the project. Anxious to guarantee a market for hydroelectric power and to obtain military support for the embattled colonial state, Portugal turned to neighboring South Africa, where sufficient capital existed to finance the dam's construction—and whose own power requirements were projected to double between 1967 and 1980.[37] Counting on the racist politics of the white minority regime, Portuguese proponents of the dam lobbied for a combined energy and military agreement with South Africa.[38]

In September 1969, after three years of negotiations, Lisbon signed a $515 million agreement with Zamco—a South African–dominated consortium with partners in West Germany, France, Italy, and Portugal—to build a dam at Cahora Bassa,[39] which reconfigured the project into a single-purpose hydroelectric scheme producing cheap power for South Africa. Lisbon continued to maintain that the dam would be instrumental in economically developing the Zambezi region, but that had become a secondary consideration. While colonial authorities believed increased economic activity in and along the river would still have a trickle-down effect on small-scale African cultivators living in the Zambezi basin—mainly in the form of the introduction of new farming techniques, new markets for their commodities, and new job opportunities[40]—these benefits were no longer necessary measures of the dam's success. The colonial state still heralded the dam as proof of its commitment to remain permanently in Africa, but its primary effect was to extend South Africa's reach into the Mozambican countryside. Mozambican energy, like Mozambican mine workers,[41] would now be expropriated to serve the interests of South African capital.

South Africa's willingness to invest in Cahora Bassa and to buy its electricity demonstrated Pretoria's commitment to incorporate Mozambique into its economic and security zone against the impending "black onslaught." Thereafter, South African, Mozambican, and Rhodesian senior military officers met regularly to plan out strategies for containing Frelimo and ZANU[42] advances in the Zambezi valley, and, in 1971, they affirmed their commitment to use all military force necessary to blunt the "terrorists" through the Alcora accord.[43]

Anxious to strengthen these new links with South Africa, Lisbon insisted that the dam be operational by January 1975. Under this tight timeline, the river had to be diverted in the 1970–71 dry season, so that the dam could be built before the 1971–72 floods, the main wall raised in the 1972–73 dry season, and the lake filled in 1974.[44] This schedule left no time for unanticipated problems, since failure to meet any deadline would necessarily cause at least a year's delay. Additionally, the slightest engineering error could, if accompanied by unanticipated peak-season flooding, sweep away the completed segments and flood the underground tunnels.[45]

Even though thousands of villagers would need to be relocated after their land was inundated by the creation of the massive 2,739-square-kilometer man-made lake behind the walls of Cahora Bassa, Portuguese officials and state planners paid little attention to the potential consequences of the hydro-electric scheme for either these local communities or the environment. While such a politically charged effort would require extensive social engineering under difficult conditions, they knew very little about the Tawara, Tonga, Nyungwe, Chikunda, Nsenga, and Pimbe communities living in the affected zone. There were few ethnographic surveys of this area conducted before the 1970s,[46] and the only monograph on the Tawara, the most populous group in the region, appeared in 1976—one year after the dam's completion.[47] Nevertheless, without detailed social and cultural data, in 1968 MFPZ researchers created a five-year plan to relocate displaced peasants into modern planned communities (aldeamentos) (see chapter 4).[48]

Portuguese planners gave even less consideration to the ecological impact of the proposed dam, either up- or downriver. Because Cahora Bassa, from its inception, reflected the political and developmentalist aims of the colonial state, there was little incentive to consider environmental costs. Additionally, the volatile security situation in the lower Zambezi valley and the general veil of secrecy surrounding the dam inhibited critical scientific inquiry. Thus, unlike the situation with Kariba,[49] the dam's environmental impacts rarely entered the promoters' field of vision.

In 1968, Rupert Fothergill, the mastermind of Kariba's wildlife removal scheme known as Operation Noah's Ark, urged the Portuguese to start such planning immediately. Failure to do so, he warned, would inevitably mean that large herds of animals would drown or starve to death on isolated Zambezi islands when the floodwaters started rising behind the proposed dam.[50] Nevertheless, it was not until 1973 that a team of GPZ researchers proposed a wildlife refuge for Chioco, adjacent to the planned lake at Cahora Bassa. They recommended that highly prized animals, such as black rhinoceroses, leopards, and red impalas, be transported there and urged the protection of the region's large game population, despite skepticism that local officials would have either the interest or the resources to implement these initiatives.[51] Their skepticism was well founded.

Nor did the Portuguese government study the dam's environmental impact before its construction, although it belatedly created an agency, the Missão de Ecologia Aplicada do Zambeze (MEAZ), under the auspices of the GPZ, for that purpose. In 1973 the MEAZ commissioned a preimpoundment survey of water quality, vegetation, soils, and climate[52] "to examine and report on the chemical and biological condition of the river and major tributaries"—information that could be used "to monitor future change" in the river's ecology.[53]

From November 1973 to October 1974, a small team of scientists affiliated with the Universidade de Lourenço Marques—researchers in chemistry, phytoplankton ecology, and stream ecology—conducted biophysical surveys of the lower Zambezi valley.[54] This was the first scientific investigation of the lower Zambezi River since the building of Kariba fifteen years earlier.[55]

According to Bryan Davies, a South African scientist who was part of this research team, its work yielded little detailed knowledge of the Zambezi ecosystems. This was due to the marked lack of resources and trained personnel available to the environmental scientists, the sporadic nature of the surveys, and the threats posed by the ongoing war[56]—all of which limited the time they spent in the region and the quality of their work.[57] Davies also decried "the lack of ecological specialists with local knowledge who should be dealing with the interdependence and interrelationships of the whole Lower Zambezi as one integrated system. This danger is compounded as authority in both land-use planning and decision-making is vested in non-ecological experts."[58]

Nevertheless, based on the preliminary research, Davies predicted that the dam's creation of reduced and regularized flows of water would have long-term devastating consequences on both downriver ecological systems and the communities whose livelihoods depended on them. He forecast a major reduction in sediment transport, changing patterns of vegetative reproduction, a rapid decline in riverine and coastal fisheries, and an increase of malaria and schistosomiasis.[59] To minimize some of these anticipated negative consequences, he and his colleagues recommended that the GPZ gradually fill the lake to permit a steady flow of water downriver. They advocated a minimum discharge of four to five hundred cubic meters per second from the dam during the filling phase, compared to the average flow in normal years of two to three thousand cubic meters per second.[60]

Civil engineers and state planners, however, were adamantly opposed to this recommendation because, with such a flow rate, filling the lake to maximum capacity would take a year or more. Since they sought to complete the dam's construction and provide cheap energy to South Africa as quickly as possible, they favored the projected four-month time frame—even though only a trickle of water would flow down the gorge during that period. Because the civil engineers, economists, and state planners had nearly all the political and cultural authority associated with the dam, they prevailed.

Davies and his colleagues could do little more than deplore the decision to rush the construction process. Years later, he wrote, "Our work was ignored by the very people who requested the survey in the first place."[61] This episode reveals how specific colonial structures and relations of power transformed one group of experts into arbiters of appropriate development, while underfunding and silencing another, whose conclusions ran counter to the state's narrative.[62] This pattern would continue throughout the century and beyond.

BUILDING CAHORA BASSA

Before actual construction could begin, colonial planners and Zamco had to overcome a myriad of logistic and technical problems. One of the most pressing was the dam site's inaccessibility. As with the building of the dam, Africans bore the physical cost of constructing the roads up the steep mountainside to the Songo plateau—the projected center of the hydroelectric complex—and down the other side, to the gorge.

When the MFPZ began its initial explorations, in 1957, the Songo plateau was a backwater region approximately one hundred kilometers north of Tete. The nearest Portuguese administrative post was at Estima, thirty kilometers away, and the administrator's only access to the plateau was by foot, bicycle, or donkey. This dirt path, the product of forced labor, which existed only because a local Portuguese merchant needed to transport goods to his small canteen on the plateau, demonstrated how inconsequential the Portuguese had considered this area.[63]

The gorge, which the dam would span, was even more inaccessible. According to Pedro da Costa Xavier, a local African MFPZ employee, who was the first person to survey the dam site, it was extremely difficult to descend the steep nine-hundred-meter escarpment from Songo to the confluence of the Zambezi and Gutu Rivers. He described his first trip there, in October 1957:

> I was taken by helicopter to fly over the area where the Gutu River falls into the Zambezi. That is where they planned to build the dam. We returned to Songo and the Portuguese officials ordered fumo Songo to select someone to accompany me on foot back to the site. The Portuguese knew there was a gorge, but they did not know exactly what was there. Our trip was very dangerous. There were many wild animals, particularly lions. It took us three hours to climb down. The vegetation was very heavy. We followed the route of the monkeys. When we arrived, I made drawings of the river, the shoreline, and the surrounding mountains. We then climbed back up the escarpment, mapping our path in great detail.[64]

A decade later little had changed. Since there was still no all-weather Tarmac road linking Songo either to the outside world or to the dam site, it was impossible to bring in the heavy equipment needed to start the project.

Between 1967 and 1972, the colonial state and Zamco instituted a crash road-building program. The GPZ brought in large bulldozers and earth-moving machinery to carve out access roads both to the Songo plateau and down to the gorge. Despite the abolition of chibalo decades earlier,[65] colonial officials conscripted peasants from surrounding communities to build these roads. Júlio Calecoetoa, an elder who had lived in the region his entire life, described the exploitation of African labor:

> The people who constructed the roads were chibalo workers. There were several hundred. They came from Zumbo, Angonia, Tete, Mukumbura, and Chicoa. They were forced to work. First, they cut the trees, and then they removed the large rocks. The engineers were in front taking the measurements, and others were building the road in the area that they had cleared. People suffered a lot. Rocks would fall on them and many lost their legs, and they would have to go to the hospital. Others went blind from rock chips. The chibalo laborers worked hard, and the *sipāes* [African police] beat them to make them work even harder. Men would arrange chickens or goats for the sipāes to keep from being beaten. There was a white foreman who told the *capitāes* [overseers] and the sipāes how much the workers had to clear each day. If there were not many rocks, they would have to clear a kilometer or so. If there were many boulders, it could take a week or even a month. When the road had to be graded, it took even longer. If they did not achieve their targets, the sipāes explained to the boss that there were many rocks, but afterward they returned and beat the workers whom they thought had been lazy.[66]

Such coercion and intimidation, combined with the imposition of a grueling work schedule, made it possible both to carve out an access road to the base camp on the Songo plateau and to build a track down the nine-hundred-meter mountainside to the gorge in less than a year (see fig. 3.1). Pedro da Costa Xavier described the challenges faced by the road crews working on the final segment of this road:

> The engineer Crispin de Sousa was in charge. He had about forty workers. They did not have sufficient equipment to build the entire road and they could not cut through the boulders. They waited for jackhammers and dynamite to break up the rocks that blocked the way. The work was very dangerous because the dynamite could explode before the workers could get far enough away. I remember one time before the construction began on the dam when many died. They were digging holes in an area where the dynamite had already been set. There was a large explosion, killing many workers.[67]

FIGURE 3.1. Road to the construction site. *CITM/AHM*

Even after the road's completion, fearsome hairpin turns, sharp bends, rainy-season washouts, and periodic rockslides made the journey to the dam site treacherous.[68] According to one observer, "it was a road in name only, continually menaced by falling boulders and landslides."[69] Despite these difficulties and a number of serious accidents, by 1971 as many as five hundred trucks crept up and down the escarpment every day, bringing heavy equipment to the dam site.[70] That same year, Zamco completed a 130-kilometer two-lane paved highway between Songo and Tete, which enabled it to bring in the bulldozers, rock drills, and other heavy equipment necessary to open up the gorge. Shortly thereafter, it built an extrawide paved road that linked the Tete highway to the gorge through the heavily wooded Mukandgadzi valley — bypassing the Songo escarpment entirely. This road allowed wide-bodied, multiwheeled trucks to transport the huge turbines, generators, and transformers directly to the dam site.[71] Conscripted African labor primarily built both roads.

RECRUITING EUROPEAN WORKERS AND THE
MAKING OF A COMPANY TOWN

With road construction under way, Zamco officials, working closely with the colonial government, turned their attention to recruiting the labor force needed to build the dam itself. Because colonial policy and an informal color bar dictated that labor be segregated along racial lines, Europeans had to hold all positions of authority. Whatever the practical skills or on-the-ground experience of African mechanics, carpenters, masons, and electricians, no African was able to occupy a supervisory post—even if, as mechanic Simões Wetela recalled, a white "boss" "did not understand how the machines worked and how labor was organized," and had to be schooled by his African subordinate.[72]

Because Mozambique's Portuguese-settler community had insufficient engineers, electricians, and mechanics willing to relocate to a remote and malaria-infested corner of the colony, Zamco recruited heavily from Portugal, France, Germany, and South Africa. It preferred married men, who were offered housing for their families and promises that their children would receive quality educations at Songo schools—in their mother tongue, if possible. Providing up to fourteen months of wages for a single year's labor and subsidized family airfares enabled Zamco, by 1973, to attract more than 150 foreign technicians from fourteen countries.[73] Many had previously worked on dam or large civil engineering projects in the developing world.[74] About six hundred Portuguese men also worked on the site, some recruited in France, where they had migrated in search of higher-paying jobs. Given the estimated construction costs of $500 million, the recruitment bonuses were just a minor, if necessary, expenditure.

In a further elaboration of the social division of labor at Cahora Bassa, Zamco assigned responsibility for planning and overseeing different spheres of the dam project by nationality. The French specialized in civil engineering, German engineers supervised the electromechanical operations, and Italian workers surveyed the routes for the transmission line. Portuguese initially filled most of the semiskilled technical and administrative positions, and South Africans oversaw the campsites and supervised the African laborers. The rationale for this last decision was that South Africans typically spoke Fanagalo, the pidgin used as the lingua franca of the South African mines, and had had substantial experience overseeing and disciplining African workers there.[75]

To stabilize this skilled labor force, Zamco made life bearable for expatriate employees and their families by turning the forests and brush of the plateau into a comfortable company town. Acutely aware that dissatisfied workers would be neither productive nor inclined to renew their contracts, it offered

European staff amenities to overcome their apprehension about living in such a remote rural setting. The transformation of Songo was thorough and swift. A South African reporter, one of the few foreign journalists allowed access to the dam, wrote admiringly in 1970 of how a desolate space "in the bush" had become a lively residential and commercial center: "Its prefabricated and concrete houses will house some 5000 people within two years. . . . The town named Songo is like a mini U.N. Its people eat at a restaurant whose dishes run a gastronomic gamut from English to Latin and German."[76] Similarly, a Rhodesian journalist in 1972 found it "hard to grasp that there was nothing here three years ago."[77]

The creation of Songo required the obliteration of the existing, African-made landscape—as a fertile farming plateau gave way to a segregated city of cement. Outsiders' representations of Songo in the early 1970s as a transformed wasteland were not only incorrect but effectively erased the histories of the several thousand Nyungwe and Tawara peasants who had resided for centuries on the highlands (see chapter 2).

The comforts provided by Zamco for its skilled labor force included modern housing at highly subsidized rents. White workers also had exclusive access to a European club offering "exquisite meals," the finest whiskies, and foreign beer at below-market prices—served on a veranda overlooking tropical gardens and a swimming pool.[78] According to the *Rhodesian Herald*,

> The township has three banks, mainly for the headquarters of the ZAMCO consortium, one hospital, a hotel and a supermarket, where you buy anything from safety pins and blankets to luxury items. . . . Outside the office of the ZAMCO club stands a glass replica of the Eiffel tower, monument of the Bastille Day celebrations which took place a fortnight before our visit. The club itself is a pleasant airy building with big veranda, a hall which is used for special occasions and the regular dining room. Outside in an area of rather dusty lawn is a good-sized swimming pool. . . . To get into the club, you must have a ZAMCO pass.[79]

Additionally, Zamco's discounted supermarkets sold a wide variety of imported commodities. Songo also offered twice-weekly movies, soccer matches, tennis, gardening, gambling, and big-game hunting to keep expatriates' boredom at bay. When white residents grew tired of Songo itself, they drove their duty-free cars on long weekends and holidays to the beaches at Beira, the Kariba casinos, or Salisbury, the capital of colonial Zimbabwe, which offered many of the attractions of a cosmopolitan European city, while counting the days until they could return home, at least for an extended visit.[80]

Concerned about the potential sexual frustration of unmarried expatriate staff and colonial soldiers, Zamco allowed African women—from a trickle in the late 1960s to nearly forty by 1974—to work as prostitutes. Most came from impoverished households in southern Mozambique, drawn to the dam site by one of the few cash jobs available to rural women with little or no formal education or wage-work experience. Officially, Zamco neither acknowledged nor made allowances for their presence, restricting them to the outskirts of town opposite the airport.[81] For security reasons, the women received identity cards; for health reasons, they underwent periodic examinations for sexually transmitted diseases. Beyond these minimal controls, however, neither Zamco nor the colonial state made any effort to ensure that sex workers had minimally acceptable living and working conditions or legal recourse against abusive clients.[82] Marginalized physically, legally, and socially, the women rarely stayed for long. Unlike many African men who came from elsewhere to work at Cahora Bassa, they tended not to marry into local families or to settle at Songo permanently—making their experiences largely invisible to historians, except through the recollections of male workers willing to discuss them.

Despite these amenities, many European employees and their families had great difficulty adjusting to life in Songo. They complained that there was no waste disposal facility, imported food was often spoiled, and letters and newspapers from home were slow to arrive. Single men grumbled about the small number of single European women.[83] For many, the long, hot rainy season proved unbearable.[84] Others, according to one French engineer, suffered from the trauma of "psychological confinement."[85]

This sense of isolation intensified in 1971 when Frelimo began attacking supply convoys and mining the roads connecting Songo to the outside world.[86] In April guerrillas kidnapped six European workers. Coming in the aftermath of a highly publicized warning in Frankfurt by a senior Frelimo official that "it could not guarantee that German workers would not be killed,"[87] the abduction sent waves of anxiety through Songo's expatriate community.

Ethnic tensions were also rampant among the Europeans. Anti-Portuguese sentiment was particularly acute. According to Keith Middlemas, one of the few foreign scholars to visit the dam site, "in the early days of isolation and poor facilities, when the easiest relief was heavy drinking, fighting frequently broke out and usually on national lines."[88] A PIDE (secret police) report highlighted the arrogance of French engineers "who treated Portuguese coworkers as servants while earning appreciably higher salaries."[89] South Africans also denigrated their Portuguese counterparts, whom they considered almost as lazy and backward as the Africans.[90] This South African snobbishness was visible to black employees, and it was common knowledge among African workers that, in the eyes of white South Africans, "the Portuguese were whites, but they were not considered whites. They were almost like Mozambicans."[91] There were also "many conflicts between the Boers and the Portuguese. Boers said that the Portuguese were stupid and did not know anything."[92] Pedro da Costa Xavier agreed that the South Africans resented "the Portuguese bosses [standing] with their arms crossed and [ordering] people around while the South African bosses actually did the work."[93] Other foreign workers complained that the Portuguese remained aloof and rarely socialized outside their own circle and that the South Africans were patronizing and short tempered.[94] There were also occasional physical confrontations between members of different expatriate groups.[95]

Combined with the other challenges in the company town, the strain of ongoing social tensions and less frequent violent interpersonal conflicts probably explains why appreciable numbers of foreign workers did not renew their lucrative contracts. Because their numbers declined by more than half between 1970 and 1974,[96] Zamco had to rely increasingly on local Portuguese men to stabilize the labor force.

RECRUITING AN AFRICAN WORKFORCE

Despite the attention Zamco devoted to its European personnel, it understood that building Cahora Bassa required a disciplined and inexpensive African labor force. African workers at the dam site were recruited—often through extralegal methods—into a highly regimented labor regime in which black men performed the most dangerous and physically demanding tasks, endured distinctly inferior conditions of employment, and had little recourse to protest. The racial dimensions of the labor process significantly undercut the partial autonomy that industrial workers typically enjoy.[97] Zamco divided its African workforce into skilled and unskilled. Drillers, dynamite blasters, solderers, masons, heavy-machinery operators, and truck drivers fell into the former category. Depending on the phase of the project, these workers constituted between 25 and 50 percent of the indigenous workforce, which doubled between 1972 and 1974.[98]

Initially, Zamco estimated that it needed to employ twelve hundred skilled African laborers per year. Almost all of them came from other parts of Mozambique, because company officials considered the local Tawara and Tonga backward, lazy, and unsuitable for all but the most menial tasks. They were, in the words of Zamco's chief labor recruiter, William Chambers, "poor physical specimens and unskilled."[99] Echoing this essentialist notion of the biologically determined capacities of African ethnic groups, Bill Smith, a South African Zamco employee who supervised African labor at Cahora Bassa, insisted that skilled positions deemed inappropriate for Europeans be reserved for "superior" Shangaan men from southern

Mozambique. Because of their long experience in the South African mines, Shangaan workers had a reputation as "good Bantus, clean, proud and well motivated."[100] The tendency of Shangaan "boss boys" and instructors from the south to use their influence to secure higher-paying jobs for relatives and neighbors reinforced this pattern.[101]

To round up sufficient Shangaan men for the dam project, Zamco opened two recruiting offices in Inhambane District, at Massinga and Vilanculos, and a third in nearby Gaza District, at Chibuto (see map 3.1).[102] These three areas in southern Mozambique were home to the thousands of migrant laborers who had spent years working in the mines or on white-owned farms in South Africa. Chambers himself personally supervised the hiring of the first laborers, using a preselection screening test, similar to one used on the South African mines, that weeded out those who lacked the appropriate mental skills, physical attributes, and work ethic.[103] Others, with "some potential," had to participate in a technical-training program before being permitted on the dam site[104]—although there was neither time nor workers to implement this requirement.[105] Simões Wetela, a skilled Shangaan migrant worker with South African experience, described his recruitment:

> I had worked in South Africa as a mechanic with a machine, which went down into the tunnels and removed the rocks in the mine. Witbank was the location and Back Block was the name of the mine. . . . It was a coal mine. I was there for three contracts. After each one, I returned home. After this, I worked in Betanie, in a quarry mine. I earned 4 rands per month as a mechanic. I also drove mine cars. After my last tour, I heard about the possibility of working at Cahora Bassa. . . . During my last visit home, recruiters from Cahora Bassa came to my village. There were many recruiters in the region. More than fifty of us signed on. . . . We were transported to Songo on a large truck. The journey lasted three days. At night we slept under the truck. We spent an additional week at the control center, where they made sure that we were not thieves or Frelimo sympathizers. We slept on the concrete; there were no tents and beds. The food was sent down there from the camp [at Songo]. Then we were given documents and assigned to a boss boy.[106]

Despite the pseudoscientific rigor of Zamco's recruitment methods, its initial efforts to attract experienced laborers were not particularly successful. Its recruiters found it difficult to compete with local agents of the Witwatersrand Native Labour Association (WNLA), the official representative of the South African mining industry. Since 125,000 legally recruited southern Mozambican workers and thousands of clandestine laborers traveled to South Africa annually, the mining industry was not about to let an interloper like Zamco undercut, even minimally, its hegemonic position in the regional labor market.[107] Moreover, Mozambican workers, having migrated to the Rand for generations, were loath to sever their ties to the South African mines.[108]

To break the WNLA's historic monopoly, Zamco advertised salaries that were higher than those prevalent on the mines. Drillers, the highest-paid African laborers at Cahora Bassa, would be paid over 12,000 escudos per month (approximately £150), truck drivers and carpenters half that amount. These salaries were several times what men could earn working locally or from their family fields.[109] Recruiters also promised overtime pay and resigning bonuses and food and transportation for the recruits traveling to Tete. Additionally, the journey to Songo was less arduous and much safer than trekking on foot across the South African border, with all its legal hassles and delays.[110] Even with such incentives, however, Zamco could not attract enough experienced African drillers, dynamite blasters, and heavy-machine operators.[111]

Zamco recruiters pursued several additional strategies in southern Mozambique to overcome this shortfall. They supplemented the modest salaries of local administrators with gifts and favors and offered state-appointed chiefs clothing, bicycles, and other incentives to encourage them to "find" labor for Cahora Bassa. These strategically placed authorities, who often enjoyed unchecked power on the ground, might encourage or pressure African men in their jurisdictions to sign with Zamco rather than the WNLA. Recruiters also used deception to expand the pool of new workers. At the office in Chibuto, for example, Jaime Chitsotso and twenty others voluntarily signed a contract with Zamco, based on promises by recruiters of high-paying construction positions at the dam site. When they arrived at Songo, however, there were no construction jobs waiting for them; instead, they were ordered to report to Ermoque-Empreiteiros, a Zamco subsidiary, to work on the road from Tete to Songo, at substantially lower wages. Chitsotso initially refused, but, being far from home, penniless, and without a local network of social support, he soon realized he had no alternative.[112]

In its search for skilled African labor, Zamco even extended its reach beyond Mozambique. It recruited Malawians, Zambians, Zimbabweans, and Sotho who had worked either in the South African mines or on the Zambian Copperbelt.[113] Chambers also brought in Pondo workers from the South African mines, whose skills were legendary, to excavate pilot shafts, cut through dangerously unstable rocks underneath, and burrow out the hangar-size chamber needed to house the generators, controls, and massive turbines.[114] Zezuru truck drivers from colonial Zimbabwe, who drove the large rigs carrying cement and petroleum, and Nyungwe carpenters and stonecutters from Tete were the only other Africans given relatively high paying jobs.

Despite disdain for the local Tawara, Tonga, and Nyungwe who lived near the dam, Zamco had to employ them to fill the ranks of its African workforce. With little access to formal education or industrial experience, they performed unskilled menial tasks—road crew laborers, stone haulers, masons' assistants, cooks, and gardeners—and worked as domestic servants for the Europeans.[115] With overtime, their starting wage hovered around 900 escudos per month—almost £9.[116]

Desperation motivated many to take these low-paying jobs. Other than on the alluvial plains, Tete District was impoverished. Thus, unless men left the area, they could not earn enough to pay their annual taxes and to buy the minimal consumer goods—such as sugar, rice, and clothing—needed for their households' survival. The escalating liberation struggle, however, made it increasingly difficult to migrate across the border seeking work on farms and mines in Rhodesia.[117] As Ereman Conforme, who came from nearby Chipalapala, bluntly explained, "I went to work in Songo because I needed money to eat."[118] Fausto Semo echoed this sense of despair: "The salaries were very low. But when a person is poor, you take even a little bit of money, so you can buy food for your family and clothes for your children."[119] Local inhabitants also sought work at the dam site, driven by their fear of the calamity that would befall them when the man-made lake inundated their homelands.[120] Such desperation precluded local workers from challenging the bosses. "If you became embroiled in a dispute with your supervisor," Francisco Alfredo recalled, "you could lose your entire month's salary."[121]

Others sought employment in Songo to avoid the threat of chibalo. Although Júlio Calecoetoa had worked for a decade on tobacco and maize farms in Rhodesia, returning home from his contracts with clothing and money, not even his status as a successful labor migrant shielded him from the gaze of the local headman. "Shortly after I returned home, I married. Then the fumo sent me to work chibalo. I worked for nine months. When I returned home I was afraid he would conscript me again. Chiefs did not allow men to remain at home. They always sent them to chibalo. So I came to Songo.'[122] Emílio Faidose's story was similar: "I started to work [at Songo] in 1972. I fled from the military recruiters, since I did not want to go into the army. So I ran away from Chicoa Velha and came to work in Songo."[123]

Neither poverty nor the threat of chibalo, however, produced sufficient unskilled African labor to satisfy Zamco's needs. To supplement this critical portion of the workforce, it turned to local administrators and régulos, who used intimidation, threats, and, when necessary, outright coercion—common in colonial Mozambique, although legally prohibited—to meet the dam's labor requirements. Administrators sent sipais to visit the régulos, or designated chiefs, who used either them or their own local retainers to round up recruits. According to Francisco Alfredo, who worked at the dam for five years, "chibalo [initially] was still very common. It only ended in 1972."[124] No one was immune, not even Africans employed by the military. A confidential

PIDE report documented the case of a houseboy who worked for a group of soldiers stationed in Tete until "the local administrator ordered him and a number of other locals to go to work at Cabora Bassa."[125]

WORKING CONDITIONS AT THE DAM SITE

Whatever one's job classification, work at the dam site was long, hard, and dangerous. It began before seven in the morning, after a short breakfast of porridge, bread, and tea,[126] and typically lasted for eight to ten hours. As Ereman Conforme, a jackhammer operator, recalled, "I would wake up very early. It was still dark. We had breakfast at six. We were taken on trucks to the dam. By seven I was on the mountain drilling holes, where we inserted the dynamite. We worked until noon. Then we would stop, cook some porridge, eat, and return to work. We stopped at five and trucks took us back to our compounds."[127] If construction was behind schedule, African workers had to toil additional hours, even on Sundays, for which they received overtime pay.[128]

Once laborers completed their assigned tasks, a second shift, which often extended into the early morning, replaced them; there would also be, if necessary, an overlapping third shift.[129] Employing workers around the clock allowed overseers to compensate both for delays resulting from periodic shortages of concrete and for unanticipated technical problems caused by unusually deep fissures in the rock.[130]

Zamco demanded that construction follow its schedule, no matter the cost. One South African overseer characterized the tyranny of work: "Life at Cahora could be summed up in three words—you work, eat, and sleep. It's a never-ending cycle with little variation."[131] Many exhausted African workers suffered even more. "The night shift," one recalled, "was very, very difficult—that is to say there were many accidents. A number of sleep-deprived workers lost their lives."[132]

Since workers excavated more than 2.5 million tons of rock, most of which they later removed from the dam site,[133] work was as grueling as it was long. Boring holes with jackhammers into dense rock, blasting tunnels, removing large boulders, pouring concrete for the massive dam walls, inserting steel girders to construct a bridge on the cliff's edge, or cutting pilot shafts deep into the mountainside would have been difficult even under the best conditions. At Cahora Bassa, however, conditions were anything but. For much of the year, the temperature in the gorge topped 100 degrees Fahrenheit (40 degrees Celsius). The sun beating down on the backs of the workers sapped their energy, and the rays reflecting off the granite cliffs were blinding.[134] Adding to the oppressive conditions, the humidity was always high, and torrential rains fell from November through February. In the excavated tunnels, nearly a kilometer into the rock, the air was heavy, and the noise from heavy machines, passing trucks,

FIGURE 3.2. Working underground. *CITM/AHM*

and shouting men deafening (see figs. 3.2–3.5). To make matters worse, the dam site was located in the heart of a malaria-infested zone, and schistosomiasis, typhoid, and yellow fever were rampant. Middlemas estimated that more than half the African workers suffered from both malaria and schistosomiasis.[135]

Zamco's serious time constraints put unrelenting pressure on Africans to work both longer and harder. To increase productivity, it used both legal and extralegal practices. Company managers, European labor overseers, and their African capitães extended the workday, harangued workers, and often disregarded prohibitions against corporal punishment.[136] The capitães played a critical role in this process—they translated their superiors' orders into Fanagalo and then brutally enforced them. Anxious to assert their authority and to please the overseers, they often "used the *chicote* [hippo-hide whip] or *palmatória* [spiked plank] to force us to work harder."[137] African laborers were helpless to object: "You could not leave even if you did not like it, and if you did not complete your work you would be beaten."[138]

While the treatment of any African worker depended, to some extent, on the temperament of his supervisor, violent abuses of supervisory authority

FIGURE 3.3. Blasting rock. *CITM/AHM*

were a systemic problem.[139] A few Europeans, such as the chief engineer Bras de Oliveira, treated Africans respectfully, but, according to Padre Gremi, they were the exception.[140] Even if "some workers were lucky and were never beaten," many others, according to Peter Size, "were whipped regularly for being lazy or engaging in work slowdowns."[141] Júlio Calecoetoa stressed that, even for those not corporally punished, the palmatória was used selectively as an instrument of collective labor control:

> The Africans who broke the boulders worked in groups of six, each with their own capitão. The capitão was African. The boss over all of them was Silva. . . . The Africans worked very hard. The capitães were chosen because they could speak Portuguese [in addition to Fanagalo]. They told the workers what to do; they did not do the work themselves. From time to time, the capitão would beat people he did not think were working hard enough. Not only did those considered lazy have to work longer; the entire group had to complete the day's tasks. There were never any strikes. If people struck, they knew they would get a beating with the palmatória.[142]

High Modernism and Building the Dam, 1965–75 ↝ 79

FIGURE 3.4. Building a tunnel. *CITM/AHM*

FIGURE 3.5. Dam wall under construction. *CITM/AHM*

Some workers recounted unexplained or random acts of violence. Peter Size, a laborer in the warehouse at Songo, recalled, "For the first year I had to work seven days a week. We all worked very hard without rest, loading and unloading trucks. Our boss, Martin, treated us very badly. He beat us for no reason, just because he was angry."[143] Padre Gremi heard a similar report from an injured worker: "I arrived at the police station and I saw a man with his hand swollen ten centimeters. He had received a beating with a palmatória. I asked him why he was beaten and he said that he did not know yet. I asked how it could be that he did not know. He said, 'I was told that I had to be beaten and after I would know why.'"[144]

Such arbitrary violence made sense to the labor overseers, white and black, who believed that not working hard was proof that Africans were under the influence of "terrorists."[145] This widely held belief structured the labor process at Cahora Bassa, and workers thought to be Frelimo sympathizers received even harsher punishments. Because the secret police feared that Frelimo agents had received falsified identity documents and infiltrated the dam workforce, they were continually on the watch for Africans behaving "suspiciously."[146] António Andrade stressed that the police "had many, many spies among us. We were afraid to even mention the name Frelimo. If they heard, you would be arrested and could be killed."[147]

Those arrested were taken to the notorious PIDE prison at Monte Bona. Padre Gremi, who was allowed to visit there, reported that "it was inside Monte Bona that the worst cases of torture took place, since it was so remote no one could hear the screams, and few impartial observers had access to the site."[148] PIDE agents bound some accused "terrorists" and threw them into the crocodile-infested river; their bodies were never found.[149]

The horrific acts described repeatedly by former workers suggest that brutality, humiliation, and a culture of terror were intrinsic to the system of domination. The message from these rituals of terror was clear—the only way a worker could hope to escape the harsh realties of the labor regime was to work longer and harder and stay away from Frelimo. Stories of violence that lived on in personal narratives, casual conversation, gossip, and rumor were a constant reminder of workers' vulnerability. So were the daily humiliations inflicted by the labor overseers—the threatening gestures, slaps, and denigrating language, such as addressing a grown man as *rapaz* (boy).

The callous labor regime and lack of effective government oversight made the work environment hazardous for all employees—skilled and unskilled, African and European. State officials reported that Zamco ignored minimal safety requirements.[150] According to Padre Gremi, for example, it failed to provide all workers with the masks needed to protect them from lung disease.[151] Additionally, dynamiters and diggers working on the edges of steep cliffs often lacked helmets, harnesses, and other safety equipment.[152]

Because of Portugal's cloak of secrecy around Songo and the inaccessibility of HCB archives, the frequency and severity of industrial accidents at Cahora Bassa are unknown. In 1971, responding to growing international support for Mozambique's independence struggle—and for an international dam boycott (see below)—Lisbon denied outside observers considered unsympathetic access to the dam site.[153] By early 1972 journalists, representatives of radio and cinema, foreign tourists, and even missionaries could visit Songo only after receiving clearance from PIDE and the GPZ.[154] This wall of silence notwithstanding, the authorities were unable to completely hide highly visible accidents from the outside world. In 1970 a premature explosion killed seven workers;[155] in 1971 an Austrian worker and four assistants were killed in an unspecified "industrial accident";[156] and in November 1973 an entire wall of the northern surge chamber suddenly collapsed—leaving eight people dead and many others seriously injured.[157] A South African magazine, relying on Portuguese sources, estimated that the total death toll in 1974 was about fifty.[158]

Portuguese colonial officials maintained that these were merely isolated incidents and that Cahora Bassa's safety record compared favorably with that of similar projects.[159] Former workers, however, told a very different story, in which "industrial accidents"—from minor to catastrophic—occurred with much greater frequency than official sources admitted. As Ereman Conforme stressed, "the work at the dam was very dangerous; many people died there."[160] Others described in vivid detail instances of bulldozers and trucks sliding off the makeshift roads, of tunnels collapsing, of workers falling off cliffs to their deaths when their harnesses snapped, of premature dynamite explosions and rockslides, and of the "many smaller accidents which occurred everyday."[161] Maurício Alemão witnessed one of these: "A white man moved one of the boulders on the top of the hill and it came crashing down, crushing a group of workers. Some said he did it on purpose."[162]

Road accidents were also common. Inexperienced truck drivers, under pressure to transport concrete and other strategic supplies to the work site as quickly as possible, failed to negotiate successfully the hairpin turns and steep descent on the crowded mountain road down to the gorge.[163] "Many," recalled António Andrade, "slid off the road and crashed to their deaths."[164] In one month, Padre Gremi reported, twenty-eight truckers were buried.[165] Truck drivers were not the only victims of driving accidents. Gervásio Chongololo, a nurse at the central hospital, remembered when an out-of-control truck plowed into a group of workers returning home from their work site—killing many of them. He treated those who were lucky enough to survive.[166]

As the following excerpts illustrate, major catastrophes remain etched in the minds of many former workers—even those fortunate enough to escape serious injury.

Pedro da Costa Xavier:

> At the intersection of two tunnels a large rock—larger than this house—fell, collapsing the tunnels and trapping the men and machines inside it. Company officials were unable to rescue the men and they ultimately had to seal off the tunnel. Many people died. It was more than twenty. [In addition,] there were smaller accidents. . . . When the ropes that were harnessing men working on the edge of the dam broke, people would fall to their deaths. Sometimes, when we were working in the tunnel, there would be rockslides, and people would be killed. Others would suffer serious injuries. It was very dangerous work, not only for the Africans, but for the Europeans who worked with them."[167]

Ereman Conforme:

> The tunnel collapsed and many mangled bodies and wrecked machines were left in the ruins. I was lucky that I was not inside when it happened. That was the biggest of them all. Then there were the ironworkers and masons [working on the dam walls] who fell from great heights into the river. I saw this happen many times.[168]

Gervásio Chongololo:

> We often had to amputate the arms and legs of workers whose limbs had been crushed in rock slides, particularly in the tunnels.[169]

Not surprisingly, the availability of medical care for workplace accident victims, like other services at Cahora Bassa, was racially determined. Severely injured Europeans were flown by helicopter to Salisbury for additional medical care and, if necessary, even back to Europe. African workers, however, generally got only minimal, local care. If their injuries were serious, they received a small indemnity[170] and either went home or were sent to the aldeamento where their family had been forcibly relocated (see chapter 4).

THE SOCIAL WORLD OF AFRICAN WORKERS

Living conditions for African workers were as inadequate as their horrendous working conditions and did little to encourage labor stabilization.[171] Whereas, for its European staff, Zamco erected homes, ranging from modest bungalows to plush residences, it spent as little as possible on housing for Africans. Most were packed into galvanized huts located on the edge of the plateau in a barren area known as COTA 90, under the control of African capitães. According to Pedro da Costa Xavier, the tin shacks were stifling in summer, freezing during winter nights, and deafeningly noisy when raining.[172] There were no toilets, hot water, or other basic amenities, and workers had to buy their own blankets at the company store. Each hut had multiple bunk beds crammed into it, and men slept in shifts to maximize space. Padre Gremi visited the camps in 1973 and reported the following: "I can only talk about the African camps down there, halfway toward the dam. There is a valley called Grande Buraco [the Big Hole]. Three thousand workers lived there [in COTA 90], but there was not enough space for three thousand people. . . . They [Zamco] would cram twelve workers into a hut. The huts were approximately two bed lengths and three or four meters in width. There were two or three bunk beds against each wall. . . . It was such a small place that people could not even breathe properly. It was a very bad life."[173] For Zamco, the organization of COTA 90 ensured that workers would be confined in a restrictive space where they could be fed, supervised, and summoned to work.

Zamco also economized on food rations for its African workers. While European employees received subsidized food allowances and had access to a wide array of imported foods and wines, African rations were hardly adequate. By statute, all African workers in Mozambique were entitled to certain daily amounts of porridge, bread, sugar, tea, and a small amount of meat, and periodically to *pombe*,[174] derisively called Bantu beer by South Africans—which government officials stationed at the dam were supposed to enforce.[175] This food was of inferior quality and poorly prepared. Simões Wetela described the barely edible meals with disgust: "Unskilled workers received porridge made from coarse flour. They did not eat it because it was very old, it had a bitter taste, and it was full of bugs. After they refused to accept the porridge, they received bread and dried fish several days a week. They also got tea, but they did not like it because the cook put his pus-tainted hands into the big teapots. For lunch, they served rotten beans that had bugs in it. Dinner was the same. . . . It was food only for pigs."[176] The ingredients did not vary, although cabbage sometimes replaced beans and there might be a bit of meat, instead of dried fish, as a condiment.[177]

Despite its poor quality, food was still a weapon to enforce the labor regime. To punish employees considered lazy or difficult, management withheld a portion of their meager rations. Although this was explicitly against the law,[178] Pedro da Costa Xavier recalled it happening regularly.[179]

Few workers could augment their inadequate diets because the long workdays left no time to grow fresh vegetables. Those who came from nearby areas periodically added produce obtained during trips home or when relatives visited.[180] Such family visits were rare, however, since both the state and Zamco discouraged them on security grounds. Inês Fondo recalled that, because she and other women lacked the right papers, the police at the gate to Songo prevented them from entering: "We slept at the police station for several days, trying to get a two-day pass."[181] Workers' wives who persevered and managed to provide foodstuffs to their husbands ended up subsidizing the wage bill of European capital.

While almost all African workers lived in squalid conditions and received inferior rations, some differentiation existed. Foremen, master technicians, and long-distance truck drivers had significantly better living conditions outside the compounds and access to more nutritious foodstuffs,[182] and some highly appreciated, better skilled employees received rations of meat, rice, and potatoes, which were not available to their less fortunate unskilled brethren.[183] Higher-paid African employees also could shop at the company stores and private supermarkets that served the expatriate community, where they could purchase food, tobacco, alcohol, and other consumer goods.

Although the number of such privileged Africans was never significant, as recruiting European workers became more problematic, Zamco began training Africans to fill some of the nonsupervisory positions.[184] This strategy had the added advantage of reducing labor costs, since reclassified African workers received less than one-third of the departing Europeans' wages.[185]

Barred from the segregated European clubs, movies, and restaurants, African laborers had few opportunities to break the monotony—or forget the hardship—of work at Cahora Bassa. Zamco did organize a soccer league for African employees and showed weekly movies at the outdoor theater.[186] It also oversaw a flourishing trade in prostitution.[187] Apart from these activities, however, the only diversions available were listening to the radio, mending clothes, attending mass, gossiping, and drinking.[188]

Management made it easy for Africans to acquire alcohol, knowing its effectiveness as a mechanism of social control. Zamco located company stores for African laborers adjacent to where they received their monthly paychecks and ensured that "on payday, the shops were brimming with wine, beer, and whatever else Africans wanted."[189] Padre Gremi, who regularly led services at the dam site, recounted meeting a parishioner "who had spent his month's earnings on forty bottles of beer and a meal." When he inquired why the worker had wasted his hard-earned income this way, the latter sheepishly replied, "to show that Africans know how to spend money like whites."[190] Many disgruntled workers escaped their grim working and living conditions through the use of beer and imported wines.

Numerous African workers also took advantage of the flourishing prostitution trade the state allowed—even encouraged. As Francisco Alfredo recounted, "[With their wives absent,] workers on weekends or during free time would go to the *baneiras* to meet their needs. They met in the backyard of Christina Abel's residence. She was one of the first prostitutes to arrive at Songo and commanded the women. The customers discussed the payment and what they desired with Christina. After some haggling, the price was typically set at 20 escudos for a single sexual encounter. Christina selected a partner from a group of young women sitting on a mat nearby. Then you went to a small hut to be satisfied."[191] According to Simões Wetela, it was the sense of sexual deprivation in COTA 90, given the Zamco-mandated absence of wives, that drove his coworkers to seek satisfaction at the baneiras: "They lined up for the prostitutes every night, not only at the end of the month. It cost 20 escudos for an hour. Each woman had her hut, where she sold beer and wine as well."[192] Here, as in other colonial African urban and industrial settings,[193] prostitution probably helped satisfy frustrated African workers' emotional, social, and sexual needs, while further enabling Zamco and the state to control a potentially restive labor force. There is also some evidence from COTA 90 of Shangaan men from Southern Mozambique engaging in same-sex practices,[194] although elders rarely spoke about such activities.

African men, however, could not compete with the better-paid European workers or Portuguese soldiers. Both of the latter were willing to pay three times the going rate for an entire night of sexual intimacy.[195] Racial tensions and drunken brawls sometimes erupted over access to these women, whom men at Songo considered a prized commodity. Generally, angry Europeans, who resented the mere presence of black men near the baneiras, started the conflicts. "Whites went to the baneiras with pistols. They would use the pistols to scare off the Africans or simply to move to the front of the line" and reacted violently if they found an African with "their women."[196]

WORKER PROTEST

Unlike at Kariba,[197] African laborers had no formal mechanisms for protesting abuses by European staff, much less the harsh working and living conditions that were an integral part of Cahora Bassa's labor regime. "If an African went to the colonial administration to complain that a European treated him badly, the administrator would become angry and respond that you are black and do not have the right to complain against Europeans," after which, according to Peter Size and Fedi Alfante, he "would beat the worker with a hippo-tail whip or a palmatória. No whites were ever imprisoned for abusing Africans."[198] Moreover, it was illegal in Mozambique for African workers to organize or strike.[199]

The hazardous working conditions and fear of physical abuse drove some locally recruited laborers to flee, although this, too, was dangerous. Numerous security checkpoints, the ever-present threat of capture by military patrols, the double barbed-wire fences that enclosed Songo, and the large minefields surrounding the dam site were all powerful deterrents. These dangers notwithstanding, "there were some recruits," as Ereman Conforme recalled, "who ran away after working for only two months, when they heard that a fellow worker had died." Others, he continued, "would stay less than a year. . . . Those who worked for a year or two were very courageous. The salary was not enough for the kind of work we did. The job kills."[200] Francisco Alfredo told a similar story: "Many Africans from Matamba and Marrara signed up, but when their coworkers began to die, they fled for Zimbabwe."[201] Others escaped to avoid corporal punishment. Padre Gremi recalled searching in the mountains for a parishioner who had fled after being severely beaten; he found the man hiding in a cave, "his back lacerated from the strokes of a whip."[202] Both the clandestine nature of this flight and Portugal's wall of silence around the dam make it difficult to determine how many actually escaped.

While colonial officials silenced public dissent with physical beatings and intimidation, they could not eliminate all worker protests. Work slowdowns were another response to abuses at the dam site.[203] "When Africans were angry [at how they were being treated], they worked more slowly, but, if the boss noticed that, he would tell the capitão to whip them."[204] Company officials and colonial authorities believed that clandestine Frelimo agents were responsible for these work slowdowns,[205] although there is no evidence to support such claims.

In small groups sitting around the fire in the evenings or huddled in their tin shacks and over morning porridge, trusted friends fanned their defiance through conversation, gossip, and rumor. They complained in hushed voices of the indignities they suffered and of food not fit for animals and mocked particularly brutal overseers, such as Bill Smith, the South African labor manager who came to personify all the evils of apartheid and colonialism.[206] Speaking softly so as not to be overheard, workers shared the deeply held view that "no one wanted the Portuguese in our land," and they "imagined a life when Frelimo would arrive to liberate them."[207] Frelimo radio broadcasts and workers' clandestine meetings with militants,[208] however irregular, reinforced the themes of these uncensored conversations.

This "private" talk was not just idle chatter. Defiant conversations behind closed doors helped sustain and give meaning to the infrequent insurgent behavior that actually occurred. Thus, for example, on May 20, 1974, African workers defied the authorities and staged a strike to protest their low wages and inadequate rations. Most refused to report to work, and an angry group pummeled to death two well-known African spies.[209] Others "broke into the food warehouses and took rice, potatoes, bananas, oil, and everything that was in it."[210] Their principal target, however, was Bill Smith, whom they wanted to kill "because he mistreated people, beat them, and continually insulted them."[211] Workers marched en masse toward his home. Terrified and humiliated, Smith managed to escape only by dressing up as a woman. In an act rich with symbolism, frustrated strikers then killed Smith's pet baboon, which they detested because it received far better food than they did. Although Portuguese soldiers in armored cars quickly suppressed the strike and reestablished control over the African compounds, the workers had made their point. Zamco agreed to increase rations of meat, fish, sugar, fruit, and cooking oil, and laborers received a modest pay raise.[212]

FRELIMO EFFORTS TO SUBVERT THE DAM

Such isolated incidents of labor unrest aside, the major struggles against the hydroelectric scheme initially took place far from Songo. Frelimo launched its diplomatic and military campaign to thwart construction in 1968 when Eduardo Mondlane, Frelimo's first president, openly condemned the unholy alliance between Pretoria and Lisbon.[213] He labeled Cabora Bassa the critical terrain of anticolonial struggle on the continent: "If we do not destroy this dam, it will destroy us, and the white regimes and racists in Africa will win definitively."[214]

Mondlane's clarion call helped unleash a well-organized and highly visible international campaign to block Western financing and construction of the dam.[215] Driving it was a diverse group of activists who shared information, developed strategically linked activities, and believed deeply that "what happens at Cahora Bassa is central to the fight for Mozambique and to the future of Southern Africa."[216] These "activists without borders"[217] included church leaders, students, trade unionists, black-power advocates, nongovernmental organizations, and other anticolonial groups operating from Lusaka to London and from Stockholm to Sydney. While their immediate objective was to convince major Western corporations—Barclays Bank, General Electric, Siemens, AEG, and the Compagnie des Constructions Internationales—to withhold equipment and capital from Cahora Bassa, most were also involved in overlapping and broader antiapartheid and anti-imperialist campaigns.

Kenneth Kaunda, Zambia's president, became the leading international spokesperson for the antidam campaign. His long opposition to Portuguese colonialism, his selection as chair of the Organization of African Unity (OAU), in 1970, and his role as a leader of the Non-aligned Movement gave him the stature and platform from which to argue that the dam was "a crime against humanity."[218] The OAU Ministerial Conference meeting in Addis Ababa shortly thereafter affirmed this position—condemning Cahora Bassa as a symbol of colonialism and an impediment to liberation in southern Africa.[219] That spring, Kaunda met with the French, British, and German heads of state to pressure them to oppose their nationals' investments in Cahora Bassa. The response from the West was unambiguously negative—after all, Portugal was a NATO ally.

Rebuffed by the Europeans, Kaunda appealed directly to the United Nations later that year. Joining him in New York was Frelimo's representative Sharfuddin Khan, who denounced the Portuguese project as "a crime not only against the Mozambican people, but also against the entire people of

Southern Africa and of Africa as a whole."[220] Some United Nations representatives from African states and the Non-aligned Movement also demanded that the dam "be stopped by the deliberate and concerted effort of the international community."[221] The South African foreign minister responded with the familiar refrain that the dam was designed to benefit Africans and that blocking its construction would be as counterproductive as destroying Egypt's Aswan High Dam or the Kariba Dam.[222]

His argument, however, was rejected, and the UN's Special Commission on Decolonization voted 14 to 2—with the United States and Great Britain in opposition—to censure Portugal, South Africa, Italy, Germany, and France for permitting their nationals to participate in the Cahora Bassa project.[223] In 1971 the UN General Assembly overwhelmingly supported, by a vote of 106 to 6, a resolution blocking economic, technical, and other assistance to Portugal and South Africa; only the United States, Britain, Canada, France, Portugal, and South Africa opposed it.[224]

Although neither vote included enforcement provisions, they were important symbolic victories for both Frelimo and the antidam forces protesting throughout Western Europe and North America during the early 1970s. In England, the Dambuster mobilizing committee occupied Barclays headquarters, picketed local branches, disrupted shareholders meetings, and pressured clients to withdraw funds.[225] In Hamburg, hundreds of students condemned German companies for "exploiting thousands of indigenous Mozambicans,"[226] and Italian trade unionists labeled the dam a repressive colonial project.[227] In Sweden, antiapartheid groups organized a public campaign against the hydroelectric project,[228] and a broad coalition of dam opponents in Canada demanded that there "be no Canadian participation whatsoever in the building or equipping of Cabora Bassa in Mozambique."[229] Senior Frelimo members, including Joaquim Chissano, Armando Guebuza, and Janet Mondlane (the widow of Eduardo Mondlane, who had been assassinated by the Portuguese in 1969), met with Western government officials and participated in some of these antidam actions.

Measured by the number of companies foregoing involvement, the boycott's impact was limited. While few major corporations withdrew their support for Cahora Bassa, moral outrage, censure by the UN Trusteeship Committee and the OAU, and threats of boycotts did motivate the Swedish electrical firm ASEA, which had been part of the original Zamco consortium, and a few Spanish and Italian companies to back out.[230] Additionally, the antidam movement in Germany, assisted by deputies in the Bundestag and the Lutheran Church, created serious public relations problems for AEG, Siemens, and Hochtief,[231] while Barclays, General Electric, and Anglo-American Contractors came under repeated attack from the Dambuster mobilization committee.

PIDE closely monitored these activities. It infiltrated opposition groups, spied on prominent activists, organized counterdemonstrations, and hired right-wing public relations firms to label the antidam campaign "communist-inspired."[232] These responses reflected Portugal's growing apprehension that the antidam campaign had breeched the wall of silence it had so carefully constructed.

The immediate threat to Cahora Bassa, however, was inside Mozambique — Frelimo's heightened efforts to subvert its construction. In 1970, Portuguese spies who had infiltrated a meeting at Nachingwea, Tanzania, confirmed Frelimo's intention of targeting the dam.[233] Interviews with guerrilla commanders published in *Mozambique Revolution*, describing how Frelimo forces had destroyed bridges and roads near the dam site and predicting that these actions would bring construction to a standstill, stoked Portugal's paranoia.[234]

Portuguese security officials were particularly concerned that the guerrillas, who were receiving modern weapons and instruction from Soviet and other Eastern Bloc advisers, would attack Cahora Bassa. One top-secret intelligence report claimed that Russian and Yugoslav commandos had trained guerrillas in the use of highly sophisticated explosives, which Frelimo soldiers would use against the dam.[235] Another strategic assessment, sent directly to the Council of Ministers in Lisbon, cited evidence that the Soviet Union had offered the "terrorists" high-speed boats so they could launch bazooka and mortar attacks from unguarded sites on the Zambezi's edge.[236] There were even reports that Frelimo had acquired portable Soviet DKZ-B missiles, which, with a range of up to twelve kilometers, would have posed an obvious threat to the dam.[237] By early 1971 intelligence circles in Mozambique were bracing for a possible attack as early as Easter.[238] They expected forces based in Makanga District and to the west, in Zumbo District, to cross to the southern bank of the Zambezi and simultaneously strike the dam site.[239]

Despite all the classified reports, public pronouncements, and rumors, however, sabotaging Cahora Bassa was probably never a realistic option. The colonial regime had heavily fortified the area around Songo, making it virtually impossible for the guerrillas to get within striking distance of the dam. A British journalist, Bruce London, who visited Cahora Bassa in 1972, described the military preparations:

> Around the entire perimeter of the dam site . . . runs a double wired fence. And within this is what must be counted one of the largest minefields laid in recent times — 85,000 mines. Two in every [square] yard around the site. Gun crews manning heavy artillery are on duty round the clock at strategic points overlooking Cabora Bassa and the construction camp a little above it at Songo, where more than 3,000 black and white workers live, [with] the guns facing out to points from

which guerrillas could come. General [Kaúlza] de Arriaga, Mozambique's commander in chief and the mastermind behind the defense of Cabora Bassa, believes that the site is now virtually impregnable.[240]

The anticipated Frelimo attack, however, never materialized.

In fact, as far back as November 1970, Joaquim Chissano, Frelimo's foreign secretary, had implied that such attacks were not central to Frelimo's long-term strategy. At a press conference on November 12, he maintained that the guerrillas were making great progress in Tete District and would consider their efforts successful "if their actions continue[d] to cause delays in the construction of the dam."[241] Frelimo president Samora Machel was even clearer. "It is not a question of preventing the building of Cabora Bassa," he told a *Newsweek* reporter two years later. "We are trying to increase the price of it four or five times."[242]

It is difficult to know whether these public pronouncements represented a shift in tactics based on military realities on the ground or whether the Frelimo leadership had known from the outset that it was neither possible nor in its interest to destroy the dam. What is clear, however, is that from the late 1960s, Frelimo forces were entering Tete District in growing numbers from bases in nearby Zambia and more distant Tanzania. In 1970 the first large Frelimo contingent crossed the Zambezi River.[243] Just one year later, according to Portuguese estimates, there were over two thousand guerrillas operating in small bands on both banks—preempting Portuguese military planners' efforts to use the man-made lake to block the "terrorists." South African military intelligence reported that guerrillas had come within twenty kilometers of the dam,[244] and Rhodesian observers opined that Frelimo's ability to open a new front in Tete was "serious and carrie[d] grave military and political dangers for all Southern Africa in the longer term."[245] While such dire predictions were likely exaggerated to justify their countries' military intervention, Frelimo forces did spread rapidly across the area south of the Zambezi,[246] transforming the dam site into a strategic military zone.

Guerrillas rocketed remote Portuguese administrative centers, attacked undermanned military posts and rural shops, and disrupted traffic by mining rural dirt roads.[247] The Mozambican newspaper *Notícias* reported that there were more than fifteen incursions in 1970.[248] The effect of these military activities was to loosen Portugal's fragile grip on this remote frontier region and to raise doubts among European workers about their own safety. A 1970 classified intelligence report warned that "security conditions around Cabora Bassa were chaotic" and questioned the colonial forces' capacity "to protect the work site."[249]

Beginning in 1971, Frelimo attacks became more brazen and started posing problems at Cahora Bassa. Moving down the forested river valley and across the Zambezi, guerrillas ambushed trucks carrying essential supplies and equipment to the dam site. Because approximately three hundred tons of food and material were needed daily to sustain the workers and the project,[250] the transport network was its Achilles' heel. By the end of the year, the insurgents were mining the principal roads and attacking traffic between Songo and the coast. London's *Daily Telegraph* described the far-reaching impact of these actions:

> For its part Frelimo seems to accept that any attempt at a direct strike against Cabora Bassa is futile. Instead, the wily insurgents have been concentrating on supply routes to the dam site, the weak point in Portugal's defences. Ambushes and land mines have become their main weapons—and very effective weapons at that.
>
> Time was when the road linking Rhodesia and Malawi, passing through the heart of the Tete district and Tete [city] itself, was a busy international connection responsible for much of the trade between those two countries. Now as a result of Frelimo's drive against Cabora-Bassa, it is known as "Hell's corridor"—an excruciating, snail's pace journey that sees traders, transport drivers and troops pitted in a daily death trap against the insurgents.[251]

Other guerrillas regularly successfully blew up trains bringing materials to Songo, since, as *Diário de Notícias* noted, it was impossible for the Portuguese to protect every mile.[252] Zamco officials acknowledged that "they blow the railway expertly now. Formerly it took three days to put it right. Now they blow it in[to] cuttings and it takes a full week to clear the rock fall."[253]

In 1971 the insurgents targeted workers at the dam site for the first time— killing nine GPZ employees on the outskirts of Songo and kidnapping six Portuguese and five African ones.[254] These attacks demoralized the expatriate community, some of whose members left without completing their contracts.[255] Frelimo also intensified its campaign against the aldeamentos, in an attempt to make Tete ungovernable.

To minimize the impact of Frelimo's offensive, the military responded quickly and brutally. It tarred the main road between Songo and Tete, making it more difficult to mine, and cleared the bush adjacent to the roads, which had provided cover for the guerrillas. It also organized daily convoys between Tete and Songo, patrolled the train tracks more aggressively, and banned civilian traffic on the Zambezi River. Additionally, to cut off Frelimo's access to the rural peasantry, local authorities forced thousands whose lands were unaffected by the dam to relocate to "rearranged communities" and enforced a free-fire-zone policy in strategic areas (see chapter 4).[256] Those villages suspected of harboring "terrorists" suffered dearly. According to Middlemas, "the most senior white officials in Tete, at least in private conversation, encouraged the practice of selective executions in villages known to have supported Frelimo."[257] The Portuguese high command increased its total force in Tete District to more than ten thousand troops and organized joint counterinsurgency campaigns with Rhodesian troops.[258] The more aggressive Frelimo's actions, the harsher the Portuguese response—especially as the dam neared completion and both Cahora Bassa and the colonial state itself appeared threatened.

These tactics, however, did little to dislodge the insurgent forces. In November 1972, Frelimo launched a mortar barrage against the provincial airbase at Tete and attacked eleven trains bringing critical materials to Cahora Bassa from the Indian Ocean port of Beira.[259] Over the next two years, it continued ambushing lorries and trains and periodically blowing up roads and bridges. Although Lisbon failed to blunt the Frelimo offensive in Tete District, the sharp increase in troops and brutal counterinsurgency measures enabled the resupply of Cahora Bassa with only minor disruptions.

By 1974 the dam was virtually complete. Lost in the shuffle were the thousands of Mozambican peasants who had been forcibly relocated from the floodplains. It is to their story that we now turn.

4 ⌒ Displaced People

Forced Eviction and Life in the Protected Villages,
1970–75

JUST AS Lisbon sought to construct a wall of silence around Cahora Bassa, it tried to render invisible the experiences of the thousands of peasants forcibly transplanted from their homelands along the life-sustaining Zambezi River to the aldeamentos. To the extent that senior officials addressed the complexities of relocating thousands of peasants whose homelands would be inundated by the dam, they framed the move in narrow technical terms, focusing on the need to establish aldeamentos on fertile lands with adequate water supplies.[1] The governor of Tete, at a 1968 strategic planning meeting, assured local administrators from the affected areas—who were concerned that uprooted peasants would react negatively to being forced to relocate—that, if these conditions were satisfied, relocated Africans would enjoy "a social transformation and elevation in the quality of their lives."[2]

Colonial planners also insisted that the long-term economic benefits to the colony of a dam at Cahora Bassa would far outweigh any short-term disruptions to the lives of displaced riverine communities, and they underestimated the extent to which resettlement would shake the very foundations of the relocated communities. Given Tete District's low population density of 1.7 people per square kilometer, they expected that relocating rural families to make way for the dam's reservoir would have only inconsequential social costs.[3] This figure was misleading, however, because the population density along the southern bank of the Zambezi—the area to be flooded—was 11.7 per square kilometer, as compared to 1.5 per square kilometer in the remainder of the district.[4] Moreover, Portuguese officials contended that moving twenty-five thousand Mozambicans was insignificant compared to the much larger numbers relocated due to dam construction elsewhere in Africa.

Written documentation chronicling the displacement of rural communities from the area of the dam is almost nonexistent, because aldeamentos were closed to all foreign observers, other than select journalists whose access was limited to several so-called model villages. Similarly, since colonial record keepers focused on the aldeamentos' military and strategic dimensions, Mozambican archives contain little about the eviction and relocation of peasant families to arid lands that were ill suited for agriculture and animal husbandry. Even less is known of the daily lives of the men, women, and children who were forced to rebuild their homes and livelihoods within these settlements virtually from scratch, of the highly regimented world in which the evacuees were forcibly embedded, or of the resulting crises of social reproduction.

To tell this important story, we rely on the voices, memories, and representations of the people driven into the resettlement camps to make way for the megadam and its company town. Their stories clearly demonstrate the highly traumatic nature of forced resettlement. Not only did those relocated lose control over their physical space, access to critical economic and cultural resources, and the power to decide where and how to live,[5] but they found themselves in a world fraught with physical suffering and new forms of social, cultural, and political conflict. In the harsh surroundings of the "protected villages," memories of the homes, communities, and livelihoods they had left behind both sustained and saddened them. While those memories are clearly nostalgic, their core narratives and images form a collective biography of Cahora Bassa's peasant victims that reveals much about the race—and gender—dynamics of both political power and environmental control in the later years of Portuguese colonialism.

DISPLACING PEASANTS: THE PLAN AND ITS ANTECEDENTS

Long before the governor of Tete made his confident pronouncements, the Portuguese colonial state had imposed a far-reaching program of forced villagization in northern Mozambique in response to the first wave of Frelimo attacks in 1964.[6] During the next four years, modeled on counterinsurgency initiatives developed in Malaysia and Vietnam,[7] it hastily constructed a network of aldeamentos into which it forcibly relocated two-thirds of the African population of Niassa and almost half the population of Cabo Delgado.[8]

The program's objective was to isolate nationalist guerrillas from their peasant base of support and to deprive them of food, critical intelligence, and new recruits. As in Malaysia and Vietnam, there were two other potential advantages to concentrating previously dispersed communities in "protected villages." Such concentration made it easier for colonial authorities to try to win the "hearts and minds" of the rural population, thereby further isolating the guerrillas, and it allowed the vast emptied areas to be designated free-fire zones, where the military could shoot moving targets on sight and engage in a scorched-earth policy.[9]

Thus, when the governor of Tete and his colleagues met in 1968 to map out a villagization initiative for Cahora Bassa, they had an example to follow. Rather than confronting a military threat from Frelimo, however, their challenge was to manage the complex and politically charged relocation of thousands of peasants whose lands would be flooded by the dam. Although colonial authorities recognized the initial hardships of resettlement, they had no plan to compensate evicted households for their losses.[10]

Alexandre da Silva Braga, a senior researcher at the MFPZ, a research arm of the GPZ, assisted by a team of fieldworkers and planners, was responsible for drawing up a five-year plan to achieve this objective.[11] His classified report, which offered a blueprint for relocating affected communities with a minimum of social disruption, significantly departed from earlier state formulations of conditions on the ground. First, it rejected government estimates that only twenty-five thousand people would be adversely impacted by the dam, because those figures excluded the nearly ten thousand migrants from the area who were temporarily working in Rhodesia and Zambia.[12] Second, it challenged the official colonial narrative depicting Tete District as a uniformly harsh, unproductive, and sparsely populated backwater region—a view that downplayed the social and economic consequences of resettlement. While its average population density was low and erratic rainfall limited agricultural production, demography and ecology varied substantially from one part of the district to another. The river-fed fields along the banks of the Zambezi River, for example, were appreciably more fertile than the upland fields, which depended on erratic rainfall. Because of their higher yields and the wider variety of crops that would thrive there, the population density was much higher than upland, where peasants had to practice shifting agriculture.[13] The river's fertile soils, which had attracted a relatively large number of peasants, may have made those living on its shores even more rooted to their land than those residing further away. One unintended consequence of building the dam, according to the report, would be the flooding of important historical and cultural sites, such as the Portuguese fort at Cachoma and the administrative post at Chicoa, both of which were "linked to the traditions and history of the occupation of the district of Tete."[14] Conspicuously absent were references to the inundation of indigenous shrine centers and burial grounds of chiefs and ancestors—sacred sites underpinning the religious system and cosmology of local communities (see below).

Nevertheless, the report expressed confidence that the dam project would be successful and that the aldeamentos would both promote a robust rural economy and produce more "civilized" colonial subjects. It predicted that peasants, working on carefully selected plots of land, with technical assistance from the government, would be integrated into the market economy; that the new villages would provide sites for training artisans and commercial fishermen and educating at least 80 percent of the resident children; and that nonliterate women living in aldeamentos would be made respectable and modern through instruction in "hygiene, proper nutrition, sewing and the domestic economy."[15]

"In the current situation," one official confidently opined, "the aldeamentos are the best way to promote the transformation of primitive structures and elevate the social, economic, political, and cultural lives of the local population."[16] This assertion rang hollow, however, given that, after five hundred years of Portugal's presence in the Zambezi valley, a mere 1,863 of the Zambezi basin's population of 93,933 had acquired sufficient Portuguese culture to be reclassified as "civilizada."[17]

Working from this report, the GPZ formulated organizing principles to guide the relocation of rural communities and to structure life inside the aldeamentos. To minimize potential disruption, it recommended the resettlement of rural families on lands as near their former villages as possible, "which had been carefully selected in terms of the quality of the soil and access to water."[18] Additionally, "each family would receive five hectares of grazing land and one hectare of cleared and graded land that they could cultivate immediately."[19] To disrupt neither the agricultural cycle nor religious practices related to agriculture, the move would take place only after peasants had harvested their crops and propitiated venerated ancestor spirits. Since winning the hearts and minds of their subjects was essential, colonial authorities were to avoid the use of force at all costs, striving instead to convince communities of the advantages of moving.[20]

Events at Kariba Dam a decade earlier underscored the dangers of a more aggressive approach to resettlement.[21] Portuguese authorities were acutely aware that British efforts to force Gwembe Tonga peasants to relocate upriver had precipitated a violent confrontation. Six thousand people refused to move over one hundred kilometers to a government-selected site. Over four hundred protesters, armed with spears, axes, and fighting sticks, defied the colonial police, who then opened fire, killing or wounding more than forty people, who ultimately became fallen martyrs in the cause of Zambian nationalism.[22] There were also a number of smaller protests in other Tonga communities.[23] Portuguese officials hoped to avoid a similar scenario.

Yet, for all this rhetoric of persuasion and modernization, the aldeamentos were to be highly organized spaces in which "primordial" ethnic loyalties would serve as instruments of social control. Ethnic mixing was to be avoided whenever possible; and, to prevent confusion and an explosion of witchcraft,

Tawara, Tonga, Nyungwe, Chikunda, Nsenga, and Serero communities would have their own aldeamentos ruled by their traditional leaders.[24] Once resettled, the GPZ would record the ethnic group, gender, age, occupation, and "defects or other characteristics of interest"[25] of each resident, and those over the age of ten would receive photo identification cards to be carried with them at all times.[26] All houses would be registered and numbered, and all streets named and mapped. Residents would also need special permission to enter or leave their aldeamento, and African militias, under the command of a Portuguese officer, would monitor their movements.[27] In short, displaced peasants would be under twenty-four-hour surveillance in their new homes—the partial autonomy they had previously enjoyed now severely restricted by the colonial state.[28] The GPZ estimated that this carefully organized relocation of the riverine communities would take approximately six years and consume only 1 percent of the project's estimated budget. After hydrological and soil studies at prospective sites, the construction of necessary infrastructure (including roads and water systems), and several pilot relocations—together expected to take several years to complete—the GPZ planned annually to move approximately eight thousand people into aldeamentos between 1970 and 1973.[29]

The reactions of Portuguese colonial officials to the GPZ plan exposed serious fault lines between civilian and military authorities and within the civil administration, especially around the use of force. Concerned about the possibility of future Frelimo incursions into Tete, military commanders rejected the GPZ's soft "psycho-social approach" and demanded that the state play a more forceful role in resettlement—herding peasants into enclosed camps—as had been done in the northern war zones.[30] In sharp contrast, during a 1970 meeting with the governor of Tete, many local administrators expressed fears that forced removals would precipitate an upsurge in clandestine migration across the porous borders into Rhodesia or Zambia.[31] Others wondered whether the régulos, on whom administrators relied, had sufficient influence to convince their followers to move voluntarily and whether a rocky resettlement would undermine their continued ability to carry out the wishes of the colonial authorities. Still others worried which régulo would rule, if two or more chieftaincies ended up in the same aldeamento.[32]

Civilian officials who worked most closely with affected communities were generally skeptical of both forced villagization and the GPZ's claim—naive, in their view—that resettlement would not be harmful. Those taking seriously their paternalistic mission to "help the natives" worried aloud that evicting peasants from their historical homelands and sacred burial sites would be highly disruptive.[33] One senior state official even warned that forcing local communities "to sever their ties to their deceased ancestors who provide a sense of order and equilibrium in tribal society" would create a profound cultural

and psychological shock with enduring consequences.[34] Some local administrators were dubious about the capacity of the land in a proposed aldeamento
to support the resettled population, while others feared that the new locations
lacked sufficient water—which could have serious economic and social consequences.[35] Several also complained that GPZ fieldworkers had usurped their
authority by visiting villages in their districts without their knowledge or prior
approval, thereby creating tension and confusion among their subjects.[36]

Frelimo's advances into Tete in 1970 rendered these concerns moot. To
blunt its offensive in the Zambezi valley, the military ordered that peasant
confinement in aldeamentos occur as quickly as possible. Despite local
authorities' strong arguments in favor of a cautious approach, forced villagization became one of the strategic cornerstones of the region's defense and
an integral part of Portugal's broader counterinsurgency policy of isolating
Frelimo forces from their rural bases of support.[37] The government intended
that here, as in the north, aldeamentos would "function as a means of combat-
ing the growth of terrorism by blocking the local population from having any
contact with the terrorists who require their support."[38] While peasants would
be encouraged to relocate, anyone resisting would face forcible eviction.

Once this position solidified, the military insisted on rapid villagization,
despite possible social costs or political disruption, and refused to tolerate dissent or foot-dragging from civilian authorities—not even from the governor
of Tete. After complaints by the military in Tete that he was not carrying out
their orders for forced villagization, he was summarily replaced; the new governor promised to rapidly increase both the number of aldeamentos and the
defoliation of strategic forest and grassland areas to blunt the movement of
"terrorists" and prevent them from ambushing convoys.[39]

Under heightened pressure from the high command and the new governor,
the GPZ became much more interventionist. Abandoning its original mandate
to resettle only those communities whose land was to be submerged, it began
to target both villages with strategic military significance and those under increasing Frelimo influence. Indicative of this shift was its decision, in 1971,
to complete twenty-three aldeamentos—only six for communities affected by
the dam—and its plan to remove eighty-three thousand peasants living in a
strategic belt stretching from Changara to Zumbo to protected villages further
from the river (see map 4.1).[40] In a not-so-subtle discursive move, these were
called rearranged communities, to distinguish them from those displaced by
the dam's lake.[41] By 1973 the GPZ had evicted more than half this latter group
from their homelands,[42] and, at Cahora Bassa's completion, over 280,000 peasants were confined in protected villages in the Zambezi valley—less than 20
percent because their villages had been flooded.[43] Forcibly resettled peasants in
both these groups had similar negative experiences in the aldeamentos.

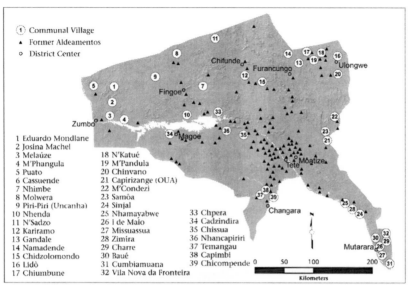

Legend:
- ① Communal Village
- ▲ Former Aldeamentos
- ○ District Center

1 Eduardo Mondlane
2 Josina Machel
3 Melaúze
4 M'Phangula
5 Puato
6 Cassuende
7 Nhimbe
8 Molwera
9 Piri-Piri (Uncanha)
10 Nhenda
11 N'Sadzo
12 Kariramo
13 Gandale
14 Namadende
15 Chidzolomondo
16 Lidö
17 Chiumbune
18 N'Katué
19 M'Pandula
20 Chinvano
21 Capirizange (OUA)
22 M'Condezi
23 Samöa
24 Sinjal
25 Nhamayabwe
26 1 de Maio
27 Missuassua
28 Zimira
29 Charre
30 Baué
31 Cumbiamuana
32 Vila Nova da Fronteira
33 Chpera
34 Cadzindira
35 Chissua
36 Nhancapiriri
37 Temangau
38 Capimbi
39 Chicompende

MAP 4.1. Aldeamentos and communal villages. *University of Minnesota Cartography*

DISPLACING PEASANTS: DESTROYING COMMUNITIES, SENSE OF PLACE, AND LIVELIHOODS

The mammoth task of evicting rural communities to make way for Cahora Bassa actually began in the late 1960s—not in the lowlands along the Zambezi but on the Songo highlands adjacent to the proposed dam site. Local agriculturalists considered the plateau extremely desirable; its fertile soils, temperate climate, and low incidence of malaria had supported prosperous agrarian livelihoods and a relatively dense population for hundreds of years. Before the dam's construction, Pedro da Costa Xavier recalled, "there were many Africans who lived on the plains here in Songo. The land was very good. People grew a lot. They cultivated maize, beans, and other products."[44] The grasslands and shrubbery also provided excellent grazing for cattle and goats. When Portugal decided to build the dam, it ordered all highland residents to leave so that a secure, racially segregated company town could be built for a bevy of GPZ officials and Zamco's 750 European employees. The several thousand Nyungwe and Tawara peasants who were evicted received compensation for neither their homes nor the land their ancestors had farmed for generations. They relocated on their own just off the plateau, in the hot, arid lowlands between Tete and Chicoa, where many suffered from malaria.[45]

The consequences for the riverine communities, whose homelands were flooded to create the lake behind the dam, were even more devastating. For the peasants of the Zambezi floodplain, resettlement entailed being herded like animals into protected villages, which were surrounded by barbed wire and guarded, around the clock, by Portuguese soldiers and African militia. Whereas other dam projects caused the relocation of several million of the rural poor and politically powerless,[46] rarely, if ever, were the relocated interned, as Mozambican peasants were, in aldeamentos.

In 1970, four years before the Zambezi's impoundment, the state began evicting peasant families from their homes along the river, under the guise of relocating vulnerable communities. Facing the pressure of an expanded war and looming construction deadlines, a small and unprepared group of local administrators hastily organized large public gatherings, known as *banjas*, to try to persuade villagers to move voluntarily. Accompanied by an entourage of armed police and interpreters, the administrators described in great detail the move's benefits—painting an excessively attractive picture of modern life in the aldeamentos—while offering only vague and sometimes deceitful explanations for why resettlement was necessary, which played on both the villagers' lack of knowledge about the dam and their fears of a possible Frelimo attack.[47]

However colonial authorities framed the move, they focused their attention on chiefs and respected male elders, ignoring the women who sat mute in the back rows. Despite the profound impact of the move on women's lives, the patriarchal assumptions of both Europeans and senior African men discouraged women from speaking up.

Most peasants—males and females alike—were skeptical they would be able to reconstruct their lives far away from their known physical environment. From childhood, they had been farming on the same fields as their parents before them, and they knew the lay of the land, the contours of the hills, and the location of the baobab trees and streams that marked the landscape. It was difficult to imagine acquiring such rich local knowledge in a new place. In public gatherings, elders complained that inland areas lacked the fertility of the river margins where, for generations, their families had enjoyed access to abundant supplies of fish and game, and they called sacrilegious the flooding of shrine centers that would alienate the *mhondoro* (royal ancestor spirits), who were the ultimate guardians of the community's health and well-being. To alleviate these worries, colonial officials sometimes took régulos and respected *svikiro* (spirit mediums) to check out the proposed new village. If these local leaders found it wanting, however, officials ignored their concerns.[48]

Since those facing resettlement feared retribution, open protest was rare. Occasional outbursts of hostility from audiences at the banjas, however, revealed deep-seated opposition to the resettlement scheme, as an incident at Estima in May 1971 demonstrated. The administrator of the Cabora Bassa locality had ordered the adult population of five chieftaincies under his jurisdiction to attend a banja. When he finished his presentation, audience members began to grumble loudly that they "would be herded into kraals like goats" and that, in the confined quarters of the aldeamentos, they would be easy targets "for the government to kill [us] all"[49]—articulating their fear that resettlement was not only dehumanizing but threatened their very existence. He dismissed these concerns as Frelimo-inspired propaganda.[50]

Colonial authorities presumed that, because régulos received salaries and other material benefits from the state, they would perform their duties faithfully. This, however, did not always happen. While many régulos initially endorsed the resettlement scheme, at least publicly, as local opposition grew that position became increasingly untenable. Some chiefs rejected relocation, due to pressure from their subjects and threats of retribution from Frelimo guerrillas with ties to community members.[51] A Portuguese informer reported, for example, that after Régulo Tomo of Chicoa shifted his position, his popularity soared, and "he enjoyed the respect of all the people, including the terrorists."[52] Intimidation, after all, was not the monopoly of the colonial state.

RESETTLEMENT: THE TURN TO VIOLENCE

Faced with widening opposition, local administrators quickly abandoned all pretenses of community input and simply ordered chiefs and their followers to relocate, resorting to coercive or openly violent tactics upon encountering any resistance. To this day, the traumatic moment the order arrived remains etched in people's memories. As Basílio Chiridzisana recalled with visible distress, "the Portuguese *chefe de posto* (local administrator) gathered all the people and told us we had to go in order to save our lives from the rising water that would soon flood our lands. We were all very angry and did not want to leave Chicoa Velha, but we had no choice."[53] "The whites forced us to leave," Chiridzisana's neighbor, Paulino Nhamizinga, recounted. "They sent armed militia with trucks and took us to Chicoa Nova."[54] Pezulani Mafalanjala and his neighbors in Masecha told a similar story: "They came and told us that the water was going to rise and that we would have to leave. . . . Among us, there were people who complained and did not want to move. They were very angry because they had fields and houses here and their whole life was here. But they had no choice."[55] Vernácio Leone concurred: "The people left Chicoa because of the water and the war. They did not want to move but the government forced them."[56]

The levels of intimidation and violence accompanying the move varied considerably. Some communities had months to prepare; others had to vacate their homes and fields right away—leaving their crops in the ground to rot.[57] When the designated day arrived, however, everyone had to leave. Pezulani Mafalanjala recalled that "they sent trucks and took us away."[58] Often, the threat of force was explicit. In Gervásio Chongololo's village, colonial soldiers "arrived very suddenly. They were heavily armed and were very impatient. They threatened to beat us, which they did. We had no choice."[59] When, for example, Régulo Metapa expressed reservations about the move, the Estima administrator sent the militia to evict him and his followers immediately and take them far away, to the Vuende aldeamento.[60]

Colonial authorities, to underscore that they would not tolerate defiance, burned the homes and possessions of anyone refusing to move.[61] Leveling homesteads also discouraged people from sneaking back there before the flooding began. Padre Gremi, who ministered to peasants living in the war zone between Songo and Maraca, recounted that "after the order was given to transfer to the aldeamentos, colonial soldiers and police literally carried people from their homes. They burned the huts and all the possessions of those who refused to leave. It was an order that everyone had to obey."[62] Some villagers who remained intransigent were subject to incarceration or even execution.[63] During an unusually frank conversation with Australian journalists, a Portuguese military commander boasted that coercion had no limits: "We give the blacks two weeks to come into fortified villages. If they don't, we shoot them."[64]

News of impending evictions and stories of official brutality caused panic in the countryside and widespread flight into neighboring colonies. As the GPZ had predicted, many peasants fled to Rhodesia or Zambia. While the clandestine nature of this migration makes it difficult to quantify, it was clearly regular and recurring. The Rhodesian Special Branch, for example, reported in early 1971 that more than one thousand peasants from three villages alone had crossed the border from Mozambique, many of whom would willingly return home if guaranteed that they would be not be forced into aldeamentos.[65] Similarly, in June of that year, according to the Portuguese secret police, more than five hundred Africans from the village of Cassepa, in the Zumbo region, escaped across the border into Zambia.[66] Others fled to the interior and joined Frelimo.[67]

There were great risks involved in such journeys. Peasants had to walk several hundred kilometers through unfamiliar territory, sometimes with children on their backs. Lack of food and shelter, attacks from marauding bandits or wild animals, and the ever-present threat of capture by African sipais or the Portuguese military posed obvious additional threats. Lofas Nsampa's account of the journey from Sena Sugar Estates, in the delta, to Zimbabwe, highlighted the multiple dangers: "We went on foot. We left our homes at night and spent the first night walking. We slept in the bush. Since we did not know the route to Rhodesia, we had to ask villagers we met on the way. . . . Many people were killed by lions. When we reached the police station near the border, we hid until we were sure that all the police were asleep. Then we swam across the river."[68] Júlio Calecoetoa of Songo told a similar story, though his journey was much shorter: "I fled at night with my twelve-year-old brother. We slept in the bush in constant terror we would be captured by the Portuguese and beaten and imprisoned."[69] According to Bento Chitima, "no one had the courage to make this trip alone. Everyone was afraid. Bandits would murder any who traveled alone."[70] To guard against these dangers, those planning to flee first propitiated the midzimu, asking for protection along the way.[71] Even when they succeeded in crossing the border, however, there was no guarantee they would be welcomed, particularly in Rhodesia, where the Ian Smith regime had established its own network of protected villages for counterinsurgency purposes.[72] Nevertheless, that such flight occurred reveals how determined these peasants were to avoid their loss of freedom in the aldeamentos.

Forced evictions became hastier and more chaotic as the independence war heated up. Entire communities were booted from their villages at a moment's notice—sometimes even before any housing was in place.[73] As Peter Size and Fedi Alfante recalled, "men, women, children and animals were loaded onto trucks at Chinyanda Velho and forced to come here to Chinyanda Nova. No one could refuse. When we arrived, there were no houses, so men had to go to the bush to construct huts. Each family received a parcel of land on which to cultivate their field."[74] These men were relatively lucky, since government-contracted tractors had already cleared some land for farming at their aldeamento site. Others were less fortunate, like the group of involuntarily displaced parishioners Padre Gremi accompanied to Mufa Kakonde:

> We arrived at Mufa Kakonde camp on the road to Tete. . . . People had been forced to abandon their farms in November [1972] after everyone had planted their fields. They lost their harvest, they lost their fields, and they lost everything they owned. They were only allowed to take four things with them. We arrived under a torrential rain and I saw hundreds of people—I say hundreds because I do not want to exaggerate; I want to be objective—maybe there were thousands. They were sitting with all their belongings under trees in the rain, without anything to protect them. They sat there for days and days.[75]

Padre Gremi stressed that the situation at Mufa Kakonde was not unique: "I can mention several other camps—Marara, Kachembe, Musha, and Estima—where there were no houses. People were brought there in trucks and told that this was their new homeland. They were literally unloaded in the bush. In some cases a Caterpillar had cleared the land into small square plots and the people were told: 'Now you make your homes.'"[76] One of Zamco's European employees confirmed that "people were just herded together; it was done too fast."[77]

The speed of the move exacerbated the trauma of the forced evictions. The authorities herded the shocked and frightened villagers into trucks—pregnant women, young mothers with newborn babies, and the elderly—with as many worldly possessions as they could gather. These evictees carried clay pots containing whatever stored grain and seeds they had been able to collect. They clung to their utensils, blankets, mats, and other personal belongings. Sometimes, but not always, there was room for chickens and goats.[78] Much personal property was lost, looted, or destroyed in the process. Bento Chitima emphasized that, in such crowded and confused conditions, "some people robbed things belonging to others, [and] many items were damaged along the way."[79]

The shortage of adequate vehicles compounded the chaos and suffering many experienced during the journey to their new homes. Some had to walk long distances in the hot sun with little to eat. A few perished even before they unpacked their meager belongings. Padre Gremi recalled a particularly tragic scene:

> It was in Catacha. I came to witness the move. I had never seen such violence. I went to visit the people and, as I moved among them, I noticed the body of an elderly woman lying under a tree. I was told that she had died that morning. Her face was parched from the sun. She had been forced to walk twenty-five kilometers from her village at Nhamajanela, which had been torched; she was all alone. She did not have family or possessions. I learned that she had not eaten on the journey. It was all that she could do to drag her tired body to a shady tree. She crumpled down and died.[80]

The total number of Africans forcibly uprooted to make way for the dam remains an open question. Because Portugal considered Cahora Bassa a strategic military project in a war zone, colonial authorities barred local journalists, international observers, and researchers, all of whom might have been able to quantify the displaced population. Government estimates of the numbers to be relocated did not include peasants who had fled to Rhodesia or to the slums and temporary camps surrounding Tete city. As occurred so often in other parts of the world, the victims of Mozambique's megadam project were undercounted and rendered invisible.[81]

One thing is clear, however—the overwhelming majority of the displaced were women and children. Of the more than 9,400 interned in the protected villages around Estima in 1973, for example, 1,455 were men, 2,591 were women, and the rest were children.[82] Gender disparities were slightly higher in the camps established in the Changara and Barue areas, where women outnumbered men two to one.[83] Although this gender imbalance was affected somewhat by the large number of men working in Rhodesia, labor migration is only part of the explanation. Villagers stressed that "many men were afraid of being killed by the Portuguese, so they fled to the bush or joined Frelimo."[84] This gender imbalance had far-reaching economic and social consequences (see "Life in the Aldeamentos," below).

LIFE IN THE ALDEAMENTOS

While there may be uncertainty about the numbers of evicted peasants, there is no doubt that life in the aldeamentos was not only harsh, but a radical departure from anything their residents had previously experienced. Because forced resettlement deprived interned peasants of the places where their identities, experiences, and livelihoods were rooted, the aldeamentos transformed the character of their daily life.[85] Having uprooted rural families from landscapes whose major features—settlements, rivers, hills—had provided order and meaning to their lives, government officials tried to minimize the loss of place by naming new villages for the ones left behind. Given an unfamiliar setting with no known landmarks, however, merely moving residents of Chicoa Velha to a village named Chicoa Nova, for example, could not re-create the feeling of home.

By 1970 heightened security concerns, rather than a commitment to improving the lives of rural families, dictated every detail of the resettlement program. General Kaúlza de Arriaga, commander in chief of military operations in Tete District, declared in an interview with a sympathetic British researcher, "The most important thing is control and defense."[86] Counterinsurgency priorities also explain the hasty selection of sites and poor organization of the first aldeamentos, which sometimes took less than three months to erect.[87] The rush to relocate peasants and the fear that Frelimo would attack GPZ fieldworkers caused many aldeamento sites to be hurriedly surveyed—sometimes in reliance on inadequate aerial photographs—or not at all.[88]

These shortcuts ensured that living conditions in most of the camps would be rudimentary at best[89]—in sharp contrast to glowing depictions of the highly publicized "model villages."[90] According to the GPZ's plan, which was communicated to the affected communities during banjas, each aldeamento was to include a school, health clinic, water pumps, grist mills, warehouses for food reserves, a social hall, and soccer fields.[91] In fact, however, the government provided at most only simple mud-and-wattle huts laid out in a grid and enclosed by a barbed-wire fence. There were few amenities, and residents were crowded into extremely tight quarters. A typical protected village consisted of roughly fifteen hundred people living in approximately 250 small, poorly constructed huts. The compounds had insufficient space for the average household of six to eight people, and huts were often less than three meters apart—leaving their occupants little privacy.[92] Overcrowding was worse for polygynous families, because each wife needed her own living quarters. Crowded conditions also left no space for cultivation of fruit trees, vegetable gardens, and the medicinal herbs on which peasants relied to protect them against sorcery and to ensure bountiful harvests and hunts. These living arrangements were nothing like the large kraals, spacious gardens, and vast commons that were typical in the villages left behind.[93] However poor they may have previously been, displaced people remembered the fertile terrain of the riverine homelands that had supported their extended families for generations.

The exigencies of war provided a convenient excuse for the gap between rhetoric and reality, and few of the protected villages ever received the amenities the state had originally promised—as official documents acknowledged without apology. According to a 1970 PIDE report, "the first group of protected villages is deficient in structure and organization. They lack water, electricity, health posts and schools. . . . It is little wonder that there [is] so much discontent among peasants transferred there."[94] Three years later, GPZ rationalized the aldeamentos' lack of physical infrastructure: "In order to relocate such a large number of people, we were forced to adjust our original plans."[95] The next year, the governor of Tete wrote that budgetary constraints had prevented the state from meeting the legally prescribed level of technical support for the aldeamentos and that "there were not sufficient funds [in the war budget] to build the schools, health centers, birth clinics, grist mills, and other infrastructures required by the GPZ [plans]."[96] Gone from the colonial discourse was any pretense of beneficial social engineering to bring the rural population into the modern world. Reflecting, twenty years later, on conditions there, the director of Tete's aldeamento program from 1972 to 1974 confessed:

> The aldeamentos had no chance. As I said, they were located in areas deprived of conditions. . . . [Insofar as foodstuffs are concerned] they always needed help. I do not know of any aldeamento [which was self-sustained]. Not to mention the aldeamentos built by the military, which were true concentration camps where we would go to try to improve the situation. But all of them needed to be fed, always. . . . They worked badly. . . . Usually the people were unhappy. They had left their homes, their lands and were humiliated. . . . They were under great pressure, submitted to great psychic violence, to say the least. . . . They were humiliated.[97]

More unsettling still, aldeamento residents were trapped in a highly militarized and controlled environment that deprived them of control over their own lives. Still reeling from the trauma of forced resettlement, they became virtual captives in their new homes, under the constant surveillance of an African militia[98] guarding, around the clock, the military checkpoints that were residents' only access to the world outside.[99] Anyone wishing to attend an important event in a neighboring community, such as a wedding or funeral, had to request written permission from colonial authorities to do so.[100] The militia also monitored residents' every move, even within the aldeamento. Peasants were no longer able to build houses where they wanted, live with whomever they chose, travel to markets to purchase basic goods, or visit in nearby villages with itinerant traders, relatives, or friends. With their movements so severely curtailed, many found it impossible to maintain contact with dispersed kin—a dramatic and upsetting rupture with past practices. Even the authorities acknowledged that the cramped quarters and spatial restrictions contributed to "the state of culture shock many peasants experienced . . . including those who had not opposed the move."[101]

The strictly regimented life of the aldeamentos extended to residents' movements in the neighboring fields and forests, where they struggled to carve out new livelihoods—always under the watchful eyes of the militia. No longer able to move freely between home and farm or from field to field, displaced peasants such as Peter Size and Fedi Alfante remember vividly the sense of living like prisoners—penned in and under constant surveillance:[102] "We were forced to live in the aldeamento surrounded by a barbed-wire fence. And there were militia who guarded it. We could not leave when we wanted to. Our movements were always controlled. Everywhere we went the militia accompanied us. When we went to cut wood, they came with us. When we went to our fields, they were there as well. They said that they were there to protect us. We worked from five in the morning until one in the afternoon, when we were ordered by the militia to return to the aldeamento."[103] Pezulani Mafalanjala stressed the dire consequences of breaking the rules:

> We started working in our machambas at six in the morning, and we were required to leave the fields between twelve and twelve thirty. We had to be back in the aldeamento by one. The patrol always accompanied us. They guarded us to make sure that we did not have any contact with strangers in the bush. If you came back late, they grilled you about where you were and what you were doing. The militia then handed over the tardy individuals to PIDE, who charged them with secretly providing food to Frelimo. The accused were severely beaten and threatened before they were allowed to return home, and some even died while being interrogated.[104]

The authorities were so worried that peasants might covertly pass supplies to Frelimo guerrillas that they permitted residents to take only small amounts of food and water with them to their fields.[105] Anyone trying to leave a field without permission or returning to the village after the midday curfew was suspected of being a Frelimo agent and was harshly interrogated and, often, beaten.[106]

AGRICULTURE, FOOD SECURITY, AND HUNGER

Military security concerns also drove restrictive new agricultural practices and policies that severely undermined food security. These included the failure of state planners to place aldeamentos near fertile lands, the government's unwillingness to clear most of the fields, the location of fields far from the aldeamentos, and prohibitions against farming multiple fields and working on others' plots. Most immediately affected were those in aldeamentos inhospitable to farming in the first place, but these policies affected peasants in virtually all of them.

Because military considerations determined the selection of settlement sites, the land's actual productivity was rarely sufficient, and most of the designated areas suffered from marginal soils and precarious or insufficient rainfall. Nor, according to Bento Chitima and Joseph Máquina, did the authorities identify the best available lands for actual plots: "The matope soils at Chicoa Nova were not fertile. When the tractors came to clear the bush, the drivers failed to select the best areas for farming. The matope soils had too many rocks and stones. They paid no attention and simply cut the trees and marked a plot for every family to occupy and farm. Most people received land that was hard and arid. These lands produced almost nothing."[107] A government agronomist agreed with their critique: "None of the sites chosen [in the Chiuta region] have the minimum conditions for agriculture."[108]

Moreover, fear of Frelimo attacks and budgetary shortfalls often prevented the private company with tractors—which was supposed to clear trees, grade the land, and till the soil—from doing so.[109] Instead, peasants using axes, machetes, and hoes had to chop down trees themselves and burn and clear the bush. This backbreaking labor caused great resentment among those already disgusted by the poor quality of the soil. In at least one instance, disgruntled villagers "fled, leaving behinds houses they had recently already built, because the government had promised to till their machambas and no tilling had been done."[110]

Compounding these problems, the fields' location far from the aldeamento caused a drastic reduction in the length of the workday. Officials in charge of the relocation program often ignored the state planners' mandate that fields be no further than three kilometers from the village.[111] It was not uncommon for peasants to leave home before six in the morning, escorted by the militia, who served as de facto labor overseers, and walk five kilometers or more to get to their designated plots.[112] The long journey could be dangerous, since they had to worry about both land mines buried in the dirt roads and Frelimo ambushes. Because peasants had to return to the protected villages by the early afternoon curfew and the trip could take over three hours,[113] they had insufficient time properly to cultivate their crops.

The hardscrabble terrain of these new fields stood in sharp contrast to the fertile, river-fed plains of the Zambezi valley, whose dark makande soils were considered the most desirable in the region. Maurício Alemão, an elderly peasant who had lived in an area later flooded by the lake, and Carlos Churo, from nearby Masecha, reminisced about the high moisture retention and rich agricultural capacity of the makande soils in their ancestral villages.[114] Peasants also remembered stretches of the river that flooded on both banks during the rainy season, which typically extended from December to March,[115] leaving behind, when the water receded, a rich deposit of nutrients along the banks and in adjacent lowland areas.[116] While not every evacuee shared identical memories of food security, all agreed that the Zambezi River had been critical to the human ecology of survival, that life on the land had been better there,[117] and that "no one ever died from hunger."[118] For the evicted, agricultural livelihoods fed by the makande soils of the Zambezi floodplain were now just a distant memory.

Official agricultural policies banning certain time-honored farming practices also contributed to the reduced harvests and increased level of food insecurity. As elsewhere in Africa, hunger resulted from both ecological crises and state policies that undermined peasant productivity.[119] For example, to minimize risk and to take advantage of variations in soils, sunlight, and moisture availability, peasants, such as Carlos Churo, had previously cultivated two or three fields strategically located in different microecological zones.[120] In the aldeamentos, however, each household was limited to one small plot—typically less than one hectare.[121] In Fedi Alfante's view, the consequences were predictable: "We had much less food here [in Chinyanda Nova] because we had only one machamba, [while] in Chinyanda Velha we had three or four near the river and scattered on the hills."[122] Maurício Alemão agreed: "We did not produce nearly as much food as we did in Chicoa Velho. There we could work in three or four fields and plant all year-round."[123]

State officials also prohibited long-standing labor exchange practices, insisting that each aldeamento household work only its parcel of land.[124] Here, colonial policy ran directly counter both to local environmental knowledge and to cultural values that prized mutual assistance networks and a reciprocal work ethic. Collective labor expedited tree cutting, bush burning, weeding, and harvesting. Before eviction from their homelands, peasants heavily utilized the services of their neighbors and kin, especially during times of labor stress.[125]

The banning of farming practices based on indigenous knowledge of local ecosystems further weakened the production capacity of households that were already living dangerously close to the edge. Dispersed fields and labor exchanges had effectively minimized the risks of crop failure in a region where uncertain and relatively short rainy seasons caused seasonal shortages. While such practices did not always prevent hunger, they had helped peasants avoid the devastating effects of subsistence crises most of the time.

Not surprisingly, resettled communities suffered from food shortages and malnutrition. Many displaced families arrived at the aldeamentos on the verge of starvation, with little or no food reserves. Ripped from the environment they knew, deposited unceremoniously in a hostile landscape with no technical support, and facing new restrictions on when, where, and how they could farm made their lives even worse. Paulino Nhamizinga recalled that "by October and November, we did not have much to eat. We were constantly hungry."[126] Joseph Máquina described how people who were starving abandoned their arid plots and covertly "went from one machamba to another offering their labor in exchange for small amounts of food."[127] Some perished even before the first harvest.[128]

Government reports confirmed that the situation was precarious—acknowledging as early as 1971 that production on the aldeamentos was extremely low and that acute food shortages were common, especially during the months before the harvest.[129] Nevertheless, they attributed hunger in the protected villages to factors largely beyond the administration's control, rather than to the effects of forced resettlement. Officials insisted that low rainfall, a "lack of peasant initiative," and the failure of displaced community members to bring adequate food reserves all contributed to the crisis.[130]

Other byproducts of forced resettlement exacerbated the food crisis. The government directive that men clear the land and construct residences in their own aldeamento before the actual move made them unavailable to work on their existing family plots, which reduced their households' ability to produce a food surplus to take with them as a strategic reserve.[131] Additionally, communities evicted in haste had to abandon not only unharvested foodstuffs but also their precious seed stores. Moreover, once settled in the aldeamento, residents, who lived far from their fields, were unable to guard their crops during the night from monkeys, baboons, wild pigs, and birds. The situation became so desperate that some peasants slipped out of their villages after dark—risking harsh punishment—to protect their fields from these predators.[132]

The substantial loss of livestock during the chaos surrounding the move also worsened the villagers' subsequent food insecurity.[133] Moreover, because most aldeamentos lacked well-watered grazing land, they were inhospitable to livestock.[134] The state's failure to clear the areas of tsetse fly and to inoculate the peasants' cattle further depleted their herds,[135] as did Frelimo's regular nocturnal raids.[136]

The decimation of livestock had significant economic and social implications for the resettled communities. Cattle, goats, and pigs were an important source of protein, even if consumed only on special occasions; cattle were also the preferred form of bridewealth and a critical marker of social status.[137] So great was the economic and cultural value of cattle for displaced communities that, as the newspaper *Voz Africana* warned, "the success of the aldeamentos depends to a large degree on the authorities recognizing and defending the principle . . . that cattle represent an important source of wealth and social prestige."[138]

For all the above reasons, food production was appreciably lower in the aldeamentos than where villagers had previously resided, and fragmentary data suggest that, over time, conditions only worsened.[139] Seasonal hunger in 1971 and 1972 gave way to a large-scale famine the following year, when, due to a prolonged drought, the entire corn crop failed. In response, the governor of Tete established a relief program that provided beans, maize, sugar, salt, and other basic commodities to supplement the uprooted peasants' meager diets.[140] For many, the supplies were too little too late, however. According to a Zamco manager who visited protected villages in 1973, "people were grossly undernourished and there was a substantial amount of death."[141] Kwashiorkor, resulting from acute protein deprivation, was reportedly endemic among children.[142]

To make matters worse, aldeamento residents had fewer opportunities to supplement their food supply through fishing and hunting, which were invaluable sources of protein, than they had enjoyed while living near the Zambezi River (see chapter 2). For most uprooted communities, fishing in the Zambezi was no longer possible. Not only were the aldeamentos far from the river, but villagers could not leave them except under guard. Additionally, the colonial government restricted fishermen's access to the Zambezi for security reasons. As Senteira Botão and his neighbors recalled, "the military controlled all movement of fishermen on the Zambezi River."[143] Nor was hunting feasible. While aldeamento residents could lay small-game traps in their fields, they could not hunt larger animals, since Portuguese military authorities prevented peasants from carrying rifles and severely restricted their movement. "Because of the war," John Paul lamented, "no one could go hunting."[144] Here again, colonial policies linked to both the dam and the war provoked food shortages and hunger.

In the past, peasants with access to hard currency could purchase food to supplement what they produced. Much of the cash came from the wages of migrant laborers working in Rhodesia or Zambia. Although there were no open borders between Mozambique and its neighbors, many males from the Zambezi valley regularly traveled back and forth between their villages and these nearby countries, where it was easy for them to find employment.[145] When they returned home to visit their families, they brought hard currency and basic commodities. Forced villagization and the increased military presence in the countryside, however, made clandestine migration almost impossible and prevented many of those working either legally or illegally outside Mozambique from coming home for visits, both of which negatively impacted their families' standard of living. Moreover, for those few peasants with access to hard currency, the requirement that they petition in writing to travel outside their aldeamento precluded them from buying commodities at the rural cantinas owned by Portuguese, Goan, or mestizo merchants.[146]

Faced with the menace of hunger, many aldeamento residents resorted to foraging for roots, bulbs, and tubers more regularly than before. Women and children collected a variety of wild fruits[147] from the forests surrounding their fields—all of which they had previously consumed, when necessary. They also set traps to snare rodents.[148] It was hard to determine which plants were poisonous, however, because foragers were unfamiliar with the microecological zones surrounding their new communities. Moreover, since they needed specific permission from the guards to go out foraging, once again official restrictions on their movement complicated efforts to close the seasonal hunger gap with gathered food.[149]

"WE ARRIVED HERE AND BEGAN TO DIE"

Among the most significant consequences of forced villagization were the acute water shortages and related public health problems of poor sanitation and disease that plagued the aldeamentos. Clean water is an essential ingredient of life—for bathing, washing, drinking, and cooking—and the free-flowing Zambezi River, along whose banks the resettled peasants had previously lived, provided an abundant supply of it. While the GPZ had intended to construct wells, fountains, water pumps, cattle ponds, and even reservoirs for the aldeamentos,[150] as with so many other dimensions of this flawed colonial project, official claims bore no relation to reality. Instead of an integrated waterworks system, most displaced communities suffered ongoing, serious water shortages.[151] In the Chitima aldeamento, for example, there were only two wells,[152] and, according to a 1972 survey of twenty-four aldeamentos in Cahora Bassa District, more than half lacked a functioning water system.[153] Two years later, access to water remained a serious problem for existing aldeamentos, and the last communities to be moved before the lake was filled were being relocated despite the GPZ hydrologists' inability to locate reliable sources of water for them.[154]

Such mismanagement forced peasants to seek out rivers, creeks, rivulets, rain-fed streams, and whatever other sources of groundwater existed. This burden fell, literally, on the backs of women. Inês Fondo recounted how she and her neighbors "had to walk for an hour or more to fetch water in large pots," which they carried back to the aldeamento on their heads.[155] Notwithstanding these efforts, serious water shortages persisted, and residents often had to draw water from stagnant pools.[156] At the Inhacaparire aldeamento the water crisis posed such a serious problem that the local population's demand to be moved to the one at Masecha, which had a secure water supply, was granted.[157]

Insufficient and unsafe water, exacerbated by overcrowding and the lack of sanitation facilities in the settlements, created obvious public health risks. Together, they explain why, during the short history of the aldeamentos, sickness and death were regular features of daily life. Heavy rains in January and February left foul pools of disease-infested water, which only intensified the sanitation problems. As early as March 1970, government reports acknowledged that overcrowded conditions and poor sanitation were causing a health crisis: "In these ill-conceived aggregations many hundreds, sometimes thousands, of people are concentrated in a restricted area. This inevitably poses a serious sanitation problem for which it is difficult to find a solution. There are no bathrooms or latrines for residents to use to satisfy themselves, so they meet their needs wherever they can. Cholera has become a very serious problem."[158] Even in the model villages, "there was cholera and many deaths from diarrhea."[159]

Although no systematic health-related data were collected from the aldeamentos,[160] both oral testimony and scattered written evidence suggest that the shortage of clean water, combined with inadequate diets and poor sanitary conditions, left many highly vulnerable to multiple diseases. John Paul and Khumbidzi Pastor confirmed the wave of illness that afflicted their community: "There were many deaths in the aldeamento. People died from cholera, hunger and malaria."[161] Aside from malaria, which posed an acute health threat, peasants relocated near the new lake also suffered from increased rates of water-borne parasitic illnesses, such as schistosomiasis, due to the stagnant waters.[162] In 1975 one investigator estimated that "malaria, bilharzia [schistosomiasis] and other debilitating diseases continue to wrack more than half the adults."[163] Taken together, this evidence supports Scudder's finding that "in the tropics and subtropics the incidence of poor nutrition and disease, as well as higher death rates, have increased immediately after [dam-related] resettlement."[164] At Cahora Bassa, as with other dam projects around the world, the very young and very old were the most vulnerable.[165]

The colonial regime tried to inoculate at-risk populations against tuberculosis and yellow fever and provided medication to curb the debilitating effects of malaria. These efforts, however, failed to convince afflicted communities that forced removal was not the source of their suffering.[166] Bernardo Potoroia expressed anger at the racialized system of oppression, which, in his view, was responsible for both the terrible circumstances of his village's involuntary resettlement and the misery that followed: "There was a great deal of hunger and many people also suffered from diseases during this period. There were serious problems with cholera, smallpox, and malaria. Many people died. No one knew why or how this happened, just that many people were dying. People bitterly complained about being forced to leave their land, which was good land. We arrived here, and people began to die. But in that time blacks were [considered] inferior to whites, and we could not do anything."[167]

THE CRISIS OF AUTHORITY IN THE ALDEAMENTOS

The destructive impact of forced villagization extended beyond the physical realm of everyday life into the spiritual and political world of uprooted peasants—tearing at the fabric of displaced communities and undermining the legitimacy of even their most sacred authorities. Throughout this Shona-speaking region, people believed that mhondoro provided a critical link between humans, the earth, and the moral order.[168] The chiefly lineage of the people who first settled in the region owned the land—a status that gave it the authority to distribute land to its family and followers. When the founding rulers died, their spirits, who became mhondoro, were revered both as guardians of all residing in their territory and as critical intermediaries in a spiritual hierarchy headed by the senior mhondoro, Dzivaguru.[169] Historically, chiefs derived their standing and power from their links to this hierarchy and to the territory protected by their mhondoro, which allowed them to rely on the mhondoro's assistance in times of drought, famine, war, or other crisis.[170]

As long as people propitiated the mhondoro—offering them locally brewed beer, tobacco, and porridge—and did not engage in witchcraft or otherwise violate the moral code, villagers were confident that these powerful spirits would ensure the fertility of the land, women, and cattle and protect them from external threats. Basílio Chiridzisana, for instance, recalled the critical interventions of Mhondoro Vulakadu in times of crisis, when "the elders would gather all the people and each family would contribute a small offering. Then the elders would take the grain and tobacco to a sacred site where they would sing and give praise to the mhondoro. If the problem was a lack of rain, by the time they returned home, it was already pouring."[171] His neighbor, Carlos Sabonete, reaffirmed the deep-seated belief that "the mhondoro was our protector."[172] Villagers also agreed, however, that this protection was contingent on good behavior; if people angered the royal ancestors, they would suffer from divinely inflicted drought, famine, or disease. As Vernácio Leone explained, "people had responsibilities to the spirits. If they forgot, there would be many illnesses. The elders would go to the sacred sites and ask why there were ill-nesses. The lion spirits [through their earthly medium, the svikiro] would tell them what they must do. The same was true if there was hunger."[173]

When disease and hunger followed the move to the aldeamentos, peasants were certain the mhondoro were angry over both the flooding of sacred shrines and burial sites and their supplicants' inability to pay homage to them in the proper places. According to Vernácio Leone, the svikiro openly objected to re-settlement on the mhondoro's behalf, but to no avail: "When the people were forced to move, the svikiro left as well. The svikiro wanted to live elsewhere, but the government forced him to live in the aldeamento. The svikiro became angry and warned of calamities. When the svikiro died, the mhondoro disap-peared and never returned."[174] Bento Estima and Joseph Ndebvuchena's ac-count revealed the profound connection between religion and place in Shona culture, and the grave consequences of severing it: "When people were told that they were going to have to leave, a number of spirit mediums selected highland sites within their spiritual domain that would not be flooded. The government rejected these options. This angered the spirit mediums of Mhon-doro Mpunzanguo, Mhondoro Ncombwe, Mhondoro Dehwe, and Mhondoro Mavula. They refused to move to the government locations. They abandoned their people."[175] Some defiant svikiros simply fled into the forest or otherwise disappeared; others died suddenly. In all these cases, "the mhondoro never returned."[176]

Desperate for help in the face of mounting misfortune, many turned to spirit mediums in nearby communities, but to no avail. As Joseph Ndebvuchena remembered, "we joined in prayer with other people in the protected village [of Estima] who came from the area of Masecha and Nhamapanda with their svikiro. It did not help. We continued to suffer. Our mhondoro was lost for-ever."[177] Peasants also kept seeking the assistance of family ancestor spirits. Maurício Alemão described how his family members "gathered the little bit of grain which they had and brewed a small amount of beer and left it as an offering under a tree. We asked the ancestors to forgive us for abandoning their graves and to protect our children from illnesses and help us to survive."[178] The midzimu, however, were not powerful enough to ward off the dangers of life in the aldeamentos. Only the mhondoro could do that—making their ab-sence devastating. The widely shared view that "there were no spirits to make it rain"[179] expressed the collective sense of loss in both literal and symbolic terms and reveals the vulnerability and cultural obliteration experienced by the uprooted peasants—a reality that even colonial officials acknowledged.[180]

Losing access to the royal ancestor spirits also undermined chiefly legitimacy. Their links to the mhondoro enabled them to seek assistance for their communi-ties in times of drought, famine, war, or other social crisis.[181] Forced resettlement broke this bond, leaving régulos without the ability to access their ancestors' sacred burial sites and the mhondoro's shrine center. In the eyes of displaced communities, this shook the cosmological foundations of chieftainship.[182]

The colonial state's demand that régulos defend and implement the unpopular forced villagization program, which left many in an untenable position, further undercut their authority. To the state, they were paid functionaries; but to their subjects, they were guardians of community resources and traditions. With both sides seeking their services, it became increasingly difficult to find a middle ground. The subjects of chiefs unwilling or unable to oppose eviction marginalized them as impotent or chastised them as collaborators. Once perceived as vacillating, untrustworthy executors of unpopular colonial policies, they lost their subordinates' trust and became the focal point of discontent. Moreover, Frelimo labeled those who collaborated as agents of colonial oppression and targeted them for attack.[183] Resisting resettlement, on the other hand, was also extremely risky. A régulo failing to support the government program could be replaced by a more pliant relative or incarcerated as a Frelimo sympathizer.

Several other factors at play in the aldeamentos reduced the legitimacy of state-appointed chiefs. By aggregating into one aldeamento previously autonomous communities, whose residents were not even always members of the same ethnic group, colonial officials seriously eroded chiefly authority by precipitating intense power struggles among the relocated régulos and their followers. In such aldeamentos, claims of seniority based on a direct blood relationship to founding ancestors carried little weight. In aldeamento Chipera, for example, régulos M'fuca, Chatala, Chatande, Alface, and Chifuca each waged fierce campaigns trying to establish his primacy.[184] Ethnic tensions among Tawara, Pimbe, and Zimba residents compounded the conflict. A similar power struggle took place in Fingoe.[185]

The régulos' inability to control the militia further compromised their positions. Most militiamen were poorly trained conscripts, lacked discipline, and often victimized members of the community they were supposed to protect. Colonial authorities regularly bemoaned the militia's destabilizing impact—especially how their arrogant and capricious behavior undermined the authority of régulos and afumo.[186] According to one report from aldeamento Sungo, "[the militia] do not fulfill their duties. . . . They spend most of the day drinking *pombe* [home-brewed beer] and going around, leaving their weapons at home. . . . They threatened the *régulo* who had to take *machambas* ready to be harvested from the civilians to give them to the militia. In conclusion, the militia unit is not helping the people in Sungo. On the contrary, they are causing serious problems between the *régulo* and the people."[187] Officials also complained that militiamen, especially when intoxicated, sexually assaulted women and young girls.[188] Carlos Sabonete, a former aldeamento resident, concurred, expressing anger and frustration that there was no recourse when incidents of abuse occurred: "The militia created havoc in the camps. They slept with our wives and daughters, but there was nothing we could say or do. If we complained, they would lock us up in the jail and beat us with the chicote."[189]

The building of Cahora Bassa frayed the social fabric of displaced communities in other ways as well. Allegations that married women were guilty of infidelity in their husband's absence were, according to Portuguese officials, a source of great social tension and unusually bitter interpersonal conflict.[190] This fixation with rumors about adulterous African women, however, may reveal more about colonial preoccupations than actual events on the ground. Nevertheless, it is not surprising that, under circumstances of unprecedented physical upheaval and resource scarcity, when adult women were bearing more responsibility than ever for the lives and livelihoods of rural families, tensions would revolve around female sexuality. Officials also worried about the sharp increase in witchcraft accusations and the use of the *mwabvi* poison ordeal[191] to identify and eliminate individuals possessed by evil spirits[192]—conflicts that underscored the traumatic psychological effects of displacement and the enduring nature of traditional institutions of conflict management. While some elders, like Gervásio Chongololo—who insisted that displaced villagers were "linked together with common problems" and did not argue seriously among themselves[193]—might have been reluctant to acknowledge these conflicts, this idealized portrait of cohesion as a strategy against community distress contradicted the testimony of other survivors, who readily described the conflicts existing in the aldeamentos.[194]

SOCIAL DIFFERENTIATION WITHIN THE ALDEAMENTOS

Although displacement adversely affected everyone, it did not affect everyone equally. Aldeamentos were not all the same. Peasants resettled in the small number of model communities,[195] for example, found life there much less daunting. They lived in cinder block homes laid out in a grid pattern and surrounded by shrubbery. They had access to running water, schools, health and social centers, and latrines. Their fields were near their homes, and, according to one visitor, "people were free to walk around; I do not see it as a concentration camp."[196] Padre Gremi, a vocal critic of the colonial regime, noted that residents in the model village at Degwe benefited from "good housing, schools, and water pumps,"[197] which was a successful propaganda ploy: "Degwe attracted a good deal of international attention because foreign journalists were invited to visit it and left deceived."[198]

In whatever protected village they were resettled, chiefs suffered less than their subjects. For all the challenges the régulos faced, as state functionaries they received material benefits that enabled them to survive the aldeamentos' harsh conditions. The colonial administration gave them uniforms, shoes, and, most important, over $100 in annual salary.[199] Although this salary was insignificant, it provided disposable income régulos could use both to purchase foodstuffs and other essential commodities and to maintain the semblance of a patronage system. They also typically received the largest houses, the most centrally located kraals, and the choicest fields. As the son of Régulo Chitima acknowledged, his father had one of the very few fertile plots in his aldeamento.[200] Additionally, chiefs were the first to get assistance from famine relief programs, and they used their access to food to reward loyalist subjects.

By contrast, forced resettlement was typically hardest on women. Displacement was anything but gender neutral.[201] Women suffered more from the stresses associated with the physical uprooting of rural households—harvesting the last crops from the fields and gathering family belongings as soldiers herded them onto trucks. Women were the ones who cared for the young and comforted the elderly on the journey to the aldeamento.[202] And, when they arrived at their destination, there was no respite, because women immediately had to channel their labor and energy into meeting the challenges of daily life. They spent much of their day walking long distances to gather firewood and fetch water and working in their machambas alongside their husbands.[203] Additionally, as always, aldeamento women had to care for children, assist the sick and elderly, and perform a wide array of household chores. What was no longer possible was earning excess income by selling surplus crops or fish or visiting neighboring villages to seek supplemental foodstuffs in times of famine.

Women forced to relocate without their spouses were even more vulnerable.[204] Forbidden to participate in labor exchanges and with little excess food for work parties in any case, many had no choice but to rely on the full-time labor of their children in the fields.[205] By the time these children were eight or nine, they were seeding, weeding, and harvesting alongside their mothers. Ironically, this use of child labor substantially reduced the number of children who attended classes—thereby undermining one of the stated objectives of the resettlement scheme. In aldeamento Massimba , for example, 180 students initially enrolled in the village school; two years later, the number had plummeted to fifty.[206] Yet, even with this assistance from their children, women struggling to maintain families alone rarely managed to produce enough food to meet their needs, and some turned to prostitution to survive. They found a ready clientele among the Portuguese soldiers and members of the militia.[207]

The only women who enjoyed a measure of food security were those married either to chiefs or to the small number of men working at the dam site who visited regularly, bringing sugar, bread, oil, and other commodities purchased at the company store.[208] Even this supply line could be tenuous, however, as

Maurício Alemão's family learned; shortly after injuring his back at Cahora Bassa, he was fired—and his family and relatives living in the aldeamento Chicoa Nova lost their only secure access to food.[209]

⌒

With independence, in 1975, the barbed wires surrounding the protected villages disappeared and the guards left. Nevertheless, life would never be the same for the displaced communities.[210] With their original homes now under water, most evacuees had little alternative but to remain where they were. After Frelimo came to power, some, under government pressure, joined communal villages,[211] as part of Frelimo's larger project of socializing the countryside (see chapter 6).[212] Others organized fishing cooperatives on the banks of newly formed Lake Cahora Bassa and managed over time to build a semblance of the livelihood they had lost (see chapter 5).

The relocated suffered a new shock two years later when Rhodesian- and South African–backed Renamo fighters began a violent destabilization campaign in the Zambezi valley. While most displaced peasants survived the Renamo onslaught, few, if any, of Cahora Bassa's victims have fully recovered from the ordeals associated with their forced resettlement, and even fewer have been able to reclaim their lives.

Despite the belief of colonial planners that the long-term economic and social benefits of the aldeamentos would far outweigh any short-term inconveniences caused by the relocation of riverine communities, forced removal, in fact, had immediate and far-reaching deleterious effects. Violent and hasty evictions, the disruption of normalcy and daily routines, the loss of place, and harsh confinement—these core images still dominate the memories of the men and women who suffered displacement for the sake of the dam. Many of the survivors live today in impoverished villages, dreaming of the world they left behind. Others have relocated to shantytowns on the edges of Tete city or have sought to create new lives as migrant workers in nearby Zimbabwe. Whatever their current circumstances, the flooding of their homelands and forced relocation remain the two critical events that irreversibly transformed their lives and collective biographies. Life before and life after the dam became one of their most important temporal divides.

5 ↪ The Lower Zambezi

Remaking Nature, Transforming the Landscape,
1975–2007

IN MOZAMBIQUE, as elsewhere, the social and ecological impact of damming on communities downriver has attracted less attention than either the
dam's construction or the forced displacement of thousands of peasants whose
homelands were submerged. While researchers studying similar megadam
projects have documented the devastating eviction of millions of rural poor
from their homelands,[1] the radical transformation of physical landscapes
around dams, and the inundation of treasured cultural sites,[2] they have often
ignored the less visible, but often more deleterious, consequences for downriver communities.[3] Thus, little is known about the millions of river basin
families who have been adversely affected around the world and even less
about dams' impact on downriver ecosystems.

With the noticeable exception of a handful of scientists, those researchers,
policymakers, and journalists who studied Cahora Bassa, have focused almost
exclusively on the political economy of the dam. Some have analyzed the diplomatic efforts of the new Mozambican government to gain ownership of the
hydroelectric project from Portugal; others have explored the complex negotiations between Maputo and Pretoria over the price for electricity exported to
South Africa. Military analysts have documented the efforts of Renamo forces,
with the support of the apartheid regime, to cut the dam's pylons and terrorize
riverine communities, while state planners and international agencies have
debated Cahora Bassa's role in the socialist or neoliberal development agendas of successive Mozambican governments.

Conspicuously absent from these discussions is examination of the environmental and social effects of Cahora Bassa on the Zambezi River basin.
Only within the past decade or so have scholars turned their attention to the

devastation of local ecosystems or the destruction of wildlife vital to the food security of riverine communities. Although Cahora Bassa produced real ecological and personal trauma for more than half a million people living in the lower Zambezi valley,[4] local stories of suffering or of stubborn resilience in the face of adversity have received little attention. As elsewhere in the world, riparian communities in central Mozambique—with their rich knowledge of environments lost in the rush to harness the river's life-giving power—were relegated to the sidelines of history.

Cahora Bassa's far-reaching negative consequences for the lower Zambezi watershed, which began the moment the steel gates closed, are beyond dispute.[5] Since late 1974 the waters of the middle Zambezi have been channeled through the turbines of Cahora Bassa, greatly diminishing, and at times reversing, the historic flooding and dry-season cycles of the river's plains. The imposed flow regime has also altered the geomorphology of the lower Zambezi valley—creating new pressures on the people and biota living there.

This damage is the direct result of Portugal's energy policy, which used Cahora Bassa to convert water, a free common resource necessary for the survival of all living things, into an export commodity created to meet the electricity demands of South Africa's mines, industries, cities, and farms. Because all that mattered under the new energy export system was the production of hydroelectric power, South Africa's needs dictated the magnitude, timing, duration, and frequency of water released from the dam, regardless of the possible effects on agriculture, fisheries, and wildlife downstream. Significantly, even during the fifteen-year period when Renamo sabotaged the dam pylons to prevent energy from being exported (see chapter 6), although the dam was generating virtually no power, the HCB kept the reservoir as full as possible to maximize hydropower generation potential. Water that could just as easily have been released to meet the survival needs of downriver communities and ecosystems was instead withheld; it was only discharged just before the rainy season to ensure that, were there a major flood, the raging river would not overtop and destroy the dam.[6] The Zambezi had become an "organic machine,"[7] controlled by operators who did not fully understand or care about the local consequences of what they had created.

This chapter explores how the dam has transformed the natural and social landscapes of the Zambezi River basin over the last three and a half decades. While physical and social worlds are always in flux and people and nature continually interact with and shape each other, what makes the postdam era—a very brief moment in the long history of the Zambezi valley—unique is the speed and scale of these changes. Because the social and ecological impacts of Cahora Bassa are inextricably intertwined and mutually reinforcing, focusing on the transformed physical landscape downriver allows us to explore how communities dwelling at or near the river's edge experienced the remaking of their environment and culture and the changing social relations.[8] We pay particular attention to the effects of damming the river on access to scarce natural resources and the livelihoods of hundreds of thousands of valley dwellers. It is difficult to know whether specific ecological changes flow directly from Cahora Bassa's construction or cumulatively from it, the opening of the Kariba Dam in 1959, and Mozambique's fifteen-year war with Renamo, which created resettlement problems of its own. Nevertheless, the processes highlighted here have been observed only since Cahora Bassa was completed. Significantly, local people attribute these changes primarily to the dam, although that might not always be the case.

FILLING LAKE CAHORA BASSA: A GLIMPSE OF THE FUTURE

As Cahora Bassa neared completion, driven by pressure from Lisbon and Pretoria to begin generating electricity for South Africa as quickly as possible, regardless of the consequences, HCB officials rushed to fill the reservoir.[9] On December 5, 1974, Lake Cahora Bassa began to rise from the Zambezi riverbed, and less than four months later it was nearly at full capacity. By comparison, it took almost four years to fill Lake Kariba.[10] This decision disregarded the warnings of environmental scientists that such action would have calamitous consequences for the hydrology and ecology of the Zambezi River valley (see chapter 2).[11]

The damage was felt almost immediately, when Lake Cahora Bassa permanently inundated 2,739 square kilometers of fertile land behind the reservoir as well as many hundreds of hectares of upriver floodplain habitats that contained resources critical to the riverine communities, drowned herds of wild animals, and irreversibly remade local ecosystems. Downstream from the dam, human, plant, and animal communities also suffered far-reaching consequences from the rapid filling of the reservoir. Without advance warning, dam engineers reduced the river to little more than a trickle. With the closing of the dam's gates, the flow rate of the Zambezi dropped to less than sixty cubic meters per second and remained there for more than three months—a rate less than 1 percent of the normal discharge of approximately eight thousand cubic meters per second at that time of year. By shutting off the river, the HCB abruptly severed the annual flood cycle and prevented the replenishment of nutrients in alluvial soils on which peasants downriver had relied for centuries. The timing could not have been worse, since it occurred during precisely those months when the Zambezi's flow normally peaked.

The Portuguese operators of Cahora Bassa demonstrated their total disregard for the well-being of downriver peoples and ecosystems even more flagrantly in April 1975, when they caused even more catastrophic results for riverine agriculturalists. The reservoir filled so quickly that by March, water appeared to be overflowing the dam's walls.[12] One month later, with construction of the dam almost complete, HCB engineers discovered a small defect in one of the turbines deep below the surface of the nearly full reservoir. To release enough water to access and repair it, without warning they completely opened the turbines and sluice gates.[13] With the sudden unleashing of a massive volume of water downstream, many small-scale agriculturalists living close to the river's edge—trying to take advantage of the strip of fertile alluvial soil—could only watch as their homes and gardens were destroyed and their cattle, goats, and pigs were swept away. Régulo Chipuazo of Caia remembered his sense of helplessness when the torrential waters "destroyed the houses and fields of all [his] followers who lived in the floodplains."[14] To make matters worse, once HCB had repaired the faulty turbine, it immediately shut off the flow, thereby again depriving downstream users of badly needed water. All of these disasters were merely harbingers of things to come.

ECOLOGICAL CHANGE IN THE LOWER ZAMBEZI VALLEY

Although Cahora Bassa irrevocably altered downstream ecosystems, even before its construction, the volume and timing of the flow of water inside Mozambique was already being held captive to the energy needs of other countries. Beginning two decades earlier, dams further upriver on the Zambezi and its tributaries (see map 4.1)[15] were responsible for a large reduction in the wet-season inflows into the lower Zambezi valley and the erratic flows that occurred at other times.[16] The most significant of these was Kariba, completed in 1959, which has one of the largest water storage areas the world.[17] Kariba controlled more than 40 percent of the total runoff of the Zambezi and dramatically changed the flow of water into Mozambique, disrupting the river's historic flooding and dry-season cycles.[18] The damming of the Kafue River—a major tributary of the Zambezi downriver from Kariba—at Kafue gorge in 1972 and at Itezhi-Tezhi in 1977, further decreased the water flows downriver by an additional 10 percent.[19] The International World Conservation Union identified some of the most pronounced ecological consequences: "After the construction of Lake Kariba, the reduction of downstream flooding dessicated the delta's alluvial soils, causing salinization and invasion of upland woody vegetation into the floodplain grasslands."[20] Villagers in the Sena-Caia area recalled that after Kariba's construction, rainy-season flooding "did not [often] occur with the same intensity."[21] Because of these three dams, the regular annual floods that nourished the Zambezi delta decreased in frequency, magnitude, and duration.[22] These reductions in overbank flooding and the loss of nutrients, however, were inconsequential compared to those caused by Cahora Bassa.

Kariba increased the ecological vulnerability of the lower Zambezi valley in other ways as well. After periods of unusually heavy rainfall, the extremely large discharges from the upriver dam posed a very real threat of flooding in the Zambezi basin. António Tchoa, who lived adjacent to the river at Caia, described one such surge in 1962, known as a cheia: "I don't know my exact age. It was around the time that I got married when the waters from Kariba inundated all our lands. We only survived from the grain and beans we received from the government."[23] Other communities were not as fortunate. "The village of Chemba [further upstream] was completely flooded and many people, including the children of [the] teacher Agostinho, perished. Others lost all their belongings, including their goats, chickens, and pigs."[24]

Even when large outpourings from Kariba did not threaten human lives, they altered physical landscapes in ways small and large. As Vale Raposo, an elder from Chemba, recalled, when "the water from Kariba descended with great velocity, the fast-moving river created a number of new channels and islands and eroded the banks of the river."[25] In 1969 prolonged releases from Kariba left river levels above the flood stage for 222 days, from early January through most of August, which was well into the dry season.[26] This atypical flooding pattern compromised agricultural production throughout the floodplain. Villagers referred to these uncertain times as cheia namwariri—"the water coming from the ground."[27]

Another factor compounding the ecological problems created by these upstream dams was the historically low and irregular rainfall in the lower Zambezi valley. With average annual precipitation in the area between Zumbo and Tete under 700 millimeters, and with drought a regular occurrence,[28] water shortfalls caused by upriver dams became extremely problematic.

THE ECOLOGICAL CONSEQUENCES OF CAHORA BASSA

While the effects of earlier dams in the Zambezi catchment area may have increased the vulnerability of delta ecosystems before 1974, Cahora Bassa had the most transformative impact[29] on downstream aquatic systems and biophysical relations.[30] By placing the lifeblood of the floodplains, delta, and estuary regions in the hands of the HCB, Portuguese colonial authorities made the success of the agricultural season in the Zambezi dependent on South African energy demands rather than on the natural cycles of rainfall and climate.

Cahora Bassa ended the movement of water that was so vital to the ecological functioning of the Zambezi basin ecosystems and hence to the livelihoods of valley residents (see fig. 5.1). The frequency, magnitude, and duration of annual flooding dramatically decreased relative to the predam period.[31] The dam greatly diminished rainy-season flooding during all but the wettest years and drastically increased dry-season flows. After 1974 the mean monthly flow

FIGURE 5.1. Mutarara bridge, 1935. *Landeg White*, Bridging the Zambezi *(cover)*

in the March rainy season dropped by 61 percent, while the minimum flow in the November dry season rose by an average of 243 percent—destroying the pronounced seasonal variations that had defined riverine farming systems for centuries. Overall, the mean monthly postdam flows declined dramatically from predam levels (see table 2.1).[32] Sediment deposition on the coastal shelf at the Zambezi River outlet to the Indian Ocean also substantially declined, as most sediment remained in the upstream reservoir, trapped there by the dam's walls.

Changes in the magnitude, timing, and duration of the river flow had profound ecological consequences. Whereas the Zambezi outflow had previously fed a number of channels, rivers, and lakes in the coastal delta region, and created high groundwater levels through seasonal runoff, after 1974 the river no longer regularly overflowed its banks during the rainy season. A Mozambican zoologist who had spent more than a decade working in Marromeu reported that "everywhere in the delta, rivers are drying up and lakes are shrinking" and that the Salone, Kunkwe, and Nhasau Rivers had vanished completely.[33] The lack of river water reduced the water table, requiring local communities to dig deeper wells. And the fertile alluvial plains shrank considerably, in some places disappearing altogether.[34]

To make matters worse, large surges of water from Cahora Bassa threatened the lower Zambezi valley anytime Pretoria's energy needs changed or the region experienced disruptive climatic events, such as torrential rains or cyclones.[35] The absence of an effective early-warning system compounded this danger. João Tesoura, a resident of Caia, on the west bank of the Zambezi, stressed that previously "we knew that the floods would come in the months of January, February, and March. Now the floods can come any time of the year and there can be more than one."[36] This unpredictability left his neighbors feeling helpless and vulnerable.[37]

The unpredictability of daily discharges from Cahora Bassa had equally adverse consequences. Even in the dry season, water levels frequently rose or fell several meters within the space of a few hours.[38] Maria Carvalho and her neighbors complained that "the runoffs never stop. Our fields can become soggy anytime of the year."[39] Milioni Lambani, an elder from Chemba, agreed that the smaller, ill-timed discharges were "constant and recurring."[40] Throughout the Zambezi valley, villagers described in painful detail how unseasonal releases harmed wetland vegetative growth and forced many of their friends and relatives to abandon valuable gardens on the river's edge.

Harnessing the Zambezi also altered the natural work of the river by severely diminishing the sediment content of the water flowing downstream. The dam trapped behind its walls rich organic and inorganic material that for centuries the river had carried downriver and deposited in the floodplains, where it provided the vital energy needed to support downstream aquatic ecosystems and human societies. In 1984 a team of United Nations scientists concluded that the dam's regulated flow regime was "catastrophic" for downstream wetlands, where vegetative growth and animal populations depended on annual flooding for nutrients. They attributed this dire situation to a lack of environmentally thoughtful planning by both the colonial and postcolonial states:

> It is clear that in the case of Cahora Bassa there was no serious attempt to ecologically optimize the dam prior to construction. . . . Furthermore, after [the] dam closure, proposals put forward by the ecological assessment team were not implemented and there has been no regular monitoring of the dam's downstream effects during its lifespan. As a result, Cahora Bassa has the dubious distinction of being the least studied and possibly least environmentally acceptable major dam project in Africa.[41]

Because the dam prevented most of the sediment from traveling downriver, the mineral-free waters sought to recapture their sediment load along the way by eroding the bed and banks of the river as well as a number of islands. Ironically, its erosive powers increased even though it now flowed at lower levels. Paulo Mayo, an elderly peasant, described the situation this way: "The river, as I see it, is really changing. In fact, it is changing very fast. It is growing in its width and it is losing more water most of the time."[42] Villagers throughout the valley told similar stories about this phenomenon, which scientists call "silt hunger."[43] It is worth noting, however, that the Zambezi, like all rivers, was naturally dynamic, with constant processes of erosion and deposition.[44] For example, before the construction of any of these dams, the coastal port of Chinde relocated twice because of the ever-changing nature of the Zambezi delta.[45]

Nevertheless, elders who had observed such changes over the previous three and a half decades provided a stinging narrative of how the dam was responsible for the Zambezi "getting bigger and bigger by eating up the river banks,"[46] and of their own powerlessness in the face of the landscape's transformation. Referring to the region of Chemba, on the southern margin of the river, Artur Medja and his neighbors recalled, "The irregular floods began after the construction of Cahora Bassa and that started the process of erosion on the islands and the banks of the river. Our fields suffered from erosion and the soils of the *mataka* [close to the river] were swept away by the floodwater, leaving only sand and gravel. As a result, the mataka was below the flood channels. We could no longer farm there."[47] Lambani added that "many families owned large trees but, after the dam, the water robbed the soil and rotted out the roots."[48] Ferreira Mangiricau and Bene Ngoca, who lived on the northern bank of the Zambezi near Mutarara, were also adamant about the harm the dam caused. After Cahora Bassa began operating, "the river swallowed the land on its banks, causing widespread erosion and increasing its width."[49] Peasants tried to prevent or slow the erosion by growing thick clusters of *maquengueres* (mangroves) as a barrier between it and their fields— the historic method of managing flood waters—but they could not contain the aggressive river, which washed away fertile soils and other vegetation in its path.[50] In the new environment created by Cahora Bassa, erosion increased, and local systems of knowledge proved wanting.

The low-lying islands dotting the river were particularly vulnerable to erosion.[51] Satellite photographs reveal that Inhangoma Island, for instance, lost several hundred hectares of extremely fertile land in less than a decade after the dam's construction.[52] Women, who spent much of their time fetching water and washing clothing at the river's edge, were acutely aware of erosion on the adjacent islands. Rita Lambique and her neighbors remembered that "when we were young there were many islands—most were ruined by the floods."[53] As Saluchepa Gelo stressed, "erosion intensified after 1980. Many islands disappeared during the period when we fled to Malawi [in 1984] because of the war. When we returned [in 1991], only the island of Nhantitiri remained."[54] According to Luís Manuel, "there were certain islands which disappeared entirely as a result of erosion from the river. Others, like José Ana, survived, but they were reduced by half."[55] That new islands sometimes emerged and some submerged islands resurfaced demonstrates the power of the harnessed river to radically alter nature.[56]

Photographs and aerial surveys graphically depict other significant changes in the geomorphology of the river valley system. Figure 5.1 shows the Zambezi River flowing freely under the pillars of the 3.7-kilometer Dona Ana railroad bridge in 1935, right after its construction.[57] When Cahora Bassa began operating, in 1975, little was visually different.[58] Two decades later, however, the reduced flows from Cahora Bassa had taken their toll, dramatically reducing wet-season flows, drying up floodplain wetlands, and narrowing the river. A photograph taken in 1996 reveals a Zambezi River limited to a few well-defined channels, with much of the floodplain desiccated and invaded by upland vegetation (see fig. 5.2).[59]

Graphic as these photographs are, they are just one example of the similar calamitous effects throughout the Zambezi basin. As satellite photographs taken in 1996 demonstrate, the geomorphology of the lower Zambezi—formerly a wide river system with "open mosaics of marsh, pond, oxbows and shallow wetlands"—had been converted to one with impoverished marshlands and "choked wetlands, tree and bulrush encroachment along the margins."[60] Without the seasonal floods to flush out vegetation and deposits of debris, many channels became clogged and stagnant.[61] Elias Januare, a fisherman who spent his entire life on the river, complained that the waterway had been strangled. "There are just too many plants that have invaded the river, unlike several years ago when the [river was clear]."[62] According to Carlos Bento, a

FIGURE 5.2. Mutarara bridge, 1996. *Richard Beilfuss*

Mozambican scientist who has been studying the Zambezi since the 1990s, invasive vegetation prevented canoemen from transporting rice and dried fish to the regional market at Marromeu.[63]

While it may be too anthropomorphic to ascribe agency to the Zambezi, it is quite clear that it continued to mediate human activity after the construction of Cahora Bassa—just in less predictable ways.[64] For instance, marked variations in erosive sculpting from one portion of the river to another left some channels substantially narrower and others wider; elsewhere, several active channels were reconfigured into one, while others disappeared altogether.[65] This realignment—combined with the emergence of new inlets, streams, and gullies and the drying up of other bodies of water—made many areas of the river more difficult for fishermen to navigate.[66] Several elders also insisted that changes in the magnitude and timing of floods destroyed numerous plants that had thrived in the predam period, providing nutrition for fish, wildlife, and livestock and medicine and food for riverine households.[67] João Raposo of Caia reported that plants, such as water lily roots, water lily bulbs, and wild mushrooms, which used to grow around Caia, could only now be found in "a place called Ngua, very far from here."[68] Across the river at Inhangoma, Armando Navalha and António Sona recalled that, after the dam's completion, "all the trees and plants were ravaged, even the big ones which we cut to make canoes."[69] For Zhili Malenje and his neighbors, the dam's most immediate effect was that vast tracts of reeds were washed away: "Places where reeds used to grow are now occupied by water . . . [and] we are unable to find material to thatch our roofs."[70] In ways such as these, the dam was transforming both the physical and social landscapes of the river.

Oral and documentary sources also highlight the pernicious impact of Cahora Bassa on fish populations in the lower Zambezi valley, caused by the river's changing flow patterns and geomorphology. More than forty species of fish in the river system before the dam's completion depended on the seasonal inundation of the floodplain, which created large stretches of warm shallow water rich in nutritious plant and insect foods and thick with protective vegetation that fish used for their reproduction and survival.[71] Because the spawning and feeding cycles of Zambezi fish populations correlated closely with the timing of the annual floods, interference with flooding necessarily had serious consequences for aquatic ecosystems. In fact, as early as 1983 scientists reported that early flooding had irretrievably interrupted the breeding cycle of many fish species in the river.[72] Local fishermen agreed that flooding outside the rainy season caused a number of species to disappear and the size and quantity of those remaining to decline drastically—because the river stopped providing adequate nourishment during the rainy season and regularly washed away fish eggs when discharges occurred at other times of the year.[73] They also explained that new species of aquatic plants that spread across the surface of some key areas of the river and estuaries deprived fish of critical oxygen.[74] Additionally, some downriver residents asserted that the dam's turbines "eat many of the biggest fish"[75]—an explanation different in detail from what was offered by Western researchers, but similar in essence to the finding that the dam's walls created a barrier that cut off the migratory patterns of fish moving downstream.[76] Moreover, the reservoir was not conducive to the perpetuation of some fish species accustomed to a riverine environment.[77]

Irregular flooding patterns, erosion, and vegetation changes similarly disrupted the breeding cycles of bird species, including the endangered wattled crane, and drove others from the region. For wattled cranes, for example, breeding is "triggered by the annual inundations and draw-downs of floodwaters. Breeding is often timed to coincide with receding water conditions, so that young chicks can feed on the explosion of fish and invertebrate life across the floodplain."[78] Because cranes feed on flood vegetation (primarily underground tubers of the spikerush, *Eleocharis*) produced only under natural flood cycles, radical changes in flood patterns rendered much of the delta uninhabitable for them.[79] Villagers reflecting on the sharp decline in local bird populations also emphasized river-related causes:

> The number of birds that come to the river has diminished. Before there were many and now there are few. . . . There are three types of aquatic birds that now rarely appear—*ngoti, dsiwe-dsiwe,* and *ntesco.* Vwe-vwe [geese] disappeared due to shortages of fish, which were their main source of food. Ducks are also very rare now. They left because they were unable to catch small fish called ntsembo and because of the decline of plants like *nenufar* [lotus] and *nhica* [water lily root]. . . . Wattled cranes have also vanished.[80]

Local elders attributed the bird decline to the disappearance of islands, which once offered friendly habitats for birds, and river gardens, where birds once fed on sweet potatoes and other crops.[81] Now, according to Aniva João, "birds do not have the opportunity to eat the remains from the harvest and as a result they migrated from here in search of nhica."[82]

The reduction in seasonal flooding and the diminished nutrient content of the river below the dam caused marked biophysical changes to the entire ecosystem—such as increased salinization of wetland soils and reduced soil fertility. All this made the Zambezi basin, especially the biologically diverse delta, much less hospitable to wildlife, whose numbers were further reduced by the increasingly dense human settlements in the riverine zone. As Marita Zhuwao sadly recounted, "the kinds of animals that were [seen] were kudu, gazelles, eland, and warthogs. Nowadays we don't see these animals."[83] Many villagers believed that uncertain flow patterns discouraged animals from "coming to the river to look for water,"[84] but they tended to disregard the negative impact of increased human settlement on wildlife migration patterns.

The desiccation of the wetlands also left the once forbidding landscape more accessible to human predators, as areas once inundated for nine months of the year could now be traversed on foot year-round. From the mid-1970s through the early 1990s, elephant poachers, illegal commercial hunters, Renamo fighters, and government troops decimated herds of elephants and other large game, whose numbers had already been reduced by dam-induced ecosystem changes.[85] While some species have recovered since the hostilities ceased, in 1992, the corruption of floodplains and the exploding human population in their key habitats, together with the extensive bushmeat trade and the clearing of riverine woodlands for charcoal, firewood, and building materials, will likely prevent wildlife communities from ever returning to prewar levels.

The increased salinization of wetland soils is part of a wider process of environmental change that scientists believe will result in a less diverse and less productive ecosystem in the Zambezi delta. Before the construction of Cahora Bassa, Zambezi flood flows maintained a relative balance between riverine freshwater and tidal saltwater in the delta; every rainy season, flood-waters flushed accumulated salt from the coastal floodplains, ensuring the survival of freshwater grasslands on which many wildlife species regularly fed. With the shift to less frequent and smaller water surges in the postdam era, the region became much drier and salt was no longer fully flushed from the landscape—sharply reducing wetlands and open water areas and correspondingly increasing the quantity of salty and stagnant water. The salinization of floodplain topsoils has caused the freshwater grasslands of the delta to be displaced by more salt-tolerant grass species that thrive in brackish environments. In the long run, these new grasses will likely have significant implications for floodplain wildlife, since they are "unpalatable to grazing species and over time may reduce the carrying capacity of the floodplain."[86]

Reduced river flows and drier conditions have, in turn, sharply increased the frequency and magnitude of floodplain grassland fires. Controlled burnings, which historically were an essential part of the local agricultural cycle, have become harder to manage because of the drier conditions in the delta, which researchers attribute to the impact of the dam: "Currently about 95% of the delta burns during the dry season, including vast areas during the early dry season, sparing only the permanently inundated floodplains and water-ways with papyrus swamps. . . . . These patterns of increasing fire are almost certainly due to the drying of floodplain, because rainfall alone in the delta region is insufficient to cause prolonged flooding that might reduce the extent and intensity of floodplain fires."[87]

While the ultimate ecological consequences of dam-induced changes on riparian forest cover remain unknown, the related social and economic costs for local communities are already obvious. This is because trees are a vital source of fuel and construction materials for the communities of the lower Zambezi valley, and forests contain wild fruits, roots, and tubers that are a critical part of local diets (see chapter 2).[88]

The substantial reduction in the volume of sediments transported to the mouth of the Zambezi has also impacted the estuary, hampering the river's important delta-building function[89] and threatening the health of shrimp populations and coastal mangrove ecosystems.[90] As silt deposition rates have declined, the estuary and natural vegetation on the coastline have been subjected to greatly increased wind and sea erosion. Although the full effects of this process are still unknown, it has undermined estuarine fisheries that depend on the annual flooding cycle for nutrient and sediment deposits.[91] The Sofala banks, for instance, is a broad and shallow shelf just outside the mouth of the Zambezi that, in predam times, was the center of a productive shrimp fishery—one of Mozambique's most important sources of foreign currency. Shrimp depend on regular, annual floods to transport them from their brackish mangrove nurseries to the open sea, where offshore commercial fisheries are able to harvest them in abundance.[92] Since the early 1980s, however, catches of the two most important shrimp species (*Fenneropenaeus indicus* and *Metapenaeus monoceros*) have fallen substantially, due to the altered seasonal pattern of runoff and the reduction in wet-season water flows. One study estimated that the catch rate declined by 60 percent between 1978 and 1998, with an annual income loss of $10 million to $30 million.[93]

Cahora Bassa may even be significantly contributing to global warming. There is no consensus among scientists studying greenhouse gases produced by dam reservoirs, but recent research at more than thirty dam sites around the world suggests that reservoirs are a significant source not only of carbon dioxide but also of methane, a much more potent greenhouse gas, which is produced by bacteria living at many of their bottoms.[94] Although emission levels vary substantially from one reservoir to another—depending on its depth and shape, local climatic conditions, aquatic plant growth, and exposure to sunlight—preliminary evidence suggests that tropical reservoirs may be especially environmentally dangerous. In fact, in 2007, Brazilian researchers estimated that methane from dams was responsible for nearly 5 percent of human-caused global warming.[95]

That both Cahora Bassa and Kariba are located in active seismic zones is also of concern to environmentalists. While the region has experienced tremors with some frequency in the recent past, the fragmentary historical record makes it impossible to predict the likelihood of future occurrences. Obviously, however, earthquake-precipitated damage to the walls of either dam could threaten the lives of countless people and wildlife downstream.[96]

Although much remains unknown, the available evidence overwhelmingly demonstrates that Cahora Bassa's construction and operation have substantially contributed to the development of a less diverse, less productive, and less sustainable freshwater ecosystem in the lower Zambezi valley.[97] Professor Davies, who participated in the environmental impact assessment for the Cahora Bassa dam in the early 1970s, revisited the lower Zambezi basin two decades later and concluded that it "has been abused to a degree that has, fortunately, few parallels anywhere else in the world."[98] In a dismal report submitted to the WCD at the turn of this century, Davies was even more pessimistic: "The changes wrought by the dam are far worse than I ever imagined," due to "the gross mismanagement of floods and low-flows in the river."[99] In short, the organic machine unleashed a massive assault on the region's biophysical systems, which, tragically, has been matched by, and inextricably linked to, the dam's devastating impact on human society.

COMMUNITIES AND LIVELIHOODS UNDER SIEGE: THE ECONOMIC AND SOCIAL CONSEQUENCES OF CAHORA BASSA

Cahora Bassa not only changed the Zambezi forever, but it also affected the lives of every individual—male and female, old and young, peasant and fisherman—who lived adjacent to the harnessed waters. Its consequences, which continue unabated, were catastrophic for over half a million people who depended on the river for their livelihoods. For most valley dwellers, the dam remains a distant and incomprehensible structure that is tampering with their river and causing tremendous havoc.

As described in chapter 2, flood recession agriculture and fishing had provided the basics of life for residents of the lower Zambezi valley for centuries. From the moment the dam's two steel gates blocked the free flow of the river, both activities were jeopardized. In this way, the hydroelectric project radically altered livelihood strategies, endangered food security, and transformed residential patterns downriver.

Changes in the Zambezi's flow patterns had an immediately disruptive impact on the agricultural practices of valley residents. The sharp reduction in the volume of the floods and the deepening river channels combined to reduce the quantity of water that overflowed its banks, diminishing the area that was regularly inundated (see fig. 5.3). Near the coast, the reduced volume and reach of the river were also insufficient to flush alluvial soils clean of ocean salt, leaving fields near its banks increasingly salinized, less productive,

FIGURE 5.3. Contemporary riverine garden. *David Morton*

and harder to farm. In some lowland areas, because discharges from the dam occurred throughout the year, the water had no chance to recede, which created new wetlands that could no longer be cultivated.[100] For those who continued to farm on the river's edge or on low-lying islands, unpredictable discharges from the dam could wash away seeds, rot crops, and devastate entire gardens.[101] Maria Faifi expressed the widespread view that "people are not happy with Cahora Bassa. How can we be happy, since all our maize fields are eaten away?"[102] Throughout the valley, women and men described the feeling of dangerous uncertainty that was now part of daily life.[103] According to Zhuwa Valera, "Sometimes our gardens are washed away unexpectedly. You may have them one year but in another year you lose them. . . . People are really suffering."[104]

Under these precarious conditions, it is not surprising that families often concluded that cultivating floodplain and island plots was not worth the risk. N'tsai António explained that many in his village at Chetcha were "no longer willing to plant near the river because the water . . . destroys the young crops."[105] Cheia Amado of Caia put it bluntly: "Because of the uncertain floods we had no choice but to leave all the fertile lands near the river."[106] Across the Zambezi, on the northern bank, villagers offered similar accounts of frustrated neighbors "who ran away . . . because of the floods."[107] In Marromeu and Luabo, it was the salinization of alluvial soils that ultimately forced them to give up their fields.[108] Changing flow patterns also made island farming untenable. Families cultivating island gardens had to abandon them when flow changes caused entire islands to disappear.[109] In other cases, while the islands remained, the gardens were destroyed by the dam's discharges. Milioni Lambani remembered that "many people had gardens on the islands near Chiramba, but as a result of the 1978 flood they were forced to abandon their plots. Only one person remained."[110]

In some areas, alluvial farming effectively collapsed. Less then four years after the completion of the dam, a government survey contrasted the absence "of river bed cultivation on the banks of the Zambezi [near Tete]" with the vibrant agricultural activity on the adjacent margins of the free-flowing Ribue.[111] To the south, at Mopeia, much of the land formerly used for a double crop of rice was also evacuated, causing rice production to drop substantially.[112]

Households that made the difficult decision to abandon floodplain, island, and wetland sites that were no longer viable for agriculture found the alternatives no better. Relocating upland and depending entirely on rain-fed fields simply substituted the vagaries of nature for the vagaries of the dam. Those on higher ground escaped the floods but were helpless in the event of drought, and the shortness and unpredictability of the rains limited their farming season. Nor could planting multiple fields in different microecological zones compensate for a lack of rainfall in bad years or the fact that upland soils were less fertile and harder to work than those near the river. Low precipitation, recurring droughts, and a lack of critical staples—such as the sweet potatoes they had cultivated in floodplain gardens—meant that upland agriculturalists with no floodplain plots faced the prospect of recurring food shortages.[113]

With the specter of hunger and even starvation ever present, rural households attempted, as best they could, to anticipate and fend off food crises.

Having lost their riverine gardens, they had a limited repertoire of strategies at their disposal to cope with food insecurity. Some women, for instance, planted more sweet potatoes, which households had relied on during difficult periods in the past. Unfortunately, because sweet potatoes grew best in the floodplain gardens that could be ruined by periodic discharges from Cahora Bassa, this was not always a viable option.[114] Other households turned to manioc (cassava), which could grow on marginal lands and was drought and pest resistant.[115] According to several villagers in Chetcha, manioc "production jumped substantially after independence [1975] in response to the increased famines, and because we could use it to make porridge and even bread."[116] Manioc, however, had serious drawbacks. While high in caloric value, it was a poor source of vitamins and proteins, and the intensive processing required to remove the poisonous hydrocyanic acid increased the labor demands on already overworked rural women (see fig. 5.4). Another common strategy—increasing the proportion of early-maturing maize in their cereal crop mix—actually heightened households' vulnerability to food shortages, since maize was much less drought and weed resistant than sorghum and millet. To overcome such disadvantages, households resorted to increased intercropping and shortened the fallow periods for their rain-fed fields.[117]

Because such coping mechanisms were often insufficient, especially during periods of serious drought, women and older children relied on wild foods growing along the Zambezi riverbed.[118] Foraging for edible roots, tubers, river plants, and berries was particularly common for hard-pressed families,

FIGURE 5.4. Women pounding maize. *Mauro Pinto*

although, due to erosion and the dam's discharges, there were now fewer fruits and edible plants, forcing women desperate to feed their families to travel long distances to find them in sufficient quantity.[119] As in the past, nyika was the most important of the foraged wild foods. Dried, pounded, and mixed with manioc flour to make a porridge, the wild lily roots could alleviate hunger — but, like manioc, had little nutritional value. Relying on nyika as a staple also posed serious health risks, particularly for undernourished babies and young children, since it could cause distended stomachs, serious cramps and diarrhea, and sometimes even death.[120] Alberto Chirembue remembered a time, in the late 1980s, "when many babies [fed nyika] had died."[121] Adults also suffered from these ailments, although less acutely.[122]

Despite the risks involved in continuing to invest scarce capital and pre-cious time in alluvial fields that could be flooded at any moment, some stubbornly refused to abandon them. They did so with the knowledge that, in the postdam era, planting near the river was a high-stakes gamble. In the drought-prone area of Chirodzi-Sanangwe, sixty-five kilometers below Cahora Bassa, for example, twenty-five years after the dam's construction one-third of the households still cultivated fields in the risky floodplains.[123] At the beginning of each agricultural cycle, they planted their seeds, which, in most years, the floods washed away. In 2008 they had not had a successful crop in more than a decade. Magamezo Tionequi hoped for a change of luck but was resigned to the harsh reality: "We seeded and planted as usual and harvested some crops, but because of the flooding we did not get nearly as much production as before Cahora Bassa was built."[124] Downriver, in Caia, João Raposo stressed that he had no alternative but to keep farming where he was, despite the obvi-ous dangers: "We continued to plant a substantial amount of sorghum, maize, beans, and onions. Now when we grow our beans and onions, the water rots out the roots and even our maize suffers."[125] Throughout the lower Zambezi valley, peasants have become bitterly reconciled to a reality in which all too often the unpredictable river sweeps away much of their crop, leaving them with little or nothing to show for their labor.[126] As Caetano Figuerido and his fellow villagers in Inhangoma complained, the water came when it pleased and "destroyed our fields on the banks of the river."[127] António Djase put this reality in historical context: "In the past, the Zambezi gave us wealth. Now it makes us poor. The waters destroy all our crops."[128]

Agriculturalists in the delta pursued a different but equally precarious option. Here, thousands of households actually moved from the predam shoreline deeper into the floodplain in search of fertile land. Perhaps trusting the claims of dam managers and state officials that Cahora Bassa provided an effective form of flood control, they believed that the ending of seasonal floods made it possible to farm safely on the moist alluvial soils. Relocating in this direction, however, placed them directly in the path of previous floods, and, when, after unseasonably heavy rains, Cahora Bassa failed to contain the surging waters, thousands of delta residents found themselves in harm's way. In 1978, 1989, 1997, 2001, and 2007 raging water destroyed their homes, inundated their fields, forced thousands to flee, and created massive food shortages. Faced with this uncertain reality, in some parts of the delta women left their homesteads to explore distant lowlands and islands on which they could still farm. Thereafter, they spent a week or two at a time working in these gardens and living in improvised shelters away from their families.[129]

Indeed, whether valley peasants found themselves displaced suddenly by the violence of a Zambezi flood or more slowly by the gradual abandonment or disappearance of alluvial plots, transformed river flow patterns profoundly disrupted rural food security. Although dam-induced food crises have only recently begun to receive serious attention, a GPZ report published in 2000 documented the growing inability of local communities to sustain themselves.[130] Anthropometric data collected in 2003—showing that almost 10 percent of the population of Tete District suffered from acute malnutrition[131]—confirmed an earlier finding that "food crop production in Tete is usually insufficient to meet households needs."[132] The situation was equally precarious in the delta, where unpredictable floods caused many to lose their crops, forcing them to rely on food aid programs.[133] Throughout the lower Zambezi valley, only those with access to the most fertile land and sufficient labor could produce enough food to meet their needs.

While villagers did not articulate that their food security had been compromised by the HCB and held captive to South African energy needs, everyone interviewed attributed the destruction of their food self-sufficiency to Cahora Bassa. Maria Faifi put it bluntly: "Cahora Bassa has given us hunger."[134] Mário Chambiça and his neighbors explained that "because the irregular discharges rot our gardens, there is not sufficient food for people to feed themselves."[135] Luís Manuel echoed this view: "Hunger became much more common after the construction of Cahora Bassa. There was never a month when discharges did not provoke some unexpected flooding and misery."[136] Many villagers stressed that even in the darkest days of the colonial forced cotton regime, "the hunger was not as acute as it is now."[137] Notwithstanding the tendency to romanticize the time before the Zambezi's impoundment, elders' detailed contrasts of predam and postdam agricultural practices and livelihood systems clearly demonstrated that Cahora Bassa left them in precarious circumstances.

Peasant households throughout the Zambezi valley worked longer and harder to produce less food after Cahora Bassa began operation, but it was women who bore the brunt of the added labor burden—since they remained primarily responsible for farming, foraging, and the social reproduction of the household—and who suffered most during periods of food scarcity.[138] Because of the decreased dam-induced flows, rural women had to travel much further to find the water they then transported back to the village in twenty-five-liter drums balanced on their heads.[139] Additionally, after Cahora Bassa, it took more time and energy for them to process and pound manioc and nyika, which were more labor intensive than the corn or sorghum that had previously served as the basis of their diets. Heightened food insecurity also led many men and older boys to leave their villages to work on the surrounding plantations and in Beira, further intensifying the labor demands on women.[140] There is no specific data on the gendered nutritional effects of Cahora Bassa, but preliminary findings published in 2002 demonstrate that in Tete, at least, rising malnutrition among women was linked to increased risks of miscarriages and stillbirths.[141] Although maternal malnutrition has many likely causes, the ongoing food shortages in this area since 1975 suggest that the dam was at least a contributing factor. In the context of displacement and acute poverty, the negative impacts of environmental changes on the well-being of women and children were particularly acute.

Between 1977 and 1992 the brutal conflict between Frelimo and Renamo compounded the dam-induced agricultural crisis in the lower Zambezi valley, especially as civilians became the principal targets of Renamo violence after 1980. Peasants, worried about traveling along paths strewn with land mines and afraid of being attacked while cultivating, stopped going to their fields.[142] "How could we farm while the war was raging around us?" asked Christopher Dozy incredulously.[143] For those who did not give up, the war compounded the already daunting production challenges created by Cahora Bassa: "To avoid the land mines, [we] farmed in the nonfertile sandy soils. It is much safer, but the yields are much lower."[144] Ultimately, many abandoned their fields entirely and sought haven in crowded refugee camps in Malawi.

Harnessing the Zambezi for the hydroelectric project also undermined food security for valley residents by causing a sharp reduction in the fish population downriver. As detailed in chapter 2, the Zambezi and its adjoining lakes, rivulets, and estuaries had previously contained a rich and varied bounty of fish, and fishing had been an important economic activity. Impounding the river impaired fish reproduction and resulted in a marked decline in the growth and survival of younger fish. As valley residents unanimously testified, "when there was little water in the river, the fish were fewer and much smaller."[145] Some fishermen maintained that the irregular floods further inhibited fish reproduction, because the eggs could be washed away at any time, while others attributed the decline to increased vegetation in the river.[146] Most were also adamant that the turbines and gates at Cahora Bassa blocked bigger fish from passing through the gates, causing several species to disappear.[147]

Four other dam-precipitated changes contributed to a substantial reduction in both the absolute number of fish in the river and the size of the catches. First, many of the richest fishing grounds were located on the edges of islands and adjacent sand bars that were submerged after Cahora Bassa began operation. Because fishermen had also used these islands as temporary fishing camps, their disappearance, by making it harder to troll regions far from home, reduced the area they could fish. Second, the high and strong dry-season flows, compared to the low-flow conditions historically, made indigenous technology, particularly fishing baskets, less effective (see fig. 5.5).[148]

The third cause of declining fish stock was overfishing. Shrinking recession agriculture forced many men to turn to fishing, causing a sharp jump in the numbers competing for fewer fish. This problem became more acute when, after Renamo laid down its arms, unemployed youth and returning refugees also started fishing.[149] In the aftermath of Mozambique's neoliberal market reforms, in the late 1980s, and privatization of large segments of the economy, truckers from Quelimane, Beira, and Maputo poured into the Zambezi in search of fish for urban markets. The spike in fish prices and the increased availability of basic consumer goods were powerful inducements to those who had few other cash-earning opportunities.[150]

A fourth, more significant, factor was the speed with which fishermen—desperate to maximize their catches in the face of fierce competition—adopted higher yielding, but unsustainable, harvesting methods.[151] They did so by replacing the coarse, locally produced fiber nets used in the past with imported finer-mesh, machine-made gill nets whose openings were less than half as

FIGURE 5.5. Men with fishing weirs. *Mauro Pinto*

wide.[152] Aniva João described why the new "mosquito" nets quickly became so popular: "The mosquito net's openings were very fine. Two fishermen entered the water, each holding one end of the net. When they placed the net below the surface, it was like putting on a *capulana* [a cloth worn by African men and women]. It covered everything. Nothing could escape. In a few hours they could fill several sacks."[153] Fishermen began to use this finer material for their larger kokota nets, which enabled them both to enclose an area of several hundred meters and to ensnarl very young fish,[154] thus depleting future populations. While such innovations enabled fishermen to increase their daily haul and their profits, they violated a long-standing cultural prohibition against overfishing. As Marita Zhuwao explained, "In the past, if one continued to fish even after one caught sufficient fish for one's family, the spirits [of the river] would get angry. Then, if one threw in the nets to catch more fish, maybe one would catch a dead baby, or some other bad omen."[155] The spirits were right. Capturing many more younger and smaller fish had a devastating effect on the reproductive capacity of numerous of species in the lower Zambezi.[156] Many areas quickly showed signs of being overfished, and yields fell even further.

While no catch statistics exist for the region as a whole, available evidence points conclusively to a radical decline in freshwater fisheries after 1975. Before the Zambezi's impoundment, the annual total catch in the delta was calculated at between thirty and fifty thousand tonnes per year; less than a decade after the dam's completion it had dropped by 25 to 50 percent.[157] The number of fishing camps and drying racks also plummeted.[158] In Marromeu, which had been a commercial fishing center, less than 20 percent of the households were engaged in this activity in 2000,[159] and many delta fisheries were abandoned, except during years of exceptional flooding.[160] Moreover, the dramatic decline in the delta's shrimp population further impoverished both local fishing families and Mozambique's major export sector.

Fishermen insist that, since Cahora Bassa began operation, they have worked longer and harder for a smaller catch. "These days," noted Artur Medja, "it is difficult to catch any fish and those that we do are very small."[161] In the formerly rich fishing area of Inhangoma, Francisco Manuel and his neighbors complained that their "nets were practically useless,"[162] and their wives mourned the old days, when "there was a lot of fish and people were catching handsomely, unlike nowadays."[163] No one summed up this shared sense of despair more powerfully than Chidasiyikwa Mavungire, who had spent his entire life fishing: "There are very few fish in the river, and it is no longer like before."[164]

For those men who persisted, however, fishing was increasingly dangerous, due to the explosion of hippopotamus and crocodile populations downriver.[165] Cheia Amado underscored the threat posed by crocodiles and his neighbors' general unwillingness to return to the river: "The number of fishermen has diminished substantially. Now they are a minority. No sooner do they put their canoes into the water than they are attacked by crocodiles."[166] Pita Araújo echoed this sense of peril: "In earlier times, fishermen could go five or six years without being attacked[.] Now five or six days rarely pass without [an attack]."[167]

While the dam affected hunting much less severely than fishing, there were significant consequences for both wildlife and human populations. As the delta dried out, so did the landscape of the Marromeu Buffalo Reserve—creating an opportunity for Renamo and government soldiers, along with European and African poachers—all armed with automatic weapons—to slaughter large herds of African buffalo, waterbuck, reedbuck, zebras, and other game that had been an important source of protein for rural communities.[168] Upriver, much of the small game that local men had trapped or hunted with spears and poisoned arrows disappeared after the completion of Cahora Bassa. While the war was certainly a contributing factor, the dried up streams and rivulets, caused by the Zambezi's impoundment, no longer attracted warthogs, hares, bushbuck, and other antelopes. As Chidasiyikwa Mavungire sadly put it, "all the game has deserted this place."[169] Villagers who set up snares and gin traps around the remaining water holes inadvertently contributed to the process of wildlife depletion, as did competition between humans and animals for the smaller areas of moist land. In fact, those who cleared land to build settlements near remaining waterways forced many animals to flee to more remote upland regions.[170]

To increase their protein intake in the absence of traditional meat options, delta residents began hunting small antelopes, warthogs, and even the giant cane rats that lived in the nearby bush. That they consumed these rodents, even though they were considered an inferior form of meat, is yet another mark of the vulnerability of rural communities.[171] Weighing between three and five kilograms, one of these rodents could feed a family for several days, if carefully cooked and rationed.[172]

The vicious circle common to all agrarian populations in crisis—food shortages contribute to illness, which reduces productivity and exacerbates food insecurity—occurred in the delta as well. Shortages of nutritious food both intensified demands on household labor and weakened human immune systems, exposing rural families to illness, even as changes in the river's ecosystem heightened the incidence of water-borne diseases. Despite the lack of sustained research on water-borne diseases in the postdam period, some villagers reported that the river became turbid and smelly after Cahora Bassa's completion.[173] Stagnant waterways used for bathing, laundry, and drinking were potent breeding grounds for disease and, combined with malnutrition, left many people vulnerable to diarrhea and cholera.[174] Watson Thamanda put it graphically: "My bowels opened from drinking the water from the river. They call it cholera."[175] According to a report compiled by Davies for the

WCD in 2000, cholera remained an acute problem in the riverine zone.[176] Risks from cholera were especially high during periods of heavy flooding.

Cholera was not the only disease that may have been associated with the river's impoundment. While malaria was common in the lower Zambezi valley even before the dam, changes in the flow regime ended the annual purging of stagnant water bodies and encouraged the formation of permanent pools on the shorelines, which became fertile breeding grounds for mosquitoes, and many villagers stressed its recent upswing.[177] Few used mosquito netting, and families living near stagnant water sources were easy prey. "To protect my children from mosquitoes," Maria Luisa told British health workers, "[I was] forced to lay all of them under the same bed, as I only had one mosquito net."[178]

Others complained that the river brought an increase in schistosomiasis.[179] This would hardly be surprising, since the snails carrying schistosomiasis prefer to live in still backwaters, usually near rooted vegetation.[180] The stagnant, grassy shoreline offered a fertile home to the parasite, and bathers provided an easy target.

The Zambezi's changing flow, which may have caused a spike in cholera, malaria, and schistosomiasis, also undermined rural health by washing away various medicinal plants used by herbal healers to treat a wide range of ailments.[181] Herbalists stressed that the altered flow pattern jeopardized the growth of medicinal plants necessary to ensure their patients' well being.[182] As Balança Casado explained, "In those areas where we previously procured many of our plants, they no longer appear. The recurring discharges, followed by the rapid retreat of the water, could not sustain them. Plants grow well when they have water. Because of the frequency of the small floods, other plants never fully mature. They rot because there are always floods."[183] In an effort to maintain their disappearing stock, herbalists Guente Escafa, Henriqueta Cascas, and Emília Joni searched year-round to recover whatever plants survived along the shoreline and traveled to remote mountainous areas seeking other remedies.[184] Although the long-term consequences of the loss of these life-sustaining plants are unknown, their absence clearly weakened the indigenous healthcare system.

The Zambezi's impoundment inflicted further damage on the physical and cultural world of riparian communities by inundating sacred shrines, burial grounds, and family graves. Most of these sites were located in the lake region, but Tawara and Tonga settlements immediately below the dam also lost sacred places when Cahora Bassa failed to prevent large-scale flooding (see chapter 4). Elders believed that because they were no longer able to propitiate the dead, they had alienated both their family ancestors (midzimu) and the royal ancestor spirits (mhondoro), thereby losing divine protection from drought, flooding, famine, disease, and Renamo.[185] Others attributed this lack of connection to the ancestors to Frelimo's policy of removing or marginalizing traditional leaders who, villagers believed, had the power to invoke the protection of the mid-zimu.[186] The decline, since the late 1970s, of rain-calling, first-fruits, and fishing ceremonies—all closely linked with historic Zambezi flow patterns—has also generated profound feelings of spiritual vulnerability and loss, especially among older villagers. It is not entirely clear, however, whether failure to conduct these ceremonies on the same scale or with the same regularity as in the past[187] was due primarily to the dam or indirectly to the social upheavals of the war with Renamo and increased conversions to Christianity,[188] most of which took place in refugee camps in Malawi. Veka Fero bemoaned that "nowadays [propitiating the ancestors] no longer happens, which is why we no longer get good rains or good crops."[189] António Ioha came to a similar conclusion about the diminished spiritual authority of the ancestors: "There was a certain place at [Marromeu] called Poska, where many canoemen drowned. To avoid this fate, [people previously sprinkled] libations into the water as an offering to the ancestor spirits. Today this is not happening."[190] A villager in Ralumbi, near Sena, confirmed that the power of the midzimu had become suspect: "In the past, before women went in work parties to catch fish, the chief and the elders would ask permission of the spirits to allow the women to enter the water and to protect them. For the past fourteen years, that is not happening. Everything of the old is falling."[191] Fajita Bemuse declared simply that "the spirits are things of the past."[192] Such sentiments would appear to reflect the combined impacts from the changes in the river and the dislocations of the war.[193]

It is revealing that, in communities where people continued to propitiate the ancestors to bring rain and ensure the fertility of the land, they never implored ancestor spirits to prevent the irregular discharges that were wreaking such havoc on local ecosystems and livelihoods. When we inquired why, villagers responded that "there are no ceremonies to protect against [these] floods; since the floods are provoked by the dam, they are caused by men."[194] Local people, in other words, understood that while the midzimu might have the power to bring rain, it was the engineers and the managers of Cahora Bassa who controlled the Zambezi and were responsible for the its catastrophic transformation. Elders in the delta distinguished between flooding from *madzi a mulungu* (god's waters) and *madzi a ku fungulu* (unnatural discharges from Cahora Bassa's dam).[195] Others blamed such flooding on the work of witches.[196] Whatever the explanation, for peasants living along the margins of the Zambezi, their world was torn asunder.

THE FAILURE OF FLOOD CONTROL

It is one of the great ironies of Cahora Bassa that flood control, heralded as an important benefit to Zambezi valley residents, failed to materialize. Proponents of the dam had touted mitigation of downstream flooding as one of the project's greatest advantages.[197] Yet, despite more than fifty years of river regulation dating back to Kariba, massive flooding remains a perilous problem along the Zambezi River. In fact, rather than eliminating floods, as the colonial authorities and civil engineers who built the dam had promised, discharges from Cahora Bassa have periodically unleashed torrential waters on downriver landscapes and human populations.

During periods of heavy rainfall, sometimes accompanied by cyclones, upriver dams, especially Kariba, had to discharge vast amounts of water to lower the level of their reservoirs. This fast-moving water cascading down the river, in turn, forced engineers at Cahora Bassa to do the same. The results downriver were predictable—larger and more catastrophic flooding than would have naturally occurred. Thus, rather than controlling floods, Cahora Bassa often exacerbated the rainy-season problems and caused greater misery, loss of property, and loss of life. As Paulo Milo, an elder from Mutarara, recounted nostalgically, "during the time we were young, the river used to flood only once a year, but today the floods are very disastrous. They are more disastrous than during the old times. Nowadays when the river floods, it reaches out very far, even to where people live. Of course, during our time, the floods could also destroy our crops and other property, but they were not as vicious as the ones we experience nowadays."[198]

In addition to the catastrophic flooding provoked by both heavy rainfall and emergency discharges from Cahora Bassa, the dam caused other flooding outside the rainy season in order to meet South Africa's energy needs. Paulo Milo spoke of this as well. What he and others seemed to sense, even if they did not articulate it openly, was that floods "nowadays" were not natural disasters caused by unusually high tropical rainfalls or cyclones. Instead, they were the result of decisions by those who built, and now control, the dam to use it to maximize hydroelectric power rather than for flood control or other downstream benefits—a political, as well as economic, calculation.

The notion that a dam optimize both flood control and hydropower generation ignores the fact that these two objectives are fundamentally incompatible. Cahora Bassa was not built to control large floods, and the reservoir's storage capacity was simply inadequate to contain huge runoffs.[199] As Beilfuss explains, "What is known about large floods is that, despite a century of river regulation and flood protection works, they are a fact of life in the Zambezi system. Cahora Bassa and Kariba Reservoirs may operate to eliminate most small- and medium-sized floods, but they do not have sufficient storage capacity to stop the great floods that periodically move through the Zambezi system, as occurred in 2001."[200] Ineffective communication between Cahora Bassa and Kariba, until recently, further increased the likelihood that large floods would be disastrous for downriver communities.[201]

Less than three years after the completion of Cahora Bassa (in 1975), a devastating flood in the lower Zambezi left forty-five people dead, ninety thousand homeless, and sixty thousand hectares of food crops destroyed.[202] Material damages surpassed $60 million. Local elders named this catastrophe Cheia Madeya—"the flood that forced us to join communal villages."[203] After the devastation, many peasants did not want to move from the fertile alluvial lands to sites they knew would be less productive. In a report from Inhangoma, one Frelimo official acknowledged, "The people's choice is the one of living on the island and not in communal villages. They were informed they would leave the island for higher areas, but their experience tells them that on the island they always have had foodstuffs, while away from it the land is not productive enough. They say they thank the Government for the help it gave to them but insist on remaining on the island."[204] For others, opposition to relocation to communal villages rested on traumatic memories from the past. According to another government official, "the people in Inhangoma . . . are not mobilized [to join the communal villages] because they consider them as new *aldeamentos* where they will carry on enduring exploitation."[205] Despite such vocal opposition, victims of the flood resettled in newly formed communal villages upland from Mutarara and Inhangoma.[206]

Tragically, the death and destruction might have been less had there been better communication about the impending release of floodwaters between dam operators at Kariba and Cahora Bassa and between Cahora Bassa managers and downstream officials. Dam engineers at Cahora Bassa did not receive sufficient notice from Kariba that it was sending abnormally large amounts of water downriver to properly prepare their own response. Similarly, when they opened all eight sluice gates and the emergency spill gates to alleviate pressure on Cahora Bassa's walls, they failed to alert downriver communities of the impending flood. The damage and human suffering caused by these acts stand in stark contrast to claims made in early Kariba and Cahora Bassa documents that the dams would usher in an age of "total control" over discharges.[207] Emergency releases to avoid overtopping also exacerbated the scale of flooding in the Zambezi in 1989 and 1997.[208]

These floods, however, were minor in comparison to the catastrophic flood of 2000–2001. First came record precipitation, heavy tropical storms, and a number of cyclones and heavy rains in southern Africa. Increased discharges from Kariba caused water to rush into Cahora Bassa, whose engineers, to reduce its water levels, opened its sluice gates. This sent a deluge downriver, about which riverine communities, again, had received no advance warning. This time, however, they were even more vulnerable, because, without the seasonal floods that had historically inundated large areas in the delta, thousands of families, anxious to farm on the river's edge and believing that Cahora Bassa could control most floods, had moved their villages and their fields closer to the river channel.[209] Several thousand returning refugees, who had fled to Malawi to escape Renamo, had also settled in this precarious zone.[210] According to the Mozambican government, these floods affected nearly half a million people—forty-four perished, more than eighty-one thousand were displaced from their homes, and thousands of hectares of maize, rice, manioc, and other basic staples were destroyed.[211]

This willingness to take risks was not unique to the riparian communities of the Zambezi. In its well-documented 2000 report, the WCD warned that large dams like Cahora Bassa often encouraged peasants to settle in lowland areas that remained subject to floods, and it questioned the effectiveness and desirability of these dams as a means of flood control.[212] Indeed, although the Mozambican government has since improved its early-warning and disaster management systems and established better flood evacuation and contingency plans, river communities remain vulnerable.

The flood of 2007–8, during which one hundred twenty thousand Zambezi residents once again fled their homes, testifies to the continued vulnerability of riverine families and the ongoing dilemma they face as they try to put order in their precarious universe.[213] The initial heavy rains, which caused flooding in the lower Zambezi, left ninety-five thousand people homeless. Subsequent torrential rainfall further upriver, in Zimbabwe, forced engineers at the Kariba Dam to open its floodgates, sending a surge down the Zambezi, with similar results at Cahora Bassa. This worsened the flooding in the lower Zambezi, creating even more homelessness.[214] As one peasant lamented, "We lost our crops and our farms in the floods last year[.] I don't know, where can we go? This place is our home. . . . We don't know anywhere else."[215] For Mozambique's president, Armando Guebuza, who visited the flooded areas on February 8, 2008, the long-term solution was to tame the river by building more dams. In addressing flood victims in Chinde District, he stressed that the Zambezi's hydroelectric potential was a source of great wealth to the country, even if, in the rainy season, "it causes problems, invading our houses and fields without our permission."[216]

༄

Many of the deleterious ecological and social consequences discussed in this chapter were predicted by earlier investigations of the megadam project,[217] although it is difficult to distinguish which environmental and social disruptions were caused by Cahora Bassa, rather than by Renamo's fifteen years of mayhem, or to determine the extent of their interconnectedness. Today, it is impoverished communities stretching from just below the dam to the Zambezi delta—many of whom were also victimized terribly during the war—who continue to suffer from operational miscalculations and the national government's ongoing fixation with exporting energy to South Africa at all costs. To this subject, we now turn our attention.

6 ✍ Displaced Energy

THAT FEW citizens of Mozambique have, to this day, derived any real benefit from the massive hydroelectric project on the Zambezi River is one of the harsh realities of Mozambique's postcolonial history. Rather than promoting national economic development or sustainable livelihoods for the people living adjacent to the river, the dam instead robbed Mozambique of precious energy. By harnessing the river's flow regime to meet the needs of the South African state, Cahora Bassa deprived rural communities in the Zambezi valley of the life-sustaining nutrients that had supported human society and local ecosystems for centuries. Additionally, peasants and the urban poor had no access to either the electricity the dam produced or the revenues it generated because, until 2007, the dam remained in Portuguese hands. While the natural energy of the river was now an export commodity that provided the South African economy, both during the apartheid era and under ANC leadership, with cheap hydroelectric power, nearly 95 percent of Mozambique's population had no access to this critical resource, including those living in villages adjacent to the power lines (see fig. 6.1). South Africa received the energy, Portugal received the income, and Zambezi valley residents paid the price.

For more than thirty years after Mozambique achieved political independence, Cahora Bassa remained a colonial project. European workers continued to fill the highest-paid jobs and enjoyed substantially better living and working conditions than their Mozambican counterparts. The HCB still owned and operated the dam, determined the outflows of water, and negotiated the sale of electricity on Lisbon's behalf. Only in 2007, after intense and contested interstate negotiations between Mozambique, Portugal, and South Africa, did Portugal reluctantly agree to cede control of the dam to Mozambique.[1]

FIGURE 6.1. Pylons passing a Tete village. *Daniel Ribeiro*

Throughout this period, South Africa continued to appropriate, at below-market value, whatever hydroelectric power Mozambique produced.[2] In 1980, concerned about Frelimo's nonracial socialist agenda and its historic ties to the African National Congress (ANC), South African security forces began a sustained military and economic campaign to destabilize Mozambique and destroy the nation's infrastructure. High on its list was Cahora Bassa. For more than a decade, South African–backed Renamo fighters repeatedly sabotaged the dam's power lines, paralyzing the hydroelectric project and terrorizing the hundreds of thousands of peasants living adjacent to the river. Since Cahora Bassa's power lines were providing only 7 percent of South Africa's energy, disabling them had relatively minor consequences for the apartheid regime.[3] Even before Mozambican independence, South Africa's public electricity utility, Eskom, had stated unambiguously that Cahora Bassa "was not envisaged as providing more than supplementary power for the Republic's energy requirements [and that] South Africa's long-term energy plan has never included Cabora Bassa as it is not our policy to depend on sources outside our border."[4]

Although the destabilization campaign ended in the early 1990s, shortly before the ANC came to power, tension over the dam persisted. The new South African government insisted that the HCB honor the existing colonial contracts that set the price of electricity artificially low. Under great pressure, it eventually agreed to pay appreciably more for the imported energy—although the rate was still well below the world price.

In this chapter, we explore the complex and often strained relationship between Mozambique, South Africa, and Portugal over control of the dam and the energy it produced. What was at stake was nothing less than Mozambique's postcolonial sovereignty and its right to use its scarce resources to insure the well-being of its citizens. This struggle over the future of Cahora Bassa illuminates the multiple ways in which human security, ecological resiliency, economic development, and national sovereignty operated within a highly contested transnational field of power over which Mozambique had little control.

FRELIMO'S SOCIALIST AGENDA

Upon gaining independence, Frelimo had to confront the existence of Cahora Bassa. Reversing its previous condemnation of the "racist project," it hailed Cahora Bassa as a symbol of liberation and an instrument for growth. In language reminiscent of Portuguese colonial discourse, Mozambique's first president, Samora Machel, and his economic advisers insisted that the dam would help the Mozambican people achieve economic prosperity, transform the Zambezi valley, and bring the fiscally strapped nation a new source of hard currency by exporting energy not just to South Africa but also to markets throughout the region. Machel's words echoed those of Gamal Abdel Nasser, Jawaharlal Nehru, Kwame Nkrumah, and other prominent third world leaders, who had heralded dams as icons of modern national development.

At Frelimo's third party congress, in 1977, two years after independence, government leaders unveiled a far-reaching plan to consolidate state power, reorganize society, and transform Mozambique's ailing economy. Based on Marxist-Leninist principles fused with nationalist ideology and developmentalist discourse[5] and reflecting the party's reverence for scientific principles—framed as "socialism with a Mozambican face"[6]—the plan would guide Mozambique forward, even as party officials acknowledged the challenges of building a new nation from "Maputo to the Rovuma."

Transforming the nation's economy took center stage. Frelimo used the party congress to set out an ambitious development agenda, underscoring the state's leading role in the economy. Party documents called for state control of private property, the implementation of a centrally planned economy, and the creation of state enterprises to implement the economic blueprint:

> The building of socialism demands that the economy be centrally planned and directed by the State. Planned management is one of its basic characteristics. It falls to the State to create a structure able to organize, direct and develop the economy, planning and rationally distributing the productive forces throughout the country. It falls to

the State to guarantee the full use of human and material resources at the regional level, linking centers of production and consumption, and therefore developing the rural areas and the towns in a balanced way. In this context, the State also creates the material conditions to guarantee the right of all citizens to work.[7]

In Frelimo discourse, it was an article of faith that state intervention was essential to dismantle the institutions of oppression deeply embedded in Mozambique after four centuries of "colonial-capitalist oppression."[8]

One of the state's highest economic priorities was "the socialization of the countryside," which, in Frelimo's Marxist lexicon, meant organizing a system of large state farms to replace abandoned or dysfunctional colonial plantations and agricultural companies and creating a vast network of communal villages. Following the European exodus,[9] Frelimo took over almost two thousand abandoned or poorly managed estates, targeting those that had produced export crops, such as tea, cotton, and rice. By 1981 nineteen of twenty-one colonial-era tea companies had been placed under the direction of Emocha (Empresa Moçambicana de Chá), a state enterprise,[10] and most cotton concessionary companies, with their long history of forced labor,[11] were also nationalized.[12]

"Socializing the countryside" also required construction of a sprawling network of communal villages (*aldeias comunais*), patterned on those established in the liberated zones during the armed struggle, that would fundamentally transform how Mozambican peasants lived and worked.[13] State planners insisted that sustained economic growth was not possible when 90 percent of the population lived in dispersed rural communities and practiced "traditional agriculture," which was viewed as chaotic and inefficient. Reorganizing peasants into agricultural cooperatives supported by technical inputs from the state would revolutionize relations of production and elevate political consciousness. It would also improve the lives of rural Mozambicans, who would thereby have access to electricity, clean water, health care, education, and other basic social services.[14]

These justifications for the establishment of communal villages, and the purported benefits of such relocations, sounded very similar to what colonial planners had proposed for the aldeamentos.[15] In fact, their similarities extended well beyond the developmentalist rhetoric that underlay them both. Like their colonial predecessors, Frelimo officials rarely consulted with local communities before organizing them into communal villages and failed either to take into account their diverse ecological conditions or to consider how such communities had historically organized their economic, social, and cultural lives. Frelimo's version of socialist high modernism rested on its belief that the countryside was the site of obscurantism and uneconomic practices, both of which it needed to transform for Mozambique to prosper. As had occurred with the aldeamentos, the establishment of many communal villages was haphazard, with insufficient consideration given to soil quality and access to water, and promised technical assistance from the government often failed to materialize. Most were overcrowded, many lacked food cooperatives, they rarely received the resources needed for their schools and health clinics, and only a few had generators to produce electricity. Not surprisingly, these new relocations generated opposition in some rural communities.[16]

While Frelimo initially did not employ the brutal tactics of the colonial regime to coerce peasants into joining communal villages, local party officials pressured, cajoled, prodded, and ordered villagers to abandon their homelands and relocate into larger communities to demonstrate their commitment to the new Mozambique.[17] In Tete Province, authorities sometimes even withheld food and agricultural assistance from reluctant peasants.[18] In other regions, such as Nampula and Manica Provinces, where Frelimo's influence before independence was more tenuous, villagers more openly opposed villagization. Due to their recalcitrance and Renamo's military activities in the area, in the name of protecting them from Renamo attacks, Frelimo cadres often forced them into hastily established communal villages.[19]

In other regions, Frelimo's transformative project went more smoothly. In much of Cabo Delgado, peasants voluntarily joined communal villages.[20] According to Otto Roach, this was also true in Gaza Province:

> Though many of the people who did resettle in communal villages [during the great wave of communal village formation in the first five years of independence] would have preferred to have remained living in traditional dispersed fashion, the vast majority accepted resettlement out of a sense of duty and obligation towards Frelimo. . . . Though this level of popular political engagement and nationalist commitment eventually evaporated and may not have been as intensely felt in other areas of Mozambique as it was in Gaza, it was initially a powerful force in large parts of the country.[21]

By 1982 the National Commission on Communal Villages reported that 1.8 million peasants, roughly 20 percent of the total population, were residing in communal villages,[22] including many peasants in Tete Province, whom the colonial authorities had previously forced into aldeamentos.[23] Interestingly, most of the communal villages there were located on the sites of former aldeamentos, and almost 60 percent of the people living in them had come from aldeamentos (see map 6.1).[24] Also relocated into communal villages were thousands of downriver Zambezi valley residents who had lost their homes and livelihoods in the 1978 flood known as Cheia Maldeia or as Cheia

Madeya ("the flood that forced us to leave our homes and move to communal villages").[25] Thereafter, internal disorganization, peasant antipathy, and Renamo's targeting of communal villages in Tete Province after 1982, led to the rapid disintegration of most of its communal villages.[26]

Because these grandiose plans for the "development of collective life" presumed the electrification of vast parts of the countryside, President Machel insisted that Cahora Bassa serve the Mozambican people as quickly as possible. In an interview by Mozambican journalist Iain Christie and Allen Isaacman, Machel stressed that South Africa was the only country benefiting from the dam.[27] He characterized the hydroelectric project as "a white elephant which doesn't have any ivory"—a creature with no value, as far as the Mozambican population was concerned[28]—and described Mozambique's challenges as follows: "We cannot irrigate without energy. The electrification of the central area of the north and of the south of our country is fundamental for us to be able to meet the needs of agriculture. We must domesticate the 'white elephant' Cahora Bassa. This 'elephant's' ivory—electricity and irrigation—should go to our agriculture and industry. . . . Within the next decade the north-bank power station [at Cahora Bassa] must begin functioning and numerous dams must be built for irrigation and electrification."[29]

DOMESTICATING THE WHITE ELEPHANT
IN THE FACE OF SOUTH AFRICAN AGGRESSION

Domesticating the white elephant proved to be impossible. Under the 1974 Lusaka peace accord, in return for assuming responsibility for the $550 million debt incurred in the dam's construction, the HCB received an 82 percent ownership share and the Mozambican state received the remainder.[30] Until repayment of the debt, the company, rather than Mozambique, would retain effective control over Cahora Bassa. Under an agreement worked out in the late 1960s and signed at the time of the dam's completion, Eskom was entitled to virtually all its electricity. The lack of an effective rural power grid, which would have been extremely expensive to construct, further limited Frelimo's ability to harness the hydroelectric project for domestic purposes.

Nevertheless, the Mozambican government, over the next several years, sought funding for several major development projects. In 1978, to provide energy from the dam to Tete city, the provincial capital, and the nearby coal mines at Moatize, it constructed a substation outside Tete. Two years later, Cahora Bassa was supplying electricity to Tete, whose obsolete thermal power station burned up to twenty thousand tons of coal annually, and to the colliery, which had relied on imported diesel for its generators.[31] None of the other projects discussed ever came to fruition,[32] due to South Africa's massive destabilization activities.

Domesticating the white elephant required extension of the power lines and provision of cheap energy to the densely populated, but energy-starved and strategically significant, provinces of Zambézia and Nampula.[33] A second set of transmission lines and substations, planned for the dam site on the northern bank of the Zambezi, would serve the coastal agricultural zones of these provinces, which produced most of the cotton, tea, and sugar for export and much of the food for domestic consumption. Provision of electricity would also satisfy the peasants there, who had been heavily pressured by Frelimo to join communal villages, that the government could produce what it had promised as an incentive—namely, electricity.[34] In 1980 a delegation led by the governor of the Bank of Mozambique concluded multimillion-dollar agreements with France and Italy to begin the first phase of this project, which would take two years to complete.[35]

South African aggression against Mozambique, however, thwarted these plans. Fearful of a socialist, independent African state on its borders, Pretoria set out to destroy it. The white minority regime's undeclared war against Mozambique, and the role of Renamo as its principal instrument of destruction, are well known.[36] As part of a broader strategy of toppling hostile governments, isolating the African National Congress, and destabilizing the entire southern African region, South Africa began its campaign within months of Mozambique's independence, when its security forces, working with their Rhodesian counterparts, created Renamo and began to train and arm it.[37] With the fall of the Rhodesian government and the independence of Zimbabwe, in 1980, Renamo headquarters and bases were moved from Rhodesia to South Africa's Transvaal Province, adjacent to Mozambique.

The South African security forces treated Renamo as a surrogate army, providing it with generous supplies of war materials—including rockets, mortars, and small arms—critical logistic support, and instructors who, according to Renamo leader Alfonso Dhlakama, would "not only teach but also participate in the attacks."[38] By 1981, South Africa was infiltrating Renamo forces into Mozambique by helicopter and resupplying them by airdrops and naval landings along Mozambique's extensive coast.[39] Once there, they sabotaged bridges and railroad lines, mined roads, destroyed warehouses, and attacked communal villages and state farms, with the aim of destroying Mozambique's infrastructure, paralyzing its economy, and bringing the young nation to its knees.[40]

Among Renamo's victims were peasants whom the colonial regime had forced into aldeamentos. Vernácio Leone, who had survived forced removal and the perilous conditions of the aldeamentos, described the additional suffering: "When Renamo would come into a village, they would call all the people together. Then they would go into the houses and steal all that was inside. They ordered the people back into their homes, which they set on fire."[41] Everywhere in the Zambezi valley, ex-aldeamento residents had to take extreme measures to survive. "We were forced to live in the mountains for four years. We slept there and only returned at daybreak to cultivate our fields."[42] Fausto Semo remembered that Renamo attacked shortly after he and others who had been interned in Chicoa Nova returned to Chipalapala to remake their lives: "There was a sense of panic; there was nothing we could do. Many of our homes were burned by [Renamo]."[43] Some fled to the mountains, while others sought shelter in squatter camps around Estima, a Frelimo base. In either case, they were once again homeless.

For the Mozambican government, the timing of these Renamo attacks could not have been worse, since most of its rural development projects were not yet underway. While Renamo deliberately targeted Cahora Bassa's power lines—which was not surprising, given that South Africa did not yet need its electricity—the dam itself was never attacked.

The pylons were especially attractive targets, and Renamo attacks on them were devastating. The Mozambican government lacked the capacity to protect the four thousand stainless-steel pylons strung across nine hundred kilometers of sparsely populated countryside. As early as 1981, Renamo forces dynamited pylons near Espungabera, which took six months to repair, reducing electricity exports by 50 percent.[44] Thereafter, it regularly destroyed power lines and towers, mining the adjacent areas to prevent their reconstruction. Neither the 1984 Nkomati peace accord nor subsequent South African promises halted these attacks,[45] since by then Renamo had its own political agenda and was escalating its campaign of destruction to force the Mozambican government into direct negotiations. By 1988, 891 pylons had been destroyed; over the next three years that number doubled.[46] The estimated cost of repairing or replacing them was $500 million—nearly three times the total value of Mozambican exports and well beyond the government's means.[47] Moreover, because the Lusaka accord envisioned that Mozambique would use the income it earned from its 18 percent ownership of the dam to gradually obtain majority control from the HCB, there were no sales of electricity to South Africa and no income for Mozambique.

Together with Renamo's military campaigns in Tete and Zambézia Provinces, the attacks on the power lines effectively blocked Frelimo's plans to develop the Zambezi valley and electrify the northern part of the country. The attacks' symbolic impact enabled both Renamo leaders and the apartheid regime to claim that Renamo was a legitimate nationalist movement motivated by opposition to Frelimo's Marxist policies, rather than merely Pretoria's puppet.[48]

From 1982 to 1997, Cahora Bassa's five massive hydroelectric generators stood idle. Because Frelimo policies placed such importance on Cahora Bassa's potential to transform the countryside, paralyzing the hydroelectric scheme not only exposed Mozambique's vulnerability—its inability to police and protect its territory—but made rural economic development impossible. Thus, as long as Renamo forces were operating, the dam remained a white elephant, benefiting neither the national economy nor local communities.

THE CHANGING POLITICAL ECONOMY OF THE DAM

In the late 1980s and early 1990s, several intersecting factors gave new life to Cahora Bassa. The implementation of Mozambique's decision, in 1987, to abandon its experiment with Marxism, privatize critical sectors of the economy, and seek new foreign investment to rebuild the country depended on the availability of cheap energy from Cahora Bassa. The 1992 peace accord signed with Renamo enabled the HCB to rebuild downed power lines so that it could again export energy. The apartheid regime's dismantling, two years later, and the ANC government's recognition that South Africa faced a serious energy shortfall provided added impetus for the speedy reconstruction of the power grid. Finally, the Southern African Power Pool, created in 1995, envisioned a robust and interconnected southern African electrical system in which Cahora Bassa figured prominently.[49]

The staggering cost of the conflict with Renamo contributed to Frelimo's decision to abandon its socialist project. In 1982, when Mozambique's economy came to a grinding halt after five years of modest growth,[50] the government estimated that South Africa's destabilization campaign had cost it $3.8 billion.[51] Between 1982 and 1986, Mozambique's gross national product fell by 40 percent, exports plummeted, and inflation skyrocketed.[52] A decade later, the cost of the war had risen to about $20 billion.

Other contributing factors were the lack of trained personnel in the country and Frelimo's limited institutional capacity to manage a command economy. Interventionist policies taxed the already understaffed bureaucracy, and the state's periodic use of force, especially in the later phases of villagization, undermined both national production levels and popular support for the ruling party.[53]

The turn to privatization, however, also reflected the realignment of international economic and political forces—the precipitous decline of the Soviet Union, the ascendancy of neoliberalism, and the rapid integration of many socialist-leaning countries into a global capitalist economy dominated by multinational corporations and transnational financial institutions, notably the International Monetary Fund and the World Bank.[54] As preconditions for Western investment, these institutions imposed on Mozambique a structural adjustment program in the late 1980s consisting of economic deregulation, currency devaluation, and draconian cuts in government spending.[55] Under siege from all sides, the government relinquished control over the economy and promoted the expansion of the private sector.

Revitalizing Cahora Bassa figured prominently in this neoliberal agenda for two reasons—because cheap electricity would lure and encourage foreign investment and because the sale of energy to South Africa, Zimbabwe, and other energy-starved neighbors, such as Malawi and Botswana, would generate badly needed hard currency.[56] The government also stressed the need to electrify the countryside, particularly the rich agricultural provinces of Nampula and Zambézia. As part of its effort to resuscitate the economy and attract foreign capital, the state announced in 1988 that it would relaunch plans to build a second set of transmission lines connecting Cahora Bassa with all of northern Mozambique.

The October 1992 cease-fire with Renamo made these ambitious plans possible. It ended fifteen years of brutal conflict, creating an opportunity for repair crews to rebuild power lines without the risk that they would be attacked or that refurbished power lines would later be destroyed. The transition from apartheid to majority rule in South Africa added urgency to the process. Although the apartheid regime had begun an electrification program in some townships in the 1980s, "serious efforts to roll out electrification infrastructure to urban and rural blacks did not begin until the early 1990s."[57] Between 1994 and 2000, Eskom connected more than 2.5 million homes to the grid,[58] which, combined with increased demand for energy from the service and financial sectors and mining's continued dependence on electricity, taxed South Africa's energy infrastructure and forced it to look beyond its borders for a cheap and secure electricity source.[59] Cahora Bassa was an obvious choice.

TUGGING ON THE CHAINS OF DEPENDENCY: FROM CAHORA BASSA TO MPHANDA NKUWA, 1994–2006

The resurgence of Cahora Bassa provoked intense competition over ownership of the dam and the energy it produced. More fundamentally, jockeying over Cahora Bassa and the possibility that Mozambique would construct a dam at Mphanda Nkuwa to export additional cheap energy raised critical questions over the meaning—and limits—of postcolonial autonomy in the neoliberal world order. At stake were the resource sovereignty of Mozambique and the extent to which the people of the Zambezi valley would benefit.

In the end, it was competing and shifting alliances among the governments of Mozambique, Portugal, and South Africa and their energy companies that determined Cahora Bassa's destiny. The ANC government and Eskom, for example, vigorously supported Mozambique's efforts to gain ownership of Cahora Bassa and construct a second dam at Mphanda Nkuwa but were reluctant to pay more for electricity. Portugal and the HCB, on the other hand, shared Frelimo's desire to raise electricity prices, even as they resisted Mozambican efforts to acquire the dam but opposed the proposed project at Mphanda Nkuwa.

To Maputo, the HCB's continued ownership of the dam and sale of electricity to South Africa at a fraction of its market value were affronts to its political and economic sovereignty and its national security.[60] Twenty-five years after independence, that Portugal still owned and operated the dam was intolerable. Cahora Bassa was a living symbol of a violent and oppressive past and a constant reminder that Mozambique was still not free from the yoke of colonialism.

Songo's continued existence as a Portuguese enclave in the heart of Mozambique, with its racialized labor hierarchy largely intact,[61] reinforced that symbolism. European managers and workers retained many of the privileges they had enjoyed in the past and continued to hold most supervisory jobs and positions of authority.[62] By contrast, the 850 African employees at Songo were almost all relegated to low-wage positions, lived in modest housing on-site or in villages adjacent to the town, and received much smaller end-of-contract bonuses.[63] Many locals could find employment only in poorly paid "ancillary" positions as guards, supermarket employees, and domestic workers,[64] where they generally lacked job security and often suffered verbal abuse.[65] Even those with extensive on-the-ground experience worked primarily as manual laborers, low-level functionaries, or in other unskilled job categories.[66] In a 1998 conversation, Simões Wetela stressed that the old colonial patterns persisted after independence: "We do the work and [the Portuguese] earn the money."[67]

Not even long-term Mozambican dam workers were able to break out of the racially defined unskilled positions to which they had been consigned. Few achieved the status of semiskilled worker, which carried additional bonuses and benefits.[68] Pedro da Costa Xavier, who labored at Songo for more than forty years, calculated that his real wages had actually decreased from 1975 to 2001.[69] Moreover, the relatively small number of Mozambicans in skilled positions continued to earn lower wages than their Portuguese counterparts.[70] Three decades after independence, local workers were still demanding "equal pay for equal work."[71] Acutely aware of their lack of progress, they attributed the status quo "to the powerful racism at Songo."[72] One worker poignantly summed up their shared sense of frustration: "As time goes on, we feel more marginalized. . . . We feel like foreigners in our own country."[73]

Recurring strike threats and periodic work stoppages, reported in detail in the media, served as a powerful reminder of how little had changed.[74] Although, by the late 1990s, a state-sanctioned union represented dam workers at Songo, HCB management was impervious to most demands to improve working conditions.[75] Negotiations were typically fruitless, since the HCB stalled, simply refused to consider issues the union brought to the table, or intimidated the union leadership. In response, the union called for work stoppages on at least four occasions between 1996 and 2003.[76] In May 2000 the union threatened to strike unless its members received the same rights granted to foreign workers.[77] Sixteen months later, after reports circulated that the HCB planned to fire four hundred workers who did not perform "core functions," which was almost half the Mozambican workforce, dam employees called for another work stoppage. The union's threat to walk off the job caused management to relent somewhat and reduce that figure by half.[78]

The HCB also disregarded the state's desire to electrify the Mozambican countryside, even after Cahora Bassa returned to full production in 1998. In that year, Eskom received 850 megawatts (60 percent) of the dam's generated electricity. Of the remainder, twice as much energy was designated for Zimbabwe's electricity utility, ZESA, as for Electricidade de Moçambique (EDM)—400 as compared with 200 megawatts.[79] To make matters worse, the HCB refused Mozambique's request to redirect unused energy to a proposed aluminum smelter in Beira, its second-largest city.[80] By 2003 less than 6 percent of Mozambican households had access to electricity—one of the lowest rates in Africa.[81] Other than in Maputo, the capital, where the rate was 23.1 percent, it hovered between 1.6 and 5.3 percent in the other provinces; and in Tete, the home of Cahora Bassa, only 3.2 percent of the population was connected to the electrical grid. Even where access existed, however, many households could not afford to pay the relatively high rates for energy, relying instead on traditional biofuels, such as wood, charcoal, and agroanimal waste (see table 6.1).[82] In short, Mozambican development needs were being held hostage to the HCB's search for new markets in the energy-starved region.[83]

TABLE 6.1 Access to electricity in Mozambique (by province), 2003

Province	Domestic customers	Population	Access
Cabo Delgado	6,192	1,584,584	1.6%
Niassa	6,704	972,391	2.8%
Nampula	28,357	3,588,348	3.2%
Zambézia	16,139	3,626,739	1.7%
Tete	11,430	1,472,728	3.2%
Manica	12,405	1,281,317	2.9%
Sofala	24,073	1,600,581	5.3%
Inhambane	8,847	1,350,372	2.4%
Gaza	20,943	1,277,307	5.0%
Maputo	128,828	2,207,136	23.1%
Total	263,918	18,961,503	5.3% (average)

Source: Electricidade de Moçambique, *Annual Report 2006* (Maputo: EDM,2006).

In the mid-1990s, Mozambican authorities began complex and contentious negotiations with their Portuguese counterparts to domesticate the white elephant that was Cahora Bassa. Meeting in Portugal in 1999, President Joaquim Chissano reminded Socialist prime minister António Gutierres, whose party had historical ties to Frelimo, that the signatories to the 1974 peace agreement had envisioned Cahora Bassa coming under Mozambican control before the end of the twentieth century.[84] That calculation reflected the shared assumption that, as revenue from electricity sales to South Africa increased, the Mozambican state would use its profits to buy shares from the HCB, thereby gradually gaining control of the dam. Chissano insisted that his country had a sovereign right to Cahora Bassa and that it should not be further penalized for Renamo's sabotage, which had prevented the ownership transfer from taking place on the original schedule.[85] After negotiations the next year in Maputo, Portuguese finance minister Joaquim Pina Moura confirmed that Lisbon was disposed to a transfer that "would meet the concerns of the three countries."[86] The price, according to Mozambican sources, was $500 million.[87]

The controversy that this proposal caused in Lisbon delayed the transfer for several years. The HCB's board of directors and a coalition of right-wing parties in the Portuguese parliament rejected the plan as unrealistic and fiscally irresponsible. They insisted that Portugal not relinquish ownership of Cahora Bassa until the Mozambican government had repaid the entire debt the HCB owed to the Portuguese treasury, including the costs incurred to repair the transmission lines—calculated at $2 billion.[88] As one senior HCB official sarcastically quipped, "Mozambique has not got the money to ask a blind man for a dance, let alone to buy a dam."[89] Despite this vocal opposition, Prime Minister Gutierres reaffirmed his government's plan to sell the dam to the consortium, and there were rumors that Lisbon might even retain a minority share. Before being able to reach a formal agreement, however, the Socialist Party suffered a major defeat at the polls, and Gutierres resigned.

The right-wing coalition that came to power in 2003, led by the Social Democratic Party, remained unenthusiastic about further negotiations.[90] Because Mozambique was unable to amass the capital needed to acquire the HCB's stake in the dam, due principally to Pretoria's refusal to pay a fair price for Cahora Bassa's electricity, the new Portuguese secretary of state for cooperation, António Lourenço, declared that "conditions still do not exist to start to carry out the transfer."[91] While Portuguese officials were periodically willing to resume talks, they refused to consider ceding control of Cahora Bassa until repayment of the entire debt to the Portuguese treasury.[92] Luís Mira Amaral, a senior government representative on the Standing Joint Committee on Cahora Bassa, warned that anyone who assumed Portugal would "stop fighting for its rights in one of its major investments [was] much mistaken."[93]

The stalled negotiations provoked a strong reaction in Mozambique. Some critics suggested that Frelimo had seriously erred by not taking control of the dam at independence,[94] and two Maputo newspapers, *Domingo* and *Zambeze*, argued that the state should simply nationalize it.[95]

At the same time as Mozambican officials began negotiations with Portugal, they turned their attention to the equally contentious issue of the artificially deflated price Eskom paid for Cahora Bassa's electricity, which was part of the historical pattern of Mozambique's resource colonization by South Africa. While agreeing about ownership, Frelimo and the ANC-led government were far apart on the thorny issue of energy pricing. Frelimo, supported by Portuguese officials, contended that the 1988 agreement governing the sale of electricity to South Africa—a legacy of the colonial-apartheid alliance—needed a radical reworking. The 1988 contract was particularly galling for several reasons. First, it guaranteed South Africa a minimum of 1,450 megawatts, or 80 percent of the dam's output, at a small fraction of the world market price. Second, included in this figure were 200 megawatts of electricity that passed through South Africa's Apollo substation, just across the Mozambican border, before being "repatriated" to Mozambique. These 200 megawatts, however, barely met the energy needs of Maputo city and the Maputo corridor, which left little energy for urban townships or rural communities in the southern provinces of Maputo, Gaza, and Inhambane.[96] To add insult to injury, the price Eskom charged its Mozambican customers for this electricity was significantly higher than what it paid for it.[97] Although the actual price was covered by confidentiality provisions and has never been disclosed publicly, the disparity was enormous—as demonstrated by the HCB chair's complaint that "South Africa is selling back to Mozambique electricity we supplied to them in the first place, but at ten times the price."[98]

The unwillingness of Eskom and the South African government to reconsider their near monopoly on the purchase of electricity from Cahora Bassa set the stage for a protracted price war. It began in 1998, when the HCB, with the support of the Mozambican government, demanded that the rate be negotiated upward to reflect market prices and to defray the cost of repairing the dam's power lines. Even though the lines were by then completely functional, Eskom's refusal to do so provoked the HCB to delay energy exports to South Africa.[99] For the cash-strapped government in Maputo, this decision proved very costly. Because of the deferral, the EDM had to pay Eskom $1.2 million per month in hard currency for South African–produced electricity, rather than accessing cheaper "repatriated" power from Cahora Bassa, for which, according to an earlier agreement, it paid with Mozambican currency.[100] Additionally, Mozambique lost its share of the revenue that would have accrued from the exported energy.

A similar conflict flared up three years later when the HCB abruptly cut off the flow of electricity to South Africa after Eskom again refused to renegotiate the price it paid for Cahora Bassa's electricity. HCB officials insisted that the 1988 agreement, which had only modestly raised the colonial rate to R2 cents per kilowatt-hour, was a "ruinous price" and a blatant attempt by Eskom to exploit its power as Cahora Bassa's almost exclusive customer.[101] Ignoring the irony of a Portuguese company voicing support for Mozambique's rights as a sovereign nation, HCB board chair Carlos Vega Angelos evoked memories of an unjust colonial past to sustain his claim that the ANC-led government was acting irresponsibly: "We have a power purchase agreement that was established between Portugal and South Africa in 1969. Many things have changed here in Africa. Portugal is no longer the colonial country. Mozambique is an independent country, and even the regime in South Africa has changed, so we need a new power purchase agreement that is more appropriate to the present situation in this region."[102] The HCB demanded, at a minimum, a doubling of the price and immediate negotiations to establish what it assumed would be an even higher rate in the future—which would reflect electricity's true market value.

Faced with rising domestic demands for electricity and the likelihood that its surplus energy capacity would run out in 2007, Eskom ultimately accepted these new terms. An interim agreement signed in 2003 raised the price for energy from Cahora Bassa to 3.6 cents per kilowatt-hour. As part of a new eighteen-year agreement signed in February 2004, the price was pegged at R7 cents per kilowatt-hour with an upward adjustment for inflation. This figure, although more than triple the 1988 rate, was still well below the market price of R15.4 cents that Zimbabwe paid for Mozambican electricity.[103]

Because Mozambique lacked sovereignty over the dam, it had no legal standing in these tortured negotiations. While the Frelimo government did favor a steep price increase, it had no say in what that price would be. It also resented HCB's unilateral decision making and failure to consider the effects of its positions on Mozambique's economy. During the price war in 1998, Prime Minister Pascoal Mocumbi publicly criticized the HCB for delaying the export of energy to South Africa, which had effectively cost the state millions of dollars, since the income could have bought down Maputo's debt to Lisbon. Five years later, he again challenged the HCB's decision to cut off power to South Africa against the express wishes of his government, which favored resolving the issue through negotiations.[104] Such public criticism reflected the frustration and anger of a government made impotent by its lack of direct control over Cahora Bassa. The minister of mineral resources and energy, Castigo Langa, summed up official sentiment when he stated that merely "solving the tariff issues on its own terms does not satisfy Mozambique's interest."[105] The ultimate issue, for Mozambique, was ownership of the dam.

Facing stiff opposition to such a transfer of ownership from powerful circles in Lisbon, the Mozambican government threatened to make the Portuguese-owned dam of little economic value to them by revitalizing colonial-era plans to build a second dam sixty kilometers downriver, at Mphanda Nkuwa, whose energy, if exported to South Africa, would dramatically reduce Cahora Bassa's income potential.[106] After receiving an encouraging feasibility report, financed by grants from Germany, Norway, and France, the Mozambican government organized an investors conference for the Mphanda Nkuwa hydroelectric project in May 2002, attended by more than two hundred government officials, consultants, and representatives of large energy companies, contracting firms, equipment manufacturers, and investment banks. Its clear intent was to mark the official launching of the dam, estimated to generate 1,300 megawatts, and to invite investors to provide funds for its construction, which, government sources indicated, would begin in 2004 or 2005.[107] In his opening address, Energy Minister Langa assured participants that his government would offer incentives to guarantee Mphanda Nkuwa's profitability.[108] Chinese, South African, and Brazilian investors all appeared interested in participating (see chapter 7).

Due to frequent changes of government in Lisbon, however, the threat of Mphanda Nkuwa did not initially achieve its purpose. In 2004, after Portuguese prime minister José Manuel Barroso was replaced by fellow conservative Pedro Santana Lopes, a senior official in Maputo complained that "it makes no sense that every time the government changes hands all the pending dossiers on Cahora Bassa are dumped into the rubbish bin."[109] A year later, Mozambique's foreign minister demanded that Portugal stop dragging its feet and speed up the transfer.[110] Armando Guebuza, the newly elected president, was even more adamant. On the eve of yet another round of talks on the dam's status, he bluntly told his Portuguese counterpart that Mozambique "would not wait another month, another day or even another hour."[111] Cahora Bassa had become more than a minor policy disagreement about finances. It now threatened to derail Portuguese efforts to expand its cultural as well as its economic ties to its former colony, which, in 1995, had entered the British Commonwealth.

In November 2006, Lisbon, seeking to solidify these ties, agreed to sell two-thirds of its holdings in Cahora Bassa to the Mozambican government for $700 million.[112] That figure was somewhat larger than the tentative offer previously floated by the Socialist-led government in 2000, but only a third of the amount Portugal had demanded in 2003. In return, Portugal received assurances that Portuguese companies would play a critical role in future hydroelectric projects and that Mozambique would support efforts to reinforce cultural ties between the two nations.[113]

At the signing of the preliminary agreement, President Guebuza put a triumphalist spin on the accord: "It removes from our soils the final redoubt of foreign domination, the landmark of 500 years of foreign domination."[114] Gue-buza elaborated on this claim at the conclusion of the November 27, 2007, ceremony marking the dam's transfer.[115] He stressed that control of Cahora Bassa was the first step toward "speeding our journey to achieve the wellbeing of Mozambicans" and that the HCB would become "a fundamental instru-ment in pursuing our objectives seeking the eradication of poverty through promoting development and making full use of the potential of the Zambezi Valley."[116] He also predicted that Mozambique's majority ownership would encourage new energy investments by international and regional companies, which had been reluctant to make them because of the stalled negotiations.[117] Under the 2007 agreement Mozambique actually acquired an 85 percent share of Cahora Bassa and will obtain the remaining 15 percent in two phases, with the transaction completed by no later than 2014.[118]

After more than forty years, Mozambique finally owned Cahora Bassa and the energy it produced. Shortly thereafter, Pretoria agreed to a further hike in energy rates.[119] Other than the formal shift in ownership and the new tariff structure, however, little has changed. The vast majority of Cahora Bassa's electricity still goes to South Africa, and, if built, Mphanda Nkuwa will reinforce this pattern. The likely continuation of preexisting practices raises troubling questions about Mozambique's actual resource sovereignty, about the mean-ing of development, and about who actually benefits from these megaprojects (see chapter 7).

⌇

Gaining ownership of Cahora Bassa and increasing the price for energy sold to South Africa were significant victories for the Mozambican state. President Guebuza's pledge that control over Cahora Bassa would "stimulate . . . rural electrification[,] improving living conditions for many more Mozambican communities"[120] also has potentially far-reaching implications for rural de-velopment. Nevertheless, the discourse of sovereignty obscures more than it reveals, and many of the concerns about livelihood security and ecological restoration in the lower Zambezi valley, particularly in the delta, remain as pressing today as they were in the past.

More than forty years after the construction of Cahora Bassa, most riverine communities still lack electricity. As peasants in Mutarara bluntly put it, "The dam brought us tears but it did not bring electricity to Inhangoma, Charre, and Doa. As a result we do not have refrigerators; we do not have anything."[121] Recognizing the bitter irony that the steel pylons on the horizon benefited people thousands of kilometers away but not them, villagers could hardly withhold their anger: "Look at the transmission lines. They are so close. The only thing they are good for is for dogs to piss on."[122]

7 ⌁ Legacies

HYDROELECTRIC DAMS in Africa are among colonialism's most enduring legacies. They stand fixed in the landscape, changing the world around
them while they stubbornly resist significant change. Almost fifty years after
its completion, the Cahora Bassa Dam continues to impoverish the more
than half a million residents of the lower Zambezi valley and to devastate
the region's local ecosystems and wildlife. Mozambique's legal sovereignty
over the dam has not significantly altered this reality. Despite the state's
assertions that Cahora Bassa and the river were now national assets, which
could reduce poverty and promote "development," its vulnerable position
in the global economy constrained its ability to act. Moreover, Frelimo's
ongoing preoccupation with the export of hydroelectric power suggests a
postcolonial regime promoting shortsighted and destructive policies that
continue to overwhelm and silence the pressing concerns of rural communities in the valley.

The construction of a second dam at Mphanda Nkuwa, if implemented,
will exacerbate these problems. Located downriver, halfway between Cahora
Bassa and the city of Tete, it is named for the mountain that juts into the
Zambezi River, creating a narrow choke point that Portuguese engineers
considered an ideal site for a dam (see map 1.3 and fig. 7.1). The Mphanda
Nkuwa Dam was a colonial project that languished for more than a quarter
of a century. The possibility of constructing a second dam resurfaced in the
late 1990s, in response to a dramatic spike in South Africa's energy needs. The
plan's recent revival reveals one of the many ways in which the postcolonial
Mozambican state has mimicked its predecessor's policies and practices—
thereby perpetuating the delusion of development.

FIGURE 7.1. Upriver from Mphanda Nkuwa. *David Morton*

In this study, we have documented how the high-modernist ideology of successive Mozambican governments gave state officials and foreign experts the authority and power to transform the majestic Zambezi. In pursuing this delusion of development, they all subverted the agronomic and economic lives of villagers and marginalized preexisting forms of knowledge and modes of social and political life.

For the residents of the Zambezi valley, the state-imposed hydroelectric project was anything but a delusion. Instead, it was a powerful reminder of their insignificance to the national debate on the meaning of development and economic progress. This situation, of course, is not unique to Mozambique. Large, postcolonial state initiatives—whether dams, agroindustrial complexes, or urban renewal—not only fail to alleviate poverty and promote sustainable livelihoods, but often violently disrupt the lives of the poor.

THE LEGACIES OF CAHORA BASSA

For the Africans who built Cahora Bassa, the dam offered few long-term benefits. Upon its completion, most workers were summarily terminated. For many others, employment was short lived. As Pedro da Costa Xavier explained, "after the dam was completed, [African workers and their families who lived in or around Songo] were expelled from here. They received no compensation. This land became the property of the company and those who were not employed could not reside here. Many were not kicked out until 1979 or even 1981. Trucks came to take them [away]. The land in the new place was good but the people were not accustomed to the conditions. Here it was cool and there it was hot. This led to malaria and colds."[1] In 1974, just before Cahora Bassa's completion, there were almost thirty-two hundred Mozambican workers on the dam site.[2] By 2000 there were fewer than nine hundred.[3] Some "semiskilled" laborers, such as Simões Wetela and Pedro da Costa Xavier, were employed by the HCB until mandatory retirement; they deplored the preferential treatment of Portuguese workers even after independence and resented being treated like foreigners in their own country.[4]

The many peasants forcibly removed to the aldeamentos fared even worse, since their worlds had been irreversibly impoverished. For them, the multiple and far-reaching consequences of forced resettlement persisted long after the barbed-wire fences were removed and the protected villages dismantled. Nevertheless, life had to go on. While some displaced peasants tried to re-build their communities on unoccupied lands in the Songo region, Renamo's periodic attacks forced many to flee to the mountains to stay alive. Frelimo's efforts to organize communal villages in this area often consigned displaced communities to live in the same inhospitable environments to which they had been relocated in the late-colonial period, while requiring other ex-aldeam-ento residents to move yet again. Additionally, the available lands in Songo were rocky and generally not well suited for agriculture, and the low rainfall and long periods of drought made farming there less profitable than it had been on the banks of the Zambezi. Those more fortunate peasants who man-aged to acquire small plots on the edge of Lake Cahora Bassa found the op-portunities for alluvial farming short lived. When the dam reopened in 1997, engineers filled the reservoir nearly to peak capacity, permanently inundating additional rich alluvial shoreline and compelling peasants to retreat to higher, less fertile ground. Even there, though, cultivated fields were still subject to periodic flooding whenever South African energy demands increased.[5] Peas-ants around Songo also faced the continuing threat posed by the existence of an estimated sixty-five thousand land mines laid by the Portuguese in the early 1970s to protect Cahora Bassa from anticipated Frelimo attacks.[6]

Forty years after their expulsion from the area of Cahora Bassa's reservoir, these victims of forced relocation continue to live in poverty and despair. They mourn the loss of the landscape that provided physical sustenance, well-being, and a deeply felt connection to their past. Robbed of royal shrines and family burial plots when their villages were flooded, they believe that neither the powerful royal lion spirits nor the ancestors spirits are presently willing or able to protect their rural communities from the vagaries of nature and ensure their long-term welfare. Many hope that the Frelimo government will live up to its promises to build more schools and hospitals so that their children, at least, will enjoy a better life. Some insist that the state should indemnify displaced families for their lost land, but few believe this will ever happen.

Without minimizing the significance for Mozambique of finally gaining ma-jority ownership of Cahora Bassa, the 2007 agreement hardly ensured that the nation would enjoy full sovereignty over—or fully benefit from—this valuable resource. Almost all the electricity generated by Cahora Bassa is still exported to South Africa, and the price Mozambique receives for it remains below both the world rate[7] and what the country pays to South Africa for energy used by industries located in the Maputo corridor. That the Mozambican countryside has not benefited from the massive hydroelectric project—remaining largely without electricity—glaringly demonstrates South Africa's continued colonization of Mozambican water resources. Even after Frelimo's recently heralded efforts to expand the electric power grid, only 15 percent of the country's population—almost all of it in major urban centers and provincial capitals—lives in areas where energy is available.[8] Availability, of course, does not guarantee that everyone in these areas actually enjoys access to electricity, which comes at a cost that is well beyond the reach of the poorest urban dwellers.

At the same time, the health of downriver Zambezi valley ecosystems continues to be held hostage to South African energy demands. Cahora Bassa's flow management regime still disrupts the seasonal flood patterns that once supported life throughout the lower Zambezi valley. More than twenty-five years after the 1984 United Nations report that described Cahora Bassa as perhaps the most environmentally damaging dam in all of Africa, little has changed—except possibly for the worse.[9]

Until the present, problems associated with catastrophic flooding persist. Virtually every year since the floods of 2007–8, downriver communities have suffered during the rainy season, although the scale of such suffering diminished appreciably after the National Operational Emergency Center introduced an effective early-warning system linking the management of Cahora Bassa with engineers at dams in neighboring countries upriver.[10] The government has also become better at informing downriver communities of impending surges from Cahora Bassa. Additionally, more villagers have acquired radios, which they use to monitor the activities of the river,[11] and, when deemed necessary, sailors from the Mozambican navy have "forcibly evacuated peasant households who were refusing to leave their homes, even though they were surrounded by water."[12]

Despite these improvements, as late as February 2012 flooding and cyclones were responsible for many fatalities in the Zambezi valley. That there were four major cyclones in the Mozambican channel in early 2012—the same number that hit Mozambique between 1980 and 1992—led Mozambique's prime minister, Aires Ali, to conclude that "the effects of climate change are already a reality in our country."[13]

Cahora Bassa's most far-reaching legacy, however, may be its destructive impact on the twin pillars of local livelihoods throughout the Zambezi valley: farming and fishing. Deprived of water and sediment after the dam began operating, the once extensive stretches of the river's productive alluvial floodplains shrank or disappeared altogether. Peasants who continued to farm along its shorelines or on its low-lying islands faced the constant risk that unpredictable discharges from the dam would wash away seeds, rot crops, or devastate entire gardens. With agricultural systems severely undermined, local food security also deteriorated. As Maria Faira bluntly put it, "Cahora Bassa has given us hunger."[14]

In like manner, Cahora Bassa had a devastating effect on the fish that lived in the Zambezi River and its adjoining lakes, rivulets, and estuaries. Altering the river's flow regime impaired fish reproduction and led to a marked decline in the growth and survival of younger fish, significantly reducing the total catch and jeopardizing a vibrant economic activity that was a way of life for many men in the region's riverine communities.[15] This not only caused a serious drop in peasants' protein intake, which adversely affected dietary quality and health, but it also appreciably reduced rural incomes, which could otherwise have been used to supplement household food supply.

Upriver, at Lake Cahora Bassa, the dam's impact on rural livelihoods differed in the details but was similarly economically devastating in the long term, as the story of the *kapenta* fishing industry illustrates. Many of the peasants displaced by the dam now live upward of forty kilometers from the reservoir, making it extremely difficult for them to fish there regularly. For those residing closer to the lake, fishing prospects initially seemed extremely favorable, since the reservoir's high water level and rich vegetation caused a substantial increase in the fish population, which the dam blocked from migrating downriver.[16] Additionally, a new type of fish, which local communities called kapenta,[17] began appearing in the reservoir in the early 1980s. According to Padre Gremi, people noticed droves of "little fish jumping out of the water. One could see them at night. They were very tiny. No one could imagine that there could be so many."[18] An official of the UN Food and Agriculture Organization identified them as Lake Tanganyika sardines that had traveled from Lake Kariba to Mozambique in large shoals.[19] Despite their small size, dried kapenta were in great demand in Zimbabwe and became an important staple in this part of Mozambique.

By the mid-1980s the fishing industry on Lake Cahora Bassa was flourishing.[20] An estimated fifteen hundred independent fishermen trolled the lake with nets and canoes or used lines, nets, and traps near the shoreline to catch both kapenta and larger fish.[21] Women fished along the reservoir's edges, using nets and scooping up fish with sheets and blankets.[22] For many impoverished peasants, fishing replaced farming as their principal economic activity.[23] As Bento Chitima recalled, "Although we could not reclaim our farmlands, which were underwater, we had access to the lake with its many fish. We began to build canoes and boats and many purchased licenses from the government to fish in the reservoir."[24] Others fished without authorization.[25] On a good night, a local fisherman could capture as many as twenty large fish.[26] Elisa Belo remembered that "we never suffered from a lack of fish. . . . Often we had enough to sell."[27] So initially promising were fishing conditions that as early as 1978, to take advantage of the reservoir's economic potential, Catholic missionaries at Boroma organized a commercial fishing cooperative, which provided jobs for forty unemployed young men residing around Tete city. Supported by French and Italian donors, cooperative members purchased a motorized fishing boat that enabled them to capture larger quantities of kapenta, which generally lived in the middle of the lake. On most nights, a group of cooperative members could catch one hundred kilograms of fish, which, after being off-loaded and dried, were sent to Zimbabwe and the local market at Tete.[28]

Local demand for kapenta grew substantially after 1992, when the cessation of hostilities with Renamo allowed many war refugees to return to the Zambezi valley. Kapenta orders from Zimbabwe were also rising in the early 1990s,[29] and for the first time in nearly two decades, shops were selling imported fishing nets and the petrol used in the antiquated motors fishermen attached to their canoes and other small boats. The local catch skyrocketed, persuading several Tete businessmen and officials to organize additional small fishing ventures, which hired local fishermen, whom they paid with a portion of the catch.[30]

This relative prosperity, however, proved short lived for local fishermen, who were rapidly displaced by foreign fishing firms. By 1994 commercial Zimbabwean and South African enterprises were pouring into the region to exploit this new opportunity. They were joined by a small number of Maputo-based firms, such as Cahora Bassa Fisheries Lda.,[31] 73 percent of which, although it was registered in Mozambique, was owned by two Zimbabwean investors.

The fortunes of Cahora Bassa Fisheries in the 1990s illustrate how the impact of the dam on peasant communities dovetailed with the forces of economic liberalization to lock local fishermen out of their one remaining possible livelihood. Cahora Bassa Fisheries began with five fishing rigs, but, with business booming, it doubled its fleet in 1996.[32] Using large motorized boats, powerful night lights, and enormous circular nets, it and other large fishing companies managed to harvest annually several thousand tonnes of kapenta, along with larger fish. By 1998 there were more than 250 boats operating on the lake, each able to haul in approximately one ton of fish per night.[33] Six years later, they estimated their total annual catch at over ten thousand tons.[34] By 2006, Mozambique was exporting sixteen thousand tons of kapenta, and the total value of exports to Zimbabwe between 2005 and 2007 was almost $15 million.[35]

The Frelimo government made little effort to protect Zambezi fishermen, whose inability to compete with the better-capitalized fisheries had dramatic economic consequences.[36] Sometimes commercial boats towed away their nets and refused to compensate them for their losses—leaving them frustrated and angry, as foreign-owned rigs brought in large hauls.[37] Luís Salicuchepa, a local fisherman, complained to a Mozambican journalist that "on many occasions, the owners of the large fishing boats catching kapenta, most of whom are white South Africans and Zimbabweans, verbally attack us and try to sink our canoes. These attacks have caused several deaths."[38]

In the face of this intensified foreign competition, the catches of local fishermen declined dramatically. While some continued to eke out a living on the lake, others abandoned fishing altogether or worked on the commercial boats for wages as low as $1 per day.[39] These men would go to work in the afternoon, labor through the night without respite or food, and return home the following morning.[40] Despite receiving numerous complaints from these exploited fishermen,[41] the state, preoccupied with attracting investors to exploit the nation's resources, took no action. Instead, it continued to license foreign-owned firms, effectively giving them carte blanche over Lake Cahora Bassa.

Local inspectors also failed to supervise conditions at the fishing camps, where a small number of women, working long hours for as little as seventy-five cents per day, dried the fish, cleaned and repaired nets, and cooked for the Zimbabwean crews who lived there.[42] Some of these women and younger girls engaged in prostitution on the side, for which white company managers and Zimbabwean overseers paid them appreciably more than what they could earn as employees.[43]

While most of the kapenta fished from Lake Cahora Bassa went to Zimbabwe, the diets of many Mozambican communities nearby were acutely short of protein.[44] Overfishing of the remaining stock compounded the local food crisis, which led to dwindling catches. One South African fisherman described a state of "anarchy where they're netting everything . . . even immature fish [in] the tributaries, where fish spawn."[45] The most desperate even robbed fish from their neighbors to survive.[46] While it is not clear whether out-of-work fisherfolk or just hungry neighbors were the ones who stole fish, these examples suggest that commercial fishing intensified food insecurity. Several foreign firms donated a portion of their profits to build schools and health clinics in the region,[47] but that they did so by appropriating another of the Zambezi's precious resources underscored, once again, the limits of Mozambique's resource sovereignty in the era of neoliberalism. Padre Gremi best summed up the irony of the situation: "When they built the dam, people were forced to leave the area. Now we own the dam, but others are doing the fishing."[48]

Development experts hailed the "kapenta revolution" and the growth of the fishing industry on the lake. The real story, however, is much more sobering. While commercial fishing created some jobs, local fishermen and riverine communities enjoyed few of its benefits. In fact, by 2001 fishing, like energy, had become commodified and was essentially sold abroad.

The devastating social, ecological, and economic consequences of Cahora Bassa throughout the lower Zambezi valley have generated much anger in rural communities both around the dam site and downriver. The litany of grievances range from the specific—such as resentment that the state no longer employs game wardens to manage the burgeoning crocodile population—to local residents' more general frustrations about their lack of access to electrical power and their sense that their poverty was unending. The experience of impoverishment associated with Cahora Bassa leads older residents such as João Raposo to hark back almost wistfully to the colonial past: "In those times [before the dam] we were afraid of the government. PIDE threatened you and you could be put in jail. But we had enough money to buy goats, pigs, and chickens and to support our family."[49]

The most glaring grievance, however, concerns the terrible economic and ecological harm caused by the dam's interruption of the Zambezi flow regime. Repeatedly, women and men, young and old, agriculturalists and fisherfolk bemoaned the loss of the river's sustenance of them, their parents, and the many generations before them.[50] They also insisted that the Frelimo government bore responsibility for restoring the river's flow.[51] When we asked how this could be done, Mário Chambiça and two other local residents asserted that "the directors of the dam [should] recognize our needs and [only discharge] water [when] we are not farming [in our river gardens]."[52] Aniva João and his neighbors were more explicit: "We want the continuation of the floods of the past. Then, we were secure because there were many fish and farming gave us a lot of food. The old flood system enabled us to plant on the fertile islands and near the river, which provided most of our food. Now the floods come any time of year and destroy our crops, and it is difficult to catch fish."[53]

By the early 2000s the intensity of local frustration over this critical livelihood issue spurred peasants and fisherfolk from throughout the Zambezi valley to join in protest with Maputo-based environmentalists (see below). Approximately seventy representatives from communities throughout the valley, at a 2004 meeting, adopted a resolution demanding restoration of predam "environmental flow releases [whose] implementation would significantly assist in recovering the different subsistence activities along the river."[54]

Government officials, however, have ignored these pleas. Even after leading international scientists demonstrated that a partial restoration of the Zambezi's predam flow regime would require only a 3 to 5 percent loss in electricity,[55] the idea gained little traction in Maputo. Government resistance appeared linked to plans to construct a second dam at Mphanda Nkuwa, because any reduction in the flow from Cahora Bassa, mimicking seasonal flooding to some extent, would reduce the new dam's ability to maximize energy output, thereby cutting into investors' potential profits.[56] Its desperation to attract foreign capital has also blinded the government to both the economic and ecological damage caused by Cahora Bassa and the likely worsening of these problems with the addition of a new dam.

MOVING FORWARD: MPHANDA NKUWA

As noted in chapter 6, a feasibility report completed in 2000 by the Technical Unit for Implementation of Hydropower Projects (UTIP)[57] signaled the state's commitment to construct a second dam at Mphanda Nkuwa.[58] Four of the findings highlighted in its executive summary and an accompanying development prospectus are particularly germane.[59] First, the report claimed that Mphanda Nkuwa could be a run-of-river dam with only limited environmental impact. Whereas Cahora Bassa created a vast lake stretching more than 2,739 square kilometers behind the dam, Mphanda Nkuwa's reservoir would be less than 4 percent as large (96.5 square kilometers), minimizing "the risks of significant adverse impacts to biodiversity from construction activities and inundation."[60] Second, since the dam would likely displace only 1,400 peasants in 260 housing units, the social and economic costs would be minimal.[61] The alleged willingness of local communities to relocate voluntarily in traditional villages, "close to the reservoir for water supplies and Mepanda Uncua for employment opportunities, provided adequate compensation was arranged,"[62] was the report's third critical finding. Finally, UTIP saw Mphanda Nkuwa as vital to closing the energy gap both within Mozambique and throughout southern Africa.[63]

While expressing confidence that Mozambique's 1995 National Water Policy protected the rights of people to basic water needs, the executive summary did acknowledge, albeit briefly, some potentially adverse effects—reduction in water quality caused by waste disposal, decay of inundated vegetation, and restricted river flow. It also conceded that the new dam would trap sediment inflows from the Luia River, thereby reducing the fertility of wetland soils downstream, and warned that fluctuations in discharges from the dam, particularly during the dry season, could affect the availability of fish, alter the river channels, and lead to unpredictable flooding of alluvial fields. To address these concerns, the consultants proposed only that there be further studies "to inform negotiations between the developer and the affected parties aimed at agreeing [on] compensation for the loss of water rights."[64]

Immediately after the study's completion, the Mozambican government officially sought international investment for the dam's construction, which it expected would begin in 2004 or 2005.[65] China was the first to respond. In April 2006, as part of Beijing's ongoing efforts to expand China's economic influence in Africa, the Export-Import Bank of China signed a memorandum of understanding with the Mozambican government to finance the Mphanda Nkuwa dam project at an estimated cost of $2.3 billion.[66]

This agreement provoked strong opposition from Justiça Ambiental (JA!), the small but vocal Maputo-based environmental organization created in the early 2000s to oppose Mphanda Nkuwa's construction.[67] JA!'s decade-long campaign against the dam has repeatedly invoked the best practices laid out in a 2000 report of the WCD, a body convened in 1998 by the World Conservation Union and the World Bank (the single largest funder of the international dams industry) to review the "development effectiveness" of large dams and create improved guidelines for dam construction.[68] Because Mozambique needed the bank's financial support—or at least its endorsement—to attract investors for the Mphanda Nkuwa project, the government could ignore these recommendations only at its peril.[69]

JA!'s opposition rested on the WCD's finding that "an unacceptable and often unnecessary price has been paid . . . by people displaced, by communities downstream, by taxpayers, and by the natural environment."[70] It supported JA!'s arguments that the new dam would exacerbate the ecological and social destruction caused by Cahora Bassa,[71] that Frelimo officials minimized these harmful impacts,[72] and that reforming Cahora Bassa's flow management plan to more closely resemble natural flooding patterns would allow peasants to resume farming along the alluvial floodplains.[73] The group also maintained that, rather than promoting public debate on Mphanda Nkuwa, the government had secretly approved the new dam project "without any public consultation, without participation of its citizens and without taking into account our preoccupations."[74] JA!'s overriding criticism was that construction of Mphanda Nkuwa would permanently preclude reversal of any of the damages caused by Cahora Bassa—widely regarded as one of the most ecologically destructive dams in Africa. According to Daniel Ribeiro, JA!'s lead organizer, "Mphanda Nkuwa could cement problems that are killing the ecosystem."[75]

Mphanda Nkuwa, however, does not have to freeze the colonial past in place. Scientists maintain that it is possible both to build this run-of-river dam and to restore pre–Cahora Bassa flood patterns, which could rehabilitate agricultural production and the delta floodplain's ecosystem.[76] Even a 3 percent reduction at Cahora Bassa "could result in very significant improvements in ecosystem-based livelihoods of downstream residents."[77] While technologically feasible, the issues are preeminently political and economic. Will the Mozambican government and investors in Cahora Bassa and Mphanda Nkuwa be willing to accept a 3-to-10 percent reduction in the amount of water discharged from Cahora Bassa to restore seasonal flooding and improve the lives of the rural poor, even though doing so would cut into the profits of both dams?[78]

Global environmental organizations, such as the World Wildlife Fund and the International Rivers Network, an antidam group based in Berkeley, California, have lent support to Mozambique's antidam campaign.[79] A number of foreign researchers, some with ties to the Mozambican activists, also joined the fray.[80] They hoped to pressure potential international investors, aid organizations, and the World Bank to withdraw from the project or at least to create enough noise to make them reassess their participation, given the social injustice and ecological devastation Mphanda Nkuwa would create.[81]

In 2006, JA! undertook its own community risk assessment to determine the likely ecological and social impact of Mphanda Nkuwa. After interviewing peasants living adjacent to the proposed project, British consultant James Morrissey concluded that displacement of peasants to higher locations would create fierce competition for the best lands and intensify existing inequalities and hierarchies of power.[82] He also expressed concern that minifloods occurring during peak power production would destroy vegetable gardens cultivated on the riverbed near Mphanda Nkuwa, which were a critical source of food during the long dry season.[83] Three years later, JA! issued a detailed report, written by Mark Hankins, an expert on renewable energy, which criticized the government for "putting all its eggs in one basket" and recommended that Mozambique focus on a combination of solar power, wind power, and smaller dams to electrify the countryside.[84]

In response to the growing outcry over Mphanda Nkuwa, the Mozambican government commissioned a new feasibility assessment, which produced a multivolume report entitled *The Scoping Study*, to rebut these criticisms.[85] State authorities also sought to discredit antidam activists, by characterizing them as irresponsible opponents of development. UTIP director Sérgio Elísio distinguished the government's position from that of the activists: "We do not agree with all the standards of the World Commission on Dams. We have our own laws. The WCD has a single agenda: to stop all development of dams. The United States has some 7,000 dams. We have one and we want to have two."[86] Mozambique's minister of energy similarly publicly criticized local environmentalists, whom he characterized as privileged urban elites—"people who live in houses with air conditioners"—trying to impose their own dogmas on the nation.[87]

Debates in the Mozambican capital were only one aspect of the struggle over Mphanda Nkuwa. In 2002, UTIP launched meetings to "gather public opinion about the proposed Mphanda Nkuwa project."[88] Of these meetings, only two—at Chirodzi-Sanangwe and Chococoma—occurred in communities that would be immediately affected by the new dam. The rest of the meetings took place at administrative and provincial capitals and in Maputo, more than fifteen hundred kilometers away.[89] Local administrators, provincial authorities, business representatives, church leaders, Renamo officials, foreign diplomats, and representatives of nongovernmental organizations attended these meetings, which ranged in size from four to thirty-eight participants. Despite concerns raised by several attendees about the challenges of relocation and what indemnification those losing their land would receive, UTIP claimed to find general support for the initiative.[90] Accounts by participants and outside observers describing a small number of subsequent conversations in Chirodzi-Sanangwe and Chococoma over the past decade, however, paint a picture of tightly scripted encounters in which officials of the Ministry of Mining and Energy—treating the construction of Mphanda Nkuwa as a foregone conclusion—set the agenda and determined the outcome.

Indeed, accounts from residents of these communities clearly demonstrate that the state made little effort to ensure peasant participation in the early decision-making process. Local communities rarely received advance notice of the few meetings that actually took place. Typically, the local Frelimo party secretary or his assistants would inform residents that they were expected to attend a meeting the following day, at which officials from Maputo would discuss new plans for "developing" the region and increasing employment. Araújo Tionequi, who lived along the Zambezi, recalled that, after a short introduction and a brief discussion of the new dam and the opportunities it would create, state officials informed them that sometime in the near future, they would have to abandon their homes and relocate. These officials provided no indication of when this move would occur, where the new homes would be, or how they would carry out this process.[91]

Peasants who attended these meetings rarely asked questions or challenged the plan in any way.[92] Their silence at the meetings in Chirodzi-Sanangwe and Chococoma reflected a top-down culture of governance. This legacy of Portuguese colonial rule, reinforced by postindependence Frelimo vanguardism and the unyielding commitment of the subsequent neoliberal state to externally dictated structural-adjustment development programs, left little room for rural Mozambicans to discuss, let alone debate, official policies. Most simply presumed that, if the state decided to move them, they had no recourse. Moreover, in direct contravention of WCD guidelines, neither before nor after these meetings did ministry officials provide local residents with information that would have enabled them to participate in the discussion in a meaningful way. All written material about Mphanda Nkuwa was in English or Portuguese—languages that few, if any, members of these communities could read—and was archived in the ministry, in Maputo.

A 2003 report by FIVAS, a Norwegian nongovernmental organization, confirmed how thoroughly the Mozambican government had marginalized riverside communities: "Today there seems to be an enormous knowledge gap between the developers and the local affected people. Generally people do not know much about the project and its consequences, and the consequences they are aware of are generally the positive ones like compensation and job opportunities. The local people have generally not been involved in the planning and decision-making process."[93] The World Wildlife Fund reached a similar conclusion the following year.[94]

Despite these various criticisms, little has changed since 2003. In 2008 the Mphanda Nkuwa consortium, led by Brazilian contractor Camargo Corrêa, contracted with the Mozambican environmental consulting firm Impacto to conduct an updated environmental impact statement—one that would rebut critics and reassure potential investors. Once again, dam planners went through the motions of holding meetings—this time in 2009 in Maputo and Tete city—to discuss the scope of the impact study and present initial findings—although the meetings were not public. Attendance at these invitation-only events was limited to political and economic elites: Impacto staff, members of the consortium, government officials, representatives of major businesses, and UTIP director Sérgio Elísio.[95] Despite the claim that Impacto was conducting an independent environmental and social assessment, the tone of the meetings was unabashedly promotional.[96] The Impacto spokesperson made it clear from the beginning that, after a preliminary study, they would find no "fatal flaw" making Mphanda Nkuwa unviable. The PowerPoint presentation that followed emphasized the positive economic impacts of the dam for Mozambique, and the accompanying written materials stressed that hydroelectric power was clean and renewable.[97]

By contrast, Justiça Ambiental made several recent efforts to inform Zambezi valley residents up and down the river about the dam and tried to involve them in decision making—a process that turned out to be more complicated than anticipated.[98] One of their major challenges, according to Ribeiro, was convincing skeptical peasants that they were not powerless against the state.[99] "Before we even talked about the dam," he recalled, "we had long discussions with villagers about their constitutional and judicial rights."[100] JA! also choreographed community-based plays and distributed comic books written only in Portuguese that graphically depicted the deleterious social, cultural, and environmental impacts of Cahora Bassa, to highlight what the future would bring were Mphanda Nkuwa constructed.[101] That the visitors were urban activists with few or no ties to the Zambezi hinterland made their task even more difficult, since, as outsiders, they often encountered high levels of confusion and distrust in rural communities. As they wrote in a 2004 report, "in some communities it took some time before people gained confidence and began to open up and discuss the issues that concerned them."[102]

The high point of JA!'s mobilizing work came in October 2004, when it helped to organize a meeting in Tete city between representatives of riverside communities throughout the lower Zambezi valley and a handful of state officials to discuss Cahora Bassa's impact on their lives.[103] Approximately seventy participants—primarily peasants, fisherfolk, and representatives of nongovernmental organizations from the four provinces through which the Zambezi River flowed—attended the three-day workshop with officials from the Zambezi Water Management Authority and the Zambezi Development Authority. Here, for the first time in a formal public venue, community members had a chance to tell their stories and even to express their outrage at the suffering Cahora Bassa had caused them.[104]

At the conference's conclusion, participants issued a twelve-point declaration entitled "Voices from the Zambezi." The document celebrated the Zambezi River as "the source of life for our families" and acknowledged "the important role of Cahora Bassa dam and its electricity as a means for economic development." It also highlighted the dam's adverse impact on peasant agriculture and fishing—caused by erosion, flooding, and the loss of enriching sediment—and the drying up of the Zambezi delta, which destroyed the mangroves and the prawn fisheries that relied on this fragile ecosystem.[105] Reflecting the sentiments of downriver communities, it further called for the reestablishment of the river's predam flow regime.

The participants also decided to form a regional association, Vozes do Zambeze (Voices of the Zambezi), to survey some thirty-eight communities along the length of the river on the Mozambican side, so it could create an inventory of concerns and advocate for them at the provincial and national levels. Afterward, JA! organizers visited various communities in the valley searching for people to join this organization. Due to bureaucratic hurdles, it took until 2007 to get the group officially registered. Because registration required all leaders be simultaneously present in Tete city to sign the necessary paperwork, the leadership team was composed solely of people who lived there, since no one else could afford the cost and inconvenience of such a trip. The entire executive board of Vozes do Zambeze was urban and male, and because the positions were unpaid, all, though not wealthy, were wage earners. The president was Chivio Cheiro, who was only twenty-seven years old.[106]

Justiça Ambiental secured some funding for the organization. According to Cheiro, the few thousand dollars provided during the first year covered nothing beyond visits to communities within Tete Province. Riddled by infighting and accusations of corruption, and crippled by lack of funds, Vozes do Zambeze did nothing after 2008 and, by 2009, had effectively ceased to exist.[107] For peasants living in the region of Chirodzi-Sanangwe, the uncertainties surrounding Mphanda Nkuwa did not.

The Zambezi River was particularly narrow adjacent to Chirodzi-Sanangwe, which made this area of regional strategic importance long before a dam was contemplated there.[108] Approximately six hundred people now live in the central village along the confluence of these two rivers, one thousand on homesteads scattered among the hills within a two-hour walk, and the remaining four hundred or so in neighborhoods on the north and south banks of the Zambezi.[109] Nearly all will have to be relocated if Mphanda Nkuwa is built, as will a few dozen families residing in Chococoma, just downriver.

Families in the upland hills grew sorghum and maize in the rainy season, and many raised cattle and goats. Those living beside the Zambezi also fished and, because the river nourished riverside soil with rich sediments, cultivated maize during the dry season. Fish and dry-season maize were sold to families who lived on higher ground, although that trade—which long sustained both parts of the community—diminished dramatically after Cahora Bassa's construction.[110] During the dry season, as grain stocks ran short, both riverside and upland families supplemented their diets with the minimally nutritious maçanica fruits that grew in bushes along the Zambezi.

The prospect of forced resettlement for the new dam provoked different responses from residents of these two communities, depending primarily on economic vulnerability and the probable costs of displacement.[111] For men with large cattle herds and access to good land, for instance, government promises of compensation for losses suffered during relocation reduced the perceived risks of displacement and encouraged a more positive attitude toward the dam. Daniel Makaza, a veteran of Frelimo's war of liberation, and Virgílio Djimo, one of Chirodzi-Sanangwe's three school teachers, both spoke approvingly about the energy Mphanda Nkuwa would generate "for everyone," the greater opportunities for fishing, the increased access to water for animals, and the possibility that the dam would improve riverine soils and crop yields.[112] Some less affluent residents also favored relocation, believing that it offered an escape from the harsh conditions along the Zambezi caused by the construction of Cahora Bassa, more than thirty-five years earlier.[113] For them, the dam offered the promise of prosperity.

Other villagers who lived near the proposed dam site, however, opposed relocation, fearing that it would jeopardize rural livelihoods. "It's reasonable living here," said Vincent Gadeni. "There, where they're going to go, they don't know what's going to happen. It could be worse there. It is possible they will not even have *malambe* [fruit of the baobab]. But even if we might have better houses, a school, a hospital, what's important is food, water."[114] Carlos Jaime, the Frelimo secretary of Chococoma's riverside neighborhood, concurred: "We are going to be relocated from here for another place. . . . There, we are going to have to request machamba from the population who lives there. Here I am a fisherman. If I go there, perhaps there will not be a place to fish."[115]

Older residents, especially women living on their own, were deeply anxious about the prospect of a move that promised them few material benefits and that they felt powerless to resist. Women, like Marialena Dique (see fig. 7.2), who was single, in her sixties, and too weak to farm on her own, did not have the resources to deal with the shock of relocation; nor were they likely to gain from any cash-earning opportunities the dam might generate. Dependent on charity and a small vegetable garden irregularly watered by the Chirodzi River, Marialena worried that in Nhasicana, where she might have to move, she would not have access to a similar field.[116] Sieda Denja, a woman in her fifties who lived with her mother, echoed this sense of anxiety: "We are accustomed to living here, to producing food here. We do not know to where we will be relocated. Since the colonial era we have always lived here, we passed all this time, until today. This place is where we are from. The little we have can keep a family going."[117] Araújo Tionequi, discussing older people's fear of relocation, highlighted the fatalistic quality of elders' attitudes toward resettlement—especially poignant given their greater control over such decisions in earlier times: "They were born here, they've been here, but they have to leave because it is an order."[118]

Ironically, even some local government and party officials were anxious about relocating for a second dam project, revealing both the deep imprint

FIGURE 7.2. Marialena Dique. *Mauro Pinto*

of Cahora Bassa on popular memory and the great distance between Zambezi valley realities and priorities in the nation's capital. For many of those interviewed, tragic memories associated with the forced resettlements of the early 1970s still affected reactions to Mphanda Nkuwa.[119] For instance, Francisco Fondo, Chirodzi-Sanangwe's thirty-eight-year-old Frelimo secretary, recounted how some people displaced during construction of Cahora Bassa had become easy prey for lions.[120] Memories of forced relocation to an aldeamento in the 1970s, and of hiding in the hills when Renamo swept through the region in the 1980s, no doubt also fed fears of what a new round of resettlement might bring.

Yet everyone we interviewed—from government representatives to the humblest peasants—shared the belief that this decision was out of their hands, and that the state alone would determine their future. "What am I going to do?" asked Fidelis Chakala, a community official. "They're going to close the dam, and we [will] have to leave."[121]

While the construction of a dam at Mphanda Nkuwa would dramatically transform the lives of residents of Chirodzi-Sanangwe and Chococoma, it would have only a negligible immediate impact on downriver communities. Not building this dam, however, could be quite significant, since it would increase the possibility of restoring the pre–Cahora Bassa flow regime.

Despite the widespread desire of rural residents throughout the lower Zambezi valley that the government mimic the river's previous flow, JA!, other environmental activists, and scientists face an uphill battle gaining the attention of state officials. The absence of a strong antidam protest movement in the valley, JA!'s weak ties to the countryside, and the state's unrelenting commitment to construct the dam reveal their lack of leverage or power. JA! organizer Ribeiro summarized their challenge: "We are like a dog who barks but has no teeth."[122]

↜

When the Portuguese colonial state conceived the Cahora Bassa project, in the mid-1960s, officials charged with its planning and construction envisioned a transformed Zambezi River, whose every drop thereafter would be used as efficiently as possible. Whether through hydroelectric generation, irrigation, or enhanced navigability, the river's waters would no longer be "wasted" by simply flowing into the sea. This is the developmentalist promise of all large dams. Yet, despite all the glossy brochures and public pronouncements about its developmental capacity to improve the lives of all Mozambicans, the real reason for Cahora Bassa's construction was to cement a security alliance between the Portuguese colonial state in Mozambique and the apartheid regime in neighboring South Africa. Constructing this dam was also part of an antiguerrilla military strategy aimed at defeating Frelimo and symbolically asserting Portugal's intention to remain in Africa indefinitely.

More relevant for this study are the ways in which the highly authoritarian colonial state, long used to stifling internal dissent, suppressed all other possible narratives about the dam—especially local accounts of violence at the dam site and the state violence employed to forcibly remove thousands of peasants to make way for the reservoir. Since the colonial state prohibited scholars, journalists, and international observers from entering the region, peasants herded into protected villages could only share stories of suffering with one another, and the lived experiences of African workers who built the massive hydroelectric project remained in the shadows of history.

The end of Portuguese rule changed neither the developmentalist thrust of official narratives of Cahora Bassa nor the willingness of the government to suppress dissident claims about the dam's disastrous effects. Although, during the liberation struggle, the nationalist leadership openly opposed Cahora Bassa's construction, once in power, Frelimo celebrated the dam as an unproblematic icon of socialist development and progress. As mounting military pressure from South Africa's destabilization campaign increasingly interfered with Frelimo's efforts to restructure the national economy, the aggrieved stories of peasants in the riverine communities most directly impacted by the dam were lost in the noise about socialist transformation and South African and Renamo destabilization. When, in 1987, the Mozambican government abandoned its socialist agenda and agreed to implement the IMF–World Bank structural adjustment program, Cahora Bassa figured prominently in a market-liberalizing development strategy that required the loosening of state control over the economy and an expanded role for the private sector. The centrality of hydroelectric power in this new economic order yet again effectively overwhelmed many of the pressing concerns of riverside communities in the lower Zambezi valley.

This study, however, is more than just the story of a state-led development initiative. Like other modernizing projects, Cahora Bassa also has a social history. Rural communities—whether in Mozambique, Brazil, China, or India—have histories that stand partly outside the logic of modernist state planning. While state planners lay out their graphs and maps, take photographs from above, and organize human settlements, these communities interact with their environment, which, in addition to being a life-sustaining resource they must carefully manage, is a site of significant social and cultural activities and a landscape of memories. Thus, Cahora Bassa was not simply an artifice of the late-colonial state; it was also a critical event in the history of local agriculture, in the reshaping of riverine environments and communities, in the reworking of social relationships, and in the reconfiguring of memories. For these reasons, the real impact of the dam on the lives of the people in the lower Zambezi valley was far more complicated than "development" experts had predicted.

With the current Mozambican government moving—inexorably, it seems—toward construction of a second dam at Mphanda Nkuwa, it is imperative that we pay attention to this history and that we listen to and learn from the men and women whose lives are so intimately bound up with the past, present, and future of the Zambezi River. Throughout this study, we have tried to shed light on the lived experiences, memories, and perspectives of those whose world was irrevocably transformed by the colossal dam because, if their stories continue to be ignored, the past is likely to be replayed in the present with devastating consequences.

The idea of building a new dam at Mphanda Nkuwa is not merely a re-enactment of the history of Cahora Bassa but the continuation of an ongoing project of colonizing the Zambezi valley and harnessing the Zambezi's power. Since dams have an extremely long life and, once built, cannot be radically altered by subsequent political regimes, their presence limits a state's available options both now and in the future. Meanwhile, it is the rural poor who must live with the consequences of this delusion of development.

When we began this project, in 1997, we knew little about dams and failed to appreciate the significance of the Zambezi River as a source of life. We never intended to offer in this book either a prescription for mitigating the damage caused by Cahora Bassa or a blueprint for preventing the construction of Mphanda Nkuwa. Nevertheless, it was necessary to raise the critical questions that flow from the stories of affected riverside communities.

Two major questions about the legal status of the river stand out. Most fundamentally, one must ask to whom the Zambezi River, with its life-sustaining water, belongs. Does ownership of the waterway reside in the hands of the seven nations upstream through which it flows, leaving Mozambique in a particularly vulnerable position, especially in times of drought? Within Mozambique, is the Zambezi the domain of those who reside along its banks and whose families lived there for centuries, of the communities living in the provinces through which it runs, of the recently constituted nation, or of the ruling elite? These are not easy questions to resolve—witness the highly contested claims to the water of the Colorado River, the conflicts in Turkey's Kurdish regions, or the tensions between Vietnam and Cambodia over the Mekong Delta Water Management for Rural Development Project.

These competing demands for water not only highlight fundamental issues about resource sovereignty, but raise a second significant question for Mozambique. How can such competing claims be resolved in a country with a long history of authoritarian rule, weak democratic institutions, a fragile civil society, and extreme poverty? In the colonial era, the answer was clear. Lisbon had exclusive power to make whatever decisions were in its imperial interests, and security, rather than poverty alleviation, was the state's paramount concern. In the years immediately after Mozambique's independence, the revolutionary state defined the domesticated Zambezi River as a national resource that would advance its socialist agenda. The Frelimo government negotiated international funding for the construction of a second set of power lines to electrify the large state farms and numerous communal villages located in central and southern Mozambique, to turn this region into the breadbasket of the country. In this era of state planning and a brutal destabilization war, the Maputo-based political leadership allowed peasants little space to voice their concerns. Neoliberalism reinforced the notions that the Zambezi River and the dam were assets that international markets could exploit and that the state's role was merely to remove impediments. According to this most recent "development" scenario, Cahora Bassa would export energy to surrounding countries, particularly South Africa, and generate additional cheap electricity to entice foreign investment in the private sector. While the nation and its citizens would be the presumed beneficiaries of this strategy, there has been no discussion of which social classes or regions would benefit. Nor is there acknowledgment of the social and ecological turmoil caused by Cahora Bassa or how to compensate its many victims for their losses.[123]

The current Mozambican government has framed the proposed new dam at Mphanda Nkuwa in similar developmentalist terms, managing at the same time to stifle both public debate about a second dam and serious national discussion of what should be done to mitigate the harm caused by the first one. At public meetings, consideration of the experiences, observations, and concerns of those who know the river best has not even been on the agenda. Not only has the government failed to recognize that local residents of riverine communities have deep knowledge of the Zambezi valley's microecologies,[124] which should be central to any environmental impact study for the new dam, but it has effectively silenced both them and the small number of Mozambican environmentalists and scientists who have spoken out against this project.

Among the contentious interrelated issues that must be tackled in serious public debates are the following: Do the multiple economic and environmental benefits of reestablishing a semblance of the predam flow regime outweigh the costs of a modest reduction in Cahora Bassa's capacity to produce electricity primarily for export? What would be the effect of such a reduction on investors in Mphanda Nkuwa? Can Cahora Bassa management minimize negative downriver consequences? Should the income generated by commodification of the Zambezi's energy be spent locally, building health clinics and schools and promoting local industry and jobs that would compensate riverside communities for the turmoil they have experienced and will continue to experience?[125] Are the anticipated social, economic, and ecological costs of Mphanda Nkuwa to riverside communities and the environment the appropriate price to pay for the possibility of electrifying much of the countryside? Is the possibility of these benefits more important than mitigating the destructive consequences of Cahora Bassa by restoring the predam flow regime? If the new dam is in the overwhelming public interest, what responsibility does the state have to provide compensation to the people of the Zambezi valley for bearing this burden of development? Conversely, are there more efficient, less costly, and less destructive ways of electrifying the countryside, with solar and wind power and smaller dams, as critics of Mphanda Nkuwa have insisted?[126]

Rather than debating these issues in public fora across the nation, the neoliberal state has decided to move forward on Mphanda Nkuwa in the name of accelerated national development, if it can secure the necessary funding.[127] While this study will not likely shift the terms of the debate in Mozambique, engaged scholars[128] have a responsibility to disseminate widely the stories and concerns of the rural poor, such as those who have suffered most from the changes wrought by Cahora Bassa. They must also continue to conceptualize how to both challenge developmentalism and "decolonize development." Development as practiced in Mozambique has meant promoting large-scale projects designed to export Mozambique's natural resources—whether energy to South Africa, coal to China, or kapenta to Zimbabwe. Decolonizing development and using the nation's resources to deliver materially better lives to all Mozambicans remain the challenges.

Notes

ACL	Academia das Ciências de Lisboa
AHD	Arquivo Histórico Diplomático de Ministério dos Negócios Estrangeiros
AHM	Arquivo Histórico de Moçambique
AHU	Arquivo Histórico Ultramarino
ANTT	Arquivo Nacional da Torre do Tombo
BPA	Biblioteca Pública de Ajuda
DGS	Direcção Geral de Segurança (General Security Directorate; successor to PIDE)
DM	David Morton
GG	Governo Geral
GPZ	Gabinete do Plano do Zambeze
HCB	Hidroeléctrica de Cabora Bassa (Cabora Bassa Hydroelectric)
HIA	Hoover Institution Archives, Stanford University
HMK	Hidroeléctrica de Mphanda Nkuwa
MC	Middlemas Collection, Hoover Institution Archives, Stanford University
MFPZ	Missão do Fomento e Povoamento do Zambeze
MNR	Mozambique National Resistance
MRB	Muwalfu Research Brigade (University of Malawi)
MRME	Ministério dos Recursos Minerais e Energia (Ministry of Mineral Resources and Energy)
PIDE	Polícia Internacional e de Defesa do Estado (International and State Defense Police)
SC	Secção Confidencial
SCCIM	Serviços de Centralização e Coordenação de Informações de Moçambique (Centralized Services for Coordination of Information from Moçambique)

UTIP   Unidade Técnica de Implementação dos Projectos Hidroeléctricos

WCD   World Commission on Dams

ARCHIVAL TERMS

caixa	box
códice	codex
fol.	folio
maço	packet
pasta	folder
processo	file

Unless otherwise indicated, all interviews have been conducted by the authors or by a research team of which one of the authors was a part.

CHAPTER 1: INTRODUCTION

1. During the colonial period, the Portuguese referred to the dam as Cabora Bassa.

2. Bryan R. Davies, Richard D. Beilfuss, and Martin C. Thoms, "Cahora Bassa Retrospective, 1974–1997: Effects of Flow Regulation on the Lower Zambezi River," *Verhandlungen—Internationale Vereinigung für theoretische und ange-wandte Limnologie* 27 (December 2000): 1.

3. Allen Isaacman and Chris Sneddon, "Toward a Social and Environmental History of the Building of Cahora Bassa Dam," *Journal of Southern African Studies* 26, no. 4 (2000): 607.

4. Portugal, Secretário de Estado da Informação e Turismo, *Cabora Bassa on the Move* (Lisbon: Agência Geral do Ultramar, n.d.), 21.

5. M. Anne Pitcher, *Transforming Mozambique: The Politics of Privatization, 1975–2000* (Cambridge: Cambridge University Press, 2002), 140–78.

6. Rhodesian intelligence forces created the Resistência Nacional Moçam-bicana (Mozambican National Resistance) in 1976. After Zimbabwe gained independence, Renamo became part of South Africa's campaign to destabilize Mozambique, and South African security forces began providing it with critical military and logistic support. Despite Renamo's history of brutal violence in the countryside, in some regions it was able to gain local support by taking advantage of social cleavages and economic and political grievances about Frelimo's heavy-handed policies. For studies of Renamo's varying political and military influence in Mozambique, see João Paulo Borges Coelho, "Protected Villages and Commu-nal Villages in the Mozambican Province of Tete (1968–1982): A History of State Resettlement Policies, Development and War" (PhD thesis, University of Brad-ford, 1993), 61–91; Christian Geffray, *A causa das armas: Antropologia da guerra contemporânea em Moçambique* (Porto: Afrontamento, 1991); Christian Geffray and Morgens Pedersen, "Sobre a guerra na província de Nampula," *Revista inter-nacional de estudos africanos* 4–5 (1986): 303–18; Margaret Hall, "The Mozambi-can National Resistance Movement (RENAMO): A Study in the Destruction of

an African Country," *Africa* 60, no. 1 (1990): 39–68; Carrie Manning, "Constructing Opposition in Mozambique: Renamo as Political Party," *Journal of Southern African Studies* 24, no. 1 (1998): 161–89; JoAnn McGregor, "Violence and Social Change in a Border Economy: War in the Maputo Hinterland, 1984–1992," *Journal of Southern African Studies* 24, no. 1 (1998): 37–60; Otto Roesch, "Renamo and the Peasantry in Southern Mozambique: A View from Gaza Province," *Canadian Journal of African Studies* 26, no. 3 (1992): 462–84; Alex Vines, *Renamo: Terrorism in Mozambique* (Bloomington: Indiana University Press, 1991).

7. Throughout the twentieth century, whatever the state's ideological position and regardless of the cost to local communities and their environments, massive dams were considered markers of modernity, economic growth, and national achievement. See Patrick McCully, *Silenced Rivers: The Ecology and Politics of Large Dams* (London: Zed Books, 2001).

8. The state, however, is never hegemonic and cannot totally silence alternate narratives—especially narratives fueled by a burning sense of injustice.

9. We, like Martin Klein, use the term *peasants* to refer to agriculturalists who spent much of their day working the land primarily to meet their household's basic human needs. Most lacked capital and relied on rudimentary agricultural technology and knowledge of local ecosystems to eke out a living. The household tended to be the central unit of production, with women providing the critical labor. Peasants were located in a specific field of power in which they were politically, economically, and socially subservient to the state or dominant classes, while often maintaining a degree of partial autonomy. See Klein, introduction to *Peasants in Africa: Historical and Contemporary Perspectives*, ed. Klein (Beverly Hills: Sage, 1980), 1–43. Allen Isaacman stresses the need to avoid homogenizing or essentializing peasants and argues that the labor process offered ways to distinguish temporally and spatially between different peasantries, all of whom were exploited economically. Isaacman, "Peasant and Rural Social Protest in Africa," *African Studies Review* 33, no. 2 (2002): 14–16. Henry Bernstein, on the other hand, contends that "classes of labor" is more analytically precise than the concept of "peasants." Bernstein, "Can Modernity Accommodate African 'Peasants'?" in *7° Congresso Ibérico de Estudos Africanos* (Lisbon, 2010), 1. For an important analysis of peasants and the agrarian myth, see Tom Brass, *Peasants, Populism and Postmodernism: The Return of the Agrarian Myth* (London: Frank Cass, 2000).

10. This, too, was not unique to Mozambique. Achille Mbembé, *On the Postcolony* (Berkeley: University of California Press, 2000), 66.

11. This formulation is derived from Bruce Braun, "Colonialism's Afterlife: Vision and Visuality on the Northwest Coast," *Cultural Geographies* 9, no. 2 (2002): 202–47.

12. For the agreement, see Hidroeléctrica de Cahora Bassa, *Our Energy Embraces Mozambique* (Lisbon: HCB, 2000).

13. This is clear from pronouncements of President Armando Guebuza, who claimed that the agreement that allowed Mozambique to take a majority holding in the Cahora Bassa dam in 2007 "did not simply mean Mozambican control over a key asset but was 'the removal of the final stronghold of foreign domination'

[and] the country's 'second independence.'" "Mozambique: Guebuza Highlights Control over Cahora Bassa," *AIM*, December 13, 2007, http://allafrica.com/stories /200712130756.html; "Mozambique: Cahora Bassa Agreement 'a Second Independence,'" *AIM*, November 30, 2005, http://allafrica.com/stories/200511300358.html.

14. Workshop on Sustainable Use of Cahora Bassa Dam and the Zambezi Valley, September 29–October 2, 1997, Songo.

15. For a summary of the proceedings, see B. R. Davies, ed., *Report on the Songo Workshop on the Sustainable Utilization of the Cahora Bassa Dam and the Valley of the Lower Zambezi* (Maputo: Arquivo do Patrimônio Cultural, 1997).

16. In one particularly moving presentation, Padre Claúdio Gremi, a Jesuit priest stationed in Songo in the early 1970s, recalled how thousands of Africans were forcibly expelled from their homelands and herded into guarded resettlement camps, known as *aldeamentos*.

17. This notion of an alternative history derives from Shahid Amin, *Event, Metaphor, and Memory: Chauri Chaura, 1922–1992* (Berkeley: University of California Press, 1995).

18. Chris Sneddon, Leila Harris, Radoslav Dimitrov, and Uygar Özesmi, "Contested Waters: Conflict, Scale, and Sustainability in Aquatic Socioecological Systems," *Society and Natural Resources* 15, no. 8 (2002): 663–75; Erik Swyngedouw, *Social Power and the Urbanization of Water* (Oxford: Oxford University Press, 2004); Vandana Shiva, *Water Wars: Privatization, Pollution, and Profit* (Cambridge, MA: South End Press, 2002).

19. Large dams are those measuring at least 18 meters (60 feet) from foundation to crest. McCully, *Silenced Rivers*, 3–4.

20. Thayer Scudder, *The Future of Large Dams: Dealing with Social, Environmental, Institutional, and Political Costs* (London: Earthscan, 2005), 1–3.

21. Kader Asmal, "Globalisation from Below," preface to *Dams and Development: A New Framework for Decision-Making*, ed. World Commission on Dams (London: Earthscan, 2000), 1.

22. McCully, *Silenced Rivers*, 1–8.

23. Ibid., 237.

24. Jawaharlal Nehru, *Jawaharlal Nehru's Speeches*, vol. 3, *March 1953–August 1957*, 3rd ed. (New Delhi: Ministry of Information and Broadcasting, Publications Division, 1983), 2.

25. McCully, *Silenced Rivers*, 8. For a revealing interior view of the World Bank, see Michael Goldman, *Imperial Nature: The World Bank and Struggle for Social Justice in the Age of Globalization* (New Haven: Yale University Press, 2005).

26. McCully, *Silenced Rivers*, 18.

27. Ibid., 19–20.

28. Because neither construction companies nor state officials collected data on the rural poor, this figure is necessarily an estimate. Ibid., 7.

29. Ibid., 8.

30. Heather Hoag, "Damming the Empire: British Attitudes on Hydropower Development in Africa," in *Program for the Study of the African Environment,*

Research Series, no. 3 (Boston: African Studies Center, 2008): 1–4; Frederick Cooper, "Modernizing Bureaucrats, Backward Africans, and the Development Concept," in *International Development and the Social Sciences: Essays on the History and Politics of Knowledge*, ed. Cooper and Randall Packard (Berkeley: University of California Press, 1997), 71–81.

31. Dzodzi Tsikata, *Living in the Shadow of the Large Dams: Long Term Responses of Downstream and Lakeside Communities of Ghana's Volta River Project* (Leiden: Brill, 2006), 43–48.

32. Quoted in ibid., 43.

33. William M. Adams, *Wasting the Rain: Rivers, People, and Planning in Africa* (Minneapolis: University of Minnesota Press, 1992), 131–34. The Aswan was an Egyptian-Sudanese undertaking, and Kariba was a project of Northern and Southern Rhodesia.

34. McCully, *Silenced Rivers*, xxvii.

35. Ibid., 5.

36. Tsikata, *Living in the Shadow*, 115; Adams, *Wasting the Rain*, 131–32.

37. Adams, *Wasting the Rain*, 131–32; Elizabeth Colson, *The Social Consequences of Resettlement: The Impact of the Kariba Resettlement upon the Gwembe Tonga* (Manchester: Manchester University Press, 1971), 20.

38. Scudder, *Large Dams*, 1–3.

39. Adams, *Wasting the Rain*, 134–36.

40. Edward Goldsmith and Nicholas Hildyard, eds., *The Social and Environmental Effects of Large Dams*, 2 vols. (San Francisco: Sierra Club Books, 1984), 1:51–66.

41. World Commission on Dams (WCD), *Dams and Development: A New Framework for Decision-Making* (London: Earthscan, 2000), xxvii.

42. Hoag, "Damming the Empire," 1–4; Cooper, "Modernizing Bureaucrats," 71–81.

43. Laos's Nam Ngum Dam, which sends all its energy to Thailand, and Canada's James Bay hydroelectric project, which transmits electricity to United States, were two of the few other hydroelectric projects also constructed to export energy. Philip Hirsch and Carol Warren, eds., *The Politics of Environment in Southeast Asia: Resources and Resistance* (London: Routledge, 1998); Boyce Richardson, *Strangers Devour the Land* (Post Mills, VT: Chelsea Green Publications, 1991).

44. Sanjeev Khagram, *Dams and Development: Transnational Struggles for Water and Power* (Ithaca: Cornell University Press, 2004), 33–65, 142–49.

45. For a discussion of Hoover Dam's celebratory representation in books, newspapers, and film, see Michael Hiltzik, *Colossus: Hoover Dam and the Making of the American Century* (New York: Free Press, 2010), 303–64.

46. See, for example, Keith Jopp, *Volta: The Story of Ghana's Volta River Project* (Accra: Volta River Authority, 1965); International Commission on Large Dams (ICOLD), *World Register of Dams* (Paris: ICOLD, 1988); John A. Dixon, Lee M. Talbot, and Guy J.-M. Le Moigne, "Dams and the Environment: Considerations in World Bank Projects," *World Bank Technical Report no.10* (Washington, DC:

World Bank, 1989); Pradip Biajal and P. K. Singh, "Large Dams, Can We Do Without Them?" *Economics and Political Weekly* 35, no. 19 (May 6–12, 2000): 1659–66; Asit K. Biswas and Cecilia Tortajada, "Development and Large Dams: A Global Perspective," *Water Resources Development* 17, no. 1 (2001): 9–21.

47. Colson, *Social Consequences*, 43–72; Scudder, *Large Dams*, 1–56; Adams, *Wasting the Rain*, 128–54. For more general discussions, see Goldsmith and Hildyard, *Large Dams*; McCully, *Silenced Rivers*; Wilson V. Binger, *Environmental Effects of Large Dams* (New York: American Society of Civil Engineers, 1978).

48. Björn Beckman, "Bakolori: Peasants versus State and Industry in Nigeria," in Goldsmith and Hildyard, *Large Dams*, 2:140–55; Barbara J. Cummings, *Dam the Rivers, Damn the People: Development and Resistance in Amazonian Brazil* (London: Earthscan, 1990); William Fisher, ed., *Toward Sustainable Development? Struggling over India's Narmada River* (Armonk, NY: M. E. Sharpe, 1994).

49. The International Rivers Network (IRN), now known as International Rivers (IR), located in Berkeley, California, played a critical role in gathering and disseminating information on rural struggles against dams and in helping to organize conferences and protests that called attention to the devastating effects of dams.

50. See, for example, McCully, *Silenced Rivers*.

51. See, for example, Goldsmith and Hildyard, *Large Dams*, 231–76.

52. Joost Fontein, "The Power of Water: Landscape, Water, and the State in Southern and Eastern Africa: An Introduction," *Journal of Southern African Studies* 34, no. 4 (2008): 738–39; McCully, *Silenced Rivers*, 296–99.

53. Thayer Scudder, "Social Anthropology, Man-Made Lakes and Population Relocation in Africa," *Anthropology Quarterly* 41, no. 1 (1968): 168–76; Scudder, "Development-Induced Impoverishment, Resistance and River Basin Development," in *Understanding Impoverishment: The Consequences of Development-Induced Displacement*, ed. Christopher McDowell (Oxford: Berghahn, 1996), 49–76.

54. Adams, *Wasting the Rain*, 128–47.

55. Timothy Mitchell, *Rule of Experts: Egypt, Techno-Politics, Modernity* (Berkeley: University of California Press, 2002).

56. JoAnn McGregor, *Crossing the Zambezi: The Politics of Landscape on a Central African Frontier* (Oxford: James Currey, 2009); Julia Tischler, "Light and Power for a Multiracial Nation: The Kariba Dam Scheme in the Central African Federation" (PhD diss., University of Cologne, 2010).

57. Tsikata, *Living in the Shadow*; Stephan Miescher, "Akosombo Stories: The Volta River Project, Modernization and Nationhood in Ghana" (unpublished book prospectus, 2010).

58. Borges Coelho, "Protected Villages."

59. Keith Middlemas, *Cabora Bassa: Engineering and Politics in Southern Africa* (London, Weidenfeld and Nicolson, 1975).

60. Peter Bolton, "The Regulation of the Zambezi in Mozambique: A Study of the Origins and Impact of the Cabora Bassa Project" (PhD thesis, University of Edinburgh, 1983).

61. Bryan Davies, "Cabora Bassa Hazards," *Nature* 254 (1975): 477; Davies, "They Pulled the Plug Out of the Lower Zambezi," *African Wildlife* 29, no. 2 (1975): 26–28; Davies, A. Hall, and P. B. N. Jackson, "Some Ecological Aspects of the Cabora Bassa Dam," *Biological Conservation* 8, no. 3 (1975): 189–201.

62. Bryan Davies, "The Zambezi River System," in *The Ecology of River Systems*, ed. Davies and K. F. Walker (Dordrecht: Kluwer Academic Publishers, 1986), 225–67; Davies and Jenny Day, *Vanishing Waters* (Cape Town: University of Cape Town Press, 1988); Davies, Beilfuss, and Thoms, "Cahora Bassa Retrospective," 1–9; Richard Beilfuss and Davies, "Prescribed Flooding and Wetland Rehabilitation in the Zambezi Delta, Mozambique," in *An International Perspective on Wetland Rehabilitation*, ed. William Streever (Dordrecht: Kluwer Academic Publishers, 1999), 143–58; Davies, "Commentary on the Cross-Check Questionnaire—Cahora Bassa Dam Moçambique" (Compiled for World Commission on Dams, Cape Town, n.d.); Davies, "Rehabilitation Programme for Cahora Bassa and the Lower Zambezi (unpublished, unpaginated background document produced for the International Crane Foundation and the Ford Foundation, 1996).

63. Richard Beilfuss, "Can This River Be Saved? Rethinking Cahora Bassa Could Make a Difference for Dam-Battered Zambezi," *World Rivers Review* 14, no. 1 (1990): 8–11; Beilfuss, "Modeling Trade-offs between Hydropower Generation and Environmental Flow Releases in the Lower Zambezi River Basin, Mozambique," *International Journal of River Basin Management* 8, no. 2 (2010): 127–38; Beilfuss, "Specialist Study—Natural Resource Utilization," in Beilfuss and Brown, *Environmental Flow Requirements*, 104–7; Beilfuss, "Understanding Extreme Floods in the Lower Zambezi River" (unpublished paper, n.d.); Beilfuss and Brown, introduction to Beilfuss and Brown, *Environmental Flow Requirements*, 1–5; Beilfuss and Brown, "Assessing Environmental Flow Requirements and Trade-offs for the Lower Zambezi River and Delta, Mozambique," *International Journal of River Basin Management* 8, no. 2 (2010): 127–38; Beilfuss and Davies, "Prescribed Flooding," 143–58; Beilfuss and David dos Santos, "Patterns of Hydrological Change in the Zambezi Delta, Mozambique" (working paper no. 2, Program for the Sustainable Management of Cahora Bassa Dam and the Lower Zambezi Valley, Maputo, 2001), 31–103; Beilfuss, Arlindo Chilundo, Allen Isaacman, and Wapu Mulwafu, "The Impact of Hydrological Changes on Subsistence Production Systems and Socio-cultural Values in the Lower Zambezi Valley" (working paper no. 6, Program of Sustainable Management of Cahora Bassa Dam and the Lower Zambezi Valley, Maputo, 2002); Beilfuss, Paul Dutton, and Dorn Moore, "Land Cover and Land Use Change in the Zambezi Delta," in *Biodiversity of the Zambezi Basin Wetlands*, vol. 3, *Land Use Change and Human Impact*, ed. Jonathan Timberlake (Bulawayo: Biodiversity Foundation for Africa, 2000), 31–105; Beilfuss, Dorn Moore, Carlos Bento, and Paul Dutton, "Patterns of Vegetation Change in the Zambezi Delta, Mozambique" (working paper no. 3, Program for the Sustainable Management of Cahora Bassa Dam and the Lower Zambezi Valley Maputo, 2001).

64. Frelimo officials, who insisted on anonymity, maintain that there is unity within the government on both Cahora Bassa and the projected dam at Mphanda

Nkuwa. Daniel Ribeiro, a leading Mozambican environmentalist who is critical of the government's position, confirmed this reality. Ribeiro, interview, Maputo, March 10, 2008.

65. James Scott, *Seeing Like a State: How Certain Schemes to Improve the Human Condition Have Failed* (New Haven: Yale University Press, 1998); Mitchell, *Rule of Experts*; James Ferguson, *The Anti-politics Machine: "Development," Depoliticization, and Bureaucratic Power in Lesotho* (Minneapolis: University of Minnesota Press, 1994).

66. Peter Vandergeest, introduction to *Development's Displacements: Ecologies, Economies and Cultures at Risk,* ed. Vandergeest, Pablo Idahosa, and Pablo Bose (Vancouver: University of British Columbia Press, 2007), 12–18.

67. Our analysis has been influenced by Gyanendra Pandey's important work *Memory, History and the Question of Violence: Reflections on the Reconstruction of Partition* (Calcutta: K. P. Bagchi, 1999).

68. For a discussion of the role of Zamco, see Middlemas, *Cabora Bassa*, 41–64.

69. Peter Bolton, "Mozambique's Cahora Bassa Project: An Environmental Assessment," in Goldsmith and Hildyard, *Large Dams,* 2:156–67; Davies, "They Pulled the Plug," 26–28.

70. For an important discussion on the colonial narrative and historical memory, see Pandey, *Memory.*

71. On December 12, 1988, President Joaquim Chissano hailed Cahora Bassa's "role in the development of Southern Africa for peace and prosperity amongst the people of the region." HCB, *Our Energy,* 14.

72. For a discussion of the historical and philosophical underpinnings of development theory, see Michael Cowen and Robert Shenton, *Doctrines of Development* (London: Routledge, 1996), 3–59; Richard Peet and Elaine Hartwick, *Theories of Development: Contentions, Arguments, Alternatives* (New York: Guilford Press, 2009), 23–52; Henry Bernstein, "Studying Development/Development Studies," *African Studies* 65, no. 1 (2006): 46–52.

73. Frederick Cooper and Randall Packard, introduction to Cooper and Packard, *International Development,* 2.

74. Arthur Lewis, *The Theory of Economic Growth* (Homewood, IL: R. D. Irwin, 1955), 9–10.

75. W. W. Rostow, *The Stages of Economic Growth: A Non-communist Manifesto* (Cambridge: Cambridge University Press, 1960).

76. Cooper and Packard, introduction, 3; Bernstein, "Studying Development," 54–57.

77. Cummings, *Dam the Rivers;* Fisher, *Toward Sustainable Development;* McCully, *Silenced Rivers.*

78. Samir Amin, *Unequal Development: An Essay on the Social Formations of Peripheral Capitalism,* trans. Brian Pearce (New York: Monthly Review Press, 1976); Andre Gunder Frank, *Capitalism and Underdevelopment in Latin America: Historical Studies of Chile and Brazil* (New York: Monthly Review Press, 1969); Celso Furtado, *Economic Development in Latin America: A Survey from Colonial*

Times to the Cuban Revolution, trans. Suzette Macedo (Cambridge: Cambridge University Press, 1970); Gavin Kitching, *Development and Underdevelopment in Historical Perspective: Populism, Nationalism, and Industrialization* (London: Methuen, 1982); Walter Rodney, *How Europe Underdeveloped Africa* (Washington, DC: Howard University Press, 1981), 16.

79. Bernstein, "Studying Development," 51.

80. Peet and Hartwick, *Theories of Development*, 143–56.

81. Ibid., 156–59.

82. Heidi Hartman, "The Unhappy Marriage of Marxism and Feminism," in *Women and Revolution: A Discussion of the Unhappy Marriage of Marxism and Feminism*, ed. Lydia Sargent (Boston: South End Press, 1981), 1–4; Vandana Shiva, *Staying Alive: Women, Ecology, and Development* (London: Zed Books, 1988); Marianne Marchand and Jane Parpart, eds., *Feminism/Postmodernism/Development* (London: Routledge, 1995); Lyla Mehta ed., *Displaced by Development: Confronting Marginalisation and Gender Injustice* (New Delhi: Sage, 2009).

83. For a review of the work of environmental economists, see Chris Sneddon, "'Sustainability' in Ecological Economics, Ecology and Livelihoods: A Review," *Progress in Human Geography* 24, no. 4 (2000): 526–29.

84. Ferguson, *Anti-politics Machine*, 3–21.

85. Arturo Escobar, *Encountering Development: The Making and Unmaking of the Third World* (Princeton: Princeton University Press, 1995). From a slightly different perspective, applying the ethnographic method and critical social theory, Donald Moore offers a powerful critique of the global discourse of development within the context of racialized land dispossession in colonial Rhodesia and Zimbabwe, where the politics of landscape and rural livelihoods complicated the challenges of decolonizing development. Moore, *Suffering for Territory: Race, Place, and Power in Zimbabwe* (Durham: Duke University Press, 2005).

86. Vinay Gidwani, "The Unbearable Modernity of 'Development'? Canal Irrigation and Development Planning in Western India," *Progress in Planning* 58, no. 1 (2002): 5–6.

87. Nancy Peluso and Michael Watts, "Violent Environments," in *Violent Environments*, ed. Peluso and Watts (Ithaca: Cornell University Press, 2001), 5.

88. Nevertheless, we share Wainright's view that, because so many people in the world lack access to food and clean water, "*rejecting* 'development' . . . is neither morally possible nor desirable." Joel Wainwright, *Decolonizing Development: Colonial Power and the Maya* (London: Blackwell, 2008), 11, emphasis in original.

89. For more detailed treatments of the concept of sustainable livelihoods, see William M. Adams, *Green Development: Environment and Sustainability in the Third World* (London: Routledge, 1990); Robert Chambers and Gordon Conway, "Sustainable Rural Livelihoods: Practical Concepts for the 21st Century" (discussion paper no. 296, Institute of Development Studies, Brighton University, March 1992); John Friedmann and Haripriya Rangan, eds., *In Defense of Livelihood: Comparative Studies on Environmental Action* (West Hartford: Kumarian Press, 1993). For its application to an African context, see Allen Isaacman, "Historical

Amnesia, or the Logic of Capital Accumulation: Cotton Production in Colonial and Postcolonial Mozambique," *Environment and Planning D: Society and Space* 15, no. 6 (1997): 757–90; A. Goldman, "Threats to Sustainability in African Agriculture: Searching for Appropriate Paradigms," *Human Ecology* 23, no. 3 (1995): 291–334; James Fairhead and Melissa Leach, *Misreading the African Landscape: Society and Ecology in a Forest-Savanna Mosaic* (Cambridge: Cambridge University Press, 1996).

90. For a critical overview of the sustainability concept, see Sneddon, "'Sustainability'"; Michael Redclift, *Sustainable Development: Exploring the Contradictions* (London: Methuen, 1987); Sharachchandra Lele, "Sustainable Development: A Critical Review," *World Development* 19, no. 6 (1991): 607–21; Richard Peet and Michael Watts, "Introduction: Development Theory and Environment in an Age of Market Triumphalism," *Economic Geography* 69, no. 3 (1993): 227–53; Timothy O'Riordan, "The Politics of Sustainability," in *Sustainable Environmental Economics and Management: Principles and Practice*, ed. R. Kerry Turner (London: Belhaven Press, 1993), 37–69; Arturo Escobar, "Constructing Nature: Elements for a Poststructural Political Ecology," in *Liberation Ecologies: Environment, Development, Social Movements*, ed. Richard Peet and Michael Watts (London: Routledge, 1996), 46–68.

91. Our work is influenced by Donald Moore's notion of "articulated assemblages" which connects "nature and culture, humans and nonhumans, symbols and substance." Moore, *Suffering for Territory*, 24.

92. Much of this documentation is also available in the Centro de Documentação e Informação do Instituto Português de Apoio ao Desenvolvimento, *Inventário de Cabora Bassa* (Lisbon: Centro de Documentação, 2004).

93. We made numerous unsuccessful attempts access the archives of the HCB, which are located at Songo and in Lisbon.

94. Premesh Lalu, "The Grammar of Domination and the Subjection of Agency: Colonial Texts and Modes of Evidence," *History and Theory* 39, no. 4 (2005): 68. See also Lalu, *The Deaths of Hintsa: Postapartheid South Africa and the Shape of Recurring Pasts* (Cape Town: HSRC Press, 2009).

95. Anne Stoler, "Rethinking Colonial Categories: European Communities and the Boundaries of Rule," *Comparative Studies in Society and History* 31, no. 1 (1989): 134–61.

96. Carlos Ramos de Oliveira, *Os Tauaras do vale do Zambeze* (Lisbon: Junta de Investigações Científicas do Ultramar, 1976), 9–10.

97. Fernando Ganhão, interview, Maputo, March 12, 2006. Ganhão was the former rector of the Universidade Eduardo Mondlane and director of the Frelimo archives.

98. Unidade Técnica de Implementação dos Projectos Hidroeléctricos, *Mepanda Uncua and Cahora Bassa North Project: Preliminary Environmental and Social Impact Assessment*, documents 012/A, 012/B (Maputo: UTIP, 1999); UTIP, *Mepanda Uncua and Cahora Bassa North Project Phase II* (Maputo: UTIP, 2001); UTIP, *Mepanda Uncua and Cahora Bassa North Project: Sumário executivo do*

relatório de viabilidade (Maputo: UTIP, 2002); Republica de Moçambique, Ministério dos Recursos Minerais e Energia, *Projecto de Mepanda Uncua e Cahora Bassa Norte: Relatório da II fase do processo de consulta pública sobre a avaliação do impacto ambiental* (Maputo: MRME, 2002); MRME, *Mphanda Nkuwa Hydropower Project, Mozambique: Development Prospect* (Maputo: MRME, 2003); Hidroeléctrica de Mphanda Nkuwa, *Mphanda Nkuwa Hydroelectric Power Plant Project HMKN* (Maputo: HMK, n.d.); Sweden, Ministry of Energy, *Cabora Bassa Hydroelectric Power Scheme—Stage II* (Stockholm: SWECO, 1986).

99. See, for example, Intermediate Technology Consultants, *Final Report For WWF, The Mphanda Nkuwa Dam Project: Is It the Best Option for Mozambique's Energy Needs?* (Washington, DC: World Wildlife Fund, 2004); International Rivers, *Damning the Zambezi: Risks Outweigh Benefits of Proposed Mphanda Nkuwa Dam* (Berkeley: IR, 2006); available online at http://www.internationalrivers.org.

100. Of particular value to us was the work of Richard Beilfuss and his colleagues, Bryan Davies, Carlos Bento, P. B. N. Jackson, and K. L. Tinley.

101. Allen Isaacman and Barbara Isaacman, *Slavery and Beyond: The Making of Men and Chikunda Ethnic Identities in the Unstable World of South-Central Africa, 1750–1920* (Portsmouth, NH: Heinemann, 2004).

102. Other members of our research group included Xavier Cadete, Germano Maússe Dimainde, Eulésio Viegas Felipe, Paulo Lopes José, and António Tovela. Together we investigated Cahora Bassa's effects on people living both in the areas around the dam (at Songo, Estima, Chicoa Nova, and Chipalapala) and downriver (at Sena, Caia, Chemba, Mutarara, and Inhangoma).

103. Padre Claúdio Gremi, interview, Songo, May 20, 1998.

104. Pedro da Costa Xavier, interviews, Songo, May 23, 27, 1998.

105. The research team worked on the northern bank of the Zambezi in the areas of Nsanje, Nyachidaza, and the Dinide marshes in Malawi, and in Inhangoma, lower Morubala, Mutarara, Vila Nova, and the Zambezi delta in Mozambique.

106. The taped interviews and their summaries are contained in the Middlemas Collection, Hoover Institution Archives, Stanford University (hereafter cited as MC).

107. Portuguese accounts confirm both that the soil along the river was more fertile than elsewhere and that natural disasters occurred somewhat regularly. AHM, Missão de Fomento e Povoamento do Zambeze, Alexandre Gomes da Silva Braga, "Plano para o reordenamento das populações da Albufeira e restantes implicações de Cabora-Bassa, Janeiro de 1968 a 1973," August 1, 1968 (hereafter cited as AHM, Silva Braga, "Plano"); AHM, Missão de Fomento e Povoamento do Zambeze: Relatório preliminar: Possibilidades de desenvolvimento (1958); Diário das sessões do Assembleia Nacional, supp. 184, March 8, 1958, quoted in Middlemas, *Cabora Bassa,* 17. See also Frederick Selous, *Travel and Adventure in South-East Africa* (London: Rowland Ward and Co., 1893), 269–74.

108. For example, oral sources are often influenced by and intertwined with written ones. See Tamara Giles-Vernick, *Cutting the Vines of the Past: Environmental*

Histories of the Central African Rain Forest (Charlottesville: University Press of Virginia, 2002).

109. Leila Harris makes a similar point in her work on southeastern Turkey. Harris, "Contested Sustainabilities: Assessing Narratives of Environmental Change in Southeastern Turkey," *Local Environment* 14, no. 8 (2009): 699–720. She also stresses that, while it is important to be attentive to local knowledge, there are often both overlaps and dissonances between different social actors in the community (699).

110. This material confirms Giles-Vernick's insight that indigenous historical knowledge is "one of several quests for historical truth." Giles-Vernick, *Cutting the Vines*, 9.

111. The other important markers were the colonial-Frelimo divide that coincided with the opening of Cahora Bassa and the beginning (1976) and end of the war (1992) between the Mozambican army and South African–backed Renamo forces. Sometimes, villagers could not distinguish the devastation caused by Cahora Bassa from that done by Renamo.

112. Luís Artur, who conducted research in the Zambezi delta communities of Cocorico and Mopeia from 2007 to 2008, came to a similar conclusion: "The perceptions of the impact of Cahora Bassa and flooding on local livelihoods are indeed fluid. They vary across the actors, but mainly with age, area of origin, education, and settlement within the delta. Elderly people who grew up along the Zambezi delta and experienced flooding before the Cahora Bassa tended to echo pro-environmental claims of unpredictable and less flooding after Cahora Bassa and its negative impacts." Artur, "Continuities in Crisis: Everyday Practices of Disaster Response and Climate Change Adaptation in Mozambique" (PhD diss., Wageningen University, 2011), 69.

113. Luise White, Stephan Miescher, and David Cohen, introduction to *African Words, African Voices: Critical Practices in Oral History*, ed. White, Miescher, and Cohen (Bloomington: Indiana University Press, 2001), 14–16.

114. John Collins, *Occupied by Memory: The Intifada Generation and the Palestinian State of Emergency* (New York: NYU Press, 2004), 8.

115. João Raposo's words typified this position: "In the old days before Frelimo, no one had to farm in the hills; we all farmed along the river. Now the unpredictable floods have forced us to abandon our fields and move to the less fertile hills." João Raposo et al., Caia (Regulado Gumançanze), July 13, 2000.

116. Bonifácio Biquane et al., interview by DM, Chirodzi-Sanangwe, August 5, 2009.

117. Marita Zhuwao, interview by MRB, Nsanje (Savieli village), April 25, 2000; António Djase, Sena (Bairro 25 de Setembro), July 5, 2000.

118. Richard Beilfuss, e-mail to authors, December 4, 2011.

119. John Kotre, *White Gloves: How We Create Ourselves through Memory* (New York: Free Press, 1995), 88.

120. Renate Siebert, "Don't Forget: Fragments of a Negative Tradition," in *Memory and Totalitarianism, International Yearbook of Oral History and Life Stories*, vol. 1, ed. Luisa Passerini (Oxford: Oxford University Press, 1992), 166–77. The

intense debates on representations of the Holocaust and the growing literature on truth commissions in South Africa underscore this point. See, for example, Lawrence Langer, *Holocaust Testimonies: The Ruins of Memory* (New Haven: Yale University Press, 1991); Primo Levi, *The Drowned and the Saved* (New York: Summit Books, 1988); James Young, *The Texture of Memory: Holocaust Memorials and Meaning* (New Haven: Yale University Press, 1993); Sara Nuttall and Carli Coetzee, eds., *Negotiating the Past: The Making of Memory in South Africa* (Cape Town: Oxford University Press, 1998); Kader Asmal, Louise Asmal, and Ronald Roberts, *Reconciliation through Truth: A Reckoning of Apartheid's Criminal Governance* (Cape Town: David Philip, 1996).

121. It is important to distinguish between silences that are intended to hide what is known and silences that reflect what is not known at all. Jan Vansina, pers. comm. November 29, 2001. For a provocative discussion of the problem of silences, see Richard Roberts, "Reversible Social Processes, Historical Memory and the Production of History," *History in Africa* 17 (1990): 341–49.

122. Jacob Climo and Maria Cattell, introduction to *Social Memory and History: Anthropological Perspectives*, ed. Climo and Cattell (Walnut Creek, CA: AltaMira Press, 2002), 21; Sara Nuttall and Carli Coetzee, introduction to Nuttall and Coetzee, *Negotiating the Past*, xii.

123. Isabel Hofmeyr, "*We Spend Our Years as a Tale That Is Told*": Oral Historical Narrative in a South African Chiefdom (Portsmouth, NH: Heinemann, 1993), 160–75.

124. Heidi Gengenbach, *Binding Memories: Women as Makers and Tellers of History in Magude, Mozambique* (New York: Columbia University Press, 2006).

125. In fact, in the postconflict era, elderly women "were openly committed to recovering 'old ways' of memory [and] were capable of making disproportionately large amounts of *pongo* [noise] on behalf of their cause." Ibid., 3.

126. Over an eighteen-month period, Gengenbach witnessed "their daily exertions to cajole, scold and remind younger women about the importance of what they had collectively lost." Ibid.

127. Senteira Botão et al., interview, Chipalapala, May 26, 1998.

128. When Caia resident Mário Chambiça was asked if he and his neighbors favored closing the dam, he said no. Instead, he insisted that we tell officials in Maputo that what the people in Caia wanted was for "those who control the dam [to] recognize that many people here practice agriculture and they should not discharge water when we are planting our fields, but only when we are not farming." Mário Chambiça et al., interview, Caia (Regulado de Gumançanze), July 13, 2000.

129. For a discussion of power relations with local elders and the researcher's positionality, see Lila Abu-Lughod, "Writing against Culture," in *Recapturing Anthropology: Working in the Present*, ed. Richard Fox (Santa Fe: School of American Research Press, 1991), 137–62.

CHAPTER 2: THE ZAMBEZI RIVER VALLEY IN MOZAMBICAN HISTORY

1. Well before the first Portuguese traveled up the river, the Zambezi demarcated the boundary between the Tawara and the Tonga, Shona-speaking patrilineal

groups living south of the rivers (Tawara, Tonga, Sena, and Barue), and the Chewa-speaking matrilineal peoples to the north (Chewa and Manganja).

2. The frontier nature of the river was both geographically defined and socially constructed. Thus, the Zambezi was a dynamic, as well as contested, space with different meanings for different social groups at distinct moments in their history. For a pioneering study on the social and cultural construction of the frontier, see Owen Lattimore, *Studies in Frontier History* (Paris: Mouton, 1962).

3. Quoted in M. D. D. Newitt, *Portuguese Settlement on the Zambesi: Exploration, Land Tenure, and Colonial Rule in East Africa* (London: Longman, 1973), 38.

4. Ibid., 44.

5. Biblioteca Nacional de Lisboa, Pombalina 721, fols. 303–5, Francisco José de Lacerda e Almeida to D. Rodrigues de Souza Coutino, March 21, 1798; Lacerda e Almeida, *Travessia de África* (Lisbon: Agência Geral das Colónias, 1936), 387; Francisco de Mello de Castro, *Descripção dos Rios de Senna, anno de 1750* (Nova Goa: Imprensa Nacional, 1861), 113.

6. ANTT, Ministério do Reino, maço 60, "Memórias da Costa da África," fol. 17, unsigned, March 21, 1762.

7. Biblioteca Pública de Ajuda, 52-X-2, no. 3, José Francisco Alves Barbosa, "Analise estatística," December 30, 1821 (hereafter cited as BPA, Barbosa, "Analyse").

8. Isaacman and Isaacman, *Slavery and Beyond*, 233–80; Newitt, *Portuguese Settlement*, 275–289; Leroy Vail and Landeg White, *Capitalism and Colonialism in Mozambique: A Study of Quelimane District* (Minneapolis: University of Minnesota Press, 1980), 29–35.

9. Isaacman and Isaacman, *Slavery and Beyond*, 233–80; Newitt, *Portuguese Settlement*, 220–23.

10. Allen Isaacman, *Mozambique: The Africanization of a European Institution: The Zambezi Prazos, 1750–1902* (Madison: University of Wisconsin Press, 1972), 89.

11. Some of these vessels were fifteen meters long and could seat up to forty people. Richard Thornton, *The Zambezi Papers of Richard Thornton*, ed. E. C. Tabler, 2 vols. (London: Chatto and Windus, 1963), 2:131.

12. Daniel J. Rankin, "The Chinde River and Zambezi Delta," *Royal Geographic Society* 12, no. 3 (1890): 142.

13. John Kirk, *The Zambezi Journal and Letters of Dr. John Kirk, 1858–63*, ed. Reginald Foskett, 2 vols. (Edinburgh: Oliver and Boyd, 1965), 2:446.

14. Ibid.

15. David Livingstone and Charles Livingstone, *Narrative of an Expedition to the Zambezi and Its Tributaries and of the Discovery of the Lakes Shirwa and Nyasa* (London: Harper and Bros., 1865), 52.

16. João dos Santos, "Ethiópia oriental," in *Records of South-Eastern Africa*, ed. G. M. Theal (Cape Town: C. Struik, 1964), 7:271; Manuel Barreto, "Informação do Estado e Conquista dos Rios de Cuama, 1667," in Theal, *South-Eastern Africa*, 3:468; Arquivo Histórico Ultramarino (hereafter cited as AHU), Moç., caixa 2,

Francisco Mateus, Conde Val de Reis et al., January 9, 1681; Isaacman, *Zambezi Prazos*, 1–23; Newitt, *Portuguese Settlement*, 55–59.

17. António Pinto de Miranda, "Memória sobre a costa de África," in *Relações de Moçambique setecentista*, ed. António Andrade (Lisbon: Agência Geral do Ultramar, 1954), 288–300.

18. Newitt, *Portuguese Settlement*, 176.

19. Miranda, "Costa de Africa," 257–63.

20. AHU, Moç., caixa 34, Francisco José Lacerda e Almeida to the Queen, March 22, 1798; BPA, Barbosa, "Analyse"; AHU, Moç., maço 24, Sebastião Xavier Botelho to Joaquim Jozé Monteiro Torres, December 30, 1835.

21. ANTT, Ministério do Reino, maço 604, Inácio Caetano Xavier to Gov. Gen., December 26, 1758.

22. AHU, Moç., caixa 35, "Mapa geral a Guarnição desta praça e artilharia della Senna," n.d.; BPA, Barbosa, "Analyse"; AHU, códice 1470, fol. 147, Izidro Manoel de Carrazedo, March 19, 1836.

23. AHU, Moç., caixa 35, "Mapa geral a Guarnição desta praça e artilharia della Senna," n.d.; BPA, Barbosa, "Analyse"; AHU, códice 1470, fol. 147, Izidro Manoel de Carrazedo, March 19, 1836.

24. Isaacman, *Zambezi Prazos*, 60.

25. Ibid., 60–63; Lacerda e Almeida, *Travessia*, 113.

26. For a discussion of hybridity, see Homi Bhabha, *The Location of Culture* (New York: Routledge, 1994), 296–97.

27. Isaacman, *Zambezi Prazos*, 114–23; Isaacman and Isaacman, *Slavery and Beyond*, 68–72; Newitt, *Portuguese Settlement*, 217–34.

28. Mozambique, *Termos de vassallagem nos territórios de Machona, Zambézia e Nyasa, 1858 a 1889* (Lisbon: Imprensa Nacional, 1890), 13.

29. AHU, Moç., maço 25, Joaquim Mendes de Vasconcelos e Cirne to Paulo Jozé Miguel, March 6, 1830.

30. Newitt, *Portuguese Settlement*, 230.

31. See Kirk, *Zambezi Journal*; Livingstone and Livingstone, *Narrative*; David Livingstone, *Missionary Travels and Researches in South Africa* (New York: Harper and Bros., 1858); Selous, *Travel and Adventure*.

32. Newitt, *Portuguese Settlement*, 231.

33. Ibid., 232; Mozambique, *Termos de vassallagem*.

34. See Elias Mandala, "The Kololo Interlude in Southern Malawi" (MA thesis, University of Malawi, 1977).

35. Allen Isaacman, in collaboration with Barbara Isaacman, *The Tradition of Resistance in Mozambique: The Zambesi Valley, 1850–1921* (Berkeley: University of California Press, 1976), 22–48; Newitt, *Portuguese Settlement*, 234–311.

36. For a discussion of the complex role of these armed slaves, see Isaacman and Isaacman, *Slavery and Beyond*, 197–280.

37. Ibid., 234–73.

38. Isaacman, *Tradition of Resistance*, 26–32.

39. Ibid., 34.

40. Ibid., 22–48.

41. Ibid., 60–62; João de Azevedo Coutinho, *A campanha do Barué em 1902* (Lisbon: Livraria Ferin, 1904).

42. Ibid.

43. Isaacman, *Tradition of Resistance*, 156–85; E. A. Azambuja Martins, *Operações militares no Barué em 1917* (Lisbon: Imprensa Nacional, 1937); Silvino Ferreira da Costa, *Governo do terrritório da Companhia de Moçambique* (Beira: Companhia de Moçambique, 1917).

44. As late as the middle of the nineteenth century, they were still searching for the Eldorado of the ancients. See Carl Peters, *The Eldorado of the Ancients (1889–1902)* (London: C. A. Pearson, 1902).

45. AHU, Moç., caixa 22, António Mello de Castro to Martinho Mello de Castro, June 15, 1785; António Candido Pedroso Gamitto, *King Kazembe and the Marave, Cheva, Bisa, Bemba, Lunda, and Other Peoples of Southern Africa*, trans. Ian Cunnison, 2 vols. (Lisbon: Junta de Investigações do Ultramar, 1960), 1:42; Isaacman, *Zambezi Prazos*, 69–71, 88; Newitt, *Portuguese Settlement*, 81–84.

46. Landeg White, *Bridging the Zambezi: A Colonial Folly* (London: McMillan, 1993), 55–56.

47. ACL, ms. 648, António Vilas Boas Truão, "Estatística dos rios de Senna," July 16, 1807; Sebastião Xavier Botelho, *Memória estatística sobre os domínios portuguezes na África oriental* (Lisbon: José Baptista Morando, 1835), 286–87.

48. ACL, Truão, "Estatística."

49. BPA, Barbosa, "Analyse."

50. David Livingstone, *African Journal*, ed. Isaac Schapera (Berkeley: University of California Press, 1963), 39, 46.

51. Between 1875 and 1891 exports from Quelimane increased by more than 500 percent, largely as a result of free peasant agriculture. Vail and White, *Capitalism*, 25–41.

52. Ibid., 83–87.

53. Under this law, "idle natives" were required to work; if they did not, "public authorities could compel them to do so." J. M. da Silva Cunha, *O trabalho indígena: Estudo do direito colonial* (Lisbon: Agência Geral das Colónias, 1949), 151.

54. Robert Nunez Lyne, *Mozambique: Its Agricultural Development* (London: T. Fisher Unwin, 1913), 201–202. Between 1907 and 1930 the approximate number of days worked by conscripted laborers jumped from 1.8 to 4.3 million. José Negrão, "One Hundred Years of African Rural Family Economy: The Zambezi Delta in Retrospective Analysis" (PhD diss., University of Lund, 1995), 57.

55. Vail and White, *Capitalism*, 128, 153–62.

56. Pedro Augusto de Sousa e Silva, *Distrito de Tete, Alta Zambézia* (Lisbon: Livraria Portugália Editora, 1927), 111.

57. Landeg White, *Bridging the Zambezi*, 15–16; Malwyn Newitt, *A History of Mozambique* (Bloomington: Indiana University Press, 1995), 404.

58. To stimulate peasant production and fuel the Portuguese textile industry, in 1938, Portugal imposed a brutal system of forced cotton cultivation throughout

the colony, which affected thousands of peasants in the Zambezi valley. See Allen Isaacman, *Cotton Is the Mother of Poverty* (Portsmouth, NH: Heinemann, 1996).

59. For a discussion of the colonial construction of the Zambezi, see McGregor, *Crossing the Zambezi*, 41–62.

60. Livingstone and Livingstone, *Narrative*, 52.

61. G. Liesegang and M. Chidiamassamba, "Alternativas e técnicas adaptadas as cheias usadas pelas comunidades ao longo do Vale de Zambeze" (paper presented at Workshop on the Sustainable Use of Cahora Bassa Dam and the Zambezi Valley, Songo, Mozambique, September 29–October 2, 1997).

62. Kirk, *Zambezi Journal*, 2:206–7.

63. Quoted in Landeg White, *Bridging the Zambezi*, 15.

64. BPA, Barbosa, "Analyse"; Botelho, *Memória*, 286–87.

65. Botelho, *Memória*, 286–87.

66. Livingstone, *Missionary Travels*, 235.

67. Joaquim Mousinho de Albuquerque, *Moçambique, 1896–1898* (Lisbon: Sociedade Geografia de Lisboa, 1913), 99.

68. Silva, *Tete*, 95.

69. Ibid., 111–12.

70. Peters, *Eldorado*, 77.

71. F. Carvalho, *Relatório do governador 1911–1912* (Lourenço Marques: Imprensa Nacional, 1912), 67–69.

72. Ibid., 59.

73. António Djase, interview, Sena (Bairro 25 de Setembro), July 5, 2000.

74. According to Tawara traditions, their ancestors, who were hunting in the region, settled in the area between Tete and the Cahora Bassa gorge in independent chieftaincies governed by chiefs, known as *amambo*. The Tonga, another Shona-speaking group, lived downriver, between the confluence of the Zambezi and Luenha Rivers and the area south of Sena, stretching inland from the southern bank into the interior. By the middle of the nineteenth century, those living around Tete and Sena thought of themselves, instead, as Nyungwe and Sena respectively. Conrado Msussa Boroma, interviews, Boroma, July 28, August 17, 20, September 29, 1968; Gaspar Cardoso, interviews, Boroma, July 15, 17, 18, 1968; João Cristóstomo, interviews, Boroma, July 18, 25, 1968; Renço Cado, interview, Chemba, August 13, 1968; Chale Lupia, interview, Massangano, September 28, 1968; Niquicicafe Presente, interview, Massangano, September 28, 1968; José Fernandes, Júnior, "Narração do distrito de Tete" (unpublished manuscript, Makanga, 1955), 4–6; Isaacman, *Zambezi Prazos*, 3–7; Oliveira, *Tauaras*, 26–28; Rob Marlin, "Possessing the Past: Legacies of Violence and Reproductive Illness in Central Mozambique" (PhD diss., Rutgers University, 2001), 19–24.

For the Chewa, the northern bank of the river marked the frontier of their territory. They arrived from the north in two major waves. The first stream—called either proto-Chewa or Banda, the name of its dominant clan—were living north of the Zambezi by at least the fifteenth century, where they practiced mixed agriculture along with iron smelting, hunting, fishing, and trading. The Maravi, led by the Phiri clan, arrived in the second major stream and were the state builders. Harry Langworthy, "A History of Undi's Kingdom to 1890: Aspects of Chewa History in East Central Africa" (PhD thesis, Boston University, 1969), 126, 173–78; Kings Phiri, "Chewa History in Central Malawi and the Use of Oral Tradition, 1600–1920" (PhD diss., University of Wisconsin, 1975), 50; Yusuf Juwayeyi, "Archaeological Excavations at Mankhamba, Malawi: An Early Settlement Site of the Maravi," *Azania: Archaeological Research in Africa* 45, no. 2 (2010): 175–202; J. Matthew Schoffeleers, *River of Blood: The Genesis of a Martyr Cult in Southern Malawi, c. A.D. 1600* (Madison: University of Wisconsin Press, 1992), 133; Barreto, "Estado e conquista," 3:470–71, 480; Newitt, *Portuguese Settlement*, 80; Isaacman and Isaacman, *Slavery and Beyond*, 68–70.

75. This summary draws from Davies, Beilfuss, and Thoms, "Cahora Bassa Retrospective," 1–3; International Crane Foundation, "The Zambezi Delta: Management Opportunities and Challenges," http://www.savingcranes.org/the-zambezi-delta -management-opportunities-and-challenges.html.

76. We distinguish the delta—the typically broad, flat zone near the mouth of a river where there are high levels of deposition—from the estuary—the zone where the river's plume extends into the ocean and where fresh and salt waters mix.

77. The area between Zumbo and Tete received less than 700 mm of rain per year on average, compared to the delta's approximately 950 mm per year. Centro de Investigação Científica Algodoeira, *Esboço reconhecimento ecológico-agrícola de Moçambique* (Lourenço Marques: CICA, 1955), 160.

78. Beilfuss and Davies, "Prescribed Flooding," fig. 4–6.

79. Beilfuss and Santos, "Hydrological Change," 31–35.

80. See Davies, Beilfuss, and Thoms, "Cahora Bassa Retrospective," 5.

81. Supia Sargento and Carlos Churo, interview, Estima, May 22, 1998.

82. Carlos Bento, interview, Maputo, March 10, 2010.

83. SWECO, *Cabora Bassa*, 77–78.

84. Jonathan Timberlake, "Biodiversity of the Zambezi Basin," Occasional Publication in Biodiversity, no. 9 (Bulawayo: Biodiversity Foundation for Africa, 2000), 17.

85. Ibid.

86. Tor Gammelsröd, "Variation in Shrimp Abundance on the Sofala Bank, Mozambique, and Its Relation to the Zambezi Runoff," *Estuarine, Coastal and Shelf Science* 35, no. 1 (1992): 91–103.

87. José Jone et al., interview, Mutarara, July 6, 2000.

88. S. Muhai, "Cahora Bassa and the Lower Zambezi" (paper presented at Workshop on the Sustainable Use of Cahora Bassa Dam and the Zambezi Valley, September 29–October 2, 1997, Songo, Mozambique), 4.

89. Liesegang and Chidiamassamba, "Alternativas."

90. Luís Artur and Dorothea Hilhorst, "Climate Change Adaptation in Mozambique," in *The Right to Water and Water Rights in a Changing World: Papers Presented at a Colloquium Held on 22 September 2010 in Delft, the Netherlands*, ed. Michael R. van der Valk and Penelope Keenan (Delft: UNESCO–International Hydrological Programme, 2012), 32.

91. Beilfuss and Santos, "Hydrological Change," 69–70.

92. Flood recession agriculture involves farming on lands adjacent to a river, which become fertile from the deposit of organic and inorganic materials by receding floodwaters.

93. Quoted in James Morrissey, *Livelihoods at Risk: The Case of Mphanda Nkuwa Dam* (Maputo: Justiça Ambiental, 2006), 55.

94. Senteira Botão et al., interview.

95. Joaquim Sacatucua, interview, Caia, July 10, 2000.

96. AHM, Silva Braga, "Plano."

97. Bonifácio Biquane et al., interview by DM; Daniel Ribeiro, interview, March 10, 2008; AHM, Silva Braga, "Plano."

98. Artur, "Continuities," 79.

99. Joaquim Sacatucua, interview.

100. Ernest Kalumbi, interview by MRB, Nsanje, April 2000.

101. AHM, Missão de Fomento e Povoamento do Zambeze, "Bacia do Zambeze, Fomento e Ocupação, Esquema Geral, Estudos Económico-sociais, Desenvolvimento económico, Estudos base para programação", vol. 1, Hidrotécnica Portuguesa, 81.

102. Oliveira, *Tauaras*, 32–34.

103. Paulo Mayo, interview by MRB, Chikoti, May 24, 2000. António da Silva Braga, a Portuguese agronomist working in the Songo area in 1961, also noted the extreme difference in agricultural productivity of these different soil types. AHM, Silva Braga, "Plano."

104. Livingstone, *African Journal*, 39, 46.

105. Selous, *Travel and Adventure*, 270.

106. Livingstone and Livingstone, *Narrative*, 239; Thornton, *Zambezi Papers*, 107; Selous, *Travel and Adventure*, 270; Miranda, "Costa de Africa," 244–45; João Baptista de Montaury, "Moçambique, Ilhas Querimbas, Rios de Sena, Villa de Tete, Villa de Zumbo, Manica, Villa de Luabo, Inhambane," in Andrade, *Relações de Moçambique*, 359; Carlos Weise, "Expedição Portugueza à Mpeseni," *Boletim da Sociedade de Geografia de Lisboa* 10 (1891), nos. 6–7: 235–73, 297–321; nos. 8–9: 331–412, 415–30; no. 12: 467–97.

107. Pezulani Mafalanjala et al., interview, Masecha, May 25, 1998.

108. Supia Sargento and Carlos Churo, interview.

109. Oliveira, *Tauaras*, 33.

110. Gamitto, *King Kazembe*, 1:97. For an important theoretical discussion on gender as practice and process, see Judith Butler, *Bodies That Matter: On the Discursive Limits of "Sex"* (New York: Routledge, 1993).

111. Oliveira, *Tauaras*, 38–40.

112. Gaspar Cardoso, interview; Luís Cebola, interview, Boroma, July 18, 1968.

113. Régulo António Chipuazo et al., interview, Caia (Regulado Chipuazo), July 7, 2000; José Inácio and Lucas Afonso, interview, Caia (Regulado Gumancanze), July 14, 2000; Miranda, "Costa de Africa," 286–300.

114. Luís Manuel et al., interview, Caia (Regulado Sangoma), July 20, 2000; Wilson Thomas, interview by MRB, Nsanje (Savieli village), April 17, 2000.

115. According to a survey of the Mphanda Nkuwa area northeast of Tete, the average floodplain plot was 0.35 hectares. UTIP, *Mepanda Uncua and Cahora Bassa North Project: Sumário*, 4–5.

116. Miranda, "Costa de Africa," 286–300; Djase, interview; Manuel Talé et al., interview, Sena (Regulado Chetcha), July 21, 2000; Luís Manuel et al., interview; Chipuazo et al., interview; José Inácio and Afonso, interview In the more arid areas of Tete, maize would grow only on river-fed fields.

117. Fatima Mbvinisa, interview by MRB, T/A Dovu (Dimingu Gashipale), May 19, 2000.

118. Oliveira, *Tauaras*, 37.

119. Botão et al., interview.

120. Henrique Conforme Mereja et al., interview, Chicoa Emboque, July 17, 2001.

121. Djase, interview; Talé et al., interview; Luís Manuel et al., interview; Chipuazo et al., interview; José Inácio and Afonso, interview.

122. Djase, interview; Talé et al., interview; Luís Manuel et al., interview; Chipuazo et al., interview; José Inácio and Afonso, interview.

123. Francisco Manuel et al., interview, Mutarara Velha (Nhancogole), July 6, 2000.

124. Chambiça et al., interview.

125. Mafalanjala et al., interview.

126. Botão et al., interview.

127. Inácio Jeremias Guta, et al., interview, Sena (Regulado Chetcha), July 21, 2000.

128. Mafalanjala et al., interview.

129. For a discussion of these cotton-created food crises, see Isaacman, *Cotton*, 150–70.

130. Sacatucua, interview.

131. Ibid.

132. Miranda, "Costa de Africa," 247; Isaacman, *Zambezi Prazos*, 119; M. D. D. Newitt, "Drought in Mozambique 1823–1831," *Journal of Southern African Studies* 15 (1988): 15–35; Elias Mandala, *Work and Control in a Peasant Economy: A History of the Lower Tchiri Valley in Malawi, 1859–1960* (Madison: University of Wisconsin Press, 1990), 74–79.

133. Novais Nhamazi et al., interview, Chemba (Regulado Chave), July 19, 2000.

134. Some recalled their parents describing a deluge (*duo-duo*) that occurred during the Makombe Wars (ca. 1917) "which killed many people." Guta et al., interview.

135. While elders often glossed over the negative features of their predam lives when comparing them with the period after Cahora Bassa's construction, when asked specifically about flooding, they gave vivid descriptions of the devastation the major floods provoked.

136. Marosse Inácio et al., interview, Chemba (Regulado Chave), July 19, 2000; Régulo Júlio Chave, interview, Chemba (Regulado Chave), July 19, 2000.

137. Nhamazi et al., interview.

138. Beilfuss and Santos, "Hydrological Change," 69.

139. Bento Estima and Joseph Ndebvuchena, interview, Estima, May 19, 1998. Because rainfall here was low and irregular—averaging only 600 mm per year—and the Zambezi River sometimes obliterated gardens when it swelled to two or three times its normal flow rate, this somewhat more sober view probably more accurately reflects historical reality.

140. José Inácio and Afonso, interview.

141. Luís Manuel et al., interview Oliva Babo and his neighbors told of similar problems. Babo et al., interview, Sena (Regulado Mwanalave), July 21, 2000.

142. Vale Raposo, interview, Chemba (Regulado Chave), July 18, 2000.

143. Vernácio Leone, interview, Estima, May 19, 1998.

144. Beilfuss, Chilundo, et al., "Hydrological Changes," 14.

145. Marialena Dique, interview by DM, Chirodzi-Sanangwe, August 8, 2009; Tilha Chafewa and Sieda Denja, interview by DM, Chirodzi-Sanangwe, August 5, 2009; Naita Siawalha, interview by DM, Chirodzi-Sanangwe, August 9, 2009.

146. Jone et al., interview; N'tsai António et al., interview, Caia (Regulado Chetcha), July 21, 2000; Bengala Mange and Zeca Sacatucua, interview, Caia (Regulado Gumançanze), July 10, 2000; Alberto Chirembue and Armando Navia, interview, Inhangoma, July 16, 2000; Vale Raposo, interview.

147. Quoted in Mandala, *Work and Control*, 245.

148. João Raposo et al., interview.

149. Gadeni Gaspar, interview by DM, Chirodzi-Sanangwe, August 3, 2009; Biquane Chazia, interview by DM, Chirodzi-Sanangwe, August 3, 2009; Marialena Dique, interview; Rabia Juma et al., interview by DM, Tete city, August 12, 2009.

150. AHM, Silva Braga, "Plano."

151. Oliveira, *Tauaras*, 49–51.

152. P. B. N. Jackson and K. H. Rogers, "Cabora Bassa Fish Populations before and during the First Filling Phase," *Zoológica Africana* 11, no. 2 (1976): 376; Selous, *Travel and Adventure*, 269.

153. SWECO, *Cabora Bassa*, 12.

154. Ibid.

155. Denis Tweddle, "Specialist Study—Freshwater Fisheries," in Beilfuss and Brown, *Environmental Flow Requirements*, 68–69. An earlier study estimated it as somewhat lower. SWECO, *Cabora Bassa*, 3, 119–22.

156. Beilfuss, Chilundo, et al., "Hydrological Changes," 11; Mange and Sacatucua, interview; Talé et al., interview.

157. John Paul and Khumbidzi Pastor, interview, Estima, May 21, 1998.

158. Ricardo Ferrão, interview, Tete, September 22, 1997; Mafalanjala et al., interview.

159. Beilfuss, Chilundo, et al., "Hydrological Changes," 11.

160. For an excellent study of fishing, see David M. Gordon, *Nachituti's Gift: Economy, Society, and Environment in Central Africa* (Madison: University of Wisconsin Press, 2006).

161. António Ioha, interview by MRB, T/A Khomelo (Matunga), May 4, 2000; Oliveira, *Tauaras*, 49–51.

162. João Raposo et al., interview; Jone et al., interview; Gina Monteiro and other women, interview, Mutarara (Bairro 25 de Dezembro), July 6, 2000; Maria Faifi, interview by MRB, Nsanje (Savieli village), April 18, 2000; Jone et al., interview.

163. Bastiana Kamuzu, interview by MRB, Madani, April 27, 2000; see also Faifi, interview.

164. Kaki Mwandipandusa, interview by MRB, Nsanje (Dominique Tom village), May 20, 2000.

165. Ioha, interview; Aniva João et al., interview, Inhangoma (Regulado Chirembwe), July 16, 2000; João Raposo et al., interview; Artur Medja et al., interview, Chemba (Regulado Chave), July 19, 2000; António Jonasse Tchoa et al., Caia (Regulado Gumançaze), July 14, 2000.

166. Aniva João, interview.

167. Ibid.; João Raposo et al., interview; Artur Medja et al., interview; António Jonasse Tchoa et al., interview.

168. Elias Januare, interview by MRB, Hapalal Kusala, April 20, 2000.

169. José Inácio and Lucas Afonso, interview.

170. António Ioha, interview.

171. Alberto Rapozolo, interview by MRB, Ralumbi, April 2000.

172. João Raposo et al., interview; Régulo António Chipuazo et al., interview.

173. Régulo António Chipuazo et al., interview.

174. Pita Araújo and Bernardo Gona, interview, Sena, July 21, 2000.

175. Ibid.

176. José Inácio and Lucas Afonso, interview; João Raposo et al., interview; Cheia Amado, interview, Caia (Regulado Magagadi), July 20, 2000.

177. Ferreira Mangiricau and Bene Ngoca, interview, Mutarara (Bairro 25 de Dezembro), July 5, 2000.

178. Mandala, *Work and Control*, 249.

179. Marita Zhuwao, interview; Oliveira, *Tauaras*, 51.

180. Marita Zhuwao, interview.

181. Jack Sobrinho and Wiseborn Benjamin, interview, Estima, May 20, 1998.

182. In 1968 approximately sixteen thousand African buffalo roamed the Marromeu reserve. K. L. Tinley, "Marromeu Wrecked by the Big Dam," *African Wildlife* 29, no. 2 (1975): 22–25; Richard Beilfuss, e-mail to the authors, May 4, 2010.

183. José António d'Abreu, interview, Tete, July 22, 1968; Diamond Mpande, interview, Bawa, September 23, 1997.

184. Zhuzi Luizhi, interview by MRB, Mhula village, April 2000.

185. Chidasiyikwa Mavungire, interview by MRB, Dimingu Thom, April 2000.

186. Maurício Alemão, interview, Masecha, May 27, 1998.

187. Pezulani Mafalanjala et al., interview.

188. Ricardo Ferrão, interview; Castro Jack et al., interview, Kajanda, October 21, 1997.

189. Mandala, *Work and Control*, 84–92.

190. Ricardo Ferrão, interview; Castro Jack et al., interview, Kajanda, October 21, 1997; Beilfuss, "Natural Resource Utilization," 104–7.

191. The word for herbalist in Portuguese is *curandeiro/curandeira*, and in Shona *gombe*.

192. Emília Joni, interview, Caia (Bairro 25 de Setembro), July 7, 2000; Balança Casado, interview, Sena (Bairro 25 de Setembro), July 11, 2000; Maria Chipwazo et al., interview, Caia (Regulado Chipuazo), July 7, 2000; Guente Escafa, interview, Sena (Bairro 25 de Setembro), July 11, 2000; Henriqueta Cascas, interview, Caia (Regulado Gumançanze), July 14, 2000.

193. Emília Joni, interview; Balança Casado, interview; Régulo António Chipuazo et al., interview; Guente Escafa, interview; João Raposo et al., interview; Gaspar Cardoso, interview; Conrado Msussa Boroma, interview; Allen Isaacman, "Madzi-Manga, Mhondoro, and the Use of Oral Traditions: A Chapter in Barue Religious and Political History," *Journal of African History* 14, no. 3 (1973): 395–409.

194. João Raposo et al., interview.

195. Selous, *Travel and Adventure*, 258.

196. Peters, *Eldorado*, 97.

CHAPTER 3: HARNESSING THE RIVER

1. It took an additional four months to fill the reservoir behind the dam.

2. For a history of the construction of Cahora Bassa, see Middlemas, *Cabora Bassa*.

3. For a discussion of high modernism, see Scott, *Seeing Like a State*.

4. Mitchell, *Rule of Experts*, 179–209.

5. As early as 1616 the Portuguese explorer Gaspar Bocarro described the majesty of the rapids in great detail. Cited in Bolton, "Regulation of the Zambezi," 49.

6. Lisbon agreed to participate in a bilateral Zambezi River Commission only after it secured guarantees that Kariba would not adversely affect either its irrigation schemes or navigation downriver.

7. Middlemas, *Cabora Bassa*, 17.

8. Diário das Sessões do Assembleia Nacional, supp. 184, March 8, 1958, quoted in Middlemas, *Cabora Bassa*, 17.

9. Middlemas, *Cabora Bassa*, 18.

10. The GPZ, established in February 1970 to oversee the Cahora Bassa project, was disbanded after Mozambique's independence. It was recreated in 1995 as the statutory agency responsible for Zambezi valley development, reporting directly to the Council of Ministers.

11. *Notícias*, August 4, 1962, 1.

12. *Notícias*, August 5, 1962, 1.

13. These reports are available in the Arquivo Histórico de Moçambique (AHM), located in Maputo.

14. Freyre expounded his theory in *O mundo que o português criou* (Rio de Janeiro: Livraria José Olympio Editora, 1940); *Um brasileiro em terras portuguêsas* (Rio de Janeiro: Livraria José Olympio Editora, 1953); *Integração portugueza nos trópicos* (Lisbon: Junta de Investigações do Ultramar, 1958); *The Masters and the*

Slaves: A Study in the Development of Brazilian Civilization, 2nd ed., abridged, trans. Samuel Putnam (New York: Knopf, 1964). For a critique of lusotropicalism, see Gerald J. Bender, *Angola under the Portuguese: The Myth and the Reality* (Berkeley: University of California Press, 1978).

15. J. M. da Silva Cunha, *Cabora-Bassa: Who Will Benefit by It?* (Lisbon: Agência-Geral do Ultramar, 1970), 12.

16. During this period, Mozambique was considered a province of Portugal and the highest administrative unit was the district. After independence, all districts became provinces. One of the districts within Tete Province is Tete District, whose capital, both then and now, is Tete city.

17. *Washington Post*, May 13, 1971, 14.

18. Scudder, *Large Dams*, 188–93; McCully, *Silenced Rivers*, 5.

19. Colson, *Social Consequences*, 1–14; McGregor, *Crossing the Zambezi*, 105–24.

20. Tischler, "Light and Power," 90.

21. The colonial regime eventually built a dam at the Kafue gorge in the late 1960s. McGregor, *Crossing the Zambezi*, 105–8.

22. Ministério do Ultramar, Missão do Fomento e Povoamento do Zambeze (MFPZ), *Plano geral de fomento e occupação do vale do Zambeze* (Lisbon: Hidro-técnica Portuguesa, 1965), 4–7; Middlemas, *Cabora Bassa*, 19–26.

23. On September 25, 1964, Frelimo launched its armed struggle, attacking a number of colonial administrative and military posts in Cabo Delgado. Eduardo Mondlane, *The Struggle for Mozambique*, 2nd ed. (London: Zed Books, 1983), 138–39.

24. Middlemas, *Cabora Bassa*, 23–28.

25. Arquivo Histórico Diplomático de Ministério dos Negócios Estrangeiros (hereafter cited as AHD), processo EAA 146, pasta 1, Domingues de Almeida, June 3, 1970.

26. Ibid.

27. Cunha, *Cabora Bassa: Benefit*, 7–13.

28. In central Mozambique, however, where only 0.25 percent of Tete District's approximately 450,000 inhabitants had been designated *civilizado*, the Salazar regime had a long way to go. Província de Moçambique, Junta Provincial de Povoamento, *Relatório-síntese da actividade da Missão de Fomento e Povoamento do Zambeze, 1957–1961* (Lourenço Marques: Junta Provincial de Povoamento, 1962), 53. Since *civilizado* referred to the European population, while *assimilado* was the term used for the minuscule number of Africans who demonstrated the ability to read and write Portuguese, had rejected "tribal" customs, and were gainfully employed in the capitalist economy, the number of assimilated Africans in Tete was almost nonexistent.

29. Cunha, *Cabora Bassa: Benefit*, 7.

30. Lewis, *Theory of Economic Growth*, 9–10.

31. Cunha, *Cabora Bassa: Discursos*, 8; Middlemas, *Cabora Bassa*, 16–22.

32. Beilfuss and Santos, "Hydrological Change," 69.

33. Cunha, *Cabora Bassa: Benefit*, 8–10; Middlemas, *Cabora Bassa*, 16–22.

34. General Venâncio Deslandes, the Portuguese military leader, stressed the urgency of "settl[ing] in the overseas territories the biggest possible number of former military people, (sic.)" since it was only through their collaboration with civilians that the colony would remain Portuguese. Quoted in Douglas Marchant, *Cabora Bassa: The Dam at Cabora Bassa—It's [sic] Implications and the International Campaign against the Project* (London: National League of Young Liberals International Department, 1971), 3–5.

35. Middlemas, *Cabora Bassa*, 16–22.

36. *Mozambique Revolution* 40 (1969): 13.

37. South Africa's need for a secure supply of cheap energy, along with new technological advances in high-voltage transmission making it possible to transmit power thirteen hundred kilometers from Cahora Bassa to Johannesburg at competitive prices without an appreciable loss of energy, combined to make investment in Cahora Bassa attractive. Middlemas, *Cabora Bassa*, 69.

38. For a detailed discussion of these negotiations, see ibid., 20–30.

39. Ibid., 80–84; William A. Hance, "Cabora Bassa Hydro Project: Portugal and South Africa Seek Political and Economic Gains From Joint Investment," *Africa Report* 15, no. 5 (1970): 20–21; Eduardo dos Santos, Júnior, "Cahora Bassa no desenvolvimento do vale do Zambeze," *Ultramar* 2, no. 5 (1973): 101–75; Wolf Radmann, "The Zambezi Development Scheme: Cabora Bassa," *Africa Report* 4, no. 2 (summer 1974): 48–54.

40. Cunha, *Cabora Bassa: Benefits*, 9–10, 13; Manuel Vidigal, "Cabora Bassa: História, Perspectivas, Justificacão, Aspectos económico-financeiros, Interesse nacional do empreendimento," *Electricidade* (Lisbon) 13 (January–February 1970): 7–20; Radmann, "Cabora Bassa"; Bolton, "Regulation of the Zambezi," 158.

41. See Ruth First, *Black Gold: The Mozambican Miner, Proletarian and Peasant* (Brighton: Harvester, 1983).

42. ZANU stands for the Zimbabwe African National Union, which, along with the Zimbabwe African People's Union (ZAPU), was fighting for Zimbabwe's independence.

43. Middlemas, *Cabora Bassa*, 280–84.

44. Ibid., 94.

45. Ibid., 95.

46. Of the handful of ethnographic surveys conducted during the first half of the twentieth century, the most significant was José Norberto Santos Jr., *Contribuição para o estudo da antropologia de Moçambique: Algumas tribos de Tete* (Lisbon: Junta das Missões Geográficas e de Investigações Coloniais, 1944).

47. Carlos Ramos de Oliveira completed the first ethnographic monograph on the Tawara in 1973, in which he acknowledged that, due to the war, he was not able to conduct extensive fieldwork. Oliveira, *Os Tauaras do vale do Zambeze* (Lisbon: Junta de Investigações Científicas do Ultramar, 1976).

48. AHM, Silva Braga, "Plano."

49. Because Kariba was the first hydroelectric megadam constructed in the tropics, it attracted considerable scholarly interest. See Colson, *Social Consequences,*

43–70; Thayer Scudder, *The Ecology of the Gwembe Tonga* (Manchester: Manchester University Press, 1962), 153–160].

50. Bolton, "Regulation of the Zambezi," 345–46.

51. AHM, Governo Geral (hereafter cited as GG), cota 864: K. Tinley and A. de Sousa Dias, Repartição dos Serviços Veterinárias, "Plano base para salvamento e transferência da fauna brâvia da albufeira de Cabora Bassa em Moçambique—Base Plan for Rescue and Translocation of Wildlife from the Cabora Bassa Dam Area in Moçambique," March 1973 (hereafter cited as AHM, Tinley and Sousa Dias, "Plano base").

52. A. Hall, I. M. Valente, and B. R. Davies, "The Zambezi River in Moçambique: the Physico-Chemical Status of the Middle and Lower Zambezi prior to the Closure of the Cabora Bassa Dam," *Freshwater Biology* 7, no. 3 (1977): 187–206.

53. Davies, "They Pulled the Plug," 26.

54. Davies, "Rehabilitation Programme." His team of researchers collected samples from the Zambezi River system on at least seven different occasions.

55. Davies, "Rehabilitation Programme"; Davies, "Cabora Bassa Hazards," 477.

56. Davies, "Rehabilitation Programme."

57. In fact, fish surveys near the reservoir were remarkably incomplete. Jackson and Rogers, "Cabora Bassa Fish Populations," 376–78.

58. Quoted in Tinley, "Morromeu Wrecked," 24.

59. Davies, Hall, and Jackson, "Ecological Aspects," 198–99.

60. The average flow through the gorge was between two and three thousand cubic meters per second. Davies, "Cabora Bassa Hazards," 478.

61. Davies, "They Pulled the Plug," 27.

62. For an important discussion on the role of experts, see Mitchell, *Rule of Experts.*

63. Due to the rugged terrain and lack of technical input from the state, the road took almost eight months to complete. One elder recalled, "the *picada* [dirt road] was built by José Vas Godinho after he decided to open a shop in Songo. At the time, he went to the administrator and requested chibalo labor, people who were not paid. Each fumo had to bring a number of his followers and clear a designated area. They used hoes. A few had pick axes. African sipais [police] supervised the workers. Some mistreated them. Sometimes the local administrator would beat them with a *palmatorio* [hand club]. This was not a road for cars; it was only for donkeys and people." Pedro da Costa Xavier, interview.

64. Ibid.

65. The local population referred to chibalo as a form of slavery.

66. Júlio Calecoetoa, interview, Songo, May 18, 1998.

67. Pedro da Costa Xavier, interview.

68. *Johannesburg Star,* June 3, 1970; *Diário popular,* November 4, 1970.

69. Middlemas, *Cabora Bassa,* 90.

70. Ibid.

71. Ibid.; Júlio Calecoetoa, interview.

72. Simões Wetela, interview, Songo, May 27–28, 1998.

73. The number of foreign technicians declined to approximately one hundred in 1972 and to sixty in 1974.

74. Middlemas, *Cabora Bassa*, 100.

75. Ibid., 99.

76. *Johannesburg Star*, June 3, 1970.

77. *Rhodesian Herald*, December 4, 1972.

78. Ibid.

79. *Rhodesian Herald*, September 12, 1972.

80. *Johannesburg Star*, June 3, 1970; *Rhodesian Herald*, December 4, 1972.

81. Pedro da Costa Xavier, interview; Padre Claúdio Gremi, interview, May 20, 1998.

82. Simões Wetela, interview; Padre Claúdio Gremi, interview, May 20, 1998.

83. *Rhodesian Herald*, September 12, 1972.

84. Bernard Bendixen, interview, 1974, MC, tape A11.

85. Horst Langer, interview, 1974, MC, tape A15; Antoine Lampiére, interview, 1973, MC, tape A11.

86. AHM, GG, caixa 860, GPZ, "Relatório da Actividade de 1971," n.d.

87. ANTT, PIDE/DGS, SC, CI(2), processo 8743, pasta 1, informação, 1.576-CI(2), December 15, 1970.

88. Middlemas, *Cabora Bassa*, 109.

89. ANTT, PIDE/DGS, SC, CI(2), processo 8743, pasta 1, relatório, 1539/70/D1/2/SC, July 31, 1970.

90. Middlemas, *Cabora Bassa*, 109; António Andrade et al., interview, Songo, July 11, 2001.

91. Simões Wetela, interview.

92. Ibid.

93. Pedro da Costa Xavier, interview.

94. Middlemas, *Cabora Bassa*, 109.

95. Ibid. See also *Johannesburg Star*, December 28, 1971, in which a Rhodesian journalist discusses these conflicts between "the white tribes."

96. In 1970, 160 non-Portuguese European nationals worked at the dam. Four years later, there were only sixty. Middlemas, *Cabora Bassa*, 100.

97. For a discussion of the labor process, see Michael Burawoy, *The Politics of Production: Factory Regimes under Capitalism and Socialism* (London: Verso, 1985); Isaacman, *Cotton*, 6–11; Isaacman and Sneddon, "Social and Environmental History," 610–15.

98. Middlemas, *Cabora Bassa*, 130.

99. William Chambers, interview, 1973, MC, tape A11.

100. Quoted in Middlemas, *Cabora Bassa*, 101.

101. Simões Wetela, interview; Pedro da Costa Xavier, interview.

102. The recruitment center at Massinga drew largely from the adjacent area and Vilanculo, the office at Maxixe attracted recruits from the Inhambane and Homoine regions, and the Chibuto office focused on the Chibuto, Chicualacuala, and Massingir regions—which were further south.

103. William Chambers, interview.

104. Simões Wetela, interview.

105. Middlemas, *Cabora Bassa*, 31.

106. Simões Wetela, interview.

107. ANTT, PIDE/DGS, SC, CI(2), processo 8743, pasta 2, informação, 62/71/01/2SC, January 12, 1971.

108. Since the beginning of the twentieth century, southern Mozambique had served as a labor reserve for South Africa. See Patrick Harries, *Work, Culture and Identity: Migrant Laborers in Mozambique and South Africa, c. 1860–1910* (Portsmouth, NH: Heinemann, 1994), 141–91; First, *Black Gold*.

109. Shangaan headman, interview, n.d., MC, tape A11; Middlemas, *Cabora Bassa*, 102–3.

110. Shangaan headman, interview; Simões Wetela, interview.

111. ANTT, PIDE/DGS, SC, CI(2), processo 8743, pasta 2, informação 62/71/01/2SC, January 12, 1971.

112. Eléusio dos Prazeres Viegas Filipe, "The Dam Brought Us Hunger" (MA thesis, University of Minnesota, 2003), 37–38.

113. António Andrade et al., interview.

114. Middlemas, *Cabora Bassa*, 133. Europeans and Africans alike "expressed open admiration for [the Pondos'] skill in this work." *Johannesburg Star*, December 28, 1971.

115. ANTT, PIDE/DGS, SC, CI(2), processo 8743, pasta 1, Delegação de Moçambique, 2013/7-DI/2, September 6, 1970; António Andrade et al., interview; Maurício Alemão, interview.

116. AHM, GG, caixa 860, GPZ, "Relatório da Actividade de 1971," n.d.; Middlemas, *Cabora Bassa*, 130.

117. Júlio Calecoetoa, interview; Senteira Botão et al., interview.

118. Ereman Conforme, interview, Chipalapala, May 26, 1998.

119. Fausto Semo, interview, Chipalapala, July 12, 2001.

120. Maurício Alemão, interview.

121. António Andrade et al, interview.

122. Júlio Calecoetoa, interview.

123. Emílio Faidose, interview, Masecha, May 25, 1998.

124. António Andrade et al., interview.

125. ANTT, PIDE/DGS, SC, CI(2), processo 8743, pasta 1, Direcção Geral de Segurança, 1783/70/D1/2/SC, September 8, 1970.

126. Pedro da Costa Xavier, interview.

127. Ereman Conforme, interview.

128. António Andrade et al., interview; Padre Cláudio Gremi, interview, May 20, 1998.

129. Ezani Sipinyo, interview, Estima, May 21, 1998; António Andrade et al., interview; *Século*, August 4, 1970.

130. Antoine Lampiére, interview.

131. Quoted in *Rhodesian Herald*, December 4, 1972, 5.

132. António Andrade et al., interview.

133. Workers crushed about 1 million rocks, which were used to make cement. Middlemas, *Cabora Bassa*, 97.

134. When the temperature rose above 120 degrees, Zamco suspended operations for health reasons.

135. Peter Size and Fedi Alfante, interview, Chinyanda Nova, May 25, 1998; *Diário popular*, November 4, 1970; Middlemas, *Cabora Bassa*, 89–116. Because the company archives located at Songo are closed, the incidence of these diseases, what treatments (if any) workers received for them, and their short- and long-term consequences remain unknown.

136. Padre Claúdio Gremi, interview, May 20, 1998; Júlio Calecoetoa, interview; Peter Size and Fedi Alfante, interview.

137. António Andrade et al., interview.

138. Simões Wetela, interview.

139. The unregulated and unrelenting use of force at Cahora Bassa contrasts sharply with labor conditions at Kariba, where colonial officials adopted policies designed to promote labor stabilization and African industrial advancement. Tischler, "Light and Power," 264–307.

140. Padre Claúdio Gremi, interview, May 20, 1998.

141. Peter Size and Fedi Alfante, interview.

142. Júlio Calecoetoa, interview.

143. Peter Size and Fedi Alfante, interview.

144. Padre Claúdio Gremi, interview, May 20, 1998.

145. Ibid.

146. ANTT, PIDE/DGS, SC, CI(2), processo 8743, pasta 1, informação, 1–073-CI(2), August 14, 1970; ANTT, PIDE/DGS, SC, CI(2), processo 8743, pasta 2, informação, 139-CI(2), June 10, 1972.

147. António Andrade et al., interview.

148. Padre Claúdio Gremi, interview, May 20, 1998.

149. Ibid.

150. ANTT, PIDE/DGS, SC, CI(2), processo 8743, pasta 2, informação, 2104/70/D/2/SC, November 17, 1970.

151. Padre Claúdio Gremi, interview, May 20, 1998.

152. For photographs of working conditions at Cahora Bassa, see Hidroeléctrica de Cahora Bassa, *A nossa energia abraça de Moçambique* (Lisbon: HCB, 2000), 94–128.

153. ANTT, PIDE/DGS, SC, CI(2), processo 8743, pasta 2, DGS RÁDIO, June 6, 1971.

154. ANTT, PIDE/DGS, SC, CI(2), processo 8743, pasta 2, Mário Luís A. Campos Costa, GPZ, Chefe de Divisão-Internacional, 659/72/01/2/SC, June 20, 1972; ANTT, PIDE/DGS, SC, CI(2), processo 8743, pasta 2, Direcção-Geral de Segurança, 1.744-CI(2), August 30, 1972.

155. Middlemas, *Cabora Bassa*, 116.

156. ANTT, PIDE/DGS, SC, CI(2), processo 8743, pasta 2, DGS RÁDIO, June 6, 1971.

157. *Notícias*, November 16, 1973; Middlemas, *Cabora Bassa*, 116.

158. *Argus*, December 6, 1974.

159. Ibid.

160. Ereman Conforme, interview.

161. António Andrade et al., interview.

162. Maurício Alemão, interview.

163. António Andrade et al., interview; Padre Claúdio Gremi, interview, May 20, 1998.

164. António Andrade et al., interview.

165. Padre Claúdio Gremi, interview, May 20, 1998.

166. Gervásio Saborinho Chongololo, interview, Estima, July 11, 2001.

167. Pedro da Costa Xavier, interview.

168. Ereman Conforme, interview.

169. Gervásio Saborinho Chongololo, interview.

170. Ibid.

171. Unlike Kariba, where African workers could bring their wives and children to live with them. Tischler, "Light and Power," 281. Zamco explicitly prohibited such practices at the Cahora Bassa dam site. Padre Claúdio Gremi, interview, May 20, 1998.

172. Pedro da Costa Xavier, interview.

173. Padre Claúdio Gremi, interview, May 20, 1998; António Andrade et al., interview.

174. Isaacman, *Cotton*, 122.

175. Júlio Calecoetoa, interview For a detailed account of the role of labor inspectors in the Zambezi Valley, see AHM, Inspecção dos Serviços Administrativos e dos Negócios Indígenas , caixa 62, José Franco Rodriguez, n.d.

176. Simões Wetela, interview; António Andrade et al., interview.

177. Some highly skilled African workers received rations of meat, rice, and potatoes cooked in oil. Pedro da Costa Xavier, interview; Ereman Conforme, interview; Simões Wetela, interview.

178. Isaacman, *Cotton*, 122.

179. Pedro da Costa Xavier, interview.

180. Ereman Conforme, interview; Simões Wetela, interview.

181. Lucrécia Arcário Luís et al., interview, Estima, July 13, 2001.

182. Simões Wetela; Padre Claúdio Gremi, interview, May 20, 1998.

183. Ereman Conforme, interview; Simões Wetela, interview.

184. Africans, however, could never fill supervisory positions.

185. Middlemas, *Cabora Bassa*, 118–19.

186. Ibid., 118.

187. Padre Claúdio Gremi, interview, May 20, 1998; Júlio Calecoetoa, interview.

188. Peter Size and Fedi Alfante, interview.

189. Padre Claúdio Gremi, interview, May 20, 1998.

190. Ibid.

191. António Andrade et al., interview.

192. Simões Wetela, interview.

193. See, for example, Luise White, *The Comforts of Home: Prostitution in Colonial Nairobi* (Chicago: University of Chicago Press, 1990); Dorothy Hodgson and Sheryl McCurdy, introduction to *"Wicked" Women and the Reconfiguration of Gender in Africa*, ed. Dorothy Hodgson and Sheryl McCurdy (Portsmouth, NH: Heinemann, 2001), 1–27; Jean Allman, "Rounding up Spinsters: Gender Chaos and Unmarried Women in Colonial Asante," in *Wicked Women and the Configuration of Gender in Africa*, ed. Dorothy Hodgson and Sheryl McCurdy (Portsmouth, NH: Heinemann, 2001), 130–48.

194. According to Pedro da Costa Xavier, "the Africans from the South often practiced homosexuality in COTA 90." Pedro da Costa Xavier, interview.

195. Simões Wetela, interview.

196. Ibid.; Padre Claúdio Gremi, interview, May 20, 1998.

197. Tischler, "Light and Power," 315–16.

198. Peter Size and Fedi Alfante, interview.

199. Middlemas, *Cabora Bassa*, 116.

200. Ereman Conforme, interview.

201. António Andrade et al., interview.

202. Padre Claúdio Gremi, interview, May 20, 1998.

203. Peter Size and Fedi Alfante, interview; Júlio Calecoetoa, interview.

204. Júlio Calecoetoa, interview.

205. ANTT, PIDE/DGS, SC, CI(2), processo 8743, pasta 1, informação, 1–073-CI(2), August 14, 1970; ANTT, PIDE/DGS, SC, CI(2), processo 8743, pasta 2, informação, 139-CI(2), June 10, 1972.

206. António Andrade et al., interview; Simões Wetela, interview; Pedro da Costa Xavier, interview; Maurício Alemão, interview; Júlio Calecoetoa, interview.

207. António Andrade et al., interview.

208. The Portuguese were very concerned about the number of Frelimo agents who had infiltrated the dam site. ANTT, PIDE/DGS, SC, CI(2), processo 8743, pasta 1, informação, 1–073-CI(2), August 14, 1970; ANTT, PIDE/DGS, SC, CI(2), processo 8743, pasta 2, informação, 139-CI(2), June 10, 1972.

209. Simões Wetela, interview.

210. Ibid.

211. Padre Claúdio Gremi, interview, May 20, 1998.

212. Ibid.; Pedro da Costa Xavier, interview; Maurício Alemão, interview; Júlio Calecoetoa, interview.

213. Mondlane, *Struggle*, 98.

214. ANTT, PIDE/DGS, SC, CI(2), processo 8743, pasta 2, Eduardo Mondlane, "Cabora Bassa contra o colonialismo contra a guerra colonial," n.d.

215. World Council of Churches, *Cabora Bassa and the Struggle for Southern Africa* (London: World Council of Churches, 1971), 2.

216. Ibid.

217. See Margaret Keck and Kathryn Sikkink, *Activists beyond Borders: Advocacy Networks in International Politics* (Ithaca: Cornell University Press, 1998).

218. *Diário de Notícias*, October 10, 1970.

219. Radmann, "Zambesi Development Scheme," 150; Middlemas, *Cabora Bassa*, 164.

220. Quoted in World Council of Churches, *Cabora Bassa*, 2. For Frelimo's official condemnation of the dam as an imperialist project, see *Mozambique Revolution* 44 (July–September 1970): 14–15.

221. A *Capital* (Lisbon), September 9, 1970.

222. Ibid.

223. Radmann, "Zambesi Development Scheme," 150; ANTT, PIDE/DGS, SC, CI(2), processo 8743, pasta 1, 1.2013/7-/DI/2, September 19, 1970.

224. *Daily News* (Tanzania), December 16, 1972.

225. ANTT, PIDE/DGS, SC, CI(2), processo 8743, pasta 1, "O Communismo Internacional," 1.2013/7-/DI/2, September 18, 1970; Middlemas, *Cabora Bassa*, 167.

226. ANTT, PIDE/DGS, SC, CI(2), processo 8743, pasta 1, *Die Welt*, July 1, 1970 (the document was a translation).

227. ANTT, PIDE/DGS, SC, CI(2), processo 8743, pasta 1, Confidencial, March 25, 1970.

228. Middlemas, *Cabora Bassa*, 164–69.

229. *Toronto Daily Star*, October 8, 1970.

230. ANTT, PIDE/DGS, SC, CI(2), processo 8743, pasta 1, Confidencial, March 25, 1970; United Nations, "Economic Conditions in Mozambique with Reference to Foreign Interests" (Conference Room Paper SCI/71/5, United Nations, New York, 1971), 38.

231. Middlemas, *Cabora Bassa*, 168.

232. Ibid.; ANTT, PIDE/DGS, SC, CI(2), processo 8743, pasta 1, "O communismo internacional," 1.2013/7/DI/2, September 18, 1970; ANTT, PIDE/DGS, SC, CI(2), processo 8743, pasta 1, "Confidencial," March 25, 1970.

233. ANTT, PIDE/DGS, SC, CI(2), processo 8743, pasta 1, informação, 1.127-CI(2), August 27, 1970.

234. *Mozambique Revolution* 44 (July–September 1970); ANTT, PIDE/DGS, SC, CI(2), processo 8743, pasta 2, informação, 278-CI(2), March 15, 1971.

235. ANTT, PIDE/DGS, SC, CI(2), processo 8743, pasta 2, relatório, 388/71/DL/2/SC, February 22, 1971.

236. ANTT, PIDE/DGS, SC, CI(2), processo 8743, pasta 2, informação, 140-CI(2), January 27, 1971.

237. Middlemas, *Cabora Bassa*, 154; ANTT, PIDE/DGS, SC, CI(2), processo 8743, pasta 2, informação, 834-CI(2), August 19, 1972.

238. ANTT, PIDE/DGS, SC, CI(2), processo 8743, pasta 1, informação, 536-CI(2), April 21, 1970; ANTT, PIDE/DGS, SC, CI(2), processo 8743, pasta 2, Ministério dos Negócios Estrangeiros, April 20, 1971; ANTT, PIDE/DGS, SC, CI(2), processo 8743, pasta 2, informação, 417-CI(2), April 8, 1971.

239. ANTT, PIDE/DGS, SC, CI(2), processo 8743, pasta 1, informação, 536-CI(2), April 17, 1970.

240. AHD, processo EAA 195, pasta 1A (1972–74): draft of 1972 article by Bruce London of the *Daily Telegraph*.

241. ANTT, PIDE/DGS, SC, CI(2), processo 8743, pasta 2, Direcção-Geral Dos Negócios Políticos, December 9, 1970.

242. *Newsweek*, November 27, 1972.

243. Borges Coelho, "Protected Villages," 241–47.

244. *Rhodesian Herald*, May 19, 1972.

245. *Rhodesian Herald*, June 21, 1972.

246. For a richly detailed military history of the escalating struggle for Tete, see Borges Coelho, "Protected Villages," 238–74.

247. ANTT, PIDE/DGS, SC, CI(2), processo 8743, pasta 1, informação, 1.196-CI(2), September 8, 1970; ANTT, PIDE/DGS, SC, CI(2), processo 8743, pasta 1, informação, 635/7/D1/2/SC, April 6, 1970; ANTT, PIDE/DGS, SC, CI(2), processo 8743, pasta 2, DGS RÁDIO, March 31, 1971; ANTT, PIDE/DGS, SC, CI(2), processo 8743, pasta 2, relatório, 1824/70/DI/2/SC, September 11, 1970.

248. *Notícias*, October 15, 1971.

249. ANTT, PIDE/DGS, SC, CI(2), processo 8743, pasta 1, informação, 635/7/D1/2/SC, April 6, 1970.

250. *Star*, December 28, 1971.

251. AHD, processo EAA 195, pasta 1A (1972–74): draft of 1972 article by Bruce London of the *Daily Telegraph* (London).

252. *Diário de Notícias*, November 16, 1971.

253. Franz Jordan, interview, 1974, MC, tape A11.

254. AHM, GG, caixa 860, GPZ, "Relatório da Actividade de 1971," Annexo Confidencial ao Relatório de Actividade do GPZ de 1971.

255. Ibid.

256. ANTT, PIDE/DGS, SC, CI(2), processo 8743, pasta 1, Director Geral do Ministério dos Negócios Estrangeiros to Director Geral de Segurança, September 9, 1970; Middlemas, *Cabora Bassa*, 147–49.

257. Middlemas, *Cabora Bassa*, 149.

258. Lieutenant Pereira, interview, 1973–74, MC, tape A12.

259. *Rhodesian Herald*, November 17, 1972.

CHAPTER 4: DISPLACED PEOPLE

1. AHM, Secção Especial (SE) a.111 p.10, caixa 237, Governo do Distrito de Tete, Serviços Distritais de Administração Civil, "Actas das Sessões da Reunião dos Administradores e do Intendente com o Governador do Distrito, realizado nos termos do art. 377 da R.A.U., que teve lugar em Tete, nos dias 27 e 28 de Dezembro de 1968."

2. Ibid. Kwame Nkrumah, the president of Ghana when the Volta River dams were constructed, supported the resettlement of eighty thousand people, residing in 739 villages, on similar grounds—that it would improve their living conditions and promote more efficient farming practices. Stephan Miescher and Dzodzi Tsikata, "Hydro Power and the Promise of Modernity and Development in Ghana: Comparing the Akosombo and Bui Dam Projects," *Ghana Studies* 12–13 (2009–10): 23–24.

3. Bolton, "Regulation of the Zambezi," 358.

4. AHM, Silva Braga, "Plano."

5. For a discussion of the stress and trauma associated with forced resettlement, see McCully, *Silenced Rivers*, 65–101; Scudder, *Large Dams*, 22–30. See also Vandergeest, Idahosa, and Bose, *Development's Displacement*.

6. Brendan Jundanian, "Resettlement Programs: Counterinsurgency in Mozambique," *Comparative Politics* 6, no. 4 (1974): 522.

7. Borges Coelho, "Protected Villages," 162–69. It is likely that Portuguese security officials, who monitored nationalist activities throughout Africa, had also studied the counterinsurgency methods used by the British against Mau Mau fighters in Kenya. For a discussion of these methods, see Caroline Elkins, *Imperial Reckoning: The Untold Story of Britain's Gulag in Kenya* (New York: Henry Holt, 2005), 154–192.

8. The colonial government forced more than 250,000 peasants in Cabo Delgado into 250 villages in a belt stretching from Montepuez to the Messalo River, while an additional 175,000 were relocated to controlled villages in Niassa. Jundanian, "Counterinsurgency," 520. See also AHM, FMA, caixa 107, Secretário Provincial de Terras e Povoamento, "Criação de um grupo de trabalho coordenador dos aldeamentos," December 22, 1971.

9. Borges Coelho, "Protected Villages," 160–69.

10. This policy stands in sharp contrast to the situation at Kariba, where those on the northern bank received compensation. Tischler, "Light and Power," 130–31.

11. AHM, Silva Braga, "Plano."

12. Ibid.

13. Ibid.

14. Ibid.

15. Ibid.

16. ANTT, SCCIM, no. 1635, Aldeamentos: Armando Gonçalves, Administrador do Concelho de Inhambane, "Reordenamento das populações em aldeamentos," August 31, 1973.

17.

Circumscription	Non-"civilized" population	"Civilized" population
Tete	65,811	1,788
Zumbo	23,495	75
Mague	29,122	—

Source: AHM, Secção Especial (SE), cota S.E. a.IV, p. 2, no. 4–12a: MFPZ, "Bacia do Zambeze: Estudos Económico–sociais, Desenvolvimento Económico, Estudos Base para Programação," vol. 1 (Lisbon, n.d.), quadro 3: População Nativa por Postos e Circunscriçoes.

18. AHM, GG, caixa 860, GPZ, "Programa de trabalho para 1973."

19. Ibid.

20. Ibid.

21. See Colson, *Social Consequences*, 35–42.

22. McGregor, *Crossing the Zambezi*, 110–17. For a detailed discussion of Gwembe Tonga opposition to the evictions, see Tischler, "Light and Power," 148–49, 185–216.

23. Tischler, "Light and Power," 147–49, 210–16.

24. A *Capital*, October 13, 1971.

25. Ibid.

26. AHM, Província de Tete, Administração do Concelho de Macanga, Arquivo Confidencial e Secreto, Administração-Secção A, caixa 97, João Gonçalves, Governador do Distrito de Tete, "Aldeamentos: Normas a observar nos aldeamentos—Identificação e controle de populações," May 20, 1970 (hereafter cited as AHM, Gonçalves, "Aldeamentos").

27. AHM, Silva Braga, "Plano"; AHM, Gonçalves, "Aldeamentos."

28. That partial autonomy stemmed from both their role as peasants and the limits of state power in the interior. See Isaacman, *Cotton*, 1–18.

29. AHM, Silva Braga, "Plano."

30. Borges Coelho, "Protected Villages," 160–211.

31. AHM, GG, caixa 2097, Governo do Distrito de Tete, Serviços de Administração Civil, "Actas das Sessões da Reuniãodos Administradores e do Intendente com o Governador do Distrito, realizada nos termos do art. 377 da RAU, que teve lugar em Tete, nos dias 28 e 29 de Dezembro de 1970" (hereafter cited as AHM, "Reuniãodos administradores"). This was not just speculation, however, since local officials documented instances where mere rumor of resettlement had precipitated widespread flight. Ibid.; AHM, Gonçalves, "Aldeamentos." To calm such fears, the administrator of Fingoe proposed a temporary moratorium on the use of force, which fell on deaf ears. ANTT, SCCIM, no. 1635, Aldeamentos, "Relatório imediato," unsigned, April 27, 1969. The governor of Tete insisted that force was essential "since these communities were unlikely to go voluntarily." ANTT, SCCIM, no. 1635, Aldeamentos: João Gonçalves, February 15, 1967.

32. AHM, "Reuniãodos administradores."

33. With these concerns in mind, colonial authorities did relocate the remains of several deceased chiefs whose graves were to be flooded by the lake, the most famous of which was Carizamimba. Jack Sobrinho and Wiseborn Benjamin, interview.

34. ANTT, SCCIM, no. 1635, Aldeamentos, João Gonçalves, February 15, 1967. See also Oliveira, *Tauaras*.

35. AHM, "Reuniãodos administradores."

36. Ibid.

37. See AHM, GG, caixa 864, GPZ, "Programa de trabalho, 1974." For a broader discussion of this policy, see Borges Coelho, "Protected Villages," 250–51; Jundanian, "Counterinsurgency," 519–40.

38. AHM, Província de Tete, Administração do Concelho de Moatize, Arquivo Confidencial e Secreto dos Processos, caixa 109, João Pinto Coelho, Administrador de Concelho de Moatize, July 28, 1970.

39. Borges Coelho, "Protected Villages," 251–52.

40. AHM, GG, caixa 860, "Relatório de actividade 1971," 24–25; Borges Coelho, "Protected Villages," 251–54; *Notícias de Beira*, June 8, 1971.

41. Borges Coelho, "Protected Villages," 253.

42. According to a state census, the actual figure was 41,857. AHM, GG, caixa 860, GPZ, "Programa de trabalho para 1973."

43. Not all the forced removals occurred under the auspices of the GPZ. Borges Coelho, "Protected Villages," 303; Middlemas, *Cabora Bassa*, 217.

44. Pedro da Costa Xavier, interview.

45. Ibid.

46. McCully, *Silenced Rivers*, 66.

47. Tablet Potroy and Maurício Alemão, interview, Masecha, July 13, 2001; Bento Chitima et al., interview, Estima, July 11, 2001.

48. Bento Estima and Joseph Ndebvuchena, interview; Supia Sargento et al., interview, Chipalapala, July 12, 2001. See also *Diário de Notícias*, July 9, 1970.

49. ANTT, SCCIM, no. 1635, Aldeamentos: António Vieira Lopes, Administrador do Concelho de Cabora Bassa, Boletim de informação, March 30, 1971.

50. Ibid.

51. ANTT, SCCIM, no. 1635, Aldeamentos: António Vieira Lopes, Administrador do Concelho de Cabora Bassa, Boletim de informação, April 30, 1971; ANTT, SCCIM, no. 1635, Aldeamentos, "Boletim de informações psicológicas," unsigned, April 17, 1971; ANTT, SCCIM, no. 1635, Aldeamentos, Relatório de notícia, unsigned, May 14, 1971.

52. ANTT, SCCIM, no. 1635, Aldeamentos, Relatório de notícia, unsigned, May 14, 1971.

53. Basílio Chiridzisana and Ragi Miguel, interview, Chicoa Nova, July 16, 2001.

54. Paulino Nhamizinga et al., interview, Chipalapala, July 12, 2001.

55. Pezulani Mafalanjala et al, interview.

56. Vernácio Leone, interview.

57. Ibid.; Pezulani Mafalanjala et al., interview.

58. Ibid.

59. Gervásio Saborinho Chongololo, interview.

60. ANTT, SCCIM, no. 1635, Aldeamentos, António Vieira Lopes, Administrador do Concelho de Cabora Bassa, Boletim de informação, March 30, May 5, 1971.

61. Padre Claúdio Gremi, interview, May 20, 1998; Middlemas, *Cabora Bassa*, 218.

62. Padre Claúdio Gremi, interview, May 20, 1998. At a 1972 press conference in Paris, Father da Costa, a Portuguese Catholic priest, confirmed that the military regularly used these tactics. *Rhodesia Herald*, November 4, 1972.

63. Padre Claúdio Gremi, interview, May 20, 1998.

64. ANTT, PIDE/DGS, SC, CI(2), processo 8743, pasta 2, *The Australian*, no. 2359, February 3, 1972 (translated).

65. ANTT, SCCIM, no. 1635, Aldeamento, Marcelo da Cruz, Boletim de informação, March 17, 1971.

66. ANTT, SCCIM, no. 1635, Aldeamentos, extracto, June 2, 1971.

67. Supia Sargento et al., interview.

68. Lofas Nsampa et al., interview by Judith Head, Luabo, November 14, 1976.

69. Júlio Calecoetoa, interview.

70. Bento Chitima et al., interview.

71. Jack Sobrinho and Wiseborn Benjamin, interview.

72. By 1973, Rhodesian authorities had interned more than eight thousand Africans, including immigrants from Mozambique. ANTT, SCCIM, no. 1635, Aldeamentos, Rhodesian government press statement, "Resettlement of Africans in the Zambesi Valley," December 7, 1973.

73. In some areas, housing was already in place because men and boys had been forcibly transported to their future aldeamento to clear the land and build their family's basic housing. Pezulani Mafalanjala et al., interview; Govate Simondeo et al., interview, Chipalapala, July 12, 2001; Basílio Chiridzisana and Ragi Miguel, interview, July 16, 2001; Peter Size and Fedi Alfante, interview.

74. Peter Size and Fedi Alfante, interview.

75. Padre Claúdio Gremi, interview, May 20, 1998.

76. Ibid.

77. S. Duncan, interview, 1973–74, MC, tape A11.

78. Govate Simondeo et al., interview.

79. Bento Chitima et al., interview.

80. Padre Claúdio Gremi, interview, Songo, May 23, 1998.

81. McCully, *Silenced Rivers*, 66–68.

82. AHM, GG, caixa 860, GPZ, "Programa de trabalho para 1973."

83. Ibid.

84. Supia Sargento et al., interview.

85. Having uprooted rural families from landscapes whose major features—settlements, rivers, hills—had provided order and meaning to their lives, government officials tried to minimize the loss of place by naming new villages for the ones left behind.

86. Gen. Kaúlza de Arriaga, interview, 1971, MC, tape A5.

87. R. Henderson, "Cabora Bassa: Who Will Benefit during the Construction Phase?" *Cultures et développement* 4, no. 2 (1972): 333.

88. Borges Coelho, "Protected Villages," 286.

89. Padre Claúdio Gremi, interview, May 23, 1998; Jundanian, "Counterinsurgency," 527. For the only extant photographs of the aldeamentos, see *Tempo* 250* (July 20, 1975). Their graininess precluded reproduction here.

90. Américo dos Santos Carvalho, *O plano do Zambeze* (Lourenço Marques: GPZ, 1974), 64–69.

91. GPZ, Relatorio de actividade, 1970 (Lisbon: GPZ, 1971), 46; GPZ, Relatorio de actividade, 1971 (Lisbon: GPZ, 1972), 20.

92. Padre Claúdio Gremi, interview, May 23, 1998.

93. Borges Coelho, "Protected Villages," 286.

94. ANTT, PIDE/DGS, SC, CI(2), NT7544, pasta 2, Director de PIDE, "Rede de informação e contra informação nos aldeamentos instalados nas zonas de intervenção," March 31, 1970.

95. AHM, GG, caixa 860, GPZ, "Programa de trabalho para 1973."

96. AHM, GG, caixa 864, GPZ, acta no. 1/74, "Comissão coordenadora districtal de Tete, 1974."

97. Arnaldo Vasconcelos, quoted in Borges Coelho, "Protected Villages," 432.

98. Typically, between six and thirty militia members—many of them conscripted—resided with their families on the periphery of each aldeamento. Recruited from as far away as Beira and Lourenço Marques, they had little in common with the population they were to protect. Carlos Sabonete, interview, Masecha, July 12, 2001. Poorly trained and undisciplined, they often plundered peasant households. Borges Coelho, "Protected Villages," 275–80; AHM, Província de Tete, Administração do Concelho de Macanga, Arquivo Confidencial e Secreto, Administração-Secção A, caixa 97, Carlos Fernandes Magalhães, Adjunto Administrador do Concelho, October 18, 1973. "They would demand goats and chickens," recalled Bento Estima, "or they would simply say, 'I want this and I want that.'" Bento Estima and Joseph Ndevuchena.

99. *Rhodesian Herald*, July 13, 1973; Crispin de Souza, interview, 1973–74, MC, tape A11.

100. Horst Langer, interview.

101. ANTT, SCCIM, no. 1635, Aldeamentos, Boletim de informação, July 19, 1971.

102. Thus, the fear voiced by Tete's governor in 1967—that peasants would view the aldeamentos as "little more than a prison"–turned out to be quite accurate. ANTT, SSCIM, no. 1635, Aldeamentos, João Gonçalves, February 5, 1967.

103. Peter Size and Fedi Alfante, interview.

104. Pezulani Mafalanjala et al., interview.

105. Padre Cláudio Gremi, May 20, 1998.

106. Pezulani Mafalanjala et al., interview.

107. Bento Chitima et al., interview.

108. Quoted in Borges Coelho, "Protected Villages," 289.

109. In 1970 the Overseas Ministry contracted with Companhia de Destroncar e Alugar de Maquinas to clear trees and grade the lands on those sites to which communities displaced by the lake would be relocated. *Diário de Notícias*, July 9, 1970.

110. Quoted in Borges Coelho, "Protected Villages," 288.

111. AHM, Província de Tete, Administração do Concelho de Macanga, Arquivo Confidencial e Secreto, Administração-Secção A, caixa 109, Rui Bastos Lacerda, Chefe de Gabinete do CDT, February 10, 1972.

112. Govate Simondeo et al., interview.

113. Peter Size and Fedi Alfante, interview; Sene Simico et al., interview, Nyatapira, May 27, 1998.

114. Pezulani Mafalanjala et al., interview; Supia Sargento and Carlos Churo, interview.

115. Ibid.

116. Senteira Botão et al., interview.

117. Pezulani Mafalanjala et al., interview.

118. Senteira Botão et al., interview.

119. Meghan Vaughan, *The Story of an African Famine: Gender and Famine in Twentieth-Century Malawi* (Cambridge: Cambridge University Press, 1983); Michael Watts, *Silent Violence: Food, Famine, and Peasantry in Northern Nigeria* (Berkeley: University of California Press, 1983).

120. Supia Sargento and Carlos Churo, interview.

121. AHM, Província de Tete, Administração do Concelho de Macanga, Arquivo Confidencial e Secreto, Administração-Secção A, caixa 109, Rui Bastos Lacerda, Chefe de Gabinete do CDT, February 10, 1972.

122. Peter Size and Fedi Alfante, interview.

123. Pezulani Mafalanjala et al., interview.

124. ANTT, PIDE/DGS, SC, CI(2), NT7544, pasta 2, Director de PIDE, "Rede de informação e contra informação nos aldeamentos instalados nas zonas de intervenção," March 31, 1970; Peter Size and Fedi Alfante, interview; Pezulani Mafalanjala et al., interview.

125. Senteira Botão et al., interview.

126. Paulino Nhamizinga et al., interview.

127. Bento Chitima et al., interview.

128. Padre Claúdio Gremi, interview, May 23, 1998.

129. AHM, Província de Tete, Administração do Concelho de Moatize, Arquivo Confidêncial e Secreto dos Processos, caixa 110, Governo do Distrito de Tete, "Colaboração do gabinete do GDT no plano de aldeamentos," November 20, 1971; Horst Langer, interview.

130. AHM, Província de Tete, Administração do Concelho de Moatize, Arquivo Confidêncial e Secreto dos Processos, caixa 110, Governo do Distrito de Tete, "Colaboração do gabinete," November 20, 1971.

131. Supia Sargento et al., interview.

132. AHM, Província de Tete, Administração do Concelho de Macanga, Arquivo Confidencial e Secreto, Administração-Secção A, caixa 97, José Rocha Dias, Administrador do Posto, April 30, 1974.

133. John Paul and Khumbidzi Pastor, interview.

134. Ibid.

135. *Voz africana*, January 29, 1974.

136. Ibid.

137. Fausto Semo, interview.

138. *Voz africana*.

139. Peasants in Chibueia, for instance, planted only 250 hectares during the 1973–74 agricultural campaign—down from 350 the previous year—and, at Nhaliuro, hectarage tumbled by 50 percent. AHM, GG, caixa 860, GPZ, "Programa de trabalho para 1973." Mapondane José remembered households in Chicoa Nova producing so little that, by November 1974, "there was nothing to eat." Govate Simondeo et al., interview.

140. Borges Coelho, "Protected Villages," 219.

141. Horst Langer, interview.

142. Ibid.

143. Senteira Botão et al., interview.

144. John Paul and Khumbidzi Pastor, interview.

145. Senteira Botão et al., interview; Supia Sargento and Carlos Churo, interview; Júlio Calecoetoa, interview.

146. Borges Coelho, "Protected Villages," 289; Middlemas, *Cabora Bassa*, 218–19.

147. These included *malambe*, a fruit from the ubiquitous baobab, *masau*, a wild fruit used to make fermented alcoholic drinks, and *myanza* roots that were pounded with a mortar to make flour or porridge.

148. Bento Estima and Joseph Ndebvuchena, interview.

149. Ibid.

150. Carvalho, *Plano do Zambeze*, 73.

151. AHM, GG, caixa 864, GPZ, "Programa de trabalho para 1974"; AHM, GG, caixa 864, GPZ, "Agenda para a reunião da commissão distrital de Tete," January 3, 1974; Borges Coelho, "Protected Villages," 288–89.

152. Fausto Semo, interview.

153. Borges Coelho, "Protected Villages," 289.

154. AHM, GG, caixa 864, GPZ, "Programa de trabalho para 1974."

155. Gervásio Saborinho Chongololo et al., interview, Estima, July 13, 2001.

156. ANTT, PIDE/DGS, SC, CI(2), NT7544, pasta 2, Director de PIDE, "Rede de informação e contra informação nos aldeamentos instalados nas zonas de intervenção," March 31, 1970.

157. AHM, GG, caixa 864, GPZ, June 5, 1973.

158. ANTT, PIDE/DGS, SC, CI(2), NT7544, pasta 2, Director de PIDE, "Rede de informação," March 31, 1970; Padre Claúdio Gremi, interview, May 20, 1998.

159. Horst Langer, interview.

160. Without such studies, we cannot know if there were increases in the rates of morbidity and mortality.

161. John Paul and Khumbidzi Pastor, interview.

162. Bolton, "Cabora Bassa Project," 161–62.

163. Middlemas, *Cabora Bassa*, 220.

164. Scudder, *Large Dams*, 24.

165. McCully, *Silenced Rivers*, 80.

166. Gabinete do Plano de Zambeze, *Relatório de Actividade*, 1973 (Lisbon: GPZ, 1974), 59–63.

167. Pezulani Mafalanjala et al., interview.

168. Basílio Chiridzisana and Ragi Miguel, interview, July 16, 2001; Carlos Sabonete, interview; Vernácio Leone, interview.

169. For a discussion of the spiritual hierarchy, see David Lan, *Guns and Rain: Guerrillas and Spirit Mediums in Zimbabwe* (Berkeley: University of California Press, 1985).

170. Gaspar Cardoso, interview; Conrado Msussa Boroma, interview.

171. Basílio Chiridzisana and Ragi Miguel, interview, July 16, 2001.

172. Carlos Sabonete, interview.

173. Vernácio Leone, interview.

174. Ibid.

175. Bento Estima and Joseph Ndebvuchena, interview.

176. Pezulani Mafalanjala et al., interview.

177. Bento Estima and Joseph Ndebvuchena, interview.

178. Tablet Potroy and Maurício Alemão, interview.

179. Sene Simico et al., interview.

180. As early as 1967 colonial authorities expressed concern about the adverse effects of separating peasants from their midzimu and mhondoro. ANTT, SCCIM, no. 1635, Aldeamentos, João Gonçalves, Aldeamentos, February 15, 1967.

181. Gaspar Cardoso, interview; Conrado Msussa Boroma, interview.

182. Tablet Potroy and Maurício Alemão, interview.

183. ANTT, SCCIM, no. 1635, Aldeamentos, José de Vilhena Ramires Ramos, Boletim de informação, April 7, 1971.

184. Borges Coelho, "Protected Villages," 286.

185. Ibid.

186. Ibid., 275–80; AHM, Província de Tete, Administração do Concelho de Macanga, Arquivo Confidêncial e Secreto, Administração-Secção A, caixa 97, Carlos Fernandes Magalhães, Adjunto Administrador do Concelho, October 18, 1973.

187. Quoted in Borges Coelho, "Protected Villages," 279.

188. AHM, Província de Tete, Administração do Concelho de Macanga, Arquivo Confidêncial e Secreto, Administração-Secção A, caixa 97, Carlos Fernandes Magalhães, Adjunto Administrador do Concelho, October 18, 1973. Borges Coelho also commented on the militia's drunkenness and violence. Borges Coelho, "Protected Villages," 279–80.

189. Carlos Sabonete, interview.

190. The mwabvi poison ordeal was practiced throughout the Zambezi valley. In periods of crisis, witchcraft accusations flourished. The person so accused was forced to drink a lethal potion made from the bark of a tree, which was pounded and mixed with water. If the accused then vomited, it was a sign from the spirits that he or she was innocent of the charge. If not, the person died, and the community no longer had to worry about witches in its midst. Gamitto, King Kazembe, 1:74-75; Isaacman, Zambezi Prazos, 92.

191. ANTT, SCCIM, no. 1635, Aldeamentos, extracto, unsigned, July 19, 1973; Padre Cláudio Gremi, interview, Songo, July 11, 2001.

192. ANTT, SCCIM, no. 1635, Aldeamentos, extracto, July 19, 1973.

193. Gervásio Saborinho Chongololo, interview. The Kariba resettlement also caused kinship solidarity to deepen. Colson, Social Consequences, 77.

194. Bento Estima and Joseph Ndebvuhchena, interview; Tablet Potroy and Maurício Alemão, interview.

195. There were only six model aldeamentos in the entire country. Thomas Henriksen, Revolution and Counterrevolution: Mozambique's War of Independence, 1964–1974 (Westport: Greenwood, 1983), 156.

196. Horst Langer, interview.

197. Padre Claúdio Gremi, interview, May 23, 1998.

198. Ibid. Middlemas came to the same conclusion. Middlemas, *Cabora Bassa*, 218.

199. For a discussion of chiefly benefits under Portuguese colonialism, see Allen Isaacman, "Chiefs, Rural Differentiation and Peasant Protest: The Mozambican Forced Cotton Regime 1938–1961," *African Economic History* 14* (1985): 15–56; Basílio Chiridzisana and Ragi Miguel, interview, July 16, 2001; Padre Claúdio Gremi, interview, May 23, 1998.

200. Bento Chitima et al., interview.

201. Because the literature on displaced people and refugee communities almost always ignored gender, the differential impact of involuntary resettlement on women was ignored. Elizabeth Colson, "Gendering Those Uprooted by 'Development,'" in *Engendering Forced Migration*, ed. Doreen Indra (New York: Berghahn, 1999), 22–39. Colson's *Social Consequences of Resettlement*, published in 1971, remains one of the few studies to treat gender seriously.

202. Padre Claúdio Gremi, interview, May 23, 1998; Peter Size and Fedi Alfante, interview; Govate Simondeo et al., interview; Basílio Chiridzisana and Ragi Miguel, interview.

203. Pezulani Mafalanjala, et al., interview; Govate Simondeo et al., interview; Supia Sargento et al., interview.

204. Govate Simondeo et al., interview; Bento Chitima et al., interview; Padre Claúdio Gremi, interview, May 23, 1998.

205. Padre Claúdio Gremi, July 11, 2001.

206. AHM, Província de Tete, Administração do Concelho de Macanga, Arquivo Confidêncial e Secreto, Administração-Secção A, caixa 97, José Rocha Dias, Administrador do Posto, April 30, 1974.

207. Basílio Chiridzisana and Ragi Miguel, interview, July 16, 2001; ANTT, SCCIM, no. 1635, Aldeamentos, extracto, unsigned, July 19, 1973.

208. Peter Size and Fedi Alfante, interview; António Andrade et al., interview.

209. Maurício Alemão, interview.

210. This is true worldwide. See Mehta, *Displaced by Development*; Vandergeest, Idahosa, and Bose, *Development's Displacements*.

211. In fact, sometimes ex-aldeamentos were simply renamed communal villages, and the inhabitants remained where they were.

212. Borges Coelho, "Protected Villages," 324–415.

CHAPTER 5: THE LOWER ZAMBEZI

1. Scudder, *Large Dams*; McCully, *Silenced Rivers*.

2. See, for example, Goldsmith and Hildyard, *Large Dams*; McCully, *Silenced Rivers*; D. L. O. Mendis, *Eppawala—Destruction of Cultural Heritage in the Name of Development* (Colombo: Sri Lanka Pugwash Group, 1999); Dai Qing, *The River Dragon Has Come! The Three Gorges Dam and the Fate of China's Yangtze River and Its People* (Armonk, NY: M. E. Sharpe, 1998); WCD, *Dams and*

Development; Margaret Barber and Gráinne Ryder, *Damming the Three Gorges: What Dam Builders Don't Want You to Know* (London: Probe International, 1993); Tsikata, *Living in the Shadow*; Khagram, *Dams*.

3. See Scudder, *Large Dams*, 211–41; Tsikata, *Living in the Shadow*, 85–279.

4. Based on government estimates of those affected by the 2001 floods, more than half a million people lived adjacent to the lower Zambezi. "Floods Claim over 100 Lives," *AIM*, April 20, 2001.

5. Some of the negative consequences began with Kariba, which blocked silt from moving downriver and, when the gates were opened after extremely heavy rains, intensified flooding from Tete city south to the mouth of the Zambezi.

6. Engineers are required to use the Design Flood Rule Curve for the life of any dam that can be overtopped during extreme floods. It models reservoir storage, outlet capacity, operational locations, overload ratios, tailwater elevation, and power efficiency, to calculate how much water to hold back or discharge. Beilfuss, "Modeling Trade-offs," 127–38. Unfortunately, because of climate change, scientists can no longer presume the curve's validity and have no idea what the new maximums might be. Richard Beilfuss, pers. comm., December 4, 2011.

7. This concept derives from Richard White, *The Organic Machine* (New York: Hill and Wang, 1995).

8. For both colonizers and colonized, the landscape is simultaneously material and a cultural image, a way of representing, structuring, or symbolizing surroundings. See Denis E. Cosgrove, *Social Formation and Symbolic Landscape* (London: Routledge, 1984); Fairhead and Leach, *Misreading the African Landscape*; James McCann, *Green Land, Brown Land, Black Land* (Portsmouth, NH: Heinemann, 1992); Giles-Vernick, *Cutting the Vines*.

9. This decision ignored the forceful recommendations of a Portuguese-led environmental research team that the reservoir's filling should be timed to match normal dry- and wet-season flows and that the release of water should never drop below four to five hundred cubic meters per second, which would make local agriculture minimally sustainable. The team further demanded several additional measures, including a two-and-a-half-year minimum filling period and a moratorium on filling during the next summer flood (December–January), which the HCB ignored. Davies, "Rehabilitation Programme"; Davies, "They Pulled the Plug," 26–28.

10. W. J. Bond, Nancy Coe, P. B. N. Jackson, and K. H. Rogers, "The Limnology of Cabora Bassa, Moçambique, during Its First Year," *Freshwater Biology* 8, no. 5 (1978): 445. That the Kariba reservoir is much larger than Lake Cahora Bassa does not explain the time differential.

11. P. B. N. Jackson, "Ecological Studies on the Middle Zambezi prior to Kariba and Cahora Bassa and the Need for Surveys of the Lower Zambezi prior to the Creation of Further Hydroelectric Dams" (paper presented at Workshop on the Sustainable Use of Cahora Bassa Dam and the Zambezi Valley, September 29–October 2, 1997, Songo); AHM, Tinley and Sousa Dias, "Plano base"; Davies, "They Pulled the Plug," 26–28.

12. Davies, "Rehabilitation Programme."

13. Ibid.

14. Régulo António Chipuazo et al., interview; N'tsai António et al., interview.

15. According to International Rivers, "the Zambezi is . . . one of the most heavily dammed rivers in Africa, with at least 30 large storage reservoirs holding back its flow." International Rivers, "Zambezi River," www.internationalrivers.org /africa/zambezi-river.

16. These upstream dams would have more significantly affected lower Zambezi River flows but for the substantial runoff from the unregulated Luangwa River, which discharges into the Zambezi just upstream from the Cahora Bassa gorge. Dry-season flows into the gorge also rose dramatically due to upstream hydropower production. Beilfuss and Santos, "Hydrological Change," 29–35.

17. Davies, Beilfuss, and Thoms, "Cahora Bassa Retrospective," 1–3.

18. In the peak flooding season (February through April), mean monthly flow declined by approximately 40 percent. Dry-season flows, on the other hand, more than tripled. Beilfuss and Santos, "Hydrological Change," 29–35.

19. Ibid., 16–20.

20. Bertha Nehrera and Lucy Emerton, *Economic Value of the Zambezi Basin Wetlands* (Harare: International World Conservation Union, Regional Office for Southern Africa, 2006), 24.

21. Mário Chambiça et al., interview; Vale Raposo, interview.

22. Nehrera and Emerton, *Economic Value*, 30.

23. António Tchoa, interview.

24. Novais Nhamazi et al., interview.

25. Ibid. The changes elders attributed to Kariba might have been due to unrelated flooding.

26. Beilfuss, Chilundo, et al., "Hydrological Changes," 8.

27. Beilfuss, "Understanding Extreme Floods," 3.

28. CICA, *Esboço*, 160.

29. All dams have far-reaching ecological repercussions. "Because all dams reduce normal flooding, they also fragment ecosystems by isolating the river from the floodplain, turning what . . . biologists term a 'floodplain river' into a 'reservoir river.' The elimination of the benefits of natural flooding may be the single most ecologically damaging impact of the dam." McCully, *Silenced Rivers*, 31.

30. The delta is exceptionally vulnerable because "it bears the cumulative effects of [river] engineering projects over a 1,375,000 km² catchment that extends over portions of eight developing countries" in south-central Africa. Beilfuss and Brown, introduction to *Environmental Flow Requirements*, 2.

31. The Kariba Dam affected the flooding regime of the Lower Zambezi somewhat, but not nearly as drastically as Cahora Bassa. Davies, "Zambezi River System," 235–42; S. Muhai, "Cahora Bassa," 4.

32. Beilfuss and Brown, "Environmental Flow Requirements," 2–3.

33. Carlos Bento, interview, March 10, 2010.

34. Ibid.; Daniel Ribeiro, interview, Maputo, March 10, 2010.

35. Government meteorological data confirm the connection between South African energy demands and erratic river flow. Between 1978 and 1980, for example, major flow peaks occurred in mid-March and early November, then in late June, and again in January. Before each, the transmission of energy to South Africa spiked. UTIP, *Mepanda uncua*, document no. 012/A, 4–12.

36. João Tesoura, interview, Caia (Aldeia 25 de Setembro), July 11, 2000.

37. José Jone et al., interview.

38. Ibid.

39. Maria Carvalho et al., interview, Sena (Regulada Mwamalavo), July 21, 2000.

40. Milioni Lambani, interview, Chemba (Regulado Chave), July 19, 2001.

41. Garry Bernacsek and Suzette Lopes, "Cahora Bassa (Mozambique)," in *Status of African Reservoir Fisheries*, ed. J. M. Kapetsky and T. Petr, CIFA Technical Paper no. 10 (Rome: FAO, 1984), 30.

42. Paulo Milo, interview by MRB, Chikoti, May 24, 2000.

43. Zhuwa Msitu, interview by MRB, T/A Kambembe (Tizola), May 6, 2000; Artur Medja et al., interview Scientists working for the GPZ actually predicted large-scale erosion in a 1974 report. Bolton, "Regulation of the Zambezi," 329; Davies, Beilfuss, and Thoms, "Cahora Bassa Retrospective," 1–3.

44. Beilfuss, Dutton, and Moore, "Land Cover Change," 52. As they emphasize, however, other factors, including "resource utilization pressures, climatic cycles, natural geomorphic processes, . . . interactions between the indigenous delta population and successive traders and colonial inhabitants[,] . . . civil war, drought and the construction of large dams on the Zambezi River [all] threaten the ecological and social fabric of the delta." Ibid., 1.

45. Richard Beilfuss, e-mail to the authors, December 4, 2011. See also Beilfuss, Dutton, and Moore, "Land Cover Change," 52; R. C. F. Maugham, *Zambezia: A General Description of the Valley of the Zambezi River, from Its Delta to the River Aroangwa, with Its History, Agriculture, Flora, Fauna, and Ethnography* (London: John Murray, 1910), 51–52.

46. Zhuwa Msitu, interview.

47. Artur Medja et al., interview.

48. Milioni Lambani, interview.

49. Ferreira Mangiricau and Bene Ngoca, interview.

50. Previously, the thick shallow roots of the maquengueres had blocked the sand and gravel carried by the river. Régulo António Chipuazo; Beilfuss, Chilundo, et al., "Hydrological Changes," 8.

51. Tchinaze João Muriana, et al., interview, Caia (Regulado Gumançanza), July 14, 2000.

52. SWECO, *Cabora Bassa*, 51.

53. Rita Lambique et al., interview, Chemba (Régulado Chave), July 19, 2000.

54. Saluchepa Gelo and Luís Nota, interview, Caia (Regulado Chave), July 18, 2000.

55. Luís Manuel et al., interview.

56. Saluchepa Gelo and Luís Nota, interview; Régulo Simão Sangoma, interview, Caia (Regulado Sangoma), July 20, 2000; Luís Manuel et al., interview; Mário Chambiça et al., interview.

57. See Landeg White, *Bridging the Zambezi*.

58. Beilfuss and Davies, "Prescribed Flooding," 147–48.

59. Ibid.

60. Davies, Beilfuss, and Thoms, "Cahora Bassa Retrospective," 5.

61. Daniel Ribeiro, interview, March 10, 2010.

62. Elias Januare, interview.

63. Carlos Bento, interview.

64. The term *mediate*, which requires purposeful decision making, better describes the river's power than *agency*, which means having a significant, if unintended, impact.

65. Carlos Bento, interview, March 10, 2010.

66. Mário Chambiça et al., interview; Simão Sangoma, interview; Régulo António Chipuazo et al., interview.

67. Armando Navalha and António Sona, interview, Inhangoma (Regulado Chirembwe), July 8, 2000; Gina Monteiro and other women, interview; João Raposo et al., interview; Inácio Guta et al., interview.

68. João Raposo et al., interview.

69. Armando Navalha and António Sona, interview.

70. Zhili Malenje, interview by MRB, T/A Dovu (Malota), May 19, 2000; Betina Biassa, interview by MRB, T/A Kambembe (Falera), May 6, 2000; Watson Thamanda, interview by MRB, T/A Malemia (Msusa), April 21, 2000. It is often difficult to separate natural changes from dam-induced ones. In fact, reed communities regularly shifted location in response to natural scouring from the river. Richard Beilfuss, e-mail to the authors, May 4, 2010.

71. SWECO, *Cabora Bassa*, 4, 12.

72. Bolton, "Regulation of the Zambezi," 395.

73. Maria Chipwazo et al., interview; Mário Chambiça et al., interview; Artur Medja et al., interview; Francisco Manuel et al., interview; Bastiana Kamuzu, interview; Chidasiyikwa Mavungire, interview.

74. Novais Nhamazi et al., interview; Régulo Júlio Chave, interview.

75. Régulo António Chipuazo et al., interview; Régulo Simão Sangoma, interview.

76. Davies and Day, *Vanishing Waters*, 248.

77. Richard Beilfuss, pers. comm., December 4, 2011.

78. Beilfuss and Santos, "Hydrological Change," 4.

79. SWECO, *Cabora Bassa*, 11.

80. Manuel Talé et al., interview.

81. During the fifteen-year war with Renamo, soldiers and hunters killed many birds for food. Bengala Mange and Zeca Sacatucua, interview; Manuel Talé et al., interview.

82. Aniva João et al., interview.

83. Marita Zhuwao, interview; António Djase, interview.

84. Benjamin Neva, interview by MRB, Nsanje (Savieli village), April 19, 2000; Lucca Phwete, interview by MRB, Nsanje (Savieli village), April 23, 2000. Today, lack of water is not the only cause of the dwindling wildlife population; local hunters and soldiers searching for bushmeat also killed or drove away many animals. Richard Beilfuss, e-mail to the authors, May 4, 2010.

85. In the late 1970s, nearly forty-five thousand African buffalo lived in the Marromeu reserve and surrounding hunting concessions. Tinley, "Morromeu Wrecked," 22–25. By 1990, there were under four thousand—a drop of more than 90 percent. Beilfuss and Davies, "Prescribed Flooding," 145–48. The number of waterbuck, zebras, hippopotami, and other mammals also fell precipitously. Beilfuss, Chilundo, et al., "Hydrological Changes," 11.

86. Beilfuss, Moore, et al., "Vegetation Change," 38. Sena Sugar Estates also reported diminishing yields due to long-term salinization. Richard Beilfuss, pers. comm., May 4, 2010.

87. Beilfuss, Moore, et al., "Vegetation Change," 34.

88. Ibid.; Beilfuss, "Natural Resource Utilization," 104–7.

89. As rivers year after year transport sediments downstream, the slow-flowing water in the delta allows the silt to settle, which typically widens and extends the semiterrestrial area of the delta itself.

90. Scientists fear the extensive tract of dead mangroves at the mouth of the Zambezi may be due to coastal erosion caused by the decreased deposition of sediment from upriver. Beilfuss, Moore, et al., "Vegetation Change," 34. Dead or dessicated mangrove forests elsewhere in the delta may also be attributable to Cahora Bassa. Davies, "Rehabilitation Programme."

91. Tinley, "Marromeu Wrecked," 23–25.

92. Tor Gammelsröd, "Improving Shrimp Production by Zambezi River Regulation," *Ambio* 21, no. 2 (1992): 145–47.

93. Ibid. For more details, see A. Hoguane, "Shrimp Abundance and River Runoff in Sofala Bank—The Role of the Zambezi" (paper presented at Workshop on the Sustainable Use of Cahora Bassa Dam and the Zambezi Valley, September 29–October 2, 1997, Songo).

94. Patrick McCully, *Flooding the Land, Warming the Earth: Greenhouse Gas Emissions from Dams* (Berkeley: International Rivers Network, 2002).

95. International Rivers, "Reservoir Emissions," http://www.internationalrivers .org/en/node/383.

96. Morrissey, *Livelihoods at Risk*, 59.

97. Davies, "Rehabilitation Programme"; Beilfuss and Davies, "Prescribed Flooding," 143–58.

98. Davies, "Zambezi River System," 258.

99. Davies, "Cross-Check Questionnaire," 1–2.

100. Daniel Ribeiro, interview, March 10, 2010.

101. Before the dam's construction, flooding was fairly predictable, although natural cycles of rainfall and climate change produced heavy flooding approximately every decade, giving the river a capricious and contingent character.

102. Maria Faifi, interview.

103. Ibid.; Zhuwa Valera and Pereira Msitu, interview by MRB, T/A Kambembe (Tizola), May 6, 2000; N'tsai António et al., interview; Cheia Amado, interview; Mário Chambiça et al., interview; Milioni Lambani, interview.

104. Zhuwa Valera and Pereira Msitu, interview.

105. N'tsai António et al., interview.

106. Cheia Amado., interview.

107. Maria Faifi, interview.

108. Ibid.

109. Mário Chambiça et al., interview; Cheia Amado, interview.

110. Milioni Lambani, interview.

111. UTIP, *Mepanda uncua*, document no. 012/A, 4–51.

112. Beilfuss, Chilundo, et al., "Hydrological Changes," 8.

113. Joaquim Sacatucua, interview; N'tsai António et al., interview; Artur Medja et al., interview; António Tchoa et al., interview.

114. Alberto Chirembue and Armando Navia, interview; Marosse Inácio et al., interview.

115. N'tsai António et al., interview; António Tchoa et al., interview.

116. N'tsai António et al., interview.

117. UTIP, *Mepanda uncua*, document no. 012/A, 4–49.

118. Beilfuss, Chilundo, et al., "Hydrological Changes," 14.

119. Liza Kabu and Fillinda Filley, interview by MRB, T/A Chilembwe (Masasu), May 5, 2000.

120. Alberto Chirembue and Armando Navia, interview; Caetano Figuerido et al., interview.

121. Ibid.

122. Ibid.

123. UTIP, *Mepanda uncua*, document no. 012/A, 4–4.

124. Maginta Cheiro et al., interview by DM, Chirodzi-Sanangwe (Bairro Luzinga), June 25, 2008.

125. João Raposo et al., interview.

126. Caetano Figuerido et al., interview, Mutarara (Inhangoma), July 18, 2000; Cheia Amado, interview.

127. Caetano Figuerido et al., interview.

128. António Djase, interview.

129. Artur, "Continuities," 78–79.

130. Cited in Lucia Scodanibbio and Gustavo Mañez, "The World Commission on Dams: A Fundamental Step towards Integrated Resources Management and Poverty Reduction? A Pilot Case in the Lower Zambezi, Mozambique," *Physics and Chemistry of the Earth* 30, nos. 11–16 (2005): 977. The four provinces through which the Zambezi runs also have the highest poverty rate. República de Moçambique, *Plano de acção para a redução da pobreza absoluta, 2001–2005* (Maputo: República de Moçambique, 2001), 23.

131. Andre Renzaho, "Mortality Rates, Prevalence of Malnutrition, and Prevalence of Lost Pregnancies among the Drought Ravaged Population of Tete Province,

Mozambique," *Prehospital and Disaster Medicine* 22, no. 1 (February 2007): 26–34, available online at http://journals.cambridge.org/action/displayAbstract?fromPage=online&aid=8236228.

132. UTIP, *Mepanda uncua*, document no. 012/A, 4–51.

133. Scodanibbio and Mañez, "World Commission on Dams," 978–79.

134. Maria Faifi, interview.

135. Mário Chambiça et al., interview.

136. Luís Manuel et al., interview.

137. Ibid.

138. Gender was, in central Mozambique, a critical determinant shaping access to and use of the scarce resources essential to the well-being of riparian households, as it was in other changing waterscapes. For a discussion of this phenomenon elsewhere, see Leila Harris, "Irrigation, Gender and Social Geographies of the Changing Waterscapes of Southeastern Anatolia," *Environment and Planning: Society and Space* 24, no. 2 (2006): 187–213; Ben Crow and Farhana Sultana, "Gender, Class and Access to Water: Three Cases in a Poor and Crowded Delta," *Society and Natural Resources* 15 (2002): 709–24.

139. In many areas women walked two to three kilometers two to three times a day to obtain water. Carlos Bento, interview.

140. Joaquim Sacatucua, interview; Maria Chipwazo et al., interview.

141. Renzaho, "Mortality Rates," 26–27.

142. Fajita Bemuse, interview with MRB, Dovu (Malone), April 2000.

143. Christopher Dozy, interview, Tete (Nyalugwe), May 1, 2000.

144. Ibid.; João Raposo et al., interview.

145. Maria Faifi, interview.

146. Inácio Guta et al., interview; Manuel Talé et al., interview.

147. Inácio Guta et al., interview; Manuel Talé et al., interview.

148. Richard Beilfuss, email to the authors, December 4, 2011.

149. Almanda Misero, interview, Mphata, August 16, 2001; Chidasiyikwa Mavungire, interview.

150. Almanda Misero, interview, Mphata, August 16, 2001; Chidasiyikwa Mavungire, interview.

151. This shift in harvesting was not solely dam induced. A similar phenomenon occurred in other parts of Africa, unrelated to water conditions, brought about by greater competition over scarce resources. Richard Beilfuss, e-mail to the authors, December 4, 2011.

152. Artur Medja et al., interview; Mandala, *Work and Control*, 250.

153. Aniva João, et al., interview.

154. Ibid.

155. Marita Zhuwao, interview.

156. Ibid.; Joaquim Sacatucua, interview.

157. Tweddle, "Freshwater Fisheries," 68–69. An earlier Swedish study came up with a lower predam estimate. SWECO, *Cahora Bassa*, 3, 119–22.

158. B. Chande and P. Dutton, "Impacts of Hydrological Change in the Zambezi Delta to Wildlife and Their Habitats with Special Attention to the Large

Mammals" (paper presented at Workshop on the Sustainable Use of Cahora Bassa Dam and the Zambezi Valley, September 29–October 2, 1997, Songo).

159. Beilfuss, Chilundo, et al., "Hydrological Changes," 10.

160. Beilfuss, "Can This River Be Saved," 8.

161. Artur Medja et al., interview.

162. Francisco Manuel et al., interview.

163. Bastiana Kamuzu, interview.

164. Chidasiyikwa Mavungire, interview.

165. During the colonial period, European hunters equipped with powerful rifles and motor-driven launches had killed many crocodiles, forcing the rest to flee to more remote parts of the river. After independence, however, these hunters disappeared and the few state game wardens were ineffectual at controlling the crocodile population, leaving local residents increasingly vulnerable. Artur Medja et al., interview; António Djase, interview; Novais Nhamazi et al., interview; Bengala Mange and Zeca Sacatucua, interview; Cheia Amado, interview.

166. Cheia Amado, interview.

167. Pita Araújo and Bernardo Gona, interview.

168. After the civil war, the government leased designated hunting areas to safari concessionary companies, which prohibited the local population from hunting within their vast holdings. Nevertheless, much bushmeat hunting still occurs. Beilfuss, Chilundo, et al., "Hydrological Changes," 12–13.

169. Chidasiyikwa Mavungire, interview.

170. Carlos Bento, interview.

171. Heidi Gengenbach, e-mail to the authors, November 20, 2010.

172. Ibid.

173. Fatima Mbvinisa, interview; Dimingu Kasenga, interview, T/A Dovu (Maloti), May 19, 2000.

174. Ibid.; N'tsai António et al., interview; Maria Chipwazo et al., interview.

175. Watson Thamanda, interview.

176. Davies, "Cross-Check Questionnaire," 9.

177. Ferreira Mangiricau and Bene Ngoca, interview; João Raposo et al., interview; Tchinaze João Muriane et al., interview To date, there have been no rigorous epidemiological studies to substantiate this anecdotal evidence. Richard Beilfuss, email to the authors, December 4, 2011.

178. Department for International Development, "Droughts, Floods and Higher Temperatures Bring More Disease to City Life," May 19, 2008, http://www.dfid.gov.uk/news/files/climate-mozambique-droughts.asp.

179. Luwichi Scanda, interview by MRB, T/A Dovu (Matola village), March 23, 2000.

180. Davies and Day, *Vanishing Waters*, 224.

181. Other medicinal plants were probably lost when riparian forests were cleared for human settlement. Richard Beilfuss, e-mail to the authors, December 4, 2011.

182. Davies and Day, *Vanishing Waters*, 224.

183. Balança Casado, interview.

184. Guente Escafa, interview; Emília Joni, interview; Henriqueta Cascas, interview.

185. Vernácio Leone, interview; Joaquim Sacatucua, interview; Maria Chipwazo et al., interview; Milioni Lambani, interview; António Ioha, interview.

186. Artur, "Continuities," 72.

187. Joaquim Sacatucua, interview; Beilfuss, Chilundo, et al., "Hydrological Changes," 16.

188. Artur, "Continuities," 72.

189. Milioni Lambani, interview.

190. António Ioha, interview.

191. Alberto Rapozolo, interview.

192. Fajita Bemuse, interview.

193. Many people from the Zambezi fled to Malawi, where they ended up in refugee camps. There, Protestant missionaries insisted that "praying to midzimu is a sin to God." Ventura Mwakwapala, interview by MRB, Mthukulo, April 17, 2000; Veka Fero, interview by MRB, Nsanje (Savieli village), April 23, 2000; Morrissey, *Livelihoods at Risk*, 35.

194. Bengala Mange and Zeca Sacatucua, interview; Régulo António Chipuazo et al., interview; Maria Chipwazo et al., interview; Caetano Figuerido et al., interview; Mário Chambiça et al., interview.

195. Artur, "Continuities," 68.

196. Ibid., 73.

197. Cunha, *Cabora Bassa: Discursos*, 21.

198. Paulo Milo, interview.

199. Like most hydroelectric projects, although Cahora Bassa had enough storage capacity to capture the smaller floods that occurred in most years, it could not contain the larger floods that, in the past, came every decade or so. Global climate change will likely make the situation worse. Richard Beilfuss, e-mail to the authors, May 30, 2011.

200. Beilfuss, "Understanding Extreme Floods," 1.

201. Richard Beilfuss, e-mail to the authors, May 30, 2011.

202. Chande and Dutton, "Impacts." Ironically, the 1978 flood, by providing moisture to water-starved soils and plant seeds, briefly returned the delta region to its previous, biologically rich, condition.

203. Régulo António Chipuazo et al., interview; Marosse Inácio et al., interview; N'tsai António et al., interview.

204. Quoted in Borges Coelho, "Protected Villages," 382.

205. Quoted in ibid., 381–82.

206. João Paulo Borges Coelho, "State Resettlement Policies in Post-colonial Rural Mozambique: The Impact of the Communal Village Programme on Tete Province, 1972–1982," *Journal of Southern African Studies* 24, no. 1 (1998): 61–91.

207. Bolton, "Regulation of the Zambezi," 397–98.

208. Although the floods would have occurred without the dam, the dam's releases were quicker and more damaging than what would have happened under

natural flood conditions. Beilfuss and Santos, "Hydrological Change," 52; Beilfuss, Chilundo, et al., "Hydrological Changes," 9.

209. Domingo Pereira, interview by MRB, Vila Nova, May 24, 2000; Shikita Njani, interview by MRB, T/A Valela (Tizoa), April 6, 2000.

210. Artur, "Continuities," 70.

211. "Death Toll Reaches 75," *AIM*, March 7, 2000; Daniel Ribeiro, "The Zambezi Valley: Damned by Dams," http://www.internationalrivers.org/files/attached-files/damnedbydams.pdf.

212. WCD, *Dams and Development*, 61.

213. "2007 Floods: Mozambique Humanitarian Situation Update," *UNICEF*, February 23, 2007, http://www.unicef.org/mozambique/humanitarian_response _3277.html.

214. "Mozambique: Flooding in Zambezi Valley Set to Worsen as Floodgates Open," *AIM*, February 11, 2008.

215. Marc Stal, *Rapid-Onset Flooding and Relocation: The Zambezi River Valley in Mozambique* (PowerPoint presentation, United Nations University Institute for Environment and Human Security, New York, 2008), 18.

216. "Mozambique: Flooding in Zambezi," *AIM*, February 11, 2008.

217. Just after completion, researchers forecasted that the "combined regulating effect" of the Kariba, Kafue, and Cahora Bassa impoundments would "result in profound long-term ecological changes in the river." Hall, Valente, and Davies, "Zambezi River," 14.

CHAPTER 6: DISPLACED ENERGY

1. Although the agreement to transfer ownership was reached in 2005, it could not become final until Eurostat, the EU's statistical agency, determined whether it complied with EU rules on budget deficits. Under the deal, Portugal wrote off more than one-half the estimated $2 billion it claimed that the HCB owed to its treasury and collected instead $950 million from Mozambique by selling it two-thirds of the dam. "Mozambique Takes Majority Ownership of Cahora Bassa," *Zambezi* 7, no. 2 (2006).

2. A 1984 agreement increased the price of electricity Cahora Bassa sold to South Africa by 50 percent, although it remained a fraction of the international price. *AIM Information Bulletin* 95* (1984): 8.

3. Vines, *Renamo*, 27. This assumption was not entirely accurate, because the power cuts, combined with a particularly severe winter in 1981, created electricity shortfalls in South Africa. Paul Fauvet and José Alves Gomes, "The Mozambican National Resistance," supplement, *AIM Information Bulletin* (Maputo) 69 (1982): 7–9.

4. *Rand Daily Mail*, May 13, 1974. This position shifted in the late 1980s, when South Africa began to electrify the townships to mollify its African population.

5. For discussion of the uncomfortable fusion of these three principles, see Pitcher, *Transforming Mozambique*, 50–58. The challenges confronted by Frelimo as it tried to restructure Mozambique are analyzed in John Saul, ed., *A

Difficult Road: The Transition to Socialism in Mozambique (New York: Monthly Review Press, 1985).

6. Machel exhorted Mozambicans to discard "traditional" values, practices, and beliefs; to create a "new man," "free for all time from ignorance and obscurantism, from superstition and prejudice"; and to combat divisive ethnic, regional, and racial tendencies, instead "reclaim[ing] our Mozambican personality [and creating] a new mentality and a new society." Frelimo, *Central Committee Report to the Third Congress of Frelimo (3–7 February 1977)*, Documento Informativo no. 6, series E, trans. Centro Nacional de Documentação e Informação de Moçambique (Maputo: CEDIMO, 1978), 35.

7. Mozambique, Angola, Guinea-Bissau Information Committee (MAGIC), *Central Committee Report to the Third Party Congress* (London: MAGIC, 1978), 43–44.

8. Ironically, Frelimo's statist prescription for socialist development sounded much like the colonial narrative concerning Cahora Bassa (see ch. 3).

9. Bitter about their lost race and class privileges and skeptical that Frelimo would follow the nonracialism it professed, departing settlers destroyed whatever they could not take with them, including farm equipment, trucks, machinery, and cattle.

10. Pitcher, *Transforming Mozambique*, 60.

11. For a history of the cotton regime, see Isaacman, *Cotton*.

12. At the same time, the Ministry of Agriculture allocated almost all the heavy equipment received in barter agreements with the socialist countries to the state-farm sector, which Frelimo optimistically projected would, by 1990, employ 10 percent of Mozambique's workforce and produce most of the country's meat, milk, eggs, and cash crops. Pitcher, *Transforming Mozambique*, 88.

13. Frelimo, whose headquarters and principal bases during the liberation struggle had been in Tanzania, patterned its communal village policy, in part, on the Tanzania's *ujamaa* village resettlement scheme. By 1976 more than 13 million Tanzanians were living in ujamaa villages, in what James Scott called "a softer version of high modernism." Scott, *Seeing Like a State*, 224.

14. MAGIC, *Central Committee Report*, 16.

15. This is especially ironic since, during the liberation struggle, Frelimo had labeled the aldeamentos "concentration camps." *Mozambique Revolution* 45 (1970–72), 10; Borges Coelho, "Protected Villages," 435.

16. Margaret Hall and Tom Young, *Confronting Leviathan: Mozambique since Independence* (London: Hurst, 1997), 84–85; Hall and Young, "Mozambique at War with Itself," in *Readings in African Politics*, ed. Young (Bloomington: Indiana University Press, 2003), 63; Carrie Manning, *The Politics of Peace in Mozambique: Post-conflict Democratization, 1992–2000* (Westport, CT: Praeger, 2002), 59–61.

17. Hall and Young, *Mozambique since Independence*, 84–85; Pitcher, *Transforming Mozambique*, 85–99.

18. Borges Coelho, "Protected Villages," 383.

19. Geffray and Pedersen, "Sobre a guerra," 303–318; Manning, *Politics of Peace*, 59–61; Victor Igreja, Bas Schreuder and Wim Kleijn, "The Cultural Dimension

of War Traumas In Central Mozambique: The Case of Gorongosa," http://priory.com/psych/traumacult.htm.

20. Manning, *Politics of Peace*, 59.

21. Roesch, "Renamo and the Peasantry," 465–66. For the varied reactions of peasants to communal villages, see Allen Isaacman and Barbara Isaacman, *Mozambique: From Colonialism to Revolution, 1900–1982* (Boulder: Westview, 1983). 153–58.

22. Isaacman and Isaacman, *Mozambique*, 155. Officials predicted that by 1990 this collective network would cover more than 5 million Mozambicans.

23. Borges Coelho, "Protected Villages," 378–92.

24. Borges Coelho, "State Resettlement Policies," 66.

25. Régulo António Chipuazo et al., interview; Marosse Inácio et al., interview; N'tsai António et al., interview; Beilfuss and Santos, "Hydrological Change," 88. To administer flood assistance and promote agricultural development, the Frelimo government required these flood victims to resettle in communal villages established on higher grounds away from the Zambezi River.

26. Borges Coelho, "State Resettlement Policies."

27. Samora Machel, interview by Iain Christie and Allen Isaacman, Maputo, May 7, 1979.

28. Ibid.

29. *AIM Information Bulletin* 38 (1979): 6.

30. Martin Zhuwakinyu, "Cahora Bassa Power Flows, but Talks to Continue," *Engineering News* (South Africa) (2002), http://www.engineeringnews.co.za/articles/cahora-bassa-power-flows-talks-continue-2002-11-15.

31. *AIM Information Bulletin* 47 (1980): 1.

32. In 1981 the government sought funding for a 110-kilowatt substation at Marromeu that would supply energy to Sena Sugar Estates, one of the nation's largest agricultural complexes. *AIM Information Bulletin* 59 (1981): 18. At the same time, the National Water Commission announced plans to use water stored by the dam to irrigate more than 210,000 hectares of choice farmland in the Lower Zambezi valley. *AIM Information Bulletin* 63 (1981): 16. Shortly thereafter, India agreed to process its bauxite at a Mozambican aluminum plant using power from Cahora Bassa, and the government began negotiating with Zimbabwe to export electricity there as well. *AIM Information Bulletin* 70 (1982): 2. State planners also received funding from Bulgaria in 1981 to develop commercial fishing, tourism, and a shipping industry on the lake created by Cahora Bassa. *AIM Information Bulletin* 58 (1981): 16.

33. "Energia de Cahora Bassa desenvolve centro-norte do pais," *Tempo* 500 (1980): 17–22.

34. Isaacman and Isaacman, *Mozambique*, 155.

35. *AIM Information Bulletin* 47 (1980): 18.

36. See William Finnegan, *A Complicated War: The Harrowing of Mozambique* (Berkeley: University of California Press, 1992); Hall and Young, *Confronting Leviathan*; Allen Isaacman, "Conflict in Southern Africa: The Case of Mozambique,"

in *Apartheid Unravels*, ed. R. Hunt Davis (Gainesville: University Press of Florida, 1991), 183–212; Vines, *Renamo*.

37. Gordon Winter, *Inside BOSS: South Africa's Secret Police* (Harmondsworth: Penguin Books, 1981), 545.

38. Alfonso Dhlakama, "Relatório referente a sessão do trabalho de RNM e do representativo do Governo Sul Africano," MNR Document, October 25, 1980.

39. Hall and Young, *Confronting Leviathan*, 129, 165–73.

40. Ibid., 129.

41. Vernácio Leone, interview.

42. Peter Size and Fedi Alfante, interview.

43. Fausto Semo, interview.

44. *AIM Information Bulletin* 58 (1981): 3.

45. Vines, *Renamo*, 28–30.

46. "Switching on to Cahora Bassa," *Mail and Guardian* 20, December 1996, http://www.mg.co.za/article/1996-12-20-switching-on-to-cahora-bassa.

47. Sabotage to the transmission lines stymied the government's plans to garner economic benefits from Cahora Bassa. The cost of replacing the more than two thousand pylons destroyed by Renamo was a significant part of Mozambique's debt to the HCB. As Castigo Langa, Mozambique's minister of mineral resources and energy, noted, "if Cahora Bassa had operated normally, and the [transmission] lines had not been sabotaged, [the debt to the HCB] would have been fully amortised by now," "Mozambique Seeks to Wrestle Power Dam from Portugal," *Pan African News Agency*, January 8, 2001, http://allafrica.com/stories/printable/200101080449.html.

48. Vines, *Renamo*, 26–28; R. Domingos, untitled summary of conversations with Orlando Christina (Renamo document in possession of authors, November 4, 1980).

49. South Africa—with its growing need for electrical power and its desire to tap into the region's vast hydroelectric potential—was the driving force behind this regional organization, the SAPP. It linked all members of the Southern African Development Community (SADC) into a supranational body, charged with developing a coherent energy strategy for the region. David A. McDonald, "Electric Capitalism: Conceptualising Electrticity and Capital Accumulation in (South) Africa," in *Electric Capitalism: Recolonising Africa on the Power Grid*, ed. McDonald (Cape Town: HSRC Press, 2009) 7–11, 31. The Zambezi River represented a prime target for this agenda.

50. "Mozambique Seeks to Wrestle Power Dam from Portugal," *Pan African News Agency* (2001); Hans Abrahamsson and Anders Nilsson, *Mozambique: The Troubled Transition: From Socialist Construction to Free Market Capitalism* (London: Zed Books, 1995), 111–30; Bertil Egerö, *Mozambique: A Dream Undone: The Political Economy of Democracy, 1975–84* (Stockholm: Almquist and Wiksell, 1987), 83–107; Hall and Young, *Confronting Leviathan*, 98–107; Pitcher, *Transforming Mozambique*, 101–6.

51. *AIM*, February 3, 1984.

52. *Financial Times*, October 21, 1986.

53. Pitcher, *Transforming Mozambique*, 109–24.

54. Ronald Aminzade, "Corruption and Boundary Politics in Socialist and Neo-Liberal Tanzania" (unpublished paper in possession of the authors, 2010), 14.

55. Isaacman, "Conflict in Southern Africa," 182–212; Joseph Hanlon, *Mozambique: Who Calls the Shots?* (Bloomington: University of Indiana Press, 1992), 113–34; John Saul, *Recolonization and Resistance: Southern Africa in the 1990s* (Trenton: Africa World Press, 1993), 74–81.

56. Programa das Nações Unidas para o Desenvolvimento/Banco Mundial, *Moçambique: Problemas e opções no sector energético* (Maputo: PNUD, 1987), 93–103.

57. McDonald, "Electric Capitalism," 14–15.

58. Ibid.

59. Ibid.

60. *East African Standard* (Nairobi), August 7, 2002.

61. *Diário de Moçambique*, August 3, 2003; Simões Wetela, interview; Pedro da Costa Xavier, interview.

62. *Diário de Moçambique*, August 3, 2003; Simões Wetela, interview; Pedro da Costa Xavier, interview; *Notícias*, September 20, 1996.

63. *Diário de Moçambique*, August 3, 2003; Simões Wetela, interview; Pedro da Costa Xavier, interview; *Notícias*, September 20, 1996. In the late 1990s, HCB management did begin to recruit a small number of Mozambicans educated at Eduardo Mondlane University for middle management. *Notícias*, September 20, 1996, September 25, 1998. By 2003 more than one hundred Mozambicans held skilled technical positions at Cahora Bassa. *AIM*, October 11, 2002.

64. *AIM Mozambiquefile* 303 (October 2001): 24.

65. Simões Wetela, interview; Pedro da Costa Xavier, interview.

66. *Savana*, May 19, 1995.

67. Simões Wetela, interview.

68. *Notícias*, September 20, 1996.

69. Simões Wetela, intrvw; Pedro da Costa Xavier, interview.

70. *AIM Mozambiquefile* 303 (October 2001): 24. Even the two Mozambicans appointed by Frelimo to sit on the HCB board of directors received substantially lower salaries than their Portuguese counterparts. *Domingo* (Maputo), October 24, 1996.

71. *Diário de Moçambique*, August 8, 2003.

72. *Notícias*, September 20, 1996.

73. Ibid. See also *Notícias*, September 19, 1995; September 20, 1996; *Domingo*, October 24, 1996; *AIM*, October 11, 2002; *Diário de Moçambique*, August 3, 2003.

74. *Notícias*, September 19, 1995; September 20, 1996; *Domingo*, October 24, 1996; *Tempo* 379 (January 8, 1998): 56–65; *Diário de Moçambique*, August 3, 2003.

75. *Notícias*, September 19, 1995; September 20, 1996; *Domingo*, October 24, 1996; *Tempo* 379 (January 8, 1998): 56–65; *Diário de Moçambique*, August 3, 2003.

76. *AIM*, October 11, 2002.

77. "Mozambique: Workers Threaten Strike at Cahora Bassa Dam," *IRIN News*, May 10, 2000, http://www.irinnews.org/Report/14356/MOZAMBIQUE-Workers -threaten-strike-at-Cahora-Bassa-Dam.

78. *AIM*, October 11, 2002.

79. Martin Zhuwakinyu, "Cahora Bassa Power Flows, but Talks to Continue," *Engineering News* (South Africa), November 15, 2002), http://www.engineering-news.co.za/article/cahora-bassa-power-flows-talks-continue-2002-11-15.

80. *AIM*, April 6, 1998; "Still No End in Sight for Cahora Bassa Tussle," *Engineering News*, June 18, 1999.

81. Hélder Chambal, *Energy Security in Mozambique*, Series on Trade and Energy Security, Policy Report 3 (Winnipeg: International Institute for Sustainable Development, 2010), 9.

82. Ibid., vii, 10.

83. *AIM*, April 6, 1998; "Still No End in Sight for Cahora Bassa Tussle," *Engineering News*, June 18, 1999. This and other similar HCB behavior infuriated the Mozambican government. In one of many of its public criticisms, Finance Minister Luisa Diogo maintained that the status quo was not acceptable and that "Cahora Bassa ha[d] a fundamental responsibility for the development of the national economy." "New Proposals on Cahora Bassa," *AIM Mozambiquefile* 293 (December 2000): 22.

84. *AIM Mozambiquefile* 316 (November 2002): 16–18; "Cahora Bassa Power Flows, but Talks to Continue," *Engineering News* (South Africa) (2000).

85. "Giant Hydroelectric Plant Threatens to Cut SA Supplies," *Sapa-LUSA* (2002), http://www.sabcnews.com/africa/southern_africa/0,1009,45254,00.html.

86. *AIM Mozambiquefile* 293 (December 2000): 21.

87. *AIM Mozambiquefile* 316 (November 2002): 6–8.

88. "Portugal to Make Fresh Offer on Cahora Bassa Dam in Mozambique," *Xinhua News Agency*, September 5, 2002.

89. Ibid., 17.

90. "Castigo Langa under Pressure," *Indian Ocean Newsletter* no.1010 (September 2002), http://www.africaintelligence.com/ION/politics-power/2002/09/21 /castigo-langa-under-pressure,4885171-ART.

91. *AIM Mozambiquefile* 325 (August 2003): 20.

92. "Portugal não querem larger Cahora Bassa," *Savana*, April 2, 2004.

93. *AIM Mozambiquefile* 325 (August 2003): 20.

94. "Portugal não querem larger Cahora Bassa," *Savana*, April 2, 2004.

95. "Mozambique Might Nationalise Cahora Bassa," *AIM*, July 24, 2004, http:// allafrica.com/stories/200407260476.html. In fact, *Zambeze* editor Salomão Moyana argued that "the continuation of the present situation makes Mozambique look like a country too weak to defend its own interests" and declared that the dam's expropriation was a "national imperative which all of Mozambican society should unconditionally support." Ibid.

96. "Cahora Bassa Power Flows, but Talks to Continue," *Engineering News* (South Africa) (2002).

97. In 1998 the Portuguese secretary of state Fernando Teixeira dos Santos announced during a visit to Maputo that the rate would drop to two South African cents: "We are practicing this [preferential] price only for the southern region of Mozambique, in an essentially political decision." "Cahora Bassa Power to the South," *AIM Mozambiquefile* 264 (1998): 15–16; Martin Zhuwakinyu, "Cahora Bassa Talks Postponed to Later Date," *Engineering News*, January 31, 2003.

98. "A Dam in Mozambique: Untapped Power: A Poor Country Is Being Ripped Off." *Economist*, March 27, 2003, http://www.economist.com/node/1667113.

99. *AIM*, April 6, 1998.

100. Before the Cahora Bassa power lines were sabotaged, Mozambique had had an agreement with Eskom that the power it supplied to southern Mozambique would be treated as Cahora Bassa's power, for which the EDM (the Mozambican electricity company) would pay the HCB in local currency. The only hard currency involved would be for the rental of the Eskom lines. "Mocumbi Criticises Cahora Bassa," *AIM Mozambiquefile* 261 (1998): 20.

101. "Vega Anjos Attacks Eskom," *AIM*, October 7, 2002. A small amount of electricity also went to Zimbabwe.

102. Quoted in Sylvia Smith, "The Cahora Bassa Dam" (2003), http://www.rnw.nl/development/html/030218cahora.html.

103. Phasiwe Khulu, "Eskom to Pay Much More for Power from Cahora Bassa," *Business Day* (Johannesburg) 10 (February 2004).

104. "Mocumbi Reacts to Cahora Bassa Decision," *AIM*, October 18, 2002.

105. *AIM Mozambiquefile* 316 (November 2002): 16.

106. "Mozambique Might Nationalise the Dam," *AIM*, July 24, 2004.

107. República de Moçambique, Minstério dos Recursos Minerais e Energia, *Mphanda Nkuwa Hydropower Project, Mozambique: Development Prospect* (Maputo: MRME, 2003), 3.

108. "Developing Mphanda Nkuwa: IWP and DC reports on the Mphanda Nkuwa hydro power project in Mozambique, as potential investors are invited to prequalify for implementation of the 1300 MW scheme," *International Water Power and Dam Construction*, October 1, 2002, 21.

109. "Mozambique Might Nationalise the Dam," *AIM*, July 24, 2004.

110. "We Want Cahora Bassa Now," *Africa News Service*, February 22, 2005.

111. *Savana*, November 5, 2005.

112. The agreement called for Mozambique to pay $250 million in 2006 and the remainder within twelve months of the signing of the final accord, although, under exceptional circumstances, the final payment could be extended up to eighteen months. "Cahora Bassa: Government Confident It Can Pay," *AIM*, November 4, 2006. To purchase an additional 67 percent of the shares in the HCB, Mozambique took out a loan of $700 million from a consortium of Portuguese and French banks. "Mozambique: Portuguese PM in Maputo to Discuss Cahora Bassa," *AIM*, April 9, 2012, http://allafrica.com/stories/201204090691.html. According to the Ministry of Energy, Mozambique will own 100 percent of the dam's shares by 2014. Ibid.

113. *Savana*, November 5, 2005. For Lisbon, maintaining cultural and economic ties to its former colonies reaffirmed its claim to be at the center of the lusophone world.

114. "Cahora Bassa, Mozambique: Agreement on Transfer of HCB Signed," *25 Degrees in Africa—News* 1 (November 2006).

115. *AIM Mozambiquefile* 351 (December 7, 2007): 1.

116. "Mozambique Takes Majority Ownership of Cahora Bassa," *Zambezi* 7, no. 2 (2006).

117. Ibid.

118. "Mozambique Acquires Full Control of Cahora Bassa Ownership Group", http://www.hydroworld.com/articles/2012/04/mozambique-acquires.html.

119. The actual rate increase remains confidential.

120. *Notícias*, October 31, 2006; *AIM*, October 31, 2006.

121. Caetano Figuerido et al., interview.

122. This common theme, that the dam did not benefit them, surfaced in informal conversation whenever members of rural communities showed us the pylons.

CHAPTER 7: LEGACIES

1. Pedro da Costa Xavier, interview.

2. Middlemas, *Cabora Bassa*, 130.

3. "Immigration in Africa," *Migration News* 3, no. 11 (November 1996).

4. Simões Wetela, interview; Pedro da Costa Xavier, interview.

5. Padre Cláudio Gremi, interview, May 20, 1998.

6. "Mozambique: Govt Needs More Funds to Demine Cahora Bassa Area," *AIM*, February 9, 2012, http://allafrica.com/stories/201202091259.html.

7. Nevertheless, Mozambique earned $257 million from the sale of electricity in 2008. "Mozambique: HCB Expects Decline in Revenue from South Africa," August 5, 2009, www.allafrica.com/stories/200908050905.html.

8. In 2011 government officials announced plans to construct a second Cahora Bassa power station on the northern bank of the Zambezi, which would play a critical role in the electrification of the rural countryside. A similar plan faltered in the 1980s due to the South African destabilization campaign. "Mozambique: Cahora Bassa Hopes to Double Its Production," *AIM*, December 1, 2011, http://allafrica.com/stories/201112010537.html.

9. Bernacsek and Lopes, "Cahora Bassa," 30.

10. "Mozambique: Prime Minister Summarizes Flood and Cyclone Damage," *AIM*, March 14, 2012, http://allafrica.com/stories/201203141135.html.

11. Artur, "Continuities," 80.

12. "Mozambique: About 6,000 Evacuated in Zambezi Valley," *AIM*, March 15, 2010, http://allafrica.com/stories/201003151665.html.

13. "Mozambique: Prime Minister Summarizes Flood and Cyclone Damage," *AIM*, March 14, 2012.

14. Maria Faifi, interview.

15. Inácio Guta et al., interview; Manuel Talé et al., interview.

16. Inácio Guta et al., interview; Manuel Talé et al., interview; Padre Claúdio Gremi, interview, May 20, 1998.

17. In Chi-Tawara, the local language spoken on the southern bank of the reservoir, they were also called *matemba*.

18. Padre Claúdio Gremi, interview, May 20, 1998.

19. Ibid.

20. Bento Chitima et al., interview; Supia Sargento et al., interview.

21. Padre Claúdio Gremi, interview, May 20, 1998; Elisa Jequessene et al., Chicoa Emboque, July 23, 2001.

22. Elisa Jequessene et al., interview.

23. Bento Chitima et al., interview.

24. Ibid.

25. Ibid.; Nembani Gémio et al., interview, Chipalapala, July 17, 2001.

26. Bento Chitima et al., interview.

27. Elisa Jequessene et al., interview.

28. Padre Claúdio Gremi, interviews, May 20, 23, 1998, July 11, 2001; António Andrade et al., interview.

29. Padre Claúdio Gremi, interviews, May 20, 23, 1998, July 11, 2001; António Andrade et al., interview; Airboat Afrika Company (AAC), *Lake Cahora Bassa*, http://www.airboatafrika.com/lake-cahora-bassa; International Finance Corporation (IFC), *Summary of Project Information 7473, AEF Cahora Bassa Fisheries Lda.*, http://www.ifc.org/ifcext/spiwebsite1.nsf/projectdisplay/dataconversion7473.

30. Elisa Jequessene et al., interview; Júlio Calecatoa, interview.

31. IFC, *Project Information*.

32. Ibid.

33. Ibid.

34. AAC, *Lake Cahora Bassa*.

35. "Mozambique: Export of Kapenta Fish Provides Mozambique with US$14.6 million since 2005," *Macau Hub*, May 30, 2008, http://www.macauhub.com.mo/en/2008/05/30/5130/.

36. "A Dam in Mozambique: Untapped Power: A Poor Country Is Being Ripped Off," *Economist*, March 27, 2003, http://www.economist.com/node/1667113; António Andrade et al.

37. Bento Chitima et al., interview; Elisa Jequessene et al., interview; Júlio Calecoetoa, interview.

38. "Tete—Albufeira de Cahora Bassa: Pescadores artesanais queixam-se de maus tratos," *Mozambique para todos*, May 4, 2011, http://macau.blogs.com/moçambique para todos/2011/05/tete=-albufeira-de-cahora-bassa-pescadores-artesanais-queixam-se-de-maus-tratos.html.

39. The basic monthly salary for unskilled laborers on these boats was 320,000 meticais, which converted to just under $30 in 2002.

40. Henrique Conforme Mereja et al., interview.

41. Ibid.

42. Supia Sargento et al., interview; Elisa Jequessene et al., interview.

43. Elisa Jequessene et al., interview.

44. The rest were either sold in local markets or transported to Maputo. Júlio Calecatoa, interview.

45. "A Dam in Mozambique," *Economist*, March 27, 2003.

46. Supia Sargento et al., interview; Elisa Jequessene et al., interview.

47. Elisa Jequessene et al., interview.

48. Padre Claúdio Gremi, interview, July 11, 2001.

49. João Raposo et al., interview.

50. Régulo António Chipuazo et al., interview; N'tsai António et al., interview; António Djase, interview; Maria Chipwazo et al., interview; Ferreira Mangiricau and Bene Ngoca, interview; Aniva João et al., interview; João Tesoura, interview; Oliva Babo et al., interview; Novais Nhamazi et al., interview; Mário Chambiça et al., interview; Alberto Chirembue and Armando Navio, interview.

51. Ironically, all these people directed their complaints at the Mozambican state, which still lacked sovereignty over the dam. Nor did they understand that the economic liberalization, which had begun in the 1980s, allowed the state less power over economic resources than it previously had had.

52. Mário Chambiça et al., interview.

53. Aniva João et al., interview.

54. Justiça Ambiental, "Report on the Workshop on Integrated Water Management in the Zambezi, Tete Meeting, October 6, 7, 8, 2004" (prepared for OXFAM, November 2004), 2.

55. Beilfuss, "Modeling Trade-offs," 331–47; Cate Brown "Drift Outputs," in Beilfuss and Brown, *Environmental Flow Requirements*, 123–25.

56. ITC, *Final Report for WWF*, 61–62; Beilfuss and Brown, "Assessing Environmental Flow," 127–38.

57. UTIP was established in 1996 to safeguard the country's interests in the river's hydropower potential and to manage its development. MRME, *Mphanda Nkuwa*, 3.

58. Much of the discussion in this section is derived from Allen Isaacman and David Morton, "Harnessing the Zambezi: How Mozambique's Planned Mphanda Nkuwa Dam Perpetuates the Colonial Past," *International Journal of African Historical Studies*, 45, no. 2 (2012): 157–90.

59. The project was undertaken in two phases. From March 1999 to July 2000 researchers defined the major issues to be explored and conducted a prefeasibility test; between October 2000 and April 2002 they conducted research on the ground.

60. UTIP, *Mepanda Uncua Feasibility Study, Environmental Impact Assessment: Executive Summary* (Maputo: UTIP, 2003), 2.

61. Ibid.

62. Ibid.

63. Ibid., 4–5.

64. Ibid., 5.

65. MRME, *Mphanda Nkuwa*, 4.

66. Pete Browne, "Debate Over Dams on Africa's Zambezi River," *Green: A Blog about Energy and the Environment, New York Times,* October 19, 2009, green.blogs.nytimes.com/2009/10/19/debate-over-dams-on-africas-zambezi-river/; *Notícias,* April 22 ,2006; "China Exim Bank Grants Loan for Hydroelectric Dam in Mozambique," *MacauHub,* April 4, 2006, http://www.macauhub.com.mo/en /2006/04/21/891. For a discussion of Chinese investment in dam building in Ghana, see Miescher and Tsikata, "Hydro Power," 15–53. By 2008, China had pulled its financing from the Mphanda Nkuwa project.

67. Livaningo, Mozambique's first legally registered environmental advocacy organization, took the lead, in the early 2000s, in opposing the construction of Mphanda Nkuwa. Some of its members later organized JA! to focus on antidam activities.

68. The WCD's two objectives were: (1) to review the effectiveness of large dams and assess the efficacy of alternatives for countries' water resources and energy development and (2) to develop criteria, guidelines, and standards for the "planning, design, appraisal, construction, operation, [and] monitoring" of dams. WCD, *Dams and Development,* xxx. Due to growing international criticism and highly publicized antidam struggles, most notably in India and Brazil, the bank had to reconsider its unequivocal support for large dams. By the late 1990s, it had reduced by half the number of dams it was funding, although it still bankrolls several large dams, as well as a number of smaller projects. McCully, *Silenced Rivers,* xvii. For a powerful critique of the World Bank in the age of globalization, see Goldman, *Imperial Nature.*

69. This is clear from the following statement contained in an official publication: "Wherever possible the guidelines of the World Commission on Dams have been followed, particularly those guidelines which relate to the conduct of feasibility studies. It is anticipated that UTIP and the selected Developers will strive to follow the WCD principles throughout the project development process." Unidade Técnica de Implementação dos Projectos Hidroeléctricos, *Mepanda Uncua Feasibility Study, no. 16* (Lisbon: UTIP, 2002).

70. WCD, *Dams and Development,* xxxviii.

71. According to these environmentalists, "The dam would cause daily fluctuations in the river, provoking mini-floods[.] Agriculture along the river would be constantly damaged by these mini-floods, and it would make navigation difficult and reduce fish resources. Important sandbanks would suffer erosion, destroying the ecological balance." "Livaningo Defends Rigorous Study," *Mediafax,* September 27, 2002.

72. There was no mention of the ecological and social damage inflicted by Cahora Bassa either in government reports or in our discussions with energy officials. See, for example, Nazário Meguigy (Ministry of Energy) and Sérgio Elísio (UTIP), interview by DM, Maputo, June 18, 2008.

73. "Livaningo Defends Rigorous Study," *Mediafax,* September 27, 2002. The well-documented scientific research conducted by Richard Beilfuss and Cate Brown stresses this possibility. Beilfuss and Brown, "Assessing Environmental Flow," 127–38.

74. "Mensagem da Direcção," *Justiça Ambiental* (2007), 3.

75. Browne, "Debate over Dams on Africa's Zambezi River."

76. According to Beilfuss and Davies, "the aim of re-establishing historic hydrologic conditions in the lower Zambezi system is [not] to re-establish a pristine, undeveloped Zambezi Delta. . . . Rather, the goal is to re-establish a hydrologic regime that will restore the dynamic processes and local production systems that were once part of the delta ecosystem." Beilfuss and Davies, "Prescribed Flooding," 147.

77. "Restoring the Zambezi: Can Dams Play a Role?" *World Rivers Review* (October 2006), reproduced by International Rivers, www.internationalrivers.org /node/1496. For a detailed analysis of how different prescribed flooding models would affect both hydroelectric output and downriver ecosystems, see Richard Beilfuss, "Prescribed Flooding and Restoration Potential in the Zambezi Delta, Mozambique" (working paper no. 4, Program for the Sustainable Management of Cahora Bassa Dam and the Lower Zambezi Valley, Maputo, 2001).

78. Beilfuss and Brown, "Assessing Environmental Flow," 137–38. As Beilfuss explained, "There is no structural or hydrological problem with flow releases if Mphanda Nkuwa is constructed—the flows would be released from Cahora Bassa and simply pass through Mphanda Nkuwa on the way downstream. However, the cost of lost hydropower sales is higher if both Cahora Bassa and Mphanda Knuwa accept reduced power generation in exchange for releasing sluice gate flow downstream." Richard Beilfuss, pers. comm., May 30, 2011.

79. See, for example, ITC, *Final Report for WWF*; IRN, Mphanda Nkuwa Dam.

80. See C. J. H. Hartnady, "Earthquake Hazard in Africa: Perspectives on the Nubia-Somalia Boundary," *South African Journal of Science* 98, nos. 9–10 (2002): 425–28; Lauren Montgomery-Rinehart, "A quem benefica o projecto?" *Livaningo* 2 (2002): 3–5; Scodanibbio and Mañez, "World Commission on Dams," 976–83.

81. For more than three decades, environmentalists and members of indigenous communities engaged in a protracted battle to prevent the construction of the massive 11,200-megawatt Belo Monte dam. "Brazil, after a Long Battle, Approves an Amazon Dam," *New York Times*, June 2, 2011, 10. While the global anti-dam movement employed a similar strategy to delay construction of major dams in India and elsewhere and was able to raise international awareness of the perils of dams, dam builders and developmentalist experts almost always prevailed, as seems to be happening in Mozambique.

82. Morrissey, *Livelihoods at Risk*, 87–88.

83. Ibid.

84. Mark Hankins, *A Renewable Energy Plan for Mozambique* (Maputo: JA!, 2009), 7–10. See Browne, "Debate Over Dams on Africa's Zambezi River."

85. The report confirmed the broad findings of the earlier UTIP study and concluded that communities at the dam site had, in fact, been informed of the dam and its consequences and that they generally welcomed the project. Impacto,

The Scoping Study: Mphanda Nkuwa HydroPower Project, volume 2 (Maputo: Impacto, 2007), 2:8.1–8.6.

86. Nazário Maguigy and Sérgio Elísio, interview Actually, Mozambique has several dams, although none are of the same magnitude as Cahora Bassa.

87. FIVAS (Oslo), November 13, 2003.

88. UTIP, *Projecto de Mepanda Uncua*, 1.

89. Ibid., 1–17.

90. Ibid.

91. Araújo Tionequi, interview by DM, Chirodzi-Sanangwe, June 25, 2008.

92. Fidelis Chakala et al., interview by DM, Chirodzi-Sanangwe, August 10, 2009.

93. Christian Hillmann and Leif Tore Trædal, *The Mepanda Unkua Project—A Planned Regulation of the Zambezi River in Mozambique: Results from a Study Trip, June 23–July 18, 2003* (Oslo: FIVAS, 2003), 15.

94. ITC, *Final Report for WWF*, 43–45.

95. The Tete meeting took place in the newly refurbished, air-conditioned conference room of the Hotel Zambeze. Present were political leaders—administrators of several districts, officials from the local water authority, and Sérgio Vieira, a longtime Frelimo cadre who was now head of the Zambezi Development Authority (known by its Portuguese initials GPZ)—and representatives of some major businesses. At the head table were Impacto employees, a representative of the consortium, and UTIP's Sérgio Elísio. Observations by David Morton, who was present at the meeting, which were transmitted in report form to Allen Isaacman.

96. Ibid.

97. Ibid.

98. Gustavo Mañez and Lucia Scodanibbio, *Mphanda Nkuwa: Dams and Development Capacity-Building Project: Report prepared for the Siemenpuu Foundation* (Maputo: Justiça Ambiental, 2004), 3.

99. Daniel Ribeiro, interview, Palo Alto, September 26, 2010.

100. Ibid.

101. Daniel Ribeiro, interview, Maputo, June 6, 2008.

102. Mañez and Scodanibbio, *Mphanda Nkuwa*, 12.

103. Justiça Ambiental, "Report on the Workshop," 1–13.

104. Ibid.

105. Justiça Ambiental, "Report on the Workshop," appendix, "Declaração: Seminário sobre a Gestão Integrada das Águas, 'Vozes do Zambeze.'"

106. Daniel Ribeiro, interview, June 6, 2008; Fabião Chazia and Chivio Cheiro, interview, Tete city, August 12, 2009.

107. Fabião Chazia and Chivio Cheiro, interview.

108. Chirodzi-Sanangwe derives its name from the two rivers that meet in the central village of the community. The Sanangwe carries on northward for another seven kilometers until it flows into the Zambezi. Because Chirodzi-Sanangwe was an easy place at which to cross to the southern bank, for much of the twentieth century Mozambicans and Malawians did so to work on commercial farms

in Zimbabwe. Gadeni Gaspar, interview; Biquane Chazia, interview; Marialena Dique, interview; Rabia Juma et al., interview.

109. Adelino Tioneque, adjunct Frelimo secretary of Chirodzi-Sanangwe, interview by DM, Chirodzi-Sanangwe, August 6, 2009.

110. Bonifácio Biquane et al., interview. See also Morrissey, *Livelihoods at Risk*, 28–36; Oliveira, *Tauaras*, 25–61.

111. Morrissey, *Livelihoods at Risk*, 87–8. For a recent gendered analysis of displacement, see Mehta, *Displaced by Development*.

112. Daniel Makaza, interview by DM, Chirodzi-Sanangwe, August 6, 2009; Virgílio Djimo, interview by DM, Chirodzi-Sanangwe, June 25, 2008.

113. Fidelis Chakala et al., interview.

114. Vincent Gadeni and Gadeni Gaspar, interview.

115. Vintina Colar et al., interview by DM, Chococoma, June 26, 2008.

116. Marialena Dique, interview.

117. Tilha Chafewa and Sieda Denja, interview. Both women were subsisting almost solely on malambe at the time of their interview. According to Sieda Denja, they had no animals, not even a chicken or a goat.

118. Araújo Tionequi, interview.

119. Francisco Fondo (Frelimo secretary), interview by DM, Chirodzi-Sanangwe, June 25, 2008; Maginta Cheiro et al., interview; Vintina Colar et al., interview.

120. Francisco Fondo, interview.

121. Fidelis Chakala et al., interview.

122. Daniel Ribeiro, interview, September 26, 2010.

123. The government recently announced that the publicly owned Zambezi Valley Development Agency will invest more than $2 million between 2012 and 2014 on a range of large-scale economic and social projects, many of which will be in the riverine zone. "Mozambique: Govt to Invest US$200 Million Dollars in Zambezi Valley," *AIM*, January 25, 2012, http://allafrica.com/stories/201201261000.html.

124. This obliteration of local knowledge is not unique to Mozambique. Scott has argued that all high modernist projects must necessarily discount or ignore indigenous systems of knowledge. Scott, *Seeing Like a State*, 6–7.

125. In the case of Mphanda Nkuwa, the cheap energy produced will primarily be exported, rather than being used for domestic development, and a share of the profits will reportedly go directly to an investment group connected to Mozambique's current president. Joseph Hanlon and Marcelo Mosse, "Mozambique's Elite—Finding Its Way in a Globalized World and Returning to Old Development Models" (working paper no. 2010/105, United Nations University, World Institute for Development Economic Research, Helsinki, 2010), 8.

126. See, for example, Hankins, *Renewable Energy Plan*.

127. In doing so, those who exercise the levers of state power continue to rely on the particular forms of developmentalist knowledge promoted by experts that helped to perpetuate the colonial and neocolonial order. This dilemma is not unique to postcolonial Mozambique. As Wainwright stresses in his provocative

study of Guatemala and Belize, "colonial knowledges have outlasted formal colonialism and live on in the present, constitute the present as such, and have ongoing political effects." Wainwright, *Decolonizing Development*, 14. Although rural communities in Mozambique were never "constituted" entirely by colonial knowledge, the image of the Zambezi as a wild and uncivilized frontier that was both a barrier to and potential site of national development certainly was an artifact of the colonial past. Given this legacy and the current alignment of political power, we remain pessimistic that such debates will take place anytime soon.

128. For an exploration of the long and rich tradition of engaged scholarship in African Studies, see Allen Isaacman, "Legacies of Engagement: Scholarship Informed by Political Commitment," *African Studies Review* 46, no. 1 (2003): 1–41.

Glossary of Select Local Terms

aldaia communal. A communal village.

aldeamento. A so-called protected village or strategic hamlet; a barbed-wire encampment for internment of victims of relocation.

aringa. A walled stockade or strategically placed fortification.

baneira. A hut where African prostitutes sold sexual favors to workers and soldiers stationed at Songo.

banja. A government-organized village meeting.

bare. An inland gold mine.

capitão (pl., *capitães*). A labor overseer.

chibalo (chibaro). The forced-labor regime.

chicote. A hippopotamus-hide whip.

colonato. A rural agricultural community of resettled Portugese peasants and ex-soldiers.

curandeiro/a (Shona: *gombe*). An herbalist.

dhomba. Collective labor.

escudo. The basic unit of Portuguese currency.

Fanagalo. A pidgin used as the lingua franca of South African mines; also spoken at Cahora Bassa.

fumo (pl., *afumo* or *mafumu*). A subordinate headman of the *mambo.*

gogoda (guguda; gogodela). A locally made muzzle-loading rifle.

kapenta. The Tanganyika sardine introduced into Lake Cahora Bassa.

kokota. A seine fishing net.

maçanica (both sing. and pl.). A wild bush yielding edible berries.

machamba (both sing. and pl.). An agricultural field.

machonga. A small triangular weir used for fishing.

maize. African corn.

makande (ndrongo, matope, mataka). River-fed soil rich in nutrients.

malambe. The fruit of the baobab.

mambo (pl., *amambo*). An indigenous territorial chief.

mboa (Chewa: *boa*). Wild mushrooms.

mestizo. A racially mixed person at least one of whose ancestors was African.

mhondoro (both sing. and pl.). Lion spirits revered as spiritual guardians within their territory.

midzimu. Ancestor spirits.

misambadzi (pl., *musambadzi*). A local-trading specialist.

mlembwe. A women's fishing technique; scooping up the catch in sheets and baskets.

mpambadza. The bulb of the wild lily.

mpumbo (tchetca). Less fertile, mixed clay-loam soils of the floodplain's upper terraces.

murope. The second harvest, typically occurring in August, on alluvial plots.

murumucheia. The upland area to which peasants moved and on which they farmed during seasonal flooding.

musonkho (mutsonko). The annual tax all peasant households were required to pay to the *prazeiros*.

nhica. See *nyika*.

nkumbalumi (pl., *mukumbalumi*). A master hunter.

nkhonga (sing. and pl.) Another type of triangular weir made out of thick grass, bound with palm strings, and baited with porridge.

ntchenga. Less fertile, often rocky, upland soil that was difficult to till.

ntsembe. The special offering fishermen made to their ancestors for protection.

nyeza. The tuber of the cocoyam.

*nyika (nhica).*The root of the water lily.

palmatório. A wood plank with spikes used by labor overseers, settlers, and officials to beat workers and the local population.

phombi (pombe). Locally brewed beer.

pombe. See *phambi.*

prazeiro. The owner of a crown estate.

prazo. A Portuguese crown estate.

psyairo. An encircling fishing fence.

regulado. A chieftaincy.

régulo. An African chief often appointed by the colonial government.

sipai (sipãe). An African policeman.

svikiro. An earthly medium through whom the *mhondoro* spoke.

tchaca. The first harvest, typically in February, on an upland field.

vwe-vwe. Geese.

Bibliography

INTERVIEWS

*Interviews Conducted by the Authors or by a Research Team
of Which One of the Authors Was a Member*

Alemão, Maurício. Masecha, May 27, 1998.

Amado, Cheia. Caia (Regulado Magagadi), July 20, 2000.

Andrade, António, George Niquisse Phiri, and Francisco Lourenço Alfredo. Songo, July 11, 2001.

António, N'tsai, Vanita Tomo, Rainhha Cardeiro, and Finegia Araúja. Caia (Regulado Chetcha), July 21, 2000.

Araújo, Pita, and Bernardo Gona. Sena, July 21, 2000.

Babo, Oliva, Ernesto Manwete, Sapanda Voro, Sapanda Saiene, Mfurunu Chave, and Fumo Isac Roda. Sena (Regulado Mwanalave), July 21, 2000.

Bento, Carlos (Museu da História Natural). Maputo, March 10, 2010.

Boroma, Conrado Msussa. Boroma, July 28, August 17, 20, September 29, 1968.

Botão, Senteira, Eliot Sargento, and Beatriz Maquina. Chipalapala, May 26, 1998.

Cado, Renço. Chemba, August 13, 1968.

Calecoetoa, Júlio. Songo, May 18, 1998.

Cardoso, Gaspar. Boroma, July 15, 17, 18, 1968.

Carvalho, Maria, Luisa Tshombe, and Rosa Nyama. Sena (Regulado Mwamalavo), July 21, 2000.

Casado, Balança. Sena (Bairro 25 de Setembro), July 11, 2000.

Cascas, Henriqueta. Caia (Regulado Gumançanze), July 14, 2000.

Cebola, Luís. Boroma, July 18, 1968.

Chambiça, Mário, Mandala Doscasaca, and António Vinte Chimgangire. Caia (Regulado de Gumançanze), July 13, 2000.

Chave, Régulo Júlio. Chemba (Regulado Chave), July 19, 2000.

Chipuazo, Régulo António, Jone Jane, and Chico Tomás Chipuazo. Caia (Regulado Chipuazo), July 7, 2000.

Chipwazo, Maria, Francisca João Chipwazo, Maria Francisco Mandala, António Moda, and Misca Joaquim. Caia (Regulado Chipuazo), July 7, 2000.

Chirembue, Alberto, and Armando Navia. Inhangoma, July 16, 2000.

Chiridzisana, Basílio, and Ragi Miguel. Chicoa Nova, July 16, August 3, 2001.

Chitima, Bento, Joseph Máquina, and Novochema. Estima, July 11, 2001.

Chongololo, Gervásio Saborinho. Estima, July 11, 2001.

Chongololo, Gervásio Saborinho, Lucrécia Arcário Luís, Inês Diamondo Fondo, and Elisa Geremias Gandali. Estima, July 13, 2001.

Conforme, Ereman. Chipalapala, May 26, 1998.

Cristóstomo, João. Boroma, July 18, 25, 1968.

d'Abreu, José António. Tete city, July 22, 1968.

Djase, António. Sena (Bairro 25 de Setembro), July 5, 2000.

Dozy, Christopher. Tete (Nyalugwe), May 1, 2000.

Escafa, Guente. Sena (Bairro 25 de Setembro), July 11, 2000.

Estima, Bento, and Joseph Ndebvuchena. Estima, May 19, 1998.

Faidose, Emílio. Masecha, May 25, 1998.

Ferrão, Ricardo António. Tete city, September 22, 1997.

Figuerido, Caetano, João Figuerido, Jalvador Carita, and Hadji Kulaminkudua, Círculo Namizula, Régulo Chirembwe. Mutarara (Inhangoma), July 18, 2000.

Ganhão, Fernando. Maputo, March 12, 2006.

Gelo, Saluchepa, and Luís Nota. Caia (Regulado Chave), July 18, 2000.

Gémio, Nembani, Lavomó Jamisse, Maique Bandera, Manuel Bicausse, and Evaristo Pacati. Chipalapala, July 17, 2001.

Gremi, Padre Claúdio. Songo, May 20, 23, 1998, July 11, 2001.

Guta, Inácio Jeremias, Bondjesse Tlonse, José Manuel António, Pedro Tomás Afonso, Duarte Tomo Lauale, and Jamson Inácio Singano. Sena (Regulado Chetcha), July 21, 2000.

Inácio, José, and Lucas Afonso. Caia (Regulado Gumançanze), July 14, 2000.

Inácio, Marosse, Artur Massangasse, and Francisco Banema e Brazão. Chemba (Regulado Chave), July 19, 2000.

Jack, Castro, Ricardo Ferrão, Senzelore Trakino, Marcos Respeito, Maria Ferrão, and Jofina Salari. Kajanda, October 21, 1997.

Jequessene, Elisa, Alegria Borada, Elisa Belo, Modesta Alone, Alisa Maganhar, Faina Piano, Eventina Salir, Lavinesse Chalequera, Talisse Enoque, Tânia Laete, Narcisa Lourenço, Acélia Aerofate, Ana Semate, Catarina João, Meji Ainero, Jusela António, Laurite Ináacio, Sara Albertino, Maria Chaideca, Celeste Mário, and Dórica Govewia. Chicoa Emboque, July 23, 2001.

João, Aniva, Regi Meque Dacomalele, and Pedro João Franque. Inhangoma (Regulado Chirembwe), July 16, 2000.

Jone, José, Tchinaze Ajase, Carlota Arminda, Cristina Monteiro, and N'tsai Mugondina. Mutarara, July 6, 2000.

Joni, Emília. Caia (Bairro 25 de Setembro), July 7, 2000.

Lambani, Milioni. Chemba (Regulado Chave), July 19, 2001.

Lambique, Rita, Verónica Simão, Amélia Jossinão, and Maria Tito. Chemba (Regulado Chave), July 19, 2000.

Leone, Vernácio. Estima, May 19, 1998.

Luís, Lucrécia Arcário, Inês Diamondo Fondo, Elisa Geremias Gandali, and Gervásio Saborinho Chongololo. Estima, July 13, 2001.

Lupia, Chale. Massangano, September 28, 1968.

Machel, Samora. Maputo, May 7, 1979.

Mafalanjala, Pezulani, Maurício Alemão, and Bernardo Tapuleta Potoroia. Masecha, May 25, 1998.

Mange, Bengala, and Zeca Sacatucua. Caia (Regulado Gumançanze), July 10, 2000.

Mangiricau, Ferreira, and Bene Ngoca. Mutarara (Bairro 25 de Dezembro), July 5, 2000.

Manuel, Francisco, et al. Mutarara Velha (Nhancogole), July 6, 2000.

Manuel, Luís, João Nhemba, and Mateus Cluimancudia. Caia (Regulado Sangoma), July 20, 2000.

Medja, Artur, Augusto Jone, and Zeca Saísse. Chemba (Regulado Chave), July 19, 2000.

Mereja, Henrique Conforme, Virgílio Manuel, João Castelo, Gabriel Albano, Peter Phiri. and Carlos Sabonete. Chicoa Emboque, July 17, 2001.

Misero, Almanda. Mphata, August 16, 2001.

Monteiro, Gina, and other women. Mutarara (Bairro 25 de Dezembro), July 6, 2000.

Mpande, Diamond. Bawa, September 23, 1997.

Muriana, Tchinaze João, Henriqueta Manuel Cascas, and Margarido João Canivete. Caia (Regulado Gumançanze), July 14, 2000.

Navalha, Armando, and António Sona. Inhangoma (Regulado Chirembwe), July 8, 2000.

Nhamazi, Novais, Quembo Kucheza, Mofozti Kastomo, Limmpo Kuche, and Amada Tomo. Chemba (Regulado Chave), July 19, 2000.

Nhamizinga, Paulino, Estêvão Argola, Mafakussene, and Romão Chasselene. Chipalapala, July 12, 2001.

Nsampa, Lofas, et al., Luabo, November 14, 1976 (interviewed by Judith Head).

Paul, John, and Khumbidzi Pastor. Estima, May 21, 1998.

Potroy, Tablet, and Maurício Alemão. Masecha, July 13, 2001.

Presente, Niquicicafe. Massangano, September 28, 1968.

Raposo, João, Maneca Fino, Gengala Chcote, Adelinno Nabeira, and Bento Katandcia. Caia (Regulado Gumançanze), July 13, 2000.

Raposo, Vale. Chemba (Regulado Chave), July 18, 2000.

Ribeiro, Daniel. Maputo, March 10, June 6, 2008, March 10, 2010; Palo Alto, September 26, 2010.

Sabonete, Carlos. Masecha, July 12, 2001.

Sacatucua, Joaquim. Caia, July 10, 2000.

Sangoma, Régulo Simão. Caia (Regulado Sangoma), July 20, 2000.

Sargento, Supia, and Carlos Churo. Estima, May 22, 1998.

Sargento, Supia, Eliot Jombo, Dionísio Laete, Muaticimbira Sargento, Fontina Caetano, and Fáusto Almeida Semo. Chipalapala, July 12, 2001.

Semo, Fausto. Chipalapala, July 12, 2001.

Simico, Sene, Mauzene Dique, and Mzwengane Mafala Njala. Nyatapira, May 27, 1998.

Simondeo, Govate, Mapondane José, Frederico Laugedone, Evaristo Pacate, and Presente Leone. Chipalapala, July 12, 2001.

Sipinyo, Ezani. Estima, May 21, 1998.
Size, Peter, and Fedi Alfante. Chinyanda Nova, May 25, 1998.
Sobrinho, Jack, and Wiseborn Benjamin. Estima, May 20, 1998.
Talé, Manuel, João John, Ernesto Navaia, and Luís Britone. Sena (Regulado Chetcha), July 21, 2000.
Tchoa, António Jonasse, Alberta Chicota Tchoa, Menes Gamo Potco, and João Charre Toranco. Caia (Regulado Gumançaze), July 14, 2000.
Tesoura, João. Caia (Aldeia 25 de Setembro), July 11, 2000.
Wetela, Simões. Songo, May 27–28, 1998.
Xavier, Pedro da Costa. Songo, May 23, 27, 1998.

Interviews Conducted by David Morton (DM in Notes)

Biquane, Bonifácio, Alexei Chipessan, and José Ferro. Chirodzi-Sanangwe, August 5, 2009.
Chafewa, Tilha, and Sieda Denja. Chirodzi-Sanangwe, August 5, 2009.
Chakala, Fidelis, Xavier Sais, and Adelino Tioneque. Chirodzi-Sanangwe, August 10, 2009.
Chazia, Biquane. Chirodzi-Sanangwe, August 3, 2009.
Chazia, Fabião Manuel, and Chivio Eliem Cheiro. Tete city, August 12, 2009.
Cheiro, Maginta, Sieda Spring, and Magamezo Tionequi. Chirodzi-Sanangwe (Bairro Luzinga), June 25, 2008.
Colar, Vintina, Macanisto Domingo, and Carlos Alfonso Jaime. Chococoma, June 26, 2008.
Dique, Marialena. Chirodzi-Sanangwe, August 8, 2009.
Djimo, Virgílio. Chirodzi-Sanangwe, June 25, 2008.
Fondo, Francisco (Frelimo secretary). Chirodzi-Sanangwe, June 25, 2008.
Gadeni, Vincent, and Gadeni Gaspar. Chirodzi-Sanangwe, August 8, 2009.
Gaspar, Gadeni. Chirodzi-Sanangwe, August 3, 2009.
Juma, Rabia, Farouk Ismael Hassam, and Abdul Gafar Ismael Hassam. Tete city, August 12, 2009.
Makaza, Daniel Ernesto. Chirodzi-Sanangwe, August 6, 2009.
Meguigy, Nazário (Ministry of Energy) and Sérgio Elísio (UTIP). Maputo, June 18, 2008.
Siawalha, Naita. Chirodzi-Sanangwe, August 9, 2009.
Tioneque, Adelino (Frelimo adjunct secretary). Chirodzi-Sanangwe, August 6, 2009.
Tionequi, Araújo. Chirodzi-Sanangwe, June 25, 2009.

Interviews Conducted by Professor Mapu Mulwafo and his Students from Chancellor College, University of Malawi (MRB in Notes)

Bemuse, Fajita. Dovu (Malone), April 2000.
Biassa, Betina. T/A Kambembe (Falera), May 6, 2000.
Faifi, Maria. Nsanje (Savieli village), April 18, 2000.
Fero, Veka. Nsanje (Savieli village), April 23, 2000.
Ioha, António. T/A Khomelo (Matunga), May 4, 2000.

Januare, Elias. Hapalal Kusala, April 20, 2000.
Kabu, Liza, and Fillinda Filley. T/A Chilembwe (Masasu), May 5, 2000.
Kalumbi, Ernest. Nsanje, April 2000.
Kamuzu, Bastiana. Madani, April 27, 2000.
Kasenga, Dimingu. T/A Dovu (Maloti), May 19, 2000.
Luizhi, Zhuzi. Mhula village, April 2000.
Malenje, Zhili. T/A Dovu (Malota), May 19, 2000.
Mavungire, Chidasiyikwa. Dimingu Thom, April 2000.
Mayo, Paulo. Chikoti, May 24, 2000.
Mbvinisa, Fatima. T/A Dovu (Dimingu Gashipale), May 19, 2000.
Milo, Paulo. Chikoti, May 24, 2000.
Msitu, Zhuwa. T/A Kambembe (Tizola), May 6, 2000.
Mwakwapala, Ventura. Mthukulo, April 17, 2000.
Mwandipandusa, Kaki. Nsanje (Dominique Tom village), May 20, 2000.
Neva, Benjamin. Nsanje (Savieli village), April 19, 2000.
Njani, Shikita. T/A Valela (Tizoa), April 6, 2000.
Pereira, Domingo. Vila Nova, May 24, 2000.
Phwete, Lucca. Nsanje (Savieli village), April 23, 2000.
Rapozolo, Alberto. Ralumbi, April 2000.
Scanda, Luwichi. T/A Dovu (Matola village), March 23, 2000.
Thamanda, Watson. T/A Malemia (Msusa), April 21, 2000.
Thomas, Wilson. Nsanje (Savieli village), April 17, 2000.
Valera, Zhuwa, and Pereira Msitu. T/A Kambembe (Tizola), May 6, 2000.
Zhuwao, Marita. Nsanje (Savieli village), April 25, 2000.

Interviews in the Middlemas Collection, Hoover Institution Archives, Stanford University

Arriaga, Gen. Kaúlza de, 1971, tape A5.
Bendixen, Bernard, 1974, tape A11.
Chambers, William, 1973, tape A11.
Duncan, S., 1973–74, tape A11.
Jordan, Franz, 1974, tape A11.
Lampiére, Antoine, 1973, tape A11.
Langer, Horst, 1974, tape A15.
Pereira, Lieutenant, 1973–74, tape A12.
Shangaan headman, n.d., tape A11.
Souza, Crispin de, 1973–74, tape A11.

BOOKS AND ARTICLES

Abrahamsson, Hans, and Anders Nilsson. *Mozambique: The Troubled Transition: From Socialist Construction to Free Market Capitalism.* London: Zed Books, 1995.
Abu-Lughod, Lila. "Writing against Culture." In *Recapturing Anthropology: Working in the Present,* edited by Richard Fox, 137–62. Santa Fe: School of American Research Press, 1991.

Adams, William M. *Green Development: Environment and Sustainability in the Third World.* London: Routledge, 1990.

———. *Wasting the Rain: Rivers, People, and Planning in Africa.* Minneapolis: University of Minnesota Press, 1992.

Airboat Afrika Company (AAC). *Cahora Bassa.* http://www.airboatafrika.com/lake-cahora-bassa.

Allman, Jean. "Rounding Up Spinsters: Gender Chaos and Unmarried Women in Colonial Asante." In Hodgson and McCurdy, *"Wicked" Women*, 130–48.

Almeida, Francisco José de Lacerda e. *Travessia de África.* Lisbon: Agência Geral das Colónias, 1936.

Amin, Samir. *Unequal Development: An Essay on the Social Formations of Peripheral Capitalism.* Translated by Brian Pearce. New York: Monthly Review Press, 1976.

Amin, Shahid. *Event, Metaphor, and Memory: Chauri Chaura, 1922–1992.* Berkeley: University of California Press, 1995.

Aminzade, Ronald. "Corruption and Boundary Politics in Socialist and Neo-Liberal Tanzania." Unpublished paper, 2010.

Andrade, António, ed. *Relações de Moçambique setecentista.* Lisbon: Agência Geral do Ultramar, 1954.

Artur, Luís. "Continuities in Crisis: Everyday Practices of Disaster Response and Climate Change Adaptation in Mozambique." PhD diss., Wageningen University, 2011.

Artur, Luís, and Dorothea Hilhorst. "Climate Change Adaptation in Mozambique." In *The Right to Water and Water Rights in a Changing World: Papers Presented at a Colloquium Held on 22 September 2010 in Delft, the Netherlands,* edited by Michael R. van der Valk and Penelope Keenan. Delft: UNESCO–International Hydrological Programme, 2012.

Asmal, Kader. "Globalisation from Below." Preface to *Dams and Development: A New Framework for Decision-Making,* edited by World Commission on Dams. London: Earthscan, 2000.

Asmal, Kader, Louise Asmal, and Ronald Roberts. *Reconciliation through Truth: A Reckoning of Apartheid's Criminal Governance.* Cape Town: David Philip, 1996.

Barber, Margaret, and Gráinne Ryder. *Damming the Three Gorges: What Dam Builders Don't Want You to Know.* London: Probe International, 1993.

Barreto, Manuel. "Informação do estado e conquista dos Rios de Cuama, 1667." In Theal, *South-Eastern Africa*, 3:436–95.

Beach, David. *The Shona and Their Neighbours.* Oxford: Blackwell, 1994.

Beckman, Björn. "Bakolori: Peasants versus State and Industry in Nigeria." In Goldsmith and Hildyard, *Large Dams*, 2:140–55.

Beilfuss, Richard. "Can This River Be Saved? Rethinking Cahora Bassa Could Make a Difference for Dam-Battered Zambezi." *World Rivers Review* 14, no. 1 (1990): 8–11.

———. "Modeling Trade-offs between Hydropower Generation and Environmental Flow Releases in the Lower Zambezi River Basin, Mozambique." *International Journal of River Basin Management* 8, no. 2 (2010): 127–38.

———. "Prescribed Flooding and Restoration Potential in the Zambezi Delta, Mozambique." Working paper no. 4, Program for the Sustainable Management of Cahora Bassa Dam and the Lower Zambezi Valley, Maputo, 2001.

———. "Specialist Study—Natural Resource Utilization." In Beilfuss and Brown, *Environmental Flow Requirements*, 104–7.

———. "Understanding Extreme Floods in the Lower Zambezi River." Unpublished paper, n.d.

Beilfuss, Richard, and Cate Brown. "Assessing Environmental Flow Requirements and Trade-offs for the Lower Zambezi River and Delta, Mozambique." *International Journal of River Basin Management* 8, no. 2 (2010): 127–38.

———, eds. *Assessing Environmental Flow Requirements for the Marromeu Complex of the Zambezi Delta: Application of the Drift Model (Downstream Response to Imposed Flow Transformations)*. Maputo: University of Eduardo Mondlane Museum of Natural History, 2006.

———. Introduction to Beilfuss and Brown, *Environmental Flow Requirements*, 1–5.

Beilfuss, Richard, Arlindo Chilundo, Allen Isaacman, and Wapu Mulwafu. "The Impact of Hydrological Changes on Subsistence Production Systems and Socio-Cultural Values in the Lower Zambezi Valley." Working paper no. 6, Program of Sustainable Management of Cahora Bassa Dam and the Lower Zambezi Valley, Maputo, 2002.

Beilfuss, Richard, and B. R. Davies. "Prescribed Flooding and Wetland Rehabilitation in the Zambezi Delta, Mozambique." In *An International Perspective on Wetland Rehabilitation*, edited by William Streever, 143–58. Dordrecht: Kluwer Academic Publishers, 1999.

Beilfuss, Richard, and David dos Santos. "Patterns of Hydrological Change in the Zambezi Delta, Mozambique." Working paper no. 2, Program for the Sustainable Management of Cahora Bassa Dam and the Lower Zambezi Valley, Maputo, 2001, 31–103.

Beilfuss, Richard, Paul Dutton, and Dorn Moore. "Land Cover and Land Use Change in the Zambezi Delta." In *Land Use Change and Human Impact*. Vol. 3 of *Biodiversity of the Zambezi Basin Wetlands*, edited by Jonathan Timberlake, 31–105. Bulawayo: Biodiversity Foundation for Africa, 2000.

Beilfuss, Richard, Dorn Moore, Carlos Bento, and Paul Dutton. "Patterns of Vegetation Change in the Zambezi Delta, Mozambique." Working paper no. 3, Program for the Sustainable Management of Cahora Bassa Dam and the Lower Zambezi Valley, Maputo, 2001.

Bender, Gerald J. *Angola under the Portuguese: The Myth and the Reality*. Berkeley: University of California Press, 1978.

Bernacsek, Garry, and Suzette Lopes. "Cabora Bassa (Mozambique)." In *Status of African Reservoir Fisheries*, edited by J. M. Kapetsky and T. Petr, CIFA Technical Paper no. 10, 21–42. Rome: FAO, 1984.

Bernstein, Henry. "Can Modernity Accommodate African 'Peasants'?" In *7° Congresso Ibérico de Estudos Africanos*, 1–17. Lisbon, 2010.

———. "Studying Development/Development Studies." *African Studies* 65, no. 1 (2006): 46–52.

Bhabha, Homi. *The Location of Culture.* New York: Routledge, 1994.

Biajal, Pradip, and P. K. Singh. "Large Dams: Can We Do Without Them?" *Economics and Political Weekly* 35, no. 19 (May 6–12, 2000): 1659–66.

Binger, Wilson V. *Environmental Effects of Large Dams.* New York: American Society of Civil Engineers, 1978.

Biswas, Asit K., and Cecilia Tortajada. "Development and Large Dams: A Global Perspective." *Water Resources Development* 17, no. 1 (2001): 9–21.

Bocarro, António, "Década da Índia." In Theal, *South-Eastern Africa*, 3:254–435.

Bolton, Peter. "Mozambique's Cahora Bassa Project: An Environmental Assessment." In Goldsmith and Hildyard, *Large Dams*, 2:156–67.

———. "The Regulation of the Zambezi in Mozambique: A Study of the Origins and Impact of the Cabora Bassa Project." PhD thesis, University of Edinburgh, 1983.

Bond, W. J., Nancy Coe, P. B. N. Jackson, and K. H. Rogers. "The Limnology of Cabora Bassa, Moçambique, during Its First Year." *Freshwater Biology* 8, no. 5 (1978): 433–47.

Borges Coelho, João Paulo. "Protected Villages and Communal Villages in the Mozambican Province of Tete (1968–1982): A History of State Resettlement Policies, Development and War." PhD thesis, University of Bradford, 1993.

———. "State Resettlement Policies in Post-Colonial Rural Mozambique: The Impact of the Communal Village Programme on Tete Province, 1972–1982." *Journal of Southern African Studies* 24, no. 1 (1998): 61–91.

Botelho, Sebastião Xavier. *Memória estatística sobre os domínios portuguezes na África oriental.* Lisbon: José Baptista Morando, 1835.

Braun, Bruce B. "Colonialism's Afterlife: Vision and Visuality on the Northwest Coast." *Cultural Geographies* 9, no. 2 (2002): 202–47.

Brass, Tom. *Peasants, Populism and Postmodernism: The Return of the Agrarian Myth.* London: Frank Cass, 2000.

Brown, Cate. "Drift Outputs." In Beilfuss and Brown, *Environmental Flow Requirements*, 116–33.

Browne, Pete. "Debate over Dams on Africa's Zambezi River." *Green: A Blog about Energy and the Environment, New York Times,* October 19, 2009. green.blogs.nytimes.com/2009/10/19/debate-over-dams-on-africas-zambezi-river/.

Burawoy, Michael. *The Politics of Production: Factory Regimes under Capitalism and Socialism.* London: Verso, 1985.

Butler, Judith. *Bodies That Matter: On the Discursive Limits of "Sex."* New York: Routledge, 1993.

Carvalho, Américo dos Santos. *O plano do Zambeze.* Lourenço Marques: GPZ, 1974.

Carvalho, F. *Relatório do governador, 1911–1912.* Lourenço Marques: Imprensa Nacional, 1912.

Castro, Francisco de Mello de. *Descripção dos Rios de Senna, anno de 1750.* Nova Goa: Imprensa Nacional, 1861.

Centro de Documentação e Informação do Instituto Português de Apoio ao Desenvolvimento. *Inventório de Cabora Bassa*. Lisbon: Centro de Documentação, 2004.

Centro de Investigação Científica Algodoeira (CICA). *Esboço reconhecimento ecológico-agrícola de Moçambique*. Lourenço Marques: CICA, 1955.

Chambal, Hélder. *Energy Security in Mozambique*. Series on Trade and Energy Security, Policy Report 3. Winnipeg: International Institute for Sustainable Development, 2010.

Chambers, Robert, and Gordon Conway. "Sustainable Rural Livelihoods: Practical Concepts for the 21st Century." Discussion paper no. 296, Institute of Development Studies, Brighton University, March 1992.

Chande, B., and P. Dutton. "Impacts of Hydrological Change in the Zambezi Delta to Wildlife and Their Habitats with Special Attention to the Large Mammals." Paper presented at Workshop on the Sustainable Use of Cahora Bassa Dam and the Zambezi Valley, September 29–October 2, 1997, Songo, Mozambique.

Climo, Jacob, and Maria Cattell. Introduction to *Social Memory and History: Anthropological Perspectives*, edited by Climo and Cattell, 1–36. Walnut Creek, CA: AltaMira Press, 2002.

Collins, John. *Occupied by Memory: The Intifada Generation and the Palestinian State of Emergency*. New York: NYU Press, 2004.

Colson, Elizabeth. "Gendering Those Uprooted by 'Development.'" In *Engendering Forced Migration*, edited by Doreen Indra, 22–39. New York: Berghahn, 1999.

———. *The Social Consequences of Resettlement: The Impact of the Kariba Resettlement upon the Gwembe Tonga*. Manchester: Manchester University Press, 1971.

Cooper, Frederick. *Africa since 1940: The Past of the Present*. Cambridge: Cambridge University Press, 2002.

———. *Decolonization and African Society: The Labor Question in French and British Africa*. Cambridge: Cambridge University Press, 1996.

———. "Modernizing Bureaucrats, Backward Africans, and the Development Concept." In Cooper and Packard, *International Development*, 71–81. Berkeley: University of California Press, 1997.

Cooper, Frederick, and Randall Packard, eds. *International Development and the Social Sciences: Essays on the History and Politics of Knowledge*. Berkeley: University of California Press, 1997.

Cosgrove, Denis E. *Social Formation and Symbolic Landscape*. London: Routledge, 1984.

Costa, Silvino Ferreira da. *Governo do território da Companhia de Moçambique*. Beira: Companhia de Moçambique, 1917.

Coutinho, João de Azevedo. *A campanha do Barué em 1902*. Lisbon: Livraria Ferin, 1904.

Cowen, Michael, and Robert Shenton. *Doctrines of Development*. London: Routledge, 1996.

Crow, Ben, and Farhana Sultana. "Gender, Class and Access to Water: Three Cases in a Poor and Crowded Delta." *Society and Natural Resources* 15 (2002): 709–24.

Cummings, Barbara J. *Dam the Rivers, Damn the People: Development and Resistance in Amazonian Brazil.* London: Earthscan, 1990.

Cunha, Joaquim Moreira da Silva. *Cabora-Bassa: Textos dos discursos proferidos em Lisboa.* Lisbon: Agência-Geral do Ultramar, 1969.

———. *Cabora Bassa: Who Will Benefit by It?* Lisbon: Agência-Geral do Ultramar, 1970.

———. *O trabalho indígena: Estudo do direito colonial.* Lisbon: Agência Geral das Colónias, 1949.

Davies, Bryan. "Cabora Bassa Hazards." *Nature* 254 (1975): 477–78.

———. "Commentary on the Cross-Check Questionnaire—Cahora Bassa Dam Moçambique." Compiled for World Commission on Dams, Cape Town, n.d.

———. "Rehabilitation Programme for Cahora Bassa and the Lower Zambezi." Unpublished, unpaginated background document produced for the International Crane Foundation and the Ford Foundation, 1996.

———, ed. *Report on the Songo Workshop on the Sustainable Utilization of the Cahora Bassa Dam and the Valley of the Lower Zambezi.* Maputo: Arquivo do Patrimônio Cultural, 1997.

———. "They Pulled the Plug Out of the Lower Zambezi." *African Wildlife* 29, no. 2 (1975): 26–28.

———. "The Zambezi River System." In *The Ecology of River Systems,* edited by B. R. Davies and K. F. Walker, 225–67. Dordrecht: Kluwer Academic Publishers, 1986.

Davies, Bryan, Richard Beilfuss, and Martin Thoms. "Cahora Bassa Retrospective, 1974–1997: Effects of Flow Regulation on the Lower Zambezi River." *Verhandlungen—Internationale Vereinigung für theoretische und angewandte Limnologie* 27 (December 2000): 1–9.

Davies, Bryan, and Jenny Day. *Vanishing Waters.* Cape Town: University of Cape Town Press, 1988.

Davies, Bryan, A. Hall, and P. B. N. Jackson. "Some Ecological Aspects of the Cabora Bassa Dam." *Biological Conservation* 8, no. 3 (1975): 189–201.

Department for International Development. "Droughts, Floods and Higher Temperatures Bring More Disease to City Life." May 19, 2008. http://www.dfid.gov.uk/news/files/climate-mozambique-droughts.asp.

Dhlakama, Alfonso. "Relatório referente a sessão do trabalho de RNM e do representativo do Governo Sul Africano." MNR document, October 25, 1980.

Dixon, John A., Lee M. Talbot, and Guy J.-M. LeMoigne. *Dams and the Environment: Considerations in World Bank Projects.* World Bank Technical Report no. 10, 1–54. Washington, DC: World Bank, 1989.

Domingos, R. Untitled summary of conversations with Orlando Christina. RENAMO document in personal possession of authors, November 4, 1980.

Egerö, Bertil. *Mozambique: A Dream Undone: The Political Economy of Democracy, 1975–84.* Stockholm: Almquist and Wiksell, 1987.

Electricidade de Moçambique (EDM). Annual Report, 2006. Maputo: EDM, 2006.

Elkins, Caroline. *Imperial Reckoning: The Untold Story of Britain's Gulag in Kenya*. New York: Henry Holt, 2005.

Escobar, Arturo. "Constructing Nature: Elements for a Poststructural Political Ecology." In *Liberation Ecologies: Environment, Development, Social Movements*, edited by Richard Peet and Michael Watts, 46–68. London: Routledge, 1996.

———. *Encountering Development: The Making and Unmaking of the Third World*. Princeton: Princeton University Press, 1995.

Fairhead, James, and Melissa Leach. *Misreading the African Landscape: Society and Ecology in a Forest-Savanna Mosaic*. Cambridge: Cambridge University Press, 1996.

Fauvet, Paul, and José Alves Gomes. "The Mozambican National Resistance." *AIM Information Bulletin* (Maputo) 69, supplement (1982): 1–12.

Ferguson, James. *The Anti-politics Machine: "Development," Depoliticization, and Bureaucratic Power in Lesotho*. Minneapolis: University of Minnesota Press, 1994.

Fernandes, José, Júnior. "Narração do distrito de Tete." Unpublished manuscript, Makanga, 1955.

Filipe, Eléusio dos Prazeres Viegas. "'The Dam Brought Us Hunger': A History of the Building of Cahora Bassa Dam." MA thesis, University of Minnesota, 2003.

Finnegan, William. *A Complicated War: The Harrowing of Mozambique*. Berkeley: University of California Press, 1992.

First, Ruth. *Black Gold: The Mozambican Miner, Proletarian and Peasant*. Brighton: Harvester, 1983.

Fisher, William, ed. *Toward Sustainable Development? Struggling over India's Narmada River*. Armonk, NY: M. E. Sharpe, 1994.

Fontein, Joost. "The Power of Water: Landscape, Water, and the State in Southern and Eastern Africa: An Introduction." *Journal of Southern African Studies* 34, no. 4 (2008): 737–56.

Frank, Andre Gunder. *Capitalism and Underdevelopment in Latin America: Historical Studies of Chile and Brazil*. New York: Monthly Review Press, 1969.

Frelimo. *Central Committee Report to the Third Congress of FRELIMO (3–7 February 1977)*. Documento Informativo no. 6, series E. Translated by Centro Nacional de Documentação e Informação de Moçambique (CEDIMO). Maputo: CEDIMO, 1978.

Freyre, Gilberto. *Um brasileiro em terras portuguêsas*. Rio de Janeiro: Livraria José Olympio Editora, 1953.

———. *Integração portugueza nos trópicos*. Lisbon: Junta de Investigações do Ultramar, 1958.

———. *The Masters and the Slaves: A Study in the Development of Brazilian Civilization*. 2nd ed., abridged. Translated by Samuel Putnam. New York: Knopf, 1964.

———. *O mundo que o português criou*. Rio de Janeiro: Livraria José Olympio Editora, 1940.

Friedmann, John, and Haripriya Rangan, eds. *In Defense of Livelihood: Comparative Studies on Environmental Action*. West Hartford: Kumarian Press, 1993.

Furtado, Celso. *Economic Development in Latin America: A Survey from Colonial Times to the Cuban Revolution*. Translated by Suzette Macedo. Cambridge: Cambridge University Press, 1970.

Gabinete do Plano de Zambeze (GPZ). *Relatório do Actividade, 1970*. Lisbon: GPZ, 1971.

———. *Relatório do Actividade, 1971*. Lisbon: GPZ, 1972.

———. *Relatório do Actividade, 1973*. Lisbon: GPZ, 1974.

Gamitto, António Candido Pedroso. *King Kazembe and the Marave, Cheva, Bisa, Bemba, Lunda, and Other Peoples of Southern Africa*. Translated by Ian Cunnison. 2 vols. Lisbon: Junta de Investigações do Ultramar, 1960.

Gammelsröd, Tor. "Improving Shrimp Production by Zambezi River Regulation." *Ambio* 21, no. 2 (1992): 145–47.

———. "Variation in Shrimp Abundance on the Sofala Bank, Mozambique, and Its Relation to the Zambezi Runoff." *Estuarine, Coastal and Shelf Science* 35, no. 1 (1992): 91–103.

Gebhardt, M. "Switching on to Cahora Bassa." *Mail and Guardian*, 20 December 1996. www.mg.co.za./article/1996-12-20-Switching-on-to-cahora-bassa.

Geffray, Christian. *A causa das armas: Antropologia da guerra contemporânea em Moçambique*. Porto: Edições Afrontamento, 1991.

Geffray, Christian, and Morgens Pedersen. "Sobre a guerra na província de Nampula." *Revista internacional de estudos africanos* 4–5 (1986): 303–18.

Gengenbach, Heidi. *Binding Memories: Women as Makers and Tellers of History in Magude, Mozambique*. New York: Columbia University Press, 2006.

Gidwani, Vinay. "The Unbearable Modernity of 'Development'? Canal Irrigation and Development Planning in Western India." *Progress in Planning* 58, no. 1 (2002): 5–6.

Giles-Vernick, Tamara. *Cutting the Vines of the Past: Environmental Histories of the Central African Rain Forest*. Charlottesville: University Press of Virginia, 2002.

Goldman, Abe. "Threats to Sustainability in African Agriculture: Searching for Appropriate Paradigms." *Human Ecology* 23, no. 3 (1995): 291–334.

Goldman, Michael. *Imperial Nature: The World Bank and Struggle for Social Justice in the Age of Globalization*. New Haven: Yale University Press, 2005.

Goldsmith, Edward, and Nicholas Hildyard, eds. *The Social and Environmental Effects of Large Dams*. 2 vols. San Francisco: Sierra Club Books, 1984.

Gordon, David M. *Nachituti's Gift: Economy, Society, and Environment in Central Africa*. Madison: University of Wisconsin Press, 2006.

Hall, A., I. M. Valente, and B. R. Davies. "The Zambezi River in Moçambique: The Physico-Chemical Status of the Middle and Lower Zambezi Prior to Closure of the Cabora Bassa Dam." *Freshwater Biology* 7, no. 3 (1977): 187–206.

Hall, Margaret. "The Mozambican National Resistance Movement (RENAMO): A Study in the Destruction of an African Country." *Africa* 60, no. 1 (1990): 39–68.

Hall, Margaret, and Tom Young. *Confronting Leviathan: Mozambique since Independence*. London: C. Hurst, 1997.

———. "Mozambique at War with Itself." In *Readings in African Politics*, edited by Tom Young, 59–67. Bloomington: Indiana University Press, 2003.

Hance, William A. "Cabora Bassa Hydro Project: Portugal and South Africa Seek Political and Economic Gains from Joint Investment." *Africa Report* 15, no. 5 (1970): 20–21.

Hankins, Mark. *A Renewable Energy Plan for Mozambique*. Maputo: Justiça Ambiental, 1999.

Hanlon, Joseph. *Mozambique: Who Calls the Shots?* Bloomington: Indiana University Press, 1992.

Hanlon, Joseph, and Marcelo Mosse. "Mozambique's Elite—Finding Its Way in a Globalized World and Returning to Old Development Models." Working paper no. 2010/105, United Nations University, World Institute for Development Economic Research, Helsinki, 2010.

Harries, Patrick. *Work, Culture, and Identity: Migrant Laborers in Mozambique and South Africa, c. 1860–1910*. Portsmouth, NH: Heinemann, 1994.

Harris, Leila. "Contested Sustainabilities: Assessing Narratives of Environmental Change in Southeastern Turkey." *Local Environment* 14, no. 8 (2009): 699–720.

———. "Irrigation, Gender and Social Geographies of the Changing Waterscapes of Southeastern Anatolia." *Environment and Planning: Society and Space* 24, no. 2 (2006); 187–213.

Hartman, Heidi. "The Unhappy Marriage of Marxism and Feminism." In *Women and Revolution: A Discussion of the Unhappy Marriage of Marxism and Feminism*, edited by Lydia Sargent, 1–4. Boston: South End Press, 1981.

Hartnady, C. J. H. "Earthquake Hazard in Africa: Perspectives on the Nubia-Somalia Boundary." *South African Journal of Science* 98, nos. 9–10 (2002): 425–28.

Harvey, David. *Justice, Nature and the Geography of Difference*. London: Blackwell, 1996.

Henderson, R. "Cabora Bassa: Who Will Benefit during the Construction Phase?" *Cultures et développement* 4, no. 2 (1972): 327–54.

Henriksen, Thomas. *Revolution and Counterrevolution: Mozambique's War of Independence, 1964–1974*. Westport, CT: Greenwood, 1983.

Hidroeléctrica de Cahora Bassa (HCB). *A nossa energia abraça de Moçambique/ Our Energy Embraces Mozambique*. Lisbon: HCB, 2000.

Hidroeléctrica de Mphanda Nkuwa (HMN). *Estudo de pré-viabilidade ambiental e definição do Mpâmbito: Resumo não técnico*. Maputo: HMN, 2009.

———. *Mphanda Nkuwa Hydroelectric Power Plant Project HMKN*. Maputo: HMK, n.d.

Hillmann, Christian, and Leif Tore Trædal. *The Mepanda Unkua Project—A Planned Regulation of the Zambezi River in Mozambique: Results from a Study Trip, June 23–July 18, 2003*. Oslo: FIVAS, 2003.

Hiltzik, Michael. *Colossus: Hoover Dam and the Making of the American Century.* New York: Free Press, 2010.

Hirsch, Philip, and Carol Warren, eds. *The Politics of Environment in Southeast Asia: Resources and Resistance.* London: Routledge, 1998.

Hoag, Heather. "Damming the Empire: British Attitudes on Hydropower Development in Africa." In *Program for the Study of the African Environment,* Research Series, no. 3, 1–4. Boston: African Studies Center, 2008.

Hodgson, Dorothy, and Sheryl McCurdy, eds. *"Wicked" Women and the Reconfiguration of Gender in Africa.* Portsmouth, NH: Heinemann, 2001.

Hofmeyr, Isabel. *"We Spend Our Years as a Tale That Is Told": Oral Historical Narrative in a South African Chiefdom.* Portsmouth, NH: Heinemann, 1993.

Hoguane, A. "Shrimp Abundance and River Runoff in Sofala Bank—the Role of the Zambezi." Paper presented at Workshop on the Sustainable Use of Cahora Bassa Dam and the Zambezi Valley, Songo, Mozambique, September 29–October 2, 1997.

Horta, Loro. "The Zambezi Valley: China's First Agricultural Colony?" *Africa Policy Forum, Center for Strategic and International Studies,* 9 June 2008. http://csis.org/publication/zambezi-valley-chinas-first-agricultural-colony.

Igrewja, Victor, Bas Schreuder, and Wim Kleijn. "The Cultural Dimension of War Traumas In Central Mozambique: The Case of Gorongosa." http://priory.com/psych/traumacult.htm.

Impacto. *The Scoping Study: Mphanda Nkuwa HydroPower Project.* Vol. 2. Maputo: Impacto, 2007.

Intermediate Technology Consultants (ITC). *Final Report for WWF, The Mphanda Nkuwa Dam Project: Is It the Best Option for Mozambique's Energy Needs?* Washington, D.C.: World Wildlife Fund, 2004.

International Commission on Large Dams (ICOLD). *World Register of Dams.* Paris: ICOLD, 1988.

International Crane Foundation, Museum of Natural History-Mozambique, the Natural Heritage Institute (USA), the University of Eduardo Mondlane (Mozambique), and Southern Waters Ecological Research and Consulting (South Africa). "The Sustainable Management of Cahora Bassa Dam and the Lower Zambezi Valley, Mozambique." Unpublished proposal.

——. "The Zambezi Delta: Management Opportunities and Challenges." www.savingcranes.org/the-zambezi-delta-management-opportunities-and-challenges.html.

International Finance Corporation. *Summary of Project Information 7473, AEF Cahora Bassa Fisheries Lda.* http://www.ifc.org/ifcext/spiwebsite1.nsf/ProjectDisplay/DataConversion74723.

International Rivers (IR). *Flooding the Land, Warming the Earth.* Berkeley: IR, 2002. www-fa.upc.es/personals/fluids/oriol/ale/2002ghreport.pdf.

——. *Damning the Zambezi: Risks Outweigh Benefits of Proposed Mphanda Nkuwa Dam.* Berkeley: IR, 2006. http://www.internationalrivers.org/files/MphandaFactSheet2006_en.pdf.

———. *Reservoir Emissions*. http://www.internationalrivers.org/en/node/383.

———. "Zambezi, River." www.internationalrivers.org/africa/zambezi-river.

Isaacman, Allen. "Chiefs, Rural Differentiation and Peasant Protest: The Mozambican Forced Cotton Regime, 1938–1961." *African Economic History* 14 (1985): 15–56.

———. "Conflict in Southern Africa: The Case of Mozambique." In *Apartheid Unravels*, edited by R. Hunt Davis, 183–212. Gainesville: University Press of Florida, 1991.

———. *Cotton Is the Mother of Poverty*. Portsmouth, NH: Heinemann, 1996.

———. "Displaced People, Displaced Energy, and Displaced Memories: The Case of Cahora Bassa, 1970–2004." *International Journal of African Historical Studies* 38, no. 2 (2005): 201–238.

———. "Domesticating a White Elephant: Sustainability and Struggles over Water, The Case of Cahora Bassa Dam." *Zambezia* 28, no. 2 (2001): 199–228.

———. "Historical Amnesia, or the Logic of Capital Accumulation: Cotton Production in Colonial and Postcolonial Mozambique." *Environment and Planning D: Society and Space* 15, no. 6 (1997): 757–90.

———. "Legacies of Engagement: Scholarship Informed by Political Commitment." *African Studies Review* 46, no. 1 (2003): 1–41.

———. "Madzi-Manga, Mhondoro, and the Use of Oral Traditions: A Chapter in Barue Religious and Political History." *Journal of African History* 14, no. 3 (1973): 395–409.

———. *Mozambique: The Africanization of a European Institution: The Zambezi Prazos, 1750–1902*. Madison: University of Wisconsin Press, 1972.

———. "Peasant and Rural Social Protest in Africa." *African Studies Review* 33, no. 2 (2002): 1–120.

———. *The Tradition of Resistance in Mozambique: The Zambesi Valley, 1850–1921*. Berkeley: University of California Press, 1976.

Isaacman, Allen, and Barbara Isaacman. *Mozambique: From Colonialism to Revolution, 1900–1982*. Boulder: Westview, 1993.

———. *Slavery and Beyond: The Making of Men and Chikunda Ethnic Identities in the Unstable World of South-Central Africa, 1750–1920*. Portsmouth, NH: Heinemann, 2004.

Isaacman, Allen, and David Morton. "Harnessing the Zambezi: How Mozambique's Planned Mphanda Nkuwa Dam Perpetuates the Colonial Past." *International Journal of African Historical Studies* 45, no. 2 (2012): 147–90.

Isaacman, Allen, and Chris Sneddon. "Portuguese Colonial Intervention, Regional Conflict and Post-colonial Amnesia: Cahora Bassa Dam, Mozambique 1965–2002." *Portuguese Studies Review* 11, no. 1 (2003): 207–36.

———. "Toward a Social and Environmental History of the Building of Cahora Bassa Dam." *Journal of Southern African Studies* 26, no. 4 (2000): 597–632.

Jackson, P. B. N. "Ecological Studies on the Middle Zambezi prior to Kariba and Cahora Bassa and the Need for Surveys of the Lower Zambezi prior to the Creation of Further Hydroelectric Dams." Paper presented at Workshop on the Sustainable Use of Cahora Bassa Dam and the Zambezi Valley, Songo, Mozambique, September 29–October 2, 1997.

Jackson, P. B. N, and K. H. Rogers. "Cabora Bassa Fish Populations before and during the First Filling Phase." *Zoológica Africana* 11, no. 2 (1976): 373–97.

Jopp, Keith. *Volta: The Story of Ghana's Volta River Project.* Accra: Volta River Authority, 1965.

Jundanian, Brendan. "Resettlement Programs: Counterinsurgency in Mozambique." *Comparative Politics* 6, no. 4 (1974): 519–540.

Justiça Ambiental. "Background Paper for the Training Process." JA!, Maputo, 2004.

——. "Report on the Workshop on Integrated Water Management in the Zambezi, Tete Meeting, October 6, 7 & 8, 2004." Report prepared for OXFAM, November 2004.

Juwayeyi, Yusuf. "Archaeological Excavations at Mankhamba, Malawi: An Early Settlement Site of the Maravi." *Azania: Archeological Research in Africa* 45, no. 2 (2010): 175–202.

Kanji, Nazneen, et al. "The Development of the 1997 Land Law in Mozambique." Unpublished document, 2002. http:\\www.caledonia.org.uk\land\mozambiq .htm.

Keck, Margaret, and Kathryn Sikkink. *Activists beyond Borders: Advocacy Networks in International Politics.* Ithaca: Cornell University Press, 1998.

Khagram, Sanjeev. *Dams and Development: Transnational Struggles for Water and Power.* Ithaca: Cornell University Press, 2004.

Kirk, John. *The Zambezi Journal and Letters of Dr. John Kirk, 1858–63.* Edited by Reginald Foskett. 2 vols. Edinburgh: Oliver and Boyd, 1965.

Kitching, Gavin. *Development and Underdevelopment in Historical Perspective: Populism, Nationalism, and Industrialization.* London: Methuen, 1982.

Klein, Martin. Introduction to *Peasants in Africa: Historical and Contemporary Perspectives,* edited by Klein, 1–43. Beverley Hills: Sage, 1980.

Kotre, John. *White Gloves: How We Create Ourselves through Memory.* New York: Free Press, 1995.

Lalu, Premesh. *The Deaths of Hintsa: Postapartheid South Africa and the Shape of Recurring Pasts.* Cape Town: HSRC Press, 2009.

——. "The Grammar of Domination and the Subjection of Agency: Colonial Texts and Modes of Evidence." *History and Theory* 39, no. 4 (2005): 45–68.

Lan, David. *Guns and Rain: Guerrillas and Spirit Mediums in Zimbabwe.* Berkeley: University of California Press, 1985.

Langer, Lawrence. *Holocaust Testimonies: The Ruins of Memory.* New Haven: Yale University Press, 1991.

Langworthy, Harry. "A History of Undi's Kingdom to 1890: Aspects of Chewa History in East Central Africa." PhD diss., Boston University, 1969.

Lattimore, Owen. *Studies in Frontier History.* Paris: Mouton, 1962.

Lele, Sharachchandra. "Sustainable Development: A Critical Review." *World Development* 19, no. 6 (1991): 607–21.

Levi, Primo. *The Drowned and the Saved.* New York: Summit Books, 1988.

Lewis, Arthur. *The Theory of Economic Growth*. Homewood, IL: R. D. Irwin, 1955.

Liesegang, G., and M. Chidiamassamba. "Alternativas e técnicas adaptadas as cheias usadas pelas comunidades ao longo do Vale de Zambeze." Paper presented at Workshop on the Sustainable Use of Cahora Bassa Dam and the Zambezi Valley, Songo, Mozambique, September 29–October 2, 1997.

Livingstone, David. *African Journal, 1853–1856*. Edited by Isaac Schapera. Berkeley: University of California Press, 1963.

——. *Missionary Travels and Researches in South Africa*. New York: Harper and Bros., 1858.

Livingstone, David, and Charles Livingstone. *Narrative of an Expedition to the Zambezi and Its Tributaries and of the Discovery of the Lakes Shirwa and Nyasa*. London: Harper and Bros., 1865.

Lyne, Robert Nunez. *Mozambique: Its Agricultural Development*. London: T. Fisher Unwin, 1913.

Mandala, Elias. "The Kololo Interlude in Southern Malawi." MA thesis, University of Malawi, 1977.

——. *Work and Control in a Peasant Economy: A History of the Lower Tchiri Valley in Malawi, 1859–1960*. Madison: University of Wisconsin Press, 1990.

Mañez, Gustavo, and Lucia Scodanibbio. *Mphanda Nkuwa: Dams and Development Capacity-Building Project*. Report Prepared for the Siemenpuu Foundation. Maputo: Justiça Ambiental, 2004.

Manning, Carrie. "Constructing Opposition in Mozambique: Renamo as Political Party." *Journal of Southern African Studies* 24, no. 1 (1998): 161–89.

——. *The Politics of Peace in Mozambique: Post-conflict Democratization, 1992–2000*. Westport, CT: Praeger, 2002.

Marchand, Marianne, and Jane Parpart, eds. *Feminism/Postmodernism/Development*. London: Routledge, 1995.

Marchant, Douglas. *Cabora Bassa: The Dam at Cabora Bassa—It's [sic] Implications and the International Campaign against the Project*. London: National League of Young Liberals International Department, 1971.

Marlin, Rob. "Possessing the Past: Legacies of Violence and Reproductive Illness in Central Mozambique." PhD diss., Rutgers University, 2001.

Martins, E. A. Azambuja. *Operações militares no Barué em 1917*. Lisbon: Imprensa Nacional, 1937.

Maugham, R. C. F. *Zambezia: A General Description of the Valley of the Zambezi River, from Its Delta to the River Aroangwa, with Its History, Agriculture, Flora, Fauna, and Ethnography*. London: John Murray, 1910.

Mbembé, Achille. *On the Postcolony*. Berkeley: University of California Press, 2000.

McCann, James. *Green Land, Brown Land, Black Land: An Environmental History of Africa, 1800–1990*. Portsmouth, NH: Heinemann, 1992.

McCully, Patrick. *Flooding the Land, Warming the Earth: Greenhouse Gas Emissions from Dams*. Berkeley: International Rivers Network, 2002.

——. *Silenced Rivers: The Ecology and Politics of Large Dams*. London: Zed Books, 2001.

McDonald, David A. "Electric Capitalism: Conceptualising Electrticity and Capital Accumulation in (South) Africa." In *Electric Capitalism: Recolonising Africa on the Power Grid*, edited by McDonald, 1–49. Cape Town: HSRC Press, 2009.

McGregor, JoAnn. "Violence and Social Change in a Border Economy: War in the Maputo Hinterland, 1984–1992." *Journal of Southern African Studies* 24, no. 1 (1998): 37–60.

——. *Crossing the Zambezi: The Politics of Landscape on a Central African Frontier*. Oxford: James Currey, 2009.

Mehta, Lyla, ed. *Displaced by Development: Confronting Marginalisation and Gender Injustice*. New Delhi: Sage, 2009.

Mendis, D. L. O. *Eppawala: Destruction of Cultural Heritage in the Name of Development*. Colombo: Sri Lanka Pugwash Group, 1999.

Middlemas, Keith. *Cabora Bassa: Engineering and Politics in Southern Africa*. London: Weidenfeld and Nicolson, 1975.

Miescher, Stephan. "Akosombo Stories: The Volta River Project, Modernization, and Nationhood in Ghana." Unpublished book prospectus, 2010.

Miescher, Stephan, and Dzodzi Tsikata. "Hydro Power and the Promise of Modernity and Development in Ghana: Comparing the Akosombo and Bui Dam Projects." *Ghana Studies* 12–13 (2009–10): 15–53.

Ministério do Ultramar, Missão de Fomento e Povoamento de Zambeze (MFPZ). *Plano geral de fomento e occupação do vale do Zambeze*. Lisbon: Hidrotécnica Portuguesa, 1965.

Miranda, António Pinto de. "Memória sobre a costa de África." In Andrade, *Relações de Moçambique setecentista*, 231–313.

Mitchell, Timothy. *Rule of Experts: Egypt, Techno-Politics, Modernity*. Berkeley: University of California Press, 2002.

Mondlane, Eduardo. *The Struggle for Mozambique*. 2nd ed. London: Zed Books, 1983.

Montaury, João Baptista de. "Moçambique, Ilhas Querimbas, Rios de Sena, Villa de Tete, Villa de Zumbo, Manica, Villa de Luabo, Inhambane." In Andrade, *Relações de Moçambique*, 339–73.

Montgomery-Rinehart, Lauren. "A quem benefica o projecto?" *Livaningo* 2 (2002): 3–5.

Moore, Donald. *Suffering for Territory: Race, Place, and Power in Zimbabwe*. Durham: Duke University Press, 2005.

Morrissey, James. *Livelihoods at Risk: The Case of Mphanda Nkuwa Dam*. Maputo: Justiça Ambiental, 2006.

Mousinho de Albuquerque, Joaquim. *Moçambique, 1896–1898*. Lisbon: Sociedade de Geografia de Lisboa, 1913.

Mozambique. *Termos de vassallagem nos territórios de Machona, Zambézia e Nyasa, 1858 a 1889*. Lisbon: Imprensa Nacional, 1890.

Mozambique, Angola, Guinea-Bissau Information Committee (MAGIC). *Central Committee Report to the Third Party Congress*. London: MAGIC, 1978.

Muhai, S. "Cahora Bassa and the Lower Zambezi." Paper presented at Workshop on the Sustainable Use of Cahora Bassa Dam and the Zambezi Valley, Songo, Mozambique, September 29–October 2, 1997.

Negrão, José. "One Hundred Years of African Rural Family Economy: The Zambezi Delta in Retrospective Analysis." PhD diss., University of Lund, 1995.

Nehrera, Bertha, and Lucy Emerton. *Economic Value of the Zambezi Basin Wetlands.* Harare: International World Conservation Union, Regional Office for Southern Africa, 2006.

Nehru, Jawaharlal. *Jawaharlal Nehru's Speeches.* Vol. 3, *March 1953–August 1957.* 3rd ed. New Delhi: Ministry of Information and Broadcasting, Publications Division, 1983.

Newitt, M. D. D. "Drought in Mozambique 1823–1831." *Journal of Southern African Studies* 15 (1998): 15–35.

———. *A History of Mozambique.* Bloomington: Indiana University Press, 1995.

———. *Portuguese Settlement on the Zambesi: Exploration, Land Tenure, and Colonial Rule in East Africa.* London: Longman, 1973.

Newsweek 80, no. 22 (November 27, 1972).

Nuttall, Sara, and Carli Coetzee. Introduction to *Negotiating the Past: The Making of Memory in South Africa,* edited by Nuttall and Coetzee, 1–19. Cape Town: Oxford University Press, 1998.

———, eds. *Negotiating the Past: The Making of Memory in South Africa.* Cape Town: Oxford University Press, 1998.

Oliveira, Carlos Ramos de. *Os Tauaras do vale do Zambeze.* Lisbon: Junta de Investigações Científicas do Ultramar, 1976.

O'Riordan, Timothy. "The Politics of Sustainability." In *Sustainable Environmental Economics and Management: Principles and Practice,* edited by R. Kerry Turner, 37–69. London: Belhaven Press, 1993.

Pandey, Gyanendra. *Memory, History and the Question of Violence: Reflections on the Reconstruction of Partition.* Calcutta: K. P. Bagchi, 1999.

Peet, Richard, and Elaine Hartwick. *Theories of Development: Contentions, Arguments, Alternatives.* New York: Guilford Press, 2009.

Peet, Richard, and Michael Watts. "Introduction: Development Theory and Environment in an Age of Market Triumphalism." *Economic Geography* 69, no. 3 (1993): 227–53.

Peluso, Nancy, and Michael Watts. "Violent Environments." In *Violent Environments,* edited by Peluso and Watts, 3–39. Ithaca: Cornell University Press, 2001.

Peters, Carl. *The Eldorado of the Ancients (1889–1902).* London: C. A. Pearson, 1902.

Phasiwe, Khuli. "Eskom to Pay Much More for Power from Cahora Bassa." *Business Day,* 10 February 2004. http://www.queensu.ca/msp/pages/IIin_the_News/2004/february/17.htm.

Phiri, Kings. "Chewa History in Central Malawi and the Use of Oral Tradition, 1600–1920." PhD diss., University of Wisconsin, 1975.

Pitcher, M. Anne. *Transforming Mozambique: The Politics of Privatization, 1975–2000.* Cambridge: Cambridge University Press, 2002.

Portugal. Secretário de Estado da Informação e Turismo. *Cabora Bassa on the Move*. Lisbon: Agência Geral do Ultramar, n.d.

Programa dos Nações Unidas para o Desenvolvimento (PNUD)/Banco Mundial. *Moçambique: Problemas e opções no sector energético*. Maputo: PNUD, 1987.

Província de Moçambique. Junta Provincial de Povoamento. *Relatório-síntese da actividade da Missão de Fomento e Povoamento do Zambeze, 1957–1961*. Lourenço Marques: Junta Provincial de Povoamento, 1962.

Qing, Dai. *The River Dragon Has Come! The Three Gorges Dam and the Fate of China's Yangtze River and Its People*. Armonk, NY: M. E. Sharpe, 1998.

Radmann, Wolf. "The Zambezi Development Scheme: Cabora Bassa." *Africa Report* 4, no. 2 (Summer 1974): 48–54.

Rankin, Daniel J. "The Chinde River and Zambezi Delta." *Royal Geographic Society* 12, no. 3 (1890): 136–46.

Redclift, Michael. *Sustainable Development: Exploring the Contradictions*. London: Methuen, 1987.

Renzaho, Andre. "Mortality Rates, Prevalence of Malnutrition, and Prevalence of Lost Pregnancies among the Drought Ravaged Population of Tete Province, Mozambique." *Prehospital and Disaster Medicine* 22, no. 1 (February 2002): 16. http:///pdm.medicine.wisc.edu.

República de Moçambique. *Plano de acção para a redução da pobreza absoluta, 2001–2005*. Maputo: República de Moçambique, 200.

República de Moçambique. Ministério dos Recursos Minerais e Energia (MRME). *Mphanda Nkuwa Hydropower Project, Mozambique: Development Prospect*. Maputo: MRME, 2003.

———. *Projecto de Mepanda Uncua e Cahora Bassa Norte: Relatório da II fase do processo de consulta pública sobre a avaliação do impacto ambiental*. Maputo: MRME, 2002.

Ribeiro, Daniel. "The Zambezi Valley: Damned by Dams." http://internationalrivers.org/files/damnedbydams.pdf.

Richardson, Boyce. *Strangers Devour the Land*. Post Mills, VT: Chelsea Green Publications, 1991.

Roberts, Richard. "Reversible Social Processes, Historical Memory and the Production of History." *History in Africa* 17 (1990): 341–49.

Rodney, Walter. *How Europe Underdeveloped Africa*. Washington, DC: Howard University Press, 1981.

Roesch, Otto. "Renamo and the Peasantry in Southern Mozambique: A View from Gaza Province." *Canadian Journal of African Studies* 26, no. 3 (1992): 462–84.

Rostow, W. W. *The Stages of Economic Growth: A Non-communist Manifesto*. Cambridge: Cambridge University Press, 1960.

Santos, Eduardo dos, Júnior. "Cahora Bassa no desenvolvimento do vale do Zambeze." *Ultramar* 2, no. 5 (1973): 101–75.

Santos, João dos. "Ethiópia oriental." In Theal, *South-Eastern Africa*, 7:1–370.

Santos, José Norberto, Jr. *Contribuição para o estudo da antropologia de Moçambique: Algumas tribos de Tete*. Lisbon: Junta das Missões Geográficas e de Investigações Coloniais, 1944.

Saul, John, ed. *A Difficult Road: The Transition to Socialism in Mozambique*. New York: Monthly Review Press, 1985.

——. *Recolonization and Resistance: Southern Africa in the 1990s*. Trenton: Africa World Press, 1993.

Schoffeleers, J. Matthew. *River of Blood: The Genesis of a Martyr Cult in Southern Malawi, c. A.D. 1600*. Madison: University of Wisconsin Press, 1992.

Scodanibbio, Lucia, and Gustavo Mañez. "The World Commission on Dams: A Fundamental Step towards Integrated Water Resources Management and Poverty Reduction? A Pilot Case in the Lower Zambezi, Mozambique." *Physics and Chemistry of the Earth* 30, nos. 11–16 (2005): 976–83.

Scott, James. *Seeing Like a State: How Certain Schemes to Improve the Human Condition Have Failed*. New Haven: Yale University Press, 1998.

Scudder, Thayer. "Development-Induced Impoverishment, Resistance and River Basin Development." In *Understanding Impoverishment: The Consequences of Development-Induced Displacement*, edited by Christopher McDowell, 49–76. Oxford: Berghahn, 1996.

——. *The Ecology of the Gwembe Tonga*. Manchester: Manchester University Press, 1962.

——. *The Future of Large Dams: Dealing with Social, Environmental, Institutional, and Political Costs*. London: Earthscan, 2005.

——. "Social Anthropology, Man-Made Lakes and Population Relocation in Africa." *Anthropology Quarterly* 41, no. 1 (1968): 168–76.

Selous, Frederick. *Travel and Adventure in South-East Africa*. London: Roland Ward and Co., 1893.

Shiva, Vandana. *Staying Alive: Women, Ecology, and Development*. London: Zed Books, 1988.

——. *Water Wars: Privatization, Pollution, and Profit*. Cambridge, MA: South End Press, 2002.

Siebert, Renate. "Don't Forget: Fragments of a Negative Tradition." In *Memory and Totalitarianism, International Yearbook of Oral History and Life Stories*, vol. 1, edited by Luisa Passerini, 166–77. Oxford: Oxford University Press, 1992.

Silva, Pedro Augusto de Sousa e. *Distrito de Tete, Alta Zambézia*. Lisbon: Livraria Portugália Editora, 1927.

Smith, Sylvia. "The Cahora Bassa Dam." Radio Netherlands Worldwide, February 18, 2003.

Sneddon, Chris. "'Sustainability' in Ecological Economics, Ecology and Livelihoods: A Review." *Progress in Human Geography* 24, no. 4 (2000): 526–29.

Sneddon, Chris, Leila Harris, Radoslav Dimitrov, and Uygar Özesmi. "Contested Waters: Conflict, Scale, and Sustainability in Aquatic Socioecological Systems." *Society and Natural Resources* 15, no. 8 (2002): 663–75.

Stal, Marc, "Rapid-Onset Flooding and Relocation: The Zambezi River Valley in Mozambique." New York: United Nations University Institute for Environment and Human Security, 2008. Power Point presentation. http://www.efmsv2008.org/file/COP14Stal.

Stoler, Anne. "Rethinking Colonial Categories: European Communities and the Boundaries of Rule." *Comparative Studies in Society and History* 31, no. 1 (1989): 134–61.

Sweden. Ministry of Energy (SWECO/SWED POWER). *Cabora Bassa Hydroelectric Power Scheme—Stage II.* Stockholm: SWECO, 1986.

Swyngedouw, Erik. *Social Power and the Urbanization of Water.* Oxford: Oxford University Press, 2004.

Theal, George M., ed. *Records of South-Eastern Africa, 1898–1903.* 9 vols. Cape Town: C. Struik, 1964.

Thornton, Richard. *The Zambezi Papers of Richard Thornton.* Edited by Edward C. Tabler. 2 vols. London: Chatto and Windus, 1963.

Timberlake, Jonathan. "Biodiversity of the Zambezi Basin." Occasional Publication in Biodiversity, no. 9. Bulawayo: Biodiversity Foundation for Africa, 2000.

Tinley, K. L. "Marromeu Wrecked by the Big Dam." *African Wildlife* 29, no. 2 (1975): 22–25.

Tischler, Julia. "Light and Power for a Multiracial Nation: The Kariba Dam Scheme in the Central African Federation." PhD diss., University of Cologne, 2010.

Tracey, Hugh. *António Fernandes, descobridor do Monomotapa, 1514–1515.* Lourenço Marques: Imprensa Nacional, 1940.

Tsikata, Dzodzi. *Living in the Shadow of the Large Dams: Long Term Responses of Downstream and Lakeside Communities of Ghana's Volta River Project.* Leiden: Brill, 2006.

Tweddle, Denis. "Specialist Study—Freshwater Fisheries," in Beilfuss and Brown, *Environmental Flow Requirements,* 68–81.

Unidade Téchnica de Implementação dos Projectos Hidroeléctricos (UTIP). *Mepanda Uncua and Cahora Bassa North Project: Preliminary Environmental and Social Impact Assessment Main Report,* Document Nos. 012/A and 012/B. Maputo: UTIP, 1999.

———. *Mepanda Uncua and Cahora Bassa North Project Phase II.* Maputo: UTIP, 2001.

———. *Mepanda Uncua and Cahora Bassa North Project: Sumário executivo do relatório de viabilidade.* Maputo: UTIP, 2002.

———. *Mepanda Uncua Feasibility Study, Environmental Impact Assessment: Executive Summary.* Maputo: UTIP, 2003.

———. *Mepanda Uncua Feasibility Study,* no. 16. Lisbon: UTIP, 2002.

United Nations. "Economic Conditions in Mozambique with Reference to Foreign Interests." Conference Room Paper SCI/71/5. New York: United Nations, 1971.

Vail, Leroy, and Landeg White. *Capitalism and Colonialism in Mozambique: A Study of Quelimane District.* Minneapolis: University of Minnesota Press, 1980.

Vandergeest, Peter, Pablo Idahosa, and Pablo Bose, eds. *Development's Displacements: Ecologies, Economies and Cultures at Risk.* Vancouver: University of British Columbia Press, 2007.

Vaughan, Meghan. *The Story of an African Famine: Gender and Famine in Twentieth-Century Malawi*. Cambridge: Cambridge University Press, 1987.

Vidigal, Manuel. "Cabora Bassa: História, Perspectivas, Justificacão, Aspectos económico-financeiros, Interesse nacional do empreendimento." *Electricidade* (Lisbon) 13 (January-February, 1970): 7–20.

Vines, Alex. *Renamo: Terrorism in Mozambique*. Bloomington: Indiana University Press, 1991.

Wainwright, Joel. *Decolonizing Development: Colonial Power and the Maya*. London: Blackwell, 2008.

Watts, Michael. *Silent Violence: Food, Famine, and Peasantry in Northern Nigeria*. Berkeley: University of California Press, 1983.

Weise, Carlos. "Expedição Portugueza à Mpeseni." *Boletim da Sociedade de Geografia de Lisboa* 10 (1891), nos. 6–7: 235–73, 297–321; nos. 8–9: 331–412, 415–30; no. 12: 467–97.

White, Landeg. *Bridging the Zambezi: A Colonial Folly*. London: Macmillan, 1993.

White, Luise. *The Comforts of Home: Prostitution in Colonial Nairobi*. Chicago: University of Chicago Press, 1990.

White, Luise, Stephan Miescher, and David Cohen. Introduction to *African Words, African Voices: Critical Practices in Oral History*, edited by White, Miescher, and Cohen, 1–16. Bloomington: Indiana University Press, 2001.

White, Richard. *The Organic Machine*. New York: Hill and Wang, 1995.

Winter, Gordon. *Inside BOSS: South Africa's Secret Police*. Harmondsworth: Penguin Books, 1981.

Worby, Eric. "Inscribing the State at the 'Edge of the Beyond': Danger and Development in Northwestern Zimbabwe." *Political and Legal Anthropology Review* 21, no. 2 (1998): 55–70.

World Commission on Dams (WCD). *Dams and Development: A New Framework for Decision-Making*. London: Earthscan, 2000.

World Council of Churches. *Cabora Bassa and the Struggle for Southern Africa*. London: World Council of Churches, 1971.

Young, James. *The Texture of Memory: Holocaust Memorials and Meaning*. New Haven: Yale University Press, 1993.

Index

Page references in italics denote illustrations.

environmental damage, 4–5; ethnic groups in, 29, 29–30; fishing in, 51–54; flood cycle, 37–38, 40–44; flora and fauna, 6, 54–56; as highway to interior, 30–33; indigenous perspective on, 39–40; maps, 2, 29, 32; natural wealth in, 35–37; oral accounts of, 5, 40, 43; and *prazos*, 33–34; soil of, 42–43, 44–47; upper, 1, 59. *See also* Lower Zambezi River/Valley

Zambezi Valley Planning Office. *See* Gabinete do Plano do Zambeze

Zamco. *See* Zambeze Consórcio Hidroeléctrico Lda.

ZANU. *See* Zimbabwe African National Union

ZAPU. *See* Zimbabwe African People's Union

ZESA. *See* Zimbabwe Electricity Supply Authority

Zhuwao, Marita, 54, 132–33, 143

Zimbabwe African National Union (ZANU), 64

Zimbabwe African People's Union (ZAPU), 64

Zimbabwe Electricity Supply Authority (ZESA), 161

Zimba community, 118

Zumbo, 31, 33, 34, 68, 126

CPSIA information can be obtained
at www.ICGtesting.com
Printed in the USA
FSOW02n0904310816
24433FS